GEDATSU-KAI
AND
RELIGION
IN
CONTEMPORARY
JAPAN

Religion in Asia and Africa
Judith Berling and Patrick Olivelle, series editors

GEDATSU-KAI
AND
RELIGION
IN
CONTEMPORARY
JAPAN

Returning to the Center

H. BYRON EARHART

INDIANA
UNIVERSITY
PRESS
Bloomington and Indianapolis

Grateful acknowledgment is made to the University of Chicago Press for permission to reprint in modified form portions of my article "Toward a Theory of the Formation of the Japanese New Religions: A Case Study of Gedatsu-kai," *History of Religions*, XX, Nos. 1–2 (August-November 1980), 175–97.

Manufactured in the United States of America

Library of Congress Cataloging-in-Publication Data

Earhart, H. Byron.
Gedatsu-Kai and religion in contemporary Japan.

(Religion in Asia and Africa series)
Bibliography: p.
Includes index.
1. Gedatsukai.   I. Title.   II. Series.
BQ9800.G432E2   1989   294.3′92   87–46409
ISBN 0–253–35007–7

1 2 3 4 5   93 92 91 90 89

This book is dedicated to
my grandparents
Harry B. and Zoe Earhart
Charles F. and Ruth Haack
and to senzo daidai

CONTENTS

ILLUSTRATIONS

TABLES

MAP

FIGURES

PREFACE

This book looks at religion in contemporary Japan by focusing on the new religion Gedatsu-kai as a microcosm of the Japanese religious tradition. This tradition has a long history and includes many individual religions and diverse beliefs and practices, but my studies over the past twenty years have convinced me that Japanese religion constitutes a unified world view. Of course, religion in contemporary Japan is an extension of this cultural transmission, and Gedatsu-kai represents a particular expression of this heritage. However, it is difficult to survey the entire history of Japanese religion or to describe the complete range of beliefs and practices; even if the subject were limited to the new religious movements of the past century or so, it would be a huge task to treat the dozen or more larger and the many smaller new religions.

My approach to Gedatsu-kai and religion in contemporary Japan has been to place it within the context of the history and dynamics of Japanese culture and religion, and to provide some comparative perspective; however, the thrust of this work is to provide a picture of the larger "macrocosmic" Japanese religious scene by viewing it through the smaller "microcosmic" example of Gedatsu-kai. In short, this work is an intensive look at Gedatsu-kai, keeping in mind but not surveying the entire Japanese religious heritage.

Special research methods and techniques have been followed, with particular emphasis on obtaining an "inside" view of Gedatsu-kai members' and leaders' beliefs and practices. We recorded many life histories of individual members, branch leaders, and executives in order to appreciate the flavor and drama of their religious experience in joining and participating in the movement; one of these life histories (that of Mr. Negishi) sets the tone for chapter 1, eight life histories are the subject of chapter 3, and a number of shorter and several lengthy life histories appear in subsequent chapters. Gedatsu-kai's own publication relating the life of the founder and the formation of the group is the basis of chapter 2, which follows the life of Okano Eizō from his early years through his spiritual crisis and eventual founding of a new religion.

The life of the founder and the life histories of a small number of members may seem too limited a sample to really speak for the whole of Gedatsu-kai; so several techniques were used to gain a more comprehensive grasp of this new religion. A nationwide survey of beliefs and practices of (and some basic demographic information about) Gedatsu-kai members enables us to go beyond the ideals of the founder and the personal accounts of life histories to write more generally about the movement's entire membership; the results of this survey form the basis of chapter 4. Observations of branch meetings in geographically diverse settings enable us to sample the social setting of Gedatsu-kai at the grassroots level; descriptions of four branch meetings and the life history of a branch leader are the subject matter of chapter 5. The organization of the movement's branches, divisions, and headquarters, which was learned from Gedatsu-kai publications and direct observation as well as through interviews with branch leaders and executives (and through the life histories of two executives), is the content of chapter 6. Our research team studied the full range of ritual life in Gedatsu-kai, observing most of it directly, and reading or interviewing about the remainder; this information is the basis for chapter 7.

All these materials, taken as a whole, form the microcosm of religion in contemporary Japan that is Gedatsu-kai. I have characterized this microcosm as a "returning to the center." In other words, Gedatsu-kai is a reformulation of the unified world view of Japanese religion that enables members to go back to the heart of their tradition while at the same time going forward into the future. Chapter 8 addresses some of the theoretical problems of dealing with the origin and nature of new religions such as Gedatsu-kai, and discusses how this microcosm represents a "returning to the center." Except for the theoretical discussion in chapter 8, my intention has been to treat the description, analysis, and interpretation of Gedatsu-kai in the text and to relegate to notes methodological, theoretical, and comparative matters. Readers who are interested primarily in the depiction of the miniature world of Gedatsu-kai and the larger world of Japanese religion can read the work through without reference to notes; those concerned with documentation of the information, and discussion of methodological, theoretical, and comparative matters, may wish to consult the notes.

Throughout this book, Japanese names are given in the Japanese fashion, family name first: for example, "Okano" is the family name in Okano Eizō.

ACKNOWLEDGMENTS

The completion of this book, from the preparation for research to the field work, the analysis of the material gathered during field work, and eventually the writing of the manuscript, was a lengthy process. None of it would have been possible without the generous assistance of many institutions and persons, whose help must be gratefully acknowledged here.

Essential financial support came from a number of sources: two summer grants from the Faculty Research Fund of Western Michigan University, one in preparation for the research and one following field work to analyze and write up the results; a sabbatical for the 1979–80 academic year from Western Michigan University; and a research grant from the Japan Society for the Promotion of Science for support in Japan during the sabbatical year. Financial support for computer analysis of survey results was provided by A. Bruce Clarke, Dean of the College of Arts and Sciences, Laurel Grotzinger, Dean of the Graduate College, and Elwood B. Ehrle, Vice-President for Academic Affairs—all of Western Michigan University.

Planning and preparation for the collecting of life histories were facilitated by the advice of three anthropologists: Alan Jacobs of Western Michigan University, David Plath of the University of Illinois, and Robert J. Smith of Cornell University.

No direct study of a religious group is possible without the permission and cooperation of that group. One reason for my decision to study Gedatsu-kai was their leaders' and members' open and enthusiastic encouragement of such an endeavor, from the time of my first meeting with them in 1969. During the period of my intensive research of the movement in 1979–80, they went beyond the bounds of well-known Japanese hospitality to open their meetings and personal lives to facilitate a thorough and comprehensive study. Such trust cannot be taken lightly, and I hope that the present book is worthy of this trust. All the members of Gedatsu-kai who aided this study, including the more than 5,000 who completed and returned a questionnaire, deserve my heartfelt thanks. Out of the many leaders of the movement who allowed and encouraged this endeavor, two should be singled out: the late Archbishop Kishida Eizan, and the head of the publications department of Gedatsu-kai, Aoyama Yūji. The Board of Directors officially gave approval for the questionnaire survey of members; thanks go to the Board of Directors and to the head (hossu) of Gedatsu-kai, Okano Seihō.

This study was planned as a joint research project with Miyake Hitoshi of Keiō University, including the application for research support from the Japan Society for the Promotion of Science. Professor Miyake and I worked together on the research design of the study; Keiō University granted me visiting professor status and the use of an office. This supportive context was crucial for the success of the research project, and is warmly appreciated.

Professor Miyake was teaching a seminar in the Department of Religious Studies at Tokyo University during the year of our joint project, and students in his seminar entered into the project. These students were Fujii Takeshi, Ishii Kenji, Kawatō

Hitoshi, Onuma Yūko, and Torii Yukiko. I had made the initial contacts with Gedatsu-kai (first in 1969, and again before the 1979–80 study), but Professor Miyake and his students participated in most aspects of the actual study. They helped plan, assemble, and distribute the questionnaire and later coded it on data sheets for computer analysis. Professor Miyake's students at Keiō University also helped complete these data sheets. (Professor Miyazaki of Gunma University, who teaches computer science and also is a member of Gedatsu-kai, provided key advice on the preparation of the questionnaire so that it would be appropriate for computer analysis.) Without the hard work of these students, the nationwide survey of more than 18,000 questionnaires would not have been completed.

The nature of our joint study requires further elaboration. In this case, "joint" research was literally true: "we"planned, observed, recorded, shared materials (such as recordings and photos), and discussed and interpreted all aspects of the research. Therefore, throughout this book, it has seemed fitting to use *we* and *our* not as editorial convention, but to indicate the true joint character of the research. From the beginning of the study, my intention was to accumulate materials for a monograph on Gedatsu-kai as an example of Japanese new religions and contemporary Japanese religion; Professor Miyake and his students used the materials we gathered as some of the content for their seminar. Because Professor Miyake was teaching at both Keiō University and Tokyo University, he was able to participate in the field work only as his schedule permitted; he gave freely of his time to me and his students, and visited both the Gedatsu-kai headquarters and the Sacred Land (Goreichi), but he did not participate directly in the observation of branch meetings or the collection of life histories.

My time in Japan from June 1979 through January 1980 was devoted almost entirely to research on Gedatsu-kai: reading the movement's publications, meeting with its officials, observing branch, regional, and national meetings, collecting life histories, and preparing and distributing the questionnaire. Professor Miyake's students also were busy with their own school schedules, but usually one or two went with me to the branch meetings and life history interviews; most or all of us (including Professor Miyake) attended national meetings. As a research team, we tended to work individually rather than as a group; for example, when collecting life histories, we paired off as a Gedatsu-kai member and researcher, rather than recording the same member's life history—this way we were able to collect more information from a wider circle, and we later shared our individually gathered materials.

My procedure after a research trip was to spend the rest of the day (or after several days of research, to spend a day or two) typing up handwritten notes. For life histories, tape recordings helped fill in missing passages from notes. Each segment of notes (for a life history or meeting) was duplicated and shared with the other individuals of the research team; my notes eventually totaled several hundred pages. During seminar meetings, we compared notes on meetings and life histories and shared photos and recordings. Professor Miyake's students made corrections and additions to my field notes.

Some of this joint research was the tedious detail familiar to all field workers, such as the assembly and distribution of the questionnaire and the checking and rechecking of the sequence of rituals and the peculiarities of Gedatsu-kai terminology. At the same time, we were interested in the theoretical issue of the nature of Japanese new religions and how they represented continuity and discontinuity with traditional Japanese religion. It was in Professor Miyake's seminar that I first introduced my criss-cross diagram analyzing the development of Gedatsu-kai out of three interrelated factors; Professor Miyake and his students criticized and helped improve this theoretical model, which was published in an article (Earhart 1980b) and is reproduced in chapter 8 as Figure 2.

Our research into Gedatsu-kai was much more profitable than we had imagined; especially because of the openness and encouragement of the movement's leaders and members, we felt that we had accumulated as much or more concrete information on any Japanese new religion than had previously been made public. We discussed the best way of communicating our research data, and considered a joint publication in English, but decided against it, partly because of the busy schedule of Professor Miyake, and partly because of the different kinds of audiences in Japan and the United States. Therefore, it seemed best to publish separately in Japanese and in English. After I returned to the United States, Professor Miyake's students continued to observe additional Gedatsu-kai activities and collected more concrete information on the religion's historical context. The students focused on various aspects of Gedatsu-kai, writing articles which formed the bulk of a book of essays on the movement, joined with several articles by Professor Miyake and me, and published under our joint editorship (Earhart and Miyake 1983).

I returned from Japan in February 1980 with a huge amount of raw material, including several hundred pages of typed field notes, tape recordings, photos, and data sheets from the survey that the students had coded (according to some categories we had agreed upon). From that point I began to sort through and analyze the material, in the midst of a busy teaching schedule. One of the first priorities was to prepare the data sheets from the nationwide survey for computer analysis: this information was placed on the mainframe computer at Western Michigan University by keyboard operators reading the data sheets, and we obtained a simple set of results. When I returned to Japan in January of 1981 for a conference (unrelated to the Gedatsu-kai research), I took with me a printout of simple results and a computer tape of the data. In the meantime, Professor Miyazaki had completed a computer file of the same data; these two files are essentially the same, with minor differences due to different manipulation of the data.

This set of material was the basis for the writing of this book. I began arranging subsets of the material, such as life histories and branch meetings, into chapters, while refining the computer analysis of the survey data. The help of the staff of the Computer Center and the Center for Statistical Services, and the advice of Thomas Van Valey of the Sociology Department of Western Michigan University were crucial for my introduction to computers and the processing of the survey data for this book. Some sections of the book, especially the life histories, were first publicly presented in lectures: at the University of Pittsburgh, Wittenberg University, and Augusta College, as well as in my own and colleagues' classes at Western Michigan University. Two life histories and the theoretical argument of chapter 8 were published previously in articles and as part of another book. After completing a rough draft of this book, I used materials from the published articles of the research team to describe aspects of Gedatsu-kai I had not researched. I was not in Japan for a full year, so I was unable to observe the complete ritual year; description of two annual festivals is taken from a published article of the research team. Other published articles by the research team provided historical background on the life of the founder and comparative data on statistics for the survey. Wherever published materials were used, they are cited either in the text or in the notes; where not cited otherwise, the book is based on my own field notes and my own handling of the computer analysis of the survey data. All photographs in the book are my own, with the exception of no. 1, courtesy of Gedatsu-kai headquarters, and no. 19, provided by the research team.

The reader is entitled to know this division of labor and the exact process of gathering and interpreting the material for this book. What should be emphasized at this point is that although this work is listed with a single author, it is in many ways a joint production of Professor Miyake and his students as well. They deserve the credit for the scope and detail of the study, but of course the responsibility for the interpretation rests with me.

Preparation of the manuscript for this book depended on the reading and editing skills of a number of people, especially colleagues at Western Michigan University: E. Thomas Lawson of the Department of Religion, Stanley Robin of the Sociology Department, and Helenan Robin of the Political Science Department read portions or drafts of the manuscript. My son David read and edited carefully an early draft of the manuscript. John DeRoo read and improved a final draft.

My thanks go to Judith Berling and Patrick Olivelle, series editors, for providing the context in which this monograph can be presented.

The help of all these people, and of others unmentioned, is gratefully acknowledged; any errors that remain are my own.

GEDATSU-KAI
AND
RELIGION
IN
CONTEMPORARY
JAPAN

1

AN INSIDE APPROACH TO JAPANESE RELIGION

Japan has a rich religious heritage with a long history. The many traditions that form this heritage include Shinto, Buddhism, Taoism, Confucianism, folk religion, Christianity, and new religions. Standard among the various approaches to Japanese religion are the treatment of individual traditions and the historical survey of the entire heritage. Because this study focuses on religious dynamics in contemporary Japan, it will emphasize a rather different, somewhat bold approach—concentration on the beliefs and practices of one new religion, Gedatsu-kai (literally Liberation or Salvation Society), as a kind of microcosm of Japanese religion. By focusing on just one movement, we are able to portray the dynamics of contemporary religion in Japan at much greater depth. In the course of this book, a more formal definition and a more precise analysis of aspects of Gedatsu-kai will be offered. But for the moment we will assume a more direct and interesting approach to this movement.

Various methods of study will be employed in the interpretation of Gedatsu-kai, including standard historical, descriptive, and survey approaches. However, our emphasis is to balance "outside" views of the new religion with "inside" views of its members. With the generous cooperation of members, we may obtain an "inside" view of a religion by asking them to relate their experience within it. Such an approach works very well within Gedatsu-kai, for a regular part of the meetings at local branches and regional centers is the giving of "testimony" or "experience" (*taiken*) by members. Thus it is possible for us to ask individual members to relate their religious experiences by retelling the kind of taiken that they have often told in meetings. This method of study is similar to the anthropological technique of collecting life histories; the major difference is that focus on taiken provides us with a more selective view of religious life, rather than the entire range of human experience. Nevertheless, in talking about their religious experiences, these people tell us a great deal about their lives generally, so we will refer to these taiken as religious life histories, or simply as life histories. Throughout this book, a number of life histories will be used to gain an "inside" view of Gedatsu-kai and Japanese religion.

The Life History of Mr. Negishi:
Religion Is Power

Perhaps the best approach to the world of contemporary Japanese religion is to listen to the taiken of one man. To protect his identity, we will call him Mr. Negishi. Mr. Negishi lives in Tokyo, has a university degree, is financially independent, and donates much of his time to Gedatsu-kai. He has long been a member of this movement, and now is an important member of its executive board. At the time of the interview, January 26, 1980, he was fifty-one years old. The following account is most of Mr. Negishi's story, which he told me, in Japanese, during a two-hour interview at the Tokyo headquarters of Gedatsu-kai. (His comments on the formal organization and future plans of the movement will be introduced in a later chapter.) We first met in 1969, when I initially began to study Gedatsu-kai, and he was the first representative of the movement who explained this new religion to me. We had also met a number of times during 1979–80, and traveled together with other executive members on an official pilgrimage to Kyoto. We were on friendly terms, and Mr. Negishi was well aware of my intentions to study Gedatsu-kai and write a book on the subject. Because he is an accomplished speaker who knows his story well, he spoke freely.

Without stealing Mr. Negishi's thunder, we have tried to indicate in the heading for his life history the general message that he tried to convey: religion is power, and the general rationale for him to join and participate in Gedatsu-kai is that it affords him the power to live. Now we turn to Mr. Negishi's story, which is recorded here in essentially the same way he told it to me. Except for very minor clarifications and additions, there has been no attempt—or need—to change or improve his narration. To retain the vividness of the human document, it is quoted here in the first-person singular—the "I" is Mr. Negishi. Brackets are used to indicate the few instances where the author interrupted with questions, and to give the Japanese original for some key terms.

Mr. Negishi speaks:

I entered Gedatsu-kai after I was ten years old—between ages ten and twenty. There was a neighbor, an older person who worked in a bank. And our family had leased land to him. This was an area formerly called Musashino—now a part of Tokyo. I am a real native of Tokyo. From ancient times, from Edo times,[1] even as far back as the Heian period,[2] my ancestors were here. They had land and rented it out. So I had a connection[3] with this person. I was still young at the time, and did not have much feeling for religion. But then there was our family situation at the time—our family was in poor health, and there was always someone sick. For example, my mother was sick for the longest period of time—she couldn't get out of bed for seven years. There were always two or three in the family sick, and it went on for ten years this way; I thought this was hard for my father.

But religion—well, in popular language, this is called newly arisen religions. As opposed to established religion, in the last hundred years or so these "newly arisen religions" had appeared as new forms of religion. And Gedatsu-kai seemed to be of a low level. This is how I felt about Gedatsu-kai. But I was told that the teaching was excellent in Gedatsu-kai. The bank person had encouraged my father to go to Gedatsu-kai, but my father didn't want to go, so I went instead. I didn't like religion. Yet at the same time I was wondering about religion. In this world— *in this world*—is religion necessary? I thought, like most people, that what is most needed in the world are such things as politics, economics, and authority or power. In this light, in this world, religion is not really good, necessary. But there were problems in this way of thinking. For example, if a law changes, then good and bad change overnight—what was good according to the law yesterday, is bad according to the law today. This was just after Japan's defeat at the end of World War II, and we had no power.

At present young people—internationally—in Russia, everywhere—in all major countries ask: What power does religion have? What purpose does religion serve? I thought this way, too, like all young people, at this time. Those who have power change their approval of religion, and the like, overnight. Of course, people said that if you believed, it would be a blessing—you would get well, and so on. There are three main types of suffering: first, economics; second, feelings, that is, the family and human relations; and third, the body, that is, sickness. To resolve these problems of suffering, you should study religion, they said, but. . . . Throughout the world, there is religion. People always fight, even over religion, I thought. Most wars are religion-based. It is an argument among different peoples.

The bank person was a fine person, so my father told me to go study Gedatsu-kai. I was against this. I had a sibling, an older sister, and because my mother was always sick, my elder sister was like a mother. So my father told my older sister, too, to go study; and because my older sister was more gentle than I, she went, and I went, too. This was just after World War II. From olden times our family lived in Musashino, so we practiced religious customs and folk religion. The local tutelary deity[4] and such beliefs were a part of our life—they were customs within daily life. One must, naturally, pay respects to the local tutelary deity, especially on the first and fifteenth of the month, when everyone went to the local Shinto shrine of the tutelary deity.

And Gedatsu-kai was good—I had heard a lot about religion, and read philosophy and religion. I had studied genetics and cytology in the university; at the end of my university work I studied economics and Japanese literature. I had also studied socialism and communism, and human character. I liked Gedatsu-kai— because I was a person from an ancient area. I had received blessings from generations of family ancestors,[5] and ancestors generally. On the first and fifteenth of the month we would go to the local Shinto shrine of the tutelary deity. "Thank you again for this month." Our ancestors were not ashamed of their efforts. This was a custom. After all, the local tutelary deity is the same as ancestors. It is like saying hello to your mother and father. My ancestors were farmers, pioneer farmers in this area—they had pioneer spirit! They prayed earnestly for the blessing of their descendants. "Thanks to you we are safe; we ask your favor again." It is like a "good morning," a greeting to parents. It is not a formal religious visit.[6]

Even today the Japanese don't understand this. The Ise Shrine and Shrine Shinto were the cause of the war, so they say, but this is irrelevant.[7] For example, the basis of religion, as we usually know it, is a teaching, ceremonies, propagation, rituals, and divinities—such as Buddhas. But this is irrelevant when we consider the local tutelary deity practices of my family. Where one lives—this is important. [At this point the author asked Mr. Negishi the name of his local Shinto shrine,

and he said it was a Hachiman shrine.] Emperor Ōjin[8] is the deity worshipped.
Also there are lots of small shrines, lots of spirits, but Emperor Ōjin is the chief
deity. My ancestors were venerating these spirits, opened up this faith. So I
followed the flesh of my parents. I had this tradition. My religion I did not think
of as an acquired "faith." My ancestors were born of this earth, they were part of
the realm of nature. We must be in harmony with the realm of nature. In other
words, the realm of nature is equal to a deity [kami]. It is nature that allows us
to live. We must live in harmony with nature. This is the basic teaching of Japan.

Gedatsu's teaching is the same. It has the same view of nature. It emphasizes
the local tutelary deity. And it stresses Buddhism. But Buddhism means our
ancestors, as well as such divinities as the Buddha—this is how Japanese Buddhism
is characteristically different from the Buddhism of other countries. So naturally
Gedatsu-kai emphasizes the local Buddhist parish temple [bodaiji]. So I was sym-
pathetic to Gedatsu-kai. I wondered about life, what a human being is. I was
twenty-two years of age when my father died. While my father was alive, and
then relatives, and even neighbors—they said about business dealings and work—
you must not do bad things—you must be honest. And they helped me affirm
this. My father died, but before he died, he taught me, and I remembered his
words and sentences, about not lying, keeping promises, and so forth. But as I
said before, I had been wondering about human beings, and how they can live.
I thought that humans do not have power. But one must have power. To protect
oneself, and one's family, one must have power. But what is one's own power?
It does not just come from one's own circumstances. How do you get power? How
can one maintain power?

In the teaching of the founder of Gedatsu-kai, and in Buddhism, there is the
law of cause and effect. It is destiny. I studied genetics in the university. This is
the scientific way of explaining it. The parents and children are the same—this
is a genetic principle. "The actions of the parents are passed on to the children."
The actions of the parents become the "result" of the children. Strong or weak,
this is the karmic connection [en] of the parent; the karma of cause and effect.[9]
This is the law of nature. This is the nature of the human race. I learned this at
school, and thought it had no relationship with religion—but then later I saw it
in the founder's teaching! The founder's disciples said that if I studied genetics,
then I should understand the founder's teaching: "If you studied genetics, then
you ought to understand Gedatsu-kai."

There were many people who didn't go on the first and fifteenth of the month
to the local Shinto shrine of the tutelary deity, but my family was a shrine parish
representative. And my family went not only on the first and fifteenth of the
month, but every day. From my youth, I went every day. My family is still parish
representative. I myself don't participate that much as parish representative, but
my mother, who is seventy-eight and healthy now, goes to the shrine as parish
representative. I go to the local shrine of the tutelary deity for "good morning"
and "good night." My teachers in Gedatsu-kai said that if I did this, then I should
understand Gedatsu-kai's teaching. In the morning, my "good morning" greeting
is "Again today your favor—blessing"; in the evening, my "good night" is "Thank
you for another safe day." I did this every day, as a custom, just as if I were
greeting my parents.

Then there is another very important aspect of Gedatsu-kai's teaching, completely different, that I studied. As you know and as I have pointed out before, Japanese Buddhism is Mahayana Buddhism. And this is fine, but in terms of human life, is the soul eternal? Worship is OK, but are there really deities [kami]? This is a doubtful matter. They say that even if the form is gone, people become kami. Is there a soul? Occasionally I practiced the ritual of *gohō shugyō*.[10] I thought the teaching was wonderful, but didn't believe in the practice of gohō shugyō. I was told to practice gohō shugyō. The branch leader of Gedatsu-kai and others urged gohō shugyō. Many times I was told this. At first when I practiced gohō shugyō, there was no spiritual communication. Then suddenly I had a spiritual experience; this was after many practices of gohō shugyō.

In the Kantō Plains[11] there was one family named Toshima that had pioneered the area. This was one major family, like the Chiba, Itabashi, Akasaka families, who opened up the Kantō Plains, and whose family names became place names. There was also a man named Ōta who built the Edo castle. There was a long battle between the Toshima and Ōta families, and the Toshima family lost out. This was at the end of the Heian period. The fallen Toshima had a residence at Shakujii—located in Nerima ward of present-day Tokyo. I saw all this during gohō shugyō. It lasted for fifteen minutes. I saw the entire struggle, the landscape, and everything. This greatly surprised me. At first I thought that the Gedatsu-kai teachers had used hypnotism. But this was a foolish idea.

There is only a little literature on this historical affair. Tokyo University has this literature. And there is some information in the *Nerima Local History*. I saw all of this because I am a native of the area. It is only eight—or six—kilometers to this place Shakujii from my house, and to the site of the Toshima mansion, it is only one kilometer. My relatives all live in this area. So the upshot is that the practice of gohō shugyō and the study of literature are all the same—in my heart I didn't know this before. I didn't know it, I practiced the sacred gohō shugyō and learned about history. Later I read literature, and was surprised to find this experience confirmed. *I heard their voices, the playing of the flute.* I still remember it clearly today. So several hundred years pass, but souls still live—in our heart. They still express this through us. We are conscious of them. The soul is immortal.

And so I became quite interested in this. And the meaning may be a little different here, but I saw this in other families: "Ah, because the father did such and such, the child becomes so and so." And because I am a native of the area, and mine is an old house, I know five or six generations of neighboring people—I can even recite the names of the heads of neighboring families going back that many generations. And I see the influence of older generations in the present. The suffering older generation affects the present generation, too. This is genetics. And when we rejoice, the ancestors do, too; this is because the ancestors are the same as deities [kami]. The soul is immortal. This is the essence of how things should be. Do good today, and it becomes tomorrow's blessing. Today's evil, tomorrow's sorrow.[12] And it is not just oneself, but one's child, and grandchild. It is the divine providence of nature. A mistake goes back to the kami. A white flower should be the same for three generations, and so on—it all goes back to the same source. And a human, even if he makes mistakes—it all returns to the kami!

The realm of nature is the way the kami have created. And we must live according to the principles of nature. For example, there are the sacred teachings of the founder—how man can live—there is destiny. But what is humanity? It is as a human being that the kami have created man. And it is according to this destiny that one matures and lives. And because we have this human quality, we must live as humans. And human nature—human quality—this quality—knowing this is a level of maturing, a level of learning—therefore we must practice this way. We must study, practice, learn. Thus we make happiness for others. The kami make everything: objects, persons, principles. We should give thanks for food—help create happiness for others. We have karmic connections [en] with all things. We give thanks to the kami for this day, for everything.

In our own hearts we grow and can understand this. Questions of what denomination we belong to, what sect—these are not important. For example, even if I take but one grain of rice and eat it, then it will never enter anyone else's mouth—this life was given just for my existence. For this we are very grateful! We must see that every day we live is given by the kami. To take good care of parents is the same thing. This is gratitude. And by this we know that it is because of the kami's heart that man lives.

In our own hearts, we grow, and can understand this. Questions of what denomination, what sect—it is not just what is "correct" according to the kami, or what the Buddha does not allow—rather, everything depends on the people, and the locale, and living in terms of this. Because this is what enables us to live. For example, take a teacup. We can use it to drink tea, or we can throw it at an enemy. So it is not the orthodox teaching, but the social, local relevance. We are *enabled* to live. So our power comes from the generations of ancestors. This is genetics. So for the descendants this is extremely important for their fortune. It is what the ancestors have done for us.

The Religious Universe of Mr. Negishi:
The Power of Kami, Ancestors, Buddhas, and Founder

If Gedatsu-kai can be seen as a kind of microcosm of Japanese religion, then Mr. Negishi's experience can be viewed as an individual sample of this microcosm. Of course, two hours out of one Japanese man's life are not sufficient evidence to depict the nature of all Japanese religion. Nevertheless, Mr. Negishi's life history is a remarkable tale of religious belief and practice in current Japan: remarkable not because it is so unusual, but because it is both representative of the history of Japanese religion and also a miniature version of the contemporary religious scene. The major outlines of Mr. Negishi's religious universe, especially his firm belief in the power of nature, kami, ancestors, Buddhas, and founder, are mirrored in the history of Japanese religion, and represent an interesting scenario of religious life in contemporary Japan.

This life history contains many key clues to the contemporary Japanese religious experience, and it provides a good case study for exploring the world of Japanese religion. By identifying the component parts of Mr. Negishi's religious universe and discussing their interrelationship, we can better appreciate its overall unity and wider significance. We will analyze features in his life history, not as a definitive conclusion to the nature of Japanese religion, but as a preview to some of the phenomena that are integral to Gedatsu-kai and central to Japanese religion. After reviewing these religious phenomena as expressed in Mr. Negishi's experience, we will look at the larger setting of the history of Japanese religion and the development of new religions, which set the context for the appearance of Gedatsu-kai and Mr. Negishi's personal philosophy of life.

The religious universe of Mr. Negishi is composed of four major objects of worship and sources of blessing: kami, ancestors, Buddhas, and founder. Directly linked to these four are both the practices by which the world view is celebrated and realized personally, and the fundamental beliefs supporting the general world view. Most of these can be found in traditional Japanese religion. Also fleshing out Mr. Negishi's religious career are some newer elements that are more typical of Japanese new religions. We will discuss Mr. Negishi's religious universe in this order, building up a more abstract and unified world view based on these elements.

One of the prominent features of Mr. Negishi's life history is his indebtedness to kami and nature. Nature as a life-giving power is divine or at least semidivine in its own right, and we as human beings owe our very existence to it. It is essential to be in harmony with nature. Kami inhabit nature, are in the earth, even form part of the local surroundings. Kami provide us with the bountifulness of life, such as rice and food. Ancestors, too, are sacred, and practically the same as tutelary kami. Just as people are indebted to the realm of nature for their creation, and receive specific blessings from kami, so they owe their particular existence to ancestors. Ancestors provide descendants with good fortune, and there is a mutually beneficial (or harmful) relation between the living and the spirits of the dead, especially within a given family.

In addition to kami and ancestors, Buddhist divinities and other spirits help grant Mr. Negishi the power to live. Buddhism for him is not so much the particular denominational tie, but the reverence of ancestors and Buddhas at one's own parish Buddhist temple (bodaiji). Reverence for the founder, too, is integral to Mr. Negishi's religious universe. In many ways the founder Okano is a model for the completion of his religious quest.

A number of practices are observed for kami, ancestors, Buddhas, and founder; these constitute the religious action by which Mr. Negishi celebrates and also realizes personally the power within the four dimensions. The most important action related to nature is the offering of gratitude. To a non-Japanese, "offering gratitude" may seem to be just an empty phrase, but in Japanese culture, it means to owe one's very existence, and thereby be indebted. The realm of nature is the ultimate level of indebtedness for all of creation, and therefore as human beings we must first pay thanks to nature. The kami are more specific, and so is the ritual action carried out for the kami. Mr. Negishi is more pious than most Japanese, since he visits the local shrine for the tutelary deity not only on the formal occasion of the first and fifteenth of the month, but also every morning and evening. His prayers are quite simple, asking for protection and giving thanks for a safe day, but they have a homey quality when he compares them to the "good morning" and "goodnight" uttered to his parents. Worship is not limited to one particular kami, but is distributed liberally to all the spirits associated with the area and the family.

Ancestors are the immediate link of humans to their worldly prosperity and fortune, so people must pay respects to the spirits of their family ancestors. One traditional practice is to visit the parish Buddhist temple of the family; Mr. Negishi does not specify the ritual concretely, but usually a trip to the temple means having a Buddhist priest recite scriptures as a kind of mass for the spirits of the dead. Another important ritual for the ancestors in Gedatsu-kai that Mr. Negishi took for granted and did not mention is pouring sweet tea over the ancestral tablets in the home—this is an innovation of the movement. Also part of this ancestral cult are acts of filial piety toward parents. Just as good fortune depends on ancestors, so will the fortune of descendants be influenced by the virtue of one's own ethical conduct.

In Japan the historical Buddha (Siddhartha Gautama) is not so important for everyday religion as many particular Buddhist divinities—Buddhas and bodhisattvas. Mr. Negishi does not mention, but assumes as part of his daily ritual in the home, worship of Gochi Nyorai (the five wisdom Buddhas). He encourages attendance at one's parish Buddhist temple (bodaiji), and interprets life through a highly concrete Buddhist notion of karma as the interconnectedness of human life, especially the fortune of a family. He is able to relate the Buddhist idea of karmic cause and effect to his university study of biology and cytology.[13]

Mr. Negishi does not say much explicitly about the founder of Gedatsu-kai, but the entire format of his life history is a paraphrase of the founder's teaching. In the next chapter, when the founder's life and teaching are treated, it will become apparent that Mr. Negishi is modeling his philosophy of life after the founder's precedent. For example, the gohō shugyō rite of meditation and mediation, which provided Mr. Negishi with his dramatic religious experience, was discovered by the founder. Likewise, Mr. Negishi's combination of otherworldly experience in gohō shugyō with ethical reflection and religious devotion is patterned after the founder's teaching.

There are many beliefs in Mr. Negishi's story that can be recognized as supporting this world view and program of action. One is the basic belief that human life is insufficient and unfulfilling by itself. Life does not contain meaning and power intrinsically, but is granted power from the realm of kami, ancestors, Buddhas, and founder. Mr. Negishi's phrasing of this principle has been translated freely, in order to provide a smooth English rendering, as "We are enabled to live." But the Japanese expression is much more forceful—*ikasarete iru*, a causative verb form which means literally, "We are caused to live," or "We are made to live." In other words, people should recognize from the outset that they are not the creators of their own destiny, so the meaning and fulfillment of human life depend on greater power. People must acknowledge the source of their life, which "causes to live," such that they have an abundant and happy life.[14]

Just as life cannot be lived apart from the sources of power, so life cannot be experienced apart from the network of karmic connections. The major force of karma, of course, is handed down immediately from family ancestors, but Mr. Negishi points out that karma also subtly colors business and personal relations, and even is present within the local history. It is not so much that one consciously contracts these relationships—rather, karmic connections are part of the givenness of human life. In order to live abundantly and meaningfully, people should practice religion as mentioned above, and follow the notions of life dependent on higher power and karmic connections. At the same time, they should pursue the traditional virtues of hard work, honesty, and patriotism. Later we will see just how important these traditional virtues are to the philosophical and ethical aspect of Gedatsu-kai.

For a person to mature religiously, it also helps to "study" religion, in the sense of reflecting on one's personal, social, and cosmic role. Sometimes this study takes specific forms, such as ascetic techniques not mentioned by Mr. Negishi. One form that he focuses on is the gohō shugyō ritual of meditation and mediation: often this becomes a means of communicating with the other world. Later we will see that this communication with the other world enables people to discover the spiritual cause of sickness, and thereby enables them to be healed.

All of the above notions, practices, and beliefs are found abundantly in traditional Japanese religion. There are some other aspects of Mr. Negishi's story that are more characteristic of the past century or so and the new religions which emerged during this time. For example, Mr. Negishi deeply experienced the changing value system after the war; from the beginning of the Meiji period in 1868, there was a rather rapid change of social structure and religious ideas, and the post-World War II dilemma is a more severe case of the search for tenable values. In pre-Meiji times there was a more natural, unconscious absorption into religious practices, and less of a sense of a break from tradition and recovery of tradition. Traditional peasants, for example, probably accepted the existence of the kami and attendance at seasonal festivals almost as commonplace, and did not agonize about such questions as the meaning of human life, the source of power, and the immortality of the soul. After World War II, the more conscious sense of a break from tradition and of a quest for "new" answers helped force Mr. Negishi to face the religious question of the meaning of life in a more "modern" or "existential" posture.

Another rather new feature of Mr. Negishi's personal experience is the central role of a charismatic founder in resolving the existential crisis. Of course, there are many founders of religious organizations in earlier Japanese history. But a striking feature of the founders of new religions is that usually they have been lay people who resolved their own quest and unified (or reunified) a pattern of belief and practice; in turn, this formed a model for individual followers, who shaped their religious philosophy after the fashion of the founder. Often the exemplary life of the founder became the means by which the individual was able to dramatically resolve his or her own crisis. In Mr. Negishi's case, the resolution came through several different modes. In the first place, he was able to think through the rationale of Gedatsu-kai, and to comprehend that it was a meaningful reordering of the traditional life he had been following. In the second place, he finally— almost against his will—had a transforming spiritual experience. That is, in contrast to deliberate reasoning out, the spiritual communication during gohō shugyō was perceived as a direct communication from the other world, transcending ordinary rational processes. As we will see later, Gedatsu-kai emphasizes this "actual experience" (*jikken*) of religion.

Usually a person joins a new religion as a result of the reconstitution of the world view (or perhaps we should say, in the process of this reconstitution): a new religion is a voluntary organization, one which at least the first generation of believers must consciously decide to join. These new religions are dominated by lay persons, both on the grassroots level and even in the higher offices. There is a high degree of participation by lay people in their ceremonies and administration.

The separate parts of Mr. Negishi's religious universe—the sources of power, the ritual practices, and the underlying beliefs—fit together to provide him a unified world view. This personal religious system does not illustrate the entirety of Japanese religion, nor does it include every aspect of Gedatsu-kai. But it affords a fascinating "inside" view of how a contemporary Japanese enters and practices religion. Remarkably, this individual's experience comes close to giving us a complete picture of Japanese religion. After we have looked at a number of other life histories—and considerable additional material, including the life of the founder, the results of a nationwide survey of Gedatsu-kai members, the organizational structure of the movement, and its ritual life—we will try to draw more comprehensive conclusions about Gedatsu-kai, Japanese new religions, and Japanese religion in general. But first we must turn briefly to the historical background of these subjects.

To understand Mr. Negishi's life history, not only do we need to examine the components of his religious universe, but also we must place his story within a general view of Japanese religious history.[15] This book has opened with an inside view of Japanese religion through one example of contemporary religious experience—Mr. Negishi's life history. The question begged here is what is the relationship of Mr. Negishi to over two thousand years of religious history in Japan. We can widen the focus from microscopic to macroscopic by tracing the religious heritage of Mr. Negishi's experience retrospectively. Mr. Negishi's taiken is a single example of religious experience similar to that of other Gedatsu-kai members. Gedatsu-kai is a medium-size Japanese new religion (claiming about 250,000 members), smaller than the dozen or so new religions with extensive memberships, but larger than the hundreds of new religions with memberships numbered in the tens of thousands and less. These new religions have been a conspicuous force in Japan since World War II, and rose to prominence from humble beginnings in the nineteenth century. Generally, these new religions are thoroughly Japanese, drawing most of their content from the heritage of more than two thousand years of Japanese tradition. In other words, Mr. Negishi's experience can be seen as the contemporary expression of the Japanese religious heritage.

A major premise of this work is that Japanese religion is the unified religious world view of the Japanese people, and Gedatsu-kai is a miniature contemporary version of this heritage. Therefore, it is important to identify more clearly what is meant by the term *Japanese religion*. Japanese religion is the distinct tradition formed from the interaction of indigenous and foreign organized religions and folk elements in the context of Japanese culture. Within Japan are found several organized religions, notably Shinto, Buddhism, and Christianity; also there are systems of thought and practice—Taoism and Confucianism (or Neo-Confucianism)—which are not so formally organized; and there are many variations of folk religion, popular thought, and local customs. Each of these elements may be viewed individually, but because the Japanese people have come to participate in several or most of these simultaneously in framing a common world view, we can call this larger heritage Japanese religion. In other words, there are many religions (in the plural) in Japan, but their totality as experienced by the people (with the possible exception of Christianity) forms one Japanese religion or religious tradition.

These various religions and folk traditions interacted with one another for many centuries, but especially during the Tokugawa period (1600–1867) they came to form a common set of social, ethical, and political as well as religious values. Such values were promoted by popular teachers such as Ishida Baigan, whose work has been interpreted by Robert Bellah in his *Tokugawa Religion*.[16] The values and practices of the late Tokugawa also found their way into various new religions. The first datable new religion (or *shinkō shūkyō*, literally "newly arisen religion") may be Nyoraikyō, claiming an 1802 founding, but the first large-scale new religion is Tenrikyō, founded in 1838. Tenrikyō is one of the thirteen popular movements which during the Meiji era (1868–1912) received the designation of Sect Shinto; after World War II such groups enjoyed complete freedom of religion and could exist as independent religious bodies. Many new religions arose in the early decades of this century and flourished especially after 1945.

These new religions are good examples of how values and practices from Tokugawa times and even previous centuries have been handed down and are continued in modified form today. Most of the "new" religions emphasize the fact that they preserve old Japanese traditions. Much of their message is the rediscovery of the "true" nature of religious life for the Japanese people. Often this rediscovery takes place in the exemplary life of a founder (or foundress) who has undergone great difficulties and/or austerities to arrive at this truth or revelation. The person becomes a founder when he or she, by virtue of resolving his or her personal dilemma, is able to show others how to resolve their personal problems. Much of the content of the religious notions and rituals borrows from past tradition, but with some cases of remarkable innovation. However, the most significantly "new" feature of the new religions is the gathering together of members into nationwide voluntary organizations (some of which are international in scope). By joining a new religion, an individual not only is able to reaffirm traditional Japanese values and practices, but often assumes a fictive relationship (parent-child) with the person who recruited him or her (or with the founding figure). In many cases the founder's charisma is aided by an efficient "organizer" who implements the founder's vision in a way that attracts followers and places them in cohesive units to mobilize their devotion and energy.

The individuals who join a new religion are linked together in both small face-to-face meetings and nationwide networks. The smaller meetings incorporate traditional beliefs and practices, such as veneration of ancestors and healing rites, with newer techniques such as counseling. The nationwide organization is a new form of universal voluntary organization, often making effective use of mass media (especially publishing) and establishing sacred centers as new sites of pilgrimage using modern transportation. There are many new religions, each with its own founder, traditions, acceptance of traditional customs, and formulation of modified practices. Amid all of their differences, the new religions generally share most of the above features.

In general, Mr. Negishi and Gedatsu-kai are part of this general trend within Japanese religious history for new religions to develop out of the general background of Japanese religion. Mr. Negishi's story in part is a reflection of his existential concern following World War II; in part it is also a continuation of religious themes that emerged from the Tokugawa era and before—such as the centrality of kami, Buddhas, ancestors, and founders—which is characteristic of other new religions. Gedatsu-kai and other new religions represent simultaneously both continuity with the Japanese religious heritage and remarkable innovation.

Just as Mr. Negishi did not create anew the religious world view that he espoused, so Gedatsu-kai (and other new religions) did not emerge in a vacuum and develop completely novel traditions. Kami, Buddhas, ancestors, and founding figures are perennial features of Japanese religion, but Gedatsu-kai reconfigured these traditional objects of worship in the context of a voluntary organization with distinctive rituals.

The leading question, of course, is exactly how a new religion such as Gedatsu-kai emerged out of the larger tradition of Japanese religion. There are many ways of approaching the origins of Gedatsu-kai, but the thread of our story begins with Mr. Negishi, and that is where we pick up the trail again. If Mr. Negishi's story is a microcosm of Japanese religion, where did he find the model for his world view? Mr. Negishi credits Gedatsu-kai with providing him with the power to live, but wherein lies the original genius of this new religion? All these questions lead us back to the founder of the movement, who was responsible for reshaping the Japanese religious heritage in the form of the voluntary organization of Gedatsu-kai, thereby making it possible for individuals such as Mr. Negishi to reconstruct their personal world views. Thus, we turn to the life of Okano Eizō and the founding of Gedatsu-kai.

2

OKANO EIZŌ
From Spiritual Crisis to
the Founding and Organization
of Gedatsu-kai

There is little in the childhood and middle years of the life of Okano Eizō that would have enabled any of his contemporaries to predict he would become the founder of a new religion with hundreds of thousands of members who view him as a deity (kami). Until his early forties, Okano lived in the same fashion as most of his contemporaries, and although he participated in many traditional religious practices, he did not spend a great deal of time in religious matters and was not involved in religion on a professional basis. From his teenage years into his forties, his main concern was seeking his fortune in the business world. His various ventures led to setbacks and outright failures, and it was not until he was about forty that he began to taste success. Ironically, just as he became successful and could repay his parents for the debts and worries he had caused them, his father died. Okano became more concerned with his sense of gratitude to his parents, especially to his father, and gave it serious thought as he recovered from sickness after his father's death. Not long after, at age forty-three, he suffered a near-fatal illness.

A deep spiritual crisis during this illness radically changed his life and inspired him to devote himself full time to the teaching and ministry of the message that was gradually revealed to him. From these experiences unfold the drama not only of Okano's life but also of the founding of Gedatsu-kai. This story is the collective memory of the founder published by Gedatsu-kai in a lavish volume (Gedatsu Shuppanbu 1979) which forms the major basis for this brief interpretation.[1] From this biography we will select the major features of Okano's life before his spiritual crisis, the key elements of his spiritual crisis, his quest for religious resolution of this crisis, the revelations and innovations that formed the basis for attracting followers, and the formative events in the development of Gedatsu-kai. This biography is useful both as a record of Okano's life and as an "inside" perception of his role as a religious founder.

Early Life of the Founder:
The Traditional Village, Business Failures and Success,
and Spiritual Crisis

Okano Eizō was born on November 28, 1881, in the village of Kitamotojuku, Saitama Prefecture, a short distance north of present-day Tokyo.[2] He was the fifth child of a landowning farm family, preceded in birth by three sisters and a brother. As young Okano grew up in this farm village, he apparently participated in the religious life of his family and the village. The nearby local Shinto shrine of the tutelary deity, Tenmanten Shrine, had originally been a small protective shrine for the Okano family, and for this reason there was a tradition for the family to participate as one of its parish representatives; Okano's father was a parish representative. His father also was a parishioner's representative for the Shingon temple Tamonji, which served as the parish temple for the Okano family. An integral part of Okano's childhood was following many traditional customs typical of the day, such as venerating the many kami present in the landscape and around their farm house. Indirectly Okano seems to have absorbed the customs of the area and of his immediate family. Both his grandfather and father had made the traditional pilgrimage to Ise, the most sacred site of Shinto, where the Sun Goddess is enshrined; in addition, his father was a leader (sendatsu) in a Fuji pilgrimage association (Fujikō) which made annual pilgrimages to Mount Fuji and brought back blessings for the local people (Gedatsu Shuppanbu 1979:27–28).[3] All of these influences must have made a great impression on young Okano, for three decades later these traditional features emerged as part of his new message.

Okano entered elementary school at age six and attended six years, which was standard for the time. Some of his textbooks survive, good examples of the "Confucian" style of education through reading praise of great personalities as models of virtue (ibid., p. 33). Okano was a good student, but he was more interested in listening to the stories of the Buddhist priest at the local Buddhist temple (Tamonji) to which his family belonged, and he spent much of his leisure time there. As he grew up, it seems that Okano absorbed traditional attitudes toward kami and Buddhas along with his acceptance of Confucian morality, without any dramatic decision or conversion experience. He gradually grew into these beliefs, practices, and customs, just as it was natural for him to participate in the family's blessing of food before meals.

It was unusual at the time for farm families to pay the money for their children to attend high school. The family tacitly understood that Okano's elder brother, as first son, would inherit the family farm. As a second son, the alternatives for Eizō were to be set up eventually as a branch family in farming, or to enter an apprenticeship in a business. At age twelve Okano was taken to Tokyo as an apprentice in a sake store, but after less than two years he was called home to work on the family farm, because his older brother had been drafted.

Okano preferred business to farming, and after his elder brother returned from military service, the father and two sons entered the expanding market of cottage-industry weaving. Most farm homes had hand looms, and could earn money in the off season by weaving cloth from thread provided by dealers such as the Okanos, who would deliver thread in the fall and collect finished goods in the spring. The father developed contacts in the countryside while the sons spent several years learning textile weaving and trading from other families. Unfortunately, just at the time when the Okano family began dealing independently with weavers, small mechanical looms began to supersede the hand looms used on farms. These mechanical looms spread throughout Japan, Korea, and Manchuria, flooding the market with cheap goods.

Struggling against the tide, the Okano family could not prevent the inevitable failure of this cottage industry.[4] For the Okanos, the collapse came when a shipment of thread did not arrive at the train station as promised to Eizō by a wholesaler; instead of returning home, he bought a ticket for Tokyo. A few months later he sailed from Tokyo to Korea to seek his fortune, at age twenty-two. After a half-year in Korea, because of the worsening of the Russo-Japanese War, his family urged him to return home, especially because the older brother had been recalled to military duty and was serving as a guard at the Ise Shrine.[5] Okano was reluctant to return home, because the failure in the weaving venture weighed heavily on him, even though it was not his fault. He worked on the family farm during his brother's absence, but still did not want to become a farmer as a branch family. When his older brother returned from military service, they decided once more to enter the textile field, but this time in the sale of cloth. He helped organize small businesses into an association which through joint sales could counteract the power of big businesses. Eizō was making some money, and when he fell in love with Aki, a young woman working in a restaurant, he asked his father for permission to marry her. His father said that his twenty-four-year-old son was ready for marriage, but absolutely refused to allow a union between him and a restaurant worker. Finally Eizō had to break off his tie with Aki, and he plunged into work again.

In spite of his hard work and organizing skills, the textile marketing association he helped form fell on difficult times, owing to double pressure from the big businesses and the general business slump after the Russo-Japanese War (1904–05). Okano arranged a large sale of goods to a wholesaler, who went bankrupt—apparently it was a deliberately planned bankruptcy, and the association had to be dissolved. The courts held Eizō responsible for evasion of taxes on the association's income, and he was a defendant in a court case that dragged on interminably. As he waited in Tokyo for the decision, Eizō was filled with remorse for the worries and difficulties he had caused his family. He wrote three letters to his parents and other family members, accepting all the blame for these failures (as due to his own evil), and apologizing profusely for the "sins" (tsumi) that had befallen the family because of his failures. None of this would have happened if he had taken up farming.[6] He wanted to improve his personal attitude and develop sincerity, and begin a new life, live as a filial son, even become an apprentice again. In the letters he hinted at welcoming death as a way of apologizing and repaying his gratitude (ongaeshi) to his parents.[7] These letters are interpreted today as a veiled suicide vow: if the court decision had been negative, he would have committed suicide to prevent further besmirching of the Okano name.

In mid-1909, the long-awaited decision of the court was handed down. Eizō was exonerated of any wrongdoing, and was required only to pay his portion of the total tax debt, in installments. This greatly relieved him, especially because it freed his parents of worry. He resolved to make a new beginning, and after visiting the Okano home in Kitamotojuku, he vowed not to return home until he was successful. He went to Tokyo to find work, hoping for an apprenticeship, and stayed for a while with relatives. However, apprentice work was hard to come by, so he took any work he could get, including odd jobs and construction work to eke out a living. In spite of severe hardships, especially during 1909 and early 1910, later he would say that it is good for people to experience such depths of misery, because this makes a person really appreciate love and duty (giri ninjō).[8]

In 1910, Okano found a better job as a laborer unloading ships; he used his leadership abilities to advance to foreman. Although apprentices usually were eleven or twelve years old, and Okano was in his late twenties, he boldly sought an apprenticeship and later was made clerk in the firm. Finally, after so many failures, Okano began to think that he was on the right path. From this point, he made a private practice of setting aside one day every month to visit the old village of Kitamotojuku, paying his respects at both the Shinto shrine of the tutelary deity (Tenmanten Shrine) and the memorial stones of the Okano family ancestors in the cemetery of the local Buddhist temple. He was able to make the trip after work and not miss time—in fact, he preferred to pay his visit at night, unnoticed, because he had not yet attained the success he had vowed. When he came before the Tenmanten Shrine, he apologized from the bottom of his heart for the impiety and unfilial behavior toward his parents, and offered his ardent thanks to the kami. He prostrated himself before the memorial stones of his ancestors, offering flowers and incense. He realized that his ancestors, with their long history preceding him, had taken good care of him. Then, facing his family home, he reflected on his past troubles, and on his own deficiencies that had caused them. In his heart he called out to his parents to forgive this unfilial son, apologizing over and over. Finally he determined to set out on a new life, and to succeed, returning privately every month until he did so.

Okano soon had a job with a shipping firm, and by 1913 he had reestablished direct contact with his family. He changed his monthly night visits to daytime visits. As his financial condition improved, he thought once more of Aki, and after eleven years of separation, they were married. While he took care of his increasing responsibilities in the shipping firm, Aki opened a geisha house. Okano and the shipping firm for which he worked benefited greatly from the worldwide shipping shortage during World War I. But as he became more prosperous through his work in Tokyo and Yokohama, he continued to think of his roots in Kitamotojuku and of the Okano family. Letters to his parents at this time were very solicitous, asking them to forgive him for lack of virtue, and inquiring about their health. Okano also concerned himself with the welfare of Kitamotojuku generally, participating in two projects: he helped provide high-quality, low-cost fertilizer for farmers (who were hard pressed by inflation), and he participated in an unsuccessful attempt to open a railroad station at Kitamotojuku. By 1919, when he was thirty-seven, Okano was financially well established.

At the same time that Okano Eizō's star was rising, his father's health was failing. The father saw himself as a restorer of the family's fortunes, which had faltered at the time of the Meiji Restoration (1868), and through his efforts and those of his seven children, he had done all he could to strengthen the family. In late 1920 he died, a severe blow to Eizō. He regretted all the trouble he had caused his father, and now that he could repay gratitude to his parents and be a filial son, his father was dead. The least he could do was to hold an elaborate funeral, which even included the scattering of money to the people attending, as an act of charity expressing symbolically the father's virtue. After his father's death, Okano became ill and went to a hot springs to recover; he spent much time reflecting on how he could improve his life as a way of thanking his father and making him happy in the next life. For Okano knew, from his family's childhood instruction, that the soul is immortal, and that death does not separate the living from the dead: his father continued to protect the family even after death. Okano and his family traced this heritage of benevolent protection through their ancestors back to the founder of this family line, Okano Hikoshirō.

For Okano Eizō, the death of his father was a turning point. He decided to work harder at being a success, and to carry this out by not just working for another firm, but becoming independent. Although there was some resistance from his firm, he was able to set up a joint agreement in which he was responsible for Hokkaido shipping. Times were difficult, but he managed the business carefully and even helped Aki build a restaurant. After the Tokyo earthquake of 1923, he became wealthy shipping building materials from Hokkaido to Tokyo; he also assisted with reconstruction in Kitamotojuku. During the next year he was active in the movement to open a railway station in Kitamotojuku, which this time succeeded.[9]

In March of 1925, exhausted by overwork, Okano caught a cold that became increasingly severe and was complicated by an unrelenting fever. His mother and wife waited on him when he became unconscious and was bothered by fierce dreams. While still unconscious, he repeatedly called out for *amacha*, which his family knew was the "sweet tea" used to bathe the statue of the infant Buddha on the Buddha's traditional birth date of April 8, and also used in Chinese herbal medicine. His mother felt this request was the wish of the Buddha, and would heal her son. Therefore the family obtained the herb and brewed this "sweet tea" for him to drink. Okano's condition was so grave that his family and the physician thought that he might die. While he was still unconscious, his dreams shifted from nightmares to a more peaceful feeling that he was returning to the innocence of his youth. He heard the voice of his father, and although he could not make out the words clearly, he was sure that his father had come to save him. As the form of his father disappeared, he saw a bright light from which the figure of the Buddha appeared, beckoning him to approach. He was told to open his mouth, and as he did, a gold-colored fluid poured forth. Instantly a shock gripped him, and he felt that everything was squeezed out of him. At this point he became conscious and was given amacha to drink. He vomited a large amount of blood mixed with pus, after which his fever dropped rapidly and he began to get better. His mother considered the sudden change a miracle, and folded her hands in prayer.

Gradually regaining consciousness and strength, Okano had plenty of time to think about his cure while in his sickbed. He thought about death, and did not want to die, because he had nothing to leave behind him, only money. He wondered about the meaning of life. He appreciated the beauty of nature, and was glad that he had been allowed to live.[10] He was vividly aware of being saved: meeting his father and ancestors, and vomiting all of the impurity in his body— this was the saving experience. All his past sins had been purified, but he wondered what the golden fluid was that he had vomited in his dream. He was brought

amacha again and was told that he had requested it when unconscious, and this
was what had made him vomit and lowered his temperature. His mother said that
the Buddha had saved him, so Okano should give thanks; Okano felt that the faith
of his mother had moved the kami and the Buddha to save him. He had not yet
digested this powerful experience, but he was much more peaceful and began to
look for a new course in life.[11]

Initial Revelations:
Discovery of the Amacha Memorial Mass
and the Decision to Initiate a Teaching

Okano Eizō and his followers came to see his critical sickness and extraordinary
recovery as both a dramatic turning point in his life and the stimulus that led to
the formation of Gedatsu-kai. Okano's entrance into religious leadership, or "conversion," was gradual and smooth. While he was recovering from his illness, he
found a new peace in his life, but at the same time he was more aware of the
disturbing social conditions around him. There was much social upheaval at this
time, and the government enacted the Peace Preservation Law to restrict radical
social movements.[12] Personally Okano was so content that he could have died in
peace because he felt reborn, but at the same time he sensed a power and purpose
within his life that was not complete. He began to experience the ability to see
into the lives of others—for example, without being told, he sensed that his maid
had a pain in the small of her back. Slowly he came to realize the miraculous
character of his rebirth through drinking amacha, and the extraordinary power
that resulted from this rebirth. While returning from a trip to a hot spring, he
stopped at the Izusan Shrine in the city of Atami. Standing peacefully in front of
it, he again recalled the golden light in his dreams, and realized that the source
of this light was kami.

Okano had more mystical experiences like the one at Izusan Shrine, and was
able not only to diagnose bodily complaints of his acquaintances but also to heal
by rubbing them with his hands. From his childhood he was familiar with this
miraculous aspect of religion, but he disliked religion that centered on requests
(gan), and he did not want to use his powers for satisfying particular requests: he
wanted a religion that conformed to his own experience of rebirth.[13] Okano did
not know exactly what this kind of religion was, so he consulted religious specialists.
He spoke to Buddhist priests, and found them to be devout, but their abstract
doctrine did not fit with his own experience (taiken). Okano was an "experiential
rationalist" in the sense of not believing what he had not experienced. He also
went to Shinto priests, but they were concerned mainly with the affairs of State
Shinto, and they could not interpret his personal experiences.

Because Okano's religious questions were not resolved by the priests of the
established religions of Buddhism and Shinto, he visited a man who practiced folk
traditions of spiritual and healing power.[14] This man immediately diagnosed Okano
as having spiritual power (reinō), and said that if Okano refined this spiritual power,
he could become a spiritual healer, too. They swapped similar stories and understood each other, but Okano did not want to become a spiritual healer, so he set
out to seek his own way to religious fulfillment. He continued to visit Buddhist

and Shinto priests as well as practitioners of folk traditions and made the rounds of temples and shrines, realizing that he was able to receive the revelation (*keiji*) of kami directly. After his sickness and recovery, his life turned increasingly to the Buddhas and kami, and the repeated revelations and increased spiritual power had a profound effect on his understanding of life.

Okano gradually came to understand that the meaning of life is given by kami, and that we should walk through life with them. His many revelations convinced him that kami are not beyond life, but within life—this was confirmed by his own powers. He knew that many diseases are caused by a person's "heart" and how that person lives, and he resolved to purify his life through ascetic practices (*shu-gyō*). He received a revelation to go to an isolated mountain area called Tanzawa (south of Tokyo) for ascetic practices and stayed there from the fall of 1927 to the spring of 1928. At shrines and temples, he formerly had sought rather lofty, "high" spiritual communication; at Tanzawa he communed directly with the spirits that inhabited the mountains—the kami protecting the mountain as well as the evil spirits known as *tengu* and spirits of dead soldiers and of other unfortunate victims. His ascetic practices at Tanzawa taught him that many of these spirits are the ones that "bother" people and cause misfortune or sickness. Okano's ascetic practices and insights gained at Tanzawa amounted to a rebirth or regeneration experience, convincing him to commit his life to religious purposes.

Okano's increasing preoccupation with religious matters did not set well with Aki, who was caught up in her own business and thought that her husband should tend to his business and moneymaking. However, Okano's critical period of practice and reflection at Tanzawa convinced him to work for the liberation of the human heart and to refine himself for this purpose. After leaving Tanzawa, he lived at a house he had built in Tokyo, and people who heard of his extraordinary powers came to him for healing of sickness or counseling of family problems. Sick people were especially numerous, and he found that most of them were possessed by wandering spirits of the dead. These spirits bothered the living because they either were *muen* (no longer memorialized by living relatives), or for some reason had not become pacified after death. He knew this directly from his practices at Tanzawa and communication with the spirits, and saw it confirmed in the lives of the people who sought help from him. In fact, such restless spirits with "dark" thoughts that cause sickness are not the exception, but the rule: through many generations of people, there have to be tragic deaths and feelings of revenge that lead to unpacified spirits' wandering about and causing trouble for the present generation. This is a crucial clue to the connection between a person's heart and the world of spirits. Hell is not just in the other world, but can be in one's own heart. When people came to Okano, usually he diagnosed the problem, had people perform the proper memorial for the spirit causing the problem, and resolved the matter; others he healed by touching with his hands.

Okano discovered that if people continued memorial rites (*kuyō*), usually the sickness did not recur; but the basic solution was due to a "healing of the heart." He was critical of people just relying on the miraculous power of kami in time of suffering: the popular saying is "kurushii toki no kamidanomi," literally "calling on kami in times of difficulty," implying that at other times kami are neglected. Okano thought that the ideal solution was to develop teaching and practice of memorial rites so that people could simultaneously pacify spirits of the dead and "heal" their own hearts. Because there was no effective practice linking these two religious goals, he resorted to standard Buddhist techniques. He advised people who sought help from him to offer candles at their *butsudan* (Buddhist altar in the home enshrining spirits of family ancestors), to make offerings, to recite Buddhist sutras, and if they did not know a sutra, to recite a simple phrase to purify the senses (*rokkon shōjō*). All people, regardless of their particular denominational ties to Buddhism, could perform these simple techniques, and they did bring some results. However, the results were inadequate, so Okano visited shrines and temples to find a better way of simultaneously pacifying spirits of the dead and healing the hearts of the living. Again there was no satisfactory answer to his questions.

As he reflected on this problem, he recalled the use of amacha, which had restored his life, and which he had been drinking since that time. He reasoned that, because he had been saved by amacha, its purpose is not simply to save the flesh but also to purify the heart. He accepted this insight as a revelation: if one's own soul is purified, the spirits of the ancestors must be pacified, because one's own soul and the spirits of the dead are the same. This was the answer to the need he felt for a kind of memorial rite for pacifying the dead: to offer amacha to the spirits of the ancestors as well as to drink it, thereby transforming the unpacified spirits of the dead into Buddhas (benevolent ancestors). This is the way of life that he decided to teach.

The first time amacha was used in this new manner was when a sick woman came to Okano complaining about her family—her dead mother-in-law who had been so cruel, her drinking husband, and her bad children. Okano told her to offer amacha to the Buddha and also to drink it; at the same time, she was to perform memorial rites for her mother-in-law and other Buddhist practices for one week. The woman returned in five days because the amacha had become thick and she couldn't drink it. Okano was happy, seeing the thickening of the amacha as a sign of communication with the spirit world. More important, the woman had even forgotten about her physical complaints. Okano attributed this to the effect of the amacha: drinking it purified her heart, and offering it pleased the spirits of the dead. Initially this spiritual experiment was successful, but Okano added the moral that she should recognize her past mistakes and work hard in life from that point on, and continue the same practice for another week. While she was performing these practices in front of her butsudan at night, she came to realize her past mistakes. She was too proud of her own family's former high position, and saw that her mother-in-law's criticism of her pride had been correct. And she realized that she had been happy when her mother-in-law died. In fact, it was her own mistaken heart that was largely responsible for her miserable family life. From that day on she was more considerate of her husband and children, and she performed memorial rites for the mother-in-law, apologizing to her. Her physical condition improved.

Okano's fame spread for "saving" people like this woman through the amacha memorial rite. An acquaintance introduced him to a Shingon Buddhist priest, Kurosawa Kōshō, who knew Buddhist doctrine but who had spiritual powers that went beyond the standard Buddhist doctrine and ritual. The two got along well, and Kurosawa was surprised at Okano's self-taught powers. Okano learned from Kurosawa some aspects of the esoteric doctrine of Shingon Buddhism to order his own experience (taiken). Another influential person for Okano at this early stage in his career was Shimada Kenshō, a popular practitioner of Nichiren Buddhism. Shimada listened to Okano's remarkable experiences and confirmed his spiritual power; at the same time, Shimada had worked with the organization of religious groups and helped Okano think about organizing his experiences into the foundation for a formal group.

Another incident with a sick woman, this time both physically and mentally ill, helped Okano complete the pattern for the amacha memorial rite. In this case he got no results from touching her, and realized that he had to put all his life into healing her if he really wanted to save people. Concentrating on this case all night, he had a revelation in which he saw an object like a memorial tablet, and was told to perform a memorial rite by pouring amacha over this tablet (on which names of the woman's ancestors were written). This new step was effective in healing the woman, and Okano was pleased that there had been revealed to him a simple and effective means of purifying the heart and pacifying the spirits of the dead, which anyone could perform. Okano combined this ritual technique with frank counseling, forcing people to face the facts of their personal situations. More and more people accepted this ritual and counseling from Okano: in effect they became the first "members" of Gedatsu-kai, although the formal organization had not yet appeared. Okano taught these people to practice self-reflection and self-effacement; for his part, he was always in the presence of kami in his daily life, not just when he visited shrines and temples.

On New Year's Day 1929, Okano returned to his family's native village at Kitamotojuku to pay his annual respects at shrines and temples. In front of the small Shinto shrine where the Okano family had long paid its respects, he felt an electric shock and could not move. A voice said, "I've been waiting," and the gist of this revelation, coming from Tenchi no Ōgami (literally "Great Kami of Heaven and Earth"), the source of the universe, was for Okano to initiate his teaching. Okano's mother was worried about this New Year's revelation, so they had his friend Shimada confirm it, since Shimada had started his own small religious movement. Shimada stood with hands clasped in prayer before the same small shrine where Okano had received the revelation to start a religion. At first Shimada could not comprehend the significance of the revelation, but he said that there certainly was a lofty spirit active here. As they were walking around the area, Shimada became possessed (kamigakari), and they took him back to the old Okano home, where he came to himself. Shimada said that there was a powerful spirit here, not only at the small shrine but in the entire area. This event was crucial for Okano personally, confirming his resolve to begin a new teaching, and Gedatsu-kai dates its founding from this point.

The Founding Year:
Revelation of the Gohō Shugyō and
the All Souls' Memorial Rite

Okano received his first inspirations and revelations long after he left his childhood home, when he lived in Tokyo and visited various shrines and temples, but more and more, especially as he sought confirmation of his earlier revelations, he returned to his native village and family home. The New Year's revelation urging him to initiate a religion occurred in front of the small shrine near the Okano home, where for generations the family had worshipped. In fact, the recurring episodes at the native village are viewed by Okano's biographers as so significant that at this juncture in the narrative they change terminology from secular to sacred.

Up to this point in the biography, they have referred to Okano Eizō by his family name (or simply as Eizō, to distinguish him from other members of the Okano family). However, from this point, because he has reached the crucial stage of deciding to found a teaching and religion, he is called Gedatsu Kongō Sonja. Although Okano Eizō did not receive this full honorific until after his death, his followers prefer to remember him by this title from the time that he decided to initiate a new religious movement. *Gedatsu* is a Buddhist term (*vimukti* in Sanskrit) meaning "freedom or release from sins or illusion," or "enlightenment" (like *nirvāna* in Sanskrit), and sometimes is translated as "salvation"; it was used by Okano to indicate the kind of religious fulfillment he taught in his movement.[15] *Kongō* is a Buddhist term (*vajra* in Sanskrit), literally "diamond, a symbol for firmness or hardness" (*Japanese-English Buddhist Dictionary* 1965:179), and used as one of the key symbols within esoteric Buddhism.[16] *Sonja* is a general term composed of two characters meaning literally "revered one," used by Gedatsu-kai to refer respectfully to Okano as the founder of their religion. In this book we will translate *Gedatsu Kongō Sonja* and abbreviations such as *Sonja* and *Kongō-sama* more freely as "the founder."

Another term that changes after this crucial foundational stage of Gedatsu-kai is *amacha*, which in the early part of the biography is written with two characters whose literal translation is "sweet tea." In subsequent appearances the second character (*cha* for "tea") remains the same, while the first character (*ama* for "sweet") is replaced with a character of the same sound *ama* but the different meaning of "heaven." The new term *amacha* is pronounced the same, but means "heaven(ly) tea." Japanese-language dictionaries contain only the "sweet tea" form of *amacha*; nevertheless, Gedatsu-kai prefers the "heavenly tea" version to indicate that when used ritually by Gedatsu-kai, this is a heaven-sent blessing, not a natural plant. Because translation of this term is awkward (the botanical name is *Hydrangea serrata*), it seems best to retain both meanings of "sweet tea" and "heavenly tea" by leaving the ambiguous *amacha* untranslated.[17]

Even the perception of space is transformed by the events surrounding Okano ("the founder"), especially the crucial confirmation of his 1929 New Year's revelation before the old family shrine to initiate a new teaching. His friend Shimada learned through possession not only that the revelation was genuine, but also that the entire area around the shrine and Okano's home was filled with a powerful spirit. For Gedatsu-kai history, the significance of this statement is the formal recognition of the founder's home and village as a holy site. Gedatsu-kai subsequently calls this area Goreichi, literally "Sacred Space" or "Holy Land." *Go* is an honorific in Japanese (preceding a term of respect), *rei* is "sacred" or "holy," and *chi* is "space" or "land." As we shall see later in greater detail, Goreichi defines a sacred center in a number of senses: revered as the source of the founder and origin of the religion he established, site of annual observances for Gedatsu-kai, and center of reality to which members return. All that need be noted for now is the changed significance of this space. Before the revelation and decision to initiate a new teaching, the founder visited his home village and paid respects to the local Shinto shrine and parish Buddhist temple at regular intervals, as was the ideal in traditional Japan. After this revelation/decision, the natal source of the founder and site of the founding event takes on the character of a "sacred space" that is different from the numerous examples of local sacred space in villages throughout Japan: this area becomes a national religious center, a "holy land" (or mecca) to which all members of Gedatsu-kai make pilgrimage.

After the revelation to start a religion and the manifestation of the Goreichi, the founder felt the guidance of even more powerful spirits than previously. The increasingly sacred character of his work and native village is borne out in the successive revelations leading to the creation of the meditation and mediation ritual called *ongohō shugyō*, or simply gohō shugyō. Unlike the explicit and complete revelations for the amacha memorial rite and for starting a religion, the revelation of gohō shugyō was fragmentary and gradual. On May 7, 1929, the founder experienced something greater than he had ever known: a strong feeling welled up within him, and an electric shock of golden light filled him. Early on the morning of May 8, with his spiritual eye he saw golden-colored spiritual letters, and at the same time he wrote them down: *ban, un, taraku, kiriku, aku*. Gedatsu-kai calls these five letters *ongohō*: *on* is an honorific, *go* is "five," and *hō* is the Japanese equivalent of *dharma* (in Sanskrit). These letters are well known as the mystic letters or "seeds" signifying a set of five Buddhist divinities.[18]

Because the usage of this revelation was not specified, and Shimada could not interpret it, the founder asked the kami who had revealed these letters how they were to be used. A voice answered the founder: "Put them between your hands clasped in prayer—this is how all people can communicate with kami" (Gedatsu Shuppanbu 1979:211).[19] This revelation clarified the form of discipline (shugyō) for using the five mystic letters (ongohō). Gedatsu-kai looks back at this revelatory experience as the moment when the founder became the embodiment of Buddhism (*gohōtai*) and achieved the boundary of oneness with kami (*shinjin goitsu*). The founder had a waitress from his wife's restaurant test the newly revealed method. She had been sick, and the founder was unable to heal her by rubbing her with his hands. He placed her in a posture of prayer before an altar and had her put between her hands a paper on which the five letters were written. The waitress's hands began to shake, and a female ancestor who had drowned three generations ago began to speak through her. The founder acted as an interpreter (*chūkaisha*, later a standard role in gohō shugyō), asking what message (*shirase*) the spirit wanted to give the waitress. The female spirit spoke through the waitress, telling the founder that the woman should perform the amacha memorial rite and pacify her spirit. The waitress did as she was told and lived peacefully thereafter.

This was the first test of gohō shugyō, and although it was successful, the complete practice and its meaning were not immediately clear. What the founder saw right away was the fact that you must understand the basic cause of personal trouble, or you will not be able to pacify a spirit that is bothering you. And he recognized that gohō shugyō was a means for anyone to commune with the spirit world. Morohashi Kakutarō helped interpret gohō shugyō by having his mentally ill father-in-law perform the rituals. The father-in-law became possessed and learned of family karma (innen), which was purified through the amacha memorial rite. This illustrates that gohō shugyō is able to uncover bad karma and extend good karma. The basic principle the founder discovered was that the mediation ritual enables one to learn the means of purifying a spirit (that is troubling a person); then through performance of memorial rituals and intense apologies to the spirit, it is possible to purify the spiritual character of oneself and the spirit. Gedatsu-kai views the greatest significance of the amacha memorial rite and the mediation ritual of gohō shugyō in the fact that anyone can perform them. It is not necessary, as in many previous Japanese religious traditions, to memorize scriptures, learn strict rules for formal memorial rites, or give up the world and enter mountains for practice of discipline. These kinds of restrictions are difficult for the lay person, but anyone can follow the practices laid down by Gedatsu-kai's founder, and this is what distinguishes Gedatsu-kai from most established Japanese religions.

The year that began with the revelation to start a religion and continued with the initial testing of the gohō shugyō was critical for the founding of Gedatsu-kai, because other central aspects of its teaching and practice came to light later in the year. After the founder began to practice gohō shugyō, he received important spiritual communications from his father in the spirit world: he was told to erect a tower to honor all the spirits of the dead (Yaoyorozu Mitama Matsuri Tō) and a monument to the spirit of the sun (Taiyō Seishin Hi). These stone structures were not actually erected until considerably later, but the fact that they were revealed at this time is another indication of the foundational character of this period. (Later, these two monuments, together with a memorial monument for the founder— Shōtoku Hi—came to be considered the three pillars of Gedatsu-kai.)[20]

During the fall of the same year, the founder once more felt the strong presence of divine spirits, who revealed the *manbu kuyō*, literally "ten thousand-fold memorial rite," which can be rendered more freely as "all souls' memorial rite." However, its contents were not specified, and he was told that this was not the time for the rite: the time and details would be made known to him later. The founder asked his friends and religious specialists Kurosawa and Shimada about this rite, but they could not interpret it. Starting in November, there were further revelations concerning this all souls' memorial rite and also the gohō shugyō. The gist of these revelations was that he should open an old stone stupa (or tower, called Hōkyōin Tō) at Tamonji, the parish Buddhist temple of the Okano family in Kitamotojuku, and spread to the world the magical formula (*darani, dhāraṇī* in Sanskrit) contained within it.[21]

The founder knew generally of the importance of this stupa, for when he made visits to his native village of Kitamotojuku, he never failed to pay his respects at it. Erected in 1731, the tower was viewed by the local people as a source of healing power and (when circumambulated) as a means of devotion for helping a person enter enlightenment.[22] When the founder visited this stupa again, he paid particular attention to it, because he found on it the five mystic characters that had appeared to him earlier as the basis of gohō shugyō. Four of the characters were on the four sides, and the fifth, *ban*, the "seed" of the Buddhist divinity Dainichi Nyorai, was on top. The founder had a relative make rubbings of the characters and later confirmed that they were the same five characters revealed to him as ongohō. This made him all the more aware of the significance of the revelation to open this stupa, although it was still unclear to him what "formula" he would find within the tower and how he would present it to the world.

Preparations to open the stupa required many permissions; the founder enlisted the help of Shimada, and temple representatives from Tamonji had to be present. When finally they were able to open it, they did find a scroll with a magical formula (darani) written in Sanskrit letters. The founder wrote and rewrote these letters until they almost wrote themselves. One night while writing them, he became possessed. The revelation that came during his possession was the gist of the manbu kuyō, the all souls' memorial rite: the darani should be recited during the rite, which would bring about the complete Buddhahood of all spirits of the dead. The all souls' memorial rite was not performed at this time, but its fundamental meaning was clear.

The founding year of 1929 was crucial for the formation of Gedatsu-kai: as the founder's biographers remind us, the basic teachings and major rituals were established during this time. New Year's Day, always an auspicious juncture in Japan, marked the revelation to the founder to establish a new teaching. The founder's friend in religion, Shimada, in the process of confirming the authenticity of this revelation, also perceived that the area around the founder's home and native village was a "sacred land" (Goreichi). In May of 1929, the five mystic letters (ongohō) were revealed to the founder, later becoming the basis for the mediation ritual of gohō shugyō. About the same time, his father in the spirit world revealed to the founder the eventual plan for a tower to honor all the spirits of the dead (Yaoyorozu Mitama Matsuri Tō) and a monument to the spirit of the sun (Taiyō Seishin Hi). This was followed by a revelation to develop an all souls' memorial rite (manbu kuyō), in connection with the magical formula in the old stupa in front of the Okano family's parish Buddhist temple; the five mystic letters previously made known to the founder were the same as those of the stupa, providing additional reinforcement for the gohō shugyō mediation ritual. These practices, together with the beliefs and teachings implicit in the practices and made explicit through the founder's counseling, constituted the foundation on which Okano Eizō built a new religious movement.

Organizing the Movement:
Forming Branches, Affiliating with an Established Religion, and Holding the First Grand Festival

Although 1929 was a good year in terms of providing the religious foundation of Gedatsu-kai, personally and socially it was an extremely difficult time for the movement's founder, Okano Eizō. The world remembers 1929 for the stock market crash and the international depression and unemployment; in Japan this economic hardship was accompanied by social disruption, the arrest of Communists, political incidents, and suppression of religion. Okano's wife was unsympathetic to his commitment to found a religion, and felt that he should share her concern for business and making money. Some of the people who had been helped by the founder gave him token gifts of money. The founder was content to receive a simple "thank you," but accepted the money as thanks to kami and Buddhas. His wife still did not understand. Gradually this irreconcilable difference in attitude drove husband and wife apart. This difficult set of personal and social conditions defined the context in which Okano Eizō began to frame an organized religious movement out of the inspirations and revelations he had recently received.

Although Gedatsu-kai now claims about a quarter-million members, it started from the most humble beginnings. Records show a membership of 4 persons in the founding year of 1929, with slow but steady growth thereafter: to 20 members in 1930, 80 in 1931, 150 in 1932, 250 in 1933, 850 in 1934, and 1,500 in 1935 (Gedatsu Shuppanbu 1979:220).

During the 1920s and 1930s, the Japanese government kept close watch on all social movements, using thought control to manipulate people, not only suppressing left-wing political movements but also harassing many religious movements.[23] Oppression and outright persecution was especially harsh for the so-called newly arisen religions (shinkō shukyō). Okano was only too aware of these liabilities as he patiently counseled people, cultivating future leaders and beginning to organize his movement—he would wait until 1934 to seek official recognition. Before the founder could apply to the authorities for official recognition, he had to carefully plan the foundation and organization of his movement: he spent several years expanding and strengthening it, which required considerable reflection on the part of him and his advisors.

Gedatsu-kai views the growth of its membership and branches as a natural, gradual process. People helped by the founder were thankful and told friends and neighbors their stories of trouble and relief; it was only natural that there would be gatherings of people to discuss this new faith and practice. The founder would set a day, and they would gather at what they called a "meeting place" (shūkaijo): this is the beginning of what later came to be called branches (shibu). At these meeting places there was no formal sermon or abstract reasoning, just frank discussion and getting to the heart of the problems of each person. On the eighth and twenty-fifth of every month, the founder paid a religious visit (omairi) to his native village of Kitamotojuku, and some of the early members went with him. These members recall that the order of this pilgrimage was always the same: first they would visit the tutelary kami shrine, next the old stupa in front of the parish Buddhist temple, then the memorial stones of his ancestors in the cemetery next to the temple, and finally the small Shinto shrine of the "great kami" (Ōgami). These are important precedents for later practice.

In the midst of his attempts to organize Gedatsu-kai more effectively, the founder was beset by many problems. He and his wife divorced in 1931, and shortly thereafter thugs threatened his life (apparently instigated by his ex-wife, who was after his money). About the same time, thought-control police were investigating religious movements, and the founder, too, came under scrutiny. Eventually he and some believers were arrested, accused by someone opposed to his teaching. Gedatsu-kai's communication with the spirit world through gohō shugyō and healing people by touching them with his hands seemed to make it a questionable religion.[24] The aim of the police was to pressure the founder into giving up his religious movement, but even after twenty-nine days of imprisonment he steadfastly refused to do so.

The founder did continue his teaching, meeting at members' houses, and the number of "meeting places" (shūkaijo) grew. However, it was difficult to organize a religious movement in the face of the increasing government control. The founder's friend Kurosawa suggested that he become formally affiliated with an established religion, and from this position of safety he could spread his distinctive teaching. Kurosawa made it possible for him to become connected with the Daigoha denomination of Shingon Buddhism.[25] The first step was for the founder to become a Buddhist priest at the Shingon temple in Yamanashi Prefecture where Kurosawa was a priest. He received the Buddhist name Seiken in March of 1931 (although he did not legally change his name from Okano Eizō to Okano Seiken until 1939); a month later he took the tonsure of a Buddhist priest at the temple Sanbōin of the Daigoji headquarters in Kyoto. From Sanbōin he also received permission to teach Buddhism. This formal connection with an officially recognized religion made it much easier for him to openly teach and organize Gedatsu-kai.

Although the founder was involved in other activities, such as the formal affiliation with an established Buddhist denomination, this did not mean that he neglected the development of his teaching and movement. In fact, this connection with recognized Buddhism made it possible for him to lay the foundation for what came to be a major event of his movement. He set the date for the first Grand Festival (Taisai) on May 8, 1931. This festival commemorates the revelation of the five mystic letters (ongohō) on May 8, 1929, and also celebrates seasonal changes. The Great Festival occurs as new life is emerging in spring, within the flow of the vast cosmos, coinciding with the founder's teaching of indebtedness to nature. This time has great significance at Kitamotojuku because it is exactly one month after a traditional spring festival (hana matsuri), and the actual day of May 8 was set aside for honoring the Buddha. The founder had in mind all of these intentions when he specified May 8 as the date of the first Grand Festival, gathering people at the Goreichi (Sacred Land) to give thanks for the protection and blessings they receive during their daily lives.

Because the old stupa containing the magical formula of the five mystic letters (at the Okano family parish temple) was so important for the founding of Gedatsu-kai, the first Great Festival was held in commemoration of this stupa. Preparations for the festival required much work both at the Goreichi and among members in Tokyo. The printed program for the event cites the commemoration of the stupa (Hōkyōin Tō) and lists the train schedule: leaving Ueno Station in northern Tokyo early in the morning and returning in late afternoon. Also included in the program is the order of pilgrimage, starting with the Okano family's tutelary kami shrine (Tenmanten Jinja) and parish Buddhist temple (Tamonji), then to the memorial stones of the ancestors (of the founder), then to the pine grove where the "great kami" (Ōgami) revealed itself to the founder and Shimada, then to the founder's home, and finally to the old stupa (Hōkyōin Tō). Fifty people were led by the founder on this round of sacred sites. This pattern of pilgrimage followed the model of the founder's life and laid the precedent for the subsequent tradition of pilgrimage at Goreichi. It is significant that on the commemorative card for participants in the initial Grand Festival, for the first time the name "Gedatsu-kai" was used. Before that time there was no official name for the group; thereafter several name changes took place, but eventually the movement returned to the title Gedatsu-kai.

The Founder as a Religious Leader:
Expansion of Membership and Branches,
and Official Recognition

By this point in the story, Okano Eizō (now Okano Seiken) has become a full-time religious leader and founder of a religious movement; Gedatsu-kai's major ritual forms and patterns of belief have been set. In this formative stage, the founder ran the movement almost single-handedly, settling all matters in a direct, face-to-face manner. The official Gedatsu-kai biography of the founder describes many of these personal exchanges, especially anecdotes of his healing and counseling, which will not be repeated here. For our purposes, the most significant aspect of this period of his career was his transformation of the movement from a one-man operation to a network of local branches guided by lay leaders who took care of the face-to-face matters. Eventually, as the membership and branches grew in number and the movement began to assume institutional character, the founder systematized the teaching and applied for official recognition.

When the founder devoted himself entirely to religious work, he retired completely from business, except for a brief venture in a lumber enterprise to improve his personal finances. Much of his time in the early years of the movement was taken up with counseling of people, frankly criticizing them and telling them to reflect on their lives; he was quite adept at this counseling and practiced it in combination with prescription of the gohō shugyō discipline and the amacha memorial ritual. When Gedatsu-kai was a budding movement, every member came into direct contact with the founder. For example, in 1932 a young man named Kishida Takeo visited a "meeting place" (shūkaijo) of Gedatsu-kai through the invitation of a fellow worker in a printing business. Kishida was attracted to the gohō shugyō, practiced it on his third visit, and "saw" the name of the divinity Shimizu Kubo Benzaiten written in gold characters. The founder himself was the interpreter (chūkaisha), and "interpreted" that this was Kishida's guardian deity. Kishida did not understand this, so the next morning he asked his mother about it. She directed him to a shrine near their home, on which were written the characters he had seen the previous night during gohō shugyō. This shrine, dedicated to the Buddhist divinity Benzaiten, had been venerated by the Kishida family for several hundred years. This confirmation of his experience in gohō shugyō convinced Kishida to become a firm believer. (Later he played a major role in the organization of branches, changed his name to Kishida Eizan, and became head of Gedatsu-kai in the United States.)

The founder was constantly busy, spending his days at home in counseling or writing out the memorial tablets (for memorial rites) for members; at night he visited various meeting places. While at these meeting places and at other times, he was called upon to help solve people's problems. Some meetings lasted until late in the night, and after returning home he wrote letters. He was so busy that some nights he got no sleep, just taking a bath in amacha and drinking amacha. He poured his efforts into personal guidance of future leaders of the movement and close contact with the meeting places, rather than being concerned with an elaborate headquarters. Not until 1936 did he build a hall at the Goreichi, followed in 1940 by a hall in Tokyo.

By 1933, the fifth year after the founding of his movement (which Gedatsu-kai dates from the 1929 New Year's revelation telling him to initiate a teaching), there were about 850 members and forty-one meeting places. At this time the founder began preparing the formal application to Saitama Prefecture authorities for formal recognition of Gedatsu-kai, which was submitted on December 15, 1933, and approved on January 12, 1934. This petition is a good representation of the early form of Gedatsu-kai teaching, belief, and practice (as a synthesis of popular Confucian, Shinto, Buddhist, and folk values).

The petition for official recognition begins with a general statement of purpose that they gather believers and spread their teaching for "spiritual peace and enlightenment" (*anshin ritsumei*), and then sets forth a number of matched values and practices. With spiritual peace and enlightenment, they strive in the occupation endowed them; in government and industry, they perceive nature's heavenly blessing and virtue; for the spiritual realization of all people, they practice reflection on self and denial of ego; for the happiness of self and others, the highest ethic is justice; for the promotion of morality, they follow the great principle of the benevolent man. The petition goes on to emphasize loyalty to superiors and love of country, which establish a person and restore the family; these values, together with the set of five virtues—loyalty, filial piety, benevolence, righteousness, and propriety—constitute the "three fundamental bonds and five cardinal virtues" (*sankō gojō*).

The term *three fundamental bonds and five cardinal virtues* calls for a brief explanation. Although the Gedatsu-kai publication does not indicate the source of the term, most people in East Asian cultures would recognize its Confucian origin; sankō gojō implies a total Confucian system of social organization and ethical behavior. The "three fundamental bonds and five cardinal virtues" are central values in the Confucian teaching codified and transmitted by the later tradition known as Neo-Confucianism, influential not only for China but also for cultures such as Korea and Japan. Crucial to Neo-Confucian teaching is the notion that social relations can be understood in terms of five major pairs: ruler-subject, father-son, husband-wife, elder brother-younger brother, friend-friend. The first four pairs are characterized by a hierarchical relationship in which the lower member (subject, son, wife, younger brother) is loyal to the higher member (ruler, father, husband, elder brother), and the higher member is benevolent to the lower. The fifth pair, friends, is governed by mutuality. Of the five relationships, the first three were considered the "three fundamental bonds" linking society.

Early Confucian teaching specified the significance of concepts such as "bonds" and "virtues." The word for "bond" is *kō* in Japanese, *kang* in Chinese, and "the literal meaning of *kang* is a major cord in a net, to which all the other strings are attached." In this sense, the higher member of each pair of relationships is the bond or "cord" that holds together the net of society (especially through loyalty) (Fung 1948:197). The five cardinal virtues are the five "constants" (*jō* in Japanese, *ch'ang* in Chinese). In Confucian teaching, "The five *ch'ang* are the virtues of an individual, and the three *kang* are the ethics of society" (ibid).[26] The Confucian (or Neo-Confucian) ideal was for all people to be mindful of these three ethical bonds and develop personally the five cardinal principles (or virtues), for the purpose of promoting a harmonious society. In short, the founder of Gedatsu-kai is subscribing to the general pattern of Neo-Confucian values when he acknowledges the "three fundamental bonds and five cardinal virtues."[27]

The petition goes on to list the objects of worship as Gochi Nyorai, Dainichi

Nyorai, Amaterasu Ōmikami, Tenchi Ōgami, and Ameyaoyorozu Ōgami. (The first two are Buddhist; the latter three are Shinto.) The general principle of revering kami and worshipping ancestors (*shinkei sūso*) is elaborated in a brief paragraph of interlocking personal and social values (Gedatsu Shuppanbu 1979:270).[28] The gist of this teaching is the supreme ethic of reflection on self and denial of ego which is summed up in the "three fundamental bonds and five cardinal virtues." Members of Gedatsu-kai strive to achieve benevolence and human perfection as set forth by Confucius and the ancestors; they strive to know and follow the way of Heaven, rectifying their lives accordingly; they are indebted and thankful for their great providential blessings; they strive to purify and refine this world and society for the edification of their individual lives and for spiritual peace and enlightenment.

This teaching is spelled out in terms of the founder's interpretation of the five cardinal virtues:

loyalty—revering the kami (of one's own accord);
filial piety—venerating the ancestors; (which in turn is)
benevolence—establishing the individual and restoring the family;
righteousness—when duty comes first, and when what comes first is duty;
propriety—possessing the way of the benevolent man, with the proper relations between ruler and subjects.

The founder treats the three "cords" (or bonds, kō) in his own fashion as nation, parents (father and mother), and society: if there were no nation, we would have no place to reside; if there were no parents, we could not be born into this world; if there were no society, we would not be able to live even one day. It is the way of heaven that gives us life. The great liberation (gedatsu) is recognizing the reason for our existence and thereby being in tune with the heavenly blessings of nature and being completely satisfied.

In the morning, gratitude (*hōon*): this is sincerity (*shin*). In the evening, thanks (*kansha*): this is discipline (*gyō*). The sincerity (*shin*) of sincere action (*shinkō*) is sincerity in what one does, and doing what is sincere.[29] Gratitude is asking to be allowed to live and work safely today; thanks is being thankful for having been allowed to live and work safely this one day. Loyalty, filial piety, benevolence, righteousness, and propriety—the dual path of loyalty and filial piety—come from Confucius—following the way of the benevolent man. All the five cardinal virtues are fulfilled in gratitude and thanks (*hōon kansha*). The way of the benevolent man benefits both the world and humans—this is "the salvation of men's hearts." When duty comes first, and what comes first is duty—this is "the great principle of the benevolent man." The way of filial piety is establishing a person and restoring the family—this is "being true to one's father and mother." Propriety is everything in accord with the great principle of the benevolent man—"everything in propriety." The sincerity of acting out completely the dual path of loyalty and filial piety, and the action of practicing sincerity, constitute sincere action.

The word *shinkō*, "sincere action," is a term developed by the founder to express his teaching, and is a play on another word of the same pronunciation, *shinkō*, meaning "belief" or "faith." In spoken Japanese, these two words (and a number of other homonyms) sound exactly the same; when *shinkō* is heard in a religious context, it calls to mind the very common term meaning "belief" or "faith." In Gedatsu-kai writings, as in this petition, even when *shinkō* as "sincere action" is read on the printed page, it brings to mind the more common term *shinkō* as "belief" or "faith." However, the founder was critical of customary belief that lacked inner sincerity and often resulted in mechanical practice of religion. According to him, the dilemma of religion is that either it is a temporary expediency in time of trouble (and then forgotten after the trouble is past), or it is a mechanical, routine performance that lacks vitality and meaning.[30] The founder's call for "sincere action" is a clever way of playing on the subconscious notion of shinkō as fleeting or routine belief, while providing the conscious critique of that notion in the positive sense of the "sincere action" that makes belief (and religion) vital, meaningful, and permanent.

As the Gedatsu-kai biography points out, this petition for official recognition, one of the oldest written forms of the founder's teaching that survives, represents a significant landmark in the formal religious organization of the movement. Prior to this time the founder handled individuals on a personal basis and counseled them "naturally"—as it occurred to him. This petition, however, formalized his teaching in a way that laid the foundation for more systematic doctrine that guides the movement down to the present day. By 1934 the number of individual members had grown to 850, with forty-one meeting places, making it almost impossible for the founder to provide personal guidance for each individual; therefore, he began to train the future leaders of the movement. On the first and fifteenth of every month, he lectured to these lay leaders, expanding upon the teachings summed up in the petition for official recognition. These lectures helped the founder systematize his informal teachings into a more formal pattern of doctrine. Prior to this time, he had focused more on spiritual practice and the amacha memorial rite, but thereafter he concentrated on doctrine.

The founder decided to systematize the doctrine first sketched in the formal petition, setting a goal of the Spring Grand Festival (May 8, 1934) for completion of this doctrinal statement. This Grand Festival (Taisai) is a landmark for Gedatsu-kai, establishing a number of significant precedents. This was the first time that the founder publicly explained his system of doctrine, focusing on the idea of "sincere action" (shinkō). The crucial character of this speech before the gathered members at the Sacred Land was recognized at the time, and recorded with a wire recorder; since that time it has been rerecorded (on tape) and is played at local, regional, and national meetings as a central feature invoking the founder's message.

This Grand Festival also marked the initial practice of the all souls' memorial rite (manbu kuyō). This ritual had been revealed to the founder by his father some time earlier, with the understanding that there would be an appropriate time to make it known to the world: this seemed to be the right time. For the all souls' memorial, held at the Sacred Land, sweet tea is poured over a five-sided pillar representing "all souls." The ethical and religious principles of Gedatsu-kai which are typified in the amacha memorial rite are completely fulfilled in the all souls' memorial rite. The spirit of the dead that through performance of the amacha memorial has been pacified and attained Buddhahood, through performance of the all souls' memorial is able to enter into the proper spiritual activities. From the viewpoint of the person performing the ritual, through the amacha memorial this person's own spirit is pacified by "earnest apology and memorial rites," and through the all soul's memorial rite this person takes the next step of participating in activities benefiting mankind and the world.

In the term *manbu kuyō*, *man* is literally "ten thousand" (*manbu* being ten thousand-part or ten thousand-fold), but here *man* means not a number but rather "everything." This "everything" includes the spirits of the entire world—of all plants and animals. In the case of people, *man* or everything means going back to the very beginning of mankind, from our ancestral figures, including all spirits of the dead with living relatives who memorialize them, as well as all spirits of the dead with no living relatives who memorialize them.[31] Every person attending the Great Festival takes his or her turn at performing the all souls' memorial (by ladling sweet tea over the five-sided pillar).

The size of the 1934 Spring Grand Festival is indicated by the fact that ten railroad cars were chartered for members to travel from Tokyo to the founder's native village of Kitamotojuku and participate in the festivities; from this year, musical entertainment was featured. The preparations were so elaborate that various branches were given responsibilities to coordinate the affair. This festival demonstrated the founder's confidence in his message and ministry, and indicated the strength of the formative organization to mobilize people from different areas to a central celebration. It helped set the pattern for annual celebrations (one in spring and one in fall) that defined high points of the Gedatsu-kai ritual year—constituting the most sacred place and the most sacred time for Gedatsu-kai believers.

Consolidating the Movement:
New Branches, Publications, and Wartime Difficulties

The slow, patient work of Okano from the momentous year of 1929 through 1934 resulted in a strong foundation for his movement; he had developed the nucleus of a religious organization that began to pick up its own momentum. The decade from 1935 until the end of World War II in 1945 was a period of consolidating the organization and strength of the movement in the face of interference from the government and the difficulties associated with wartime conditions. The early geographical center for Gedatsu-kai had been the area immediately around Tokyo and nearby Kitamotojuku (in Saitama Prefecture). As the religion grew in numbers, it also expanded into neighboring prefectures on Honshu, and even to Shikoku. The founder encouraged members to recruit (*michibiku*) other members, and when there was a sufficient number of members in an area, they formed a branch, along the lines of the previously established branch organization. He continued his efforts in spite of difficult social times, even after a personal attack which almost cost him his life (Gedatsu Shuppanbu 1979:280).

About this time, the emergence of Gedatsu-kai was stimulated by capable early members. An energetic member named Kishida (mentioned earlier) suggested a brief report be published of branch news. The founder accepted this suggestion, but told Kishida that it would be better to publish a monthly report for all of Gedatsu-kai. The first issue of this monthly magazine, *Gedatsu-kyō* (Gedatsu religion), was released February 18, 1935. The initial volume included the founder's teachings, testimonial accounts (*taikendan*) by members, and announcements. This general format set the tone for further issues, and was continued until 1945, when it was stopped because of paper shortages at the end of World War II. (Publication resumed in 1949.) This magazine became the means for the founder to disseminate his message to a wider audience, stressing his themes of thank-fulness to the kami and parents who gave life to people, and of apologies to ancestors for wrongs (tsumi). He criticized improper faith as "superstition" (*meishin*), because too many people at the time practiced blind faith and mechanical offerings to the objects of their beliefs (ibid., p. 282).

As Gedatsu-kai grew, its facilities and structure became more elaborate. Even the informal visits to the sacred sites of the founder's native village became more formal and expansive. The founder bought the woods around the shrine of the Ōgami, and the celebration of New Year's and the Grand Festival came to be held in this woods, making it possible for circles of friends to gather in a more festive atmosphere. More branches were formed, and activities such as women's meetings, youth meetings, and young women's meetings were initiated. The founder was especially concerned with the role of women, and felt that some imported values of European and American culture were to blame for the increase of social problems.[32] He taught that women are the foundation of the family, which in turn is the basis of society. In the face of considerable social change and increasing governmental suppression of religion, Okano felt it was important to systematize his teaching; from October 1935 to May 1939, seven major volumes of Gedatsu doctrine were published. Gradually Gedatsu-kai was assuming the dimensions of a major religion with more elaborate internal organization and more comprehensive teachings.

The Gedatsu biography devotes considerable space to the founder's attitude toward war, and documents his peaceful concern for all people with the 1940 erection of the All Souls' Memorial Tower (Yaoyorozu Mitama Matsuri Tō) at the Sacred Land (Goreichi). This tower is a symbol of world peace, because it, along with the all souls' memorial rite, has the purpose of bringing all souls to complete Buddhahood. From 1937, when war with China began, the founder preached the equality of friend and enemy in memorial rites; he continued these observances throughout World War II.

With the war came even more severe thought control, and the founder moved in vain to avoid persecution, attempting to strengthen the ties with the Daigo denomination of the Shingon sect. Nevertheless, people who did not study Gedatsu-kai teaching made complaints to the police about the mediation ritual gohō shugyō. The special police launched an investigation of Gedatsu-kai, and because its connection with the Daigo denomination was unclear, a warning was sent to the Daigo headquarters; in turn the Daigo authorities, who oversaw more than five-hundred branch temples and more than a thousand "churches" of Shugendō practice sites, called in the founder. Apparently the intention was for both the Daigo denomination and Gedatsu-kai to avoid harassment by the authorities through organizing Gedatsu-kai as a standard subdivision of Daigo. When the founder and his friend in religion Kurosawa went to the Daigo headquarters at Kyoto, the Daigo authorities proposed uniformity of Gedatsu-kai with Daigo's rituals and giving up worship of kami, such that only the Buddhist deity Dainichi (central to Shingon teaching and practice) be honored. Further demands were that the name of the religion be changed to Shingonshū Daigoha Gedatsu Bun-kyōkai (Shingon Sect Daigo Denomination Gedatsu Branch Church): in other words, Gedatsu-kai would be totally subservient to this Buddhist organization, from name to object of worship to ritual pattern. The Gedatsu-kai biographers recognize that this demand for conformity to Daigo was not unreasonable, because government suppression was severe, and Daigo was being held legally responsible for Gedatsu-kai's activities, even though Okano had set up his teaching and practice independently of Daigo.

In these negotiations with the Daigo denomination authorities, the founder agreed to incorporate their standard ritual and adopt their name—although he wanted to include the words *hōon kansha* (thanks and gratitude) in the name. The major difference of opinion was about objects of worship within Gedatsu-kai; up to this point the kami with the name Tenchi Ōgami (literally "heaven and earth great kami") had been the central figure, and was worshipped by forty branches, so it was not a simple matter to remove this deity. However, he felt that this deity could be considered the same as Tenjin Chigi (literally "kami [or gods] of heaven and earth").[33] Formerly in Gedatsu-kai they had respected the Buddhist deity Dainichi, although not as the main object of worship (*honzon*). However, the founder felt it was consistent with his revelation from the divine spirits, and also with the viewpoint of En no Gyōja, the founding figure of Shugendō, to worship both kami and Buddhas. En no Gyōja is a legendary figure who combined especially Buddhist and Taoist magical and ascetic practices with worship of kami in the context of Japanese sacred mountains to form Shugendō, the "way of mastering extraordinary power."[34] Because the Daigo denomination was within the Shugendō tradition and honored En no Gyōja as a founding figure, Okano as the founder of Gedatsu-kai was able to win his argument to worship both Tenjin Chigi and Dainichi. In a special issue of the monthly magazine, the founder reported these changes, and he used subsequent issues to explain the nature of the Buddhist scriptures and the Shugendō adopted from the Daigo denomination. They had to use the name Shingonshū Daigoha Gedatsu Bunkyōkai (Shingon Sect Daigo Denomination Gedatsu Branch Church), but also used their preferred name Gedatsu Hōon Kansha-kai (Liberation Gratitude and Thanks Society).

From the present vantage point, this minor revision of Gedatsu-kai under government and ecclesiastical pressure may appear trivial; however, such apparently trivial interference might well have derailed and even permanently blocked the development of the movement. The ability of the founder to accept a crisis such as this and turn it into an opportunity to strengthen his movement is a hallmark of a successful religious leader; the ability of the movement to absorb this shock and to adapt quickly to changing conditions demonstrates its organizational power and flexibility.[35]

As the war effort intensified, the founder became more involved in war-related activities. He helped prepare young men mentally for battle by helping them achieve inner peace; he held special memorial rites for the war dead and consoled the bereaved families. He and Gedatsu-kai members were effective in collecting donations for the war; they contributed materials for soldiers (such as magazines and musical records) and donated enough money for two airplanes (one was called gratitude—*Hōon*, the other thanks—*Kansha*). Special rituals were conducted during wartime Great Festivals, such as memorial rites for the war dead in China, including army horses, dogs, and doves as well as human dead. The founder went with others to pay respects at the Yasukuni Shrine in Tokyo, the special shrine for spirits of soldiers and sailors who died in the service of the country. He also went with Kurosawa to Kyoto to pay respects at Sennyūji, a Buddhist temple that since medieval times has memorialized and enshrined the spirits of previous emperors.

An incident in 1939 demonstrates the depths of the founder's sincerity and the extent to which he would go to act out his principles. He visited Sennyūji again, this time with a high-ranking Shugendō priest named Ōmiwa Shinya. At this time, because Sennyūji was closely connected with the imperial line, commoners could not enter the temple compounds and pay respects; therefore, it was practically impossible for organizations of commoners (such voluntary organizations as Gedatsu-kai) to lend support and protection to the temple. But the founder felt that common people should be allowed to give support to the temple and pay respects there. Ōmiwa agreed, saying that "if Sennyūji's status as the ancestral temple of the imperial line is respected too much, such that it results in the relation of the common people to Sennyūji becoming weak, then this is really not respect. Only when the people's attitude of respect and veneration is gathered from wide and far are we able to preserve the dignity and majesty of Sennyūji" (Gedatsu Shuppanbu 1979:343). Through Ōmiwa, a meeting was arranged with a high-ranking priest of Sennyūji on April 17, 1939. During this four-hour meeting, Ōmiwa and the founder requested permission for commoners to enter the temple compounds, pay respects, and make direct donations. Permission was refused. The temple authorities appreciated the founder's intentions, but felt that they could not break the rules forbidding commoners to enter the compounds.

However, the founder did not relent. He gave the Sennyūji priest the same rationale he taught to members of Gedatsu-kai: because the emperor is the parent of the people, the people are children of the emperor; and for a child to render filial piety to a parent—how can this be seen as impiety? In this way the founder was begging the question of Sennyūji's refusal to allow commoners to come into more direct contact with ancestral spirits of the imperial line because of "impiety."[36] The founder said he was so firm in his resolve that if he was refused permission to enter, he was determined to camp outside the main gate of the temple. Finally the Sennyūji priest consented, because of the founder's sincerity, taking upon himself the responsibility for allowing commoners to come into more direct contact with the imperial spirits enshrined within the temple grounds. The founder formed a support group for the temple, and Gedatsu-kai has continued to have a special relationship with this temple down to the present time.[37]

About the same time, he visited Yasukuni Shrine with children who had lost their fathers in the war. He encouraged all members to console war orphans in their areas. He said that other people shared the guilt of indirectly rejoicing that the dead person was not from their own family. On a number of occasions he took groups of members to visit the Yasukuni Shrine.

As the Gedatsu-kai biography points out, 1940 was undoubtedly the most memorable year in the founder's life, because of all the achievements and honors realized then. On February 15, the traditional holiday for the founding of the Japanese nation, Gedatsu-kai held a formal ceremony celebrating the erection of the Sun Monument (Taiyō Seishin Hi, literally "Sun Spirit Monument") at the Sacred Land. In a revelation he had learned that this monument should be erected as a symbol of man's fundamental spirit. It represents the sun (a symbol of the

Japanese nation) as well as life and thankfulness. On this day the founder distributed 10,000 pictures of Emperor Jinmu (traditionally considered the first Japanese emperor). The founder was so moved that he cried at the dedication of this monument; in some respects his biographers consider this a climax to his achievements.

Nevertheless, he was not able to rest from the constant governmental pressures, and in fact at this time the enactment of the Religious Organizations Law[38] caused considerable problems for the founder and especially the local branches. For Gedatsu-kai, this law meant that every local branch had to register with the government. Branch leaders had little experience with such regulations, so the founder had the forms printed at Gedatsu-kai headquarters and helped branch leaders fill them in. There were 208 such local branches at the time, and they had to be very careful not to make any mistakes in the face of increasingly severe thought control.

In spite of such pressing problems and the scarcity of commodities and materials caused by the war, Gedatsu-kai continued to flourish and make plans. In 1940 the Tokyo Practice Hall (Dōjō) was completed; because it has been the administrative center for the movement since it was erected, this building signifies a new departure for Gedatsu-kai as a fully mature religious organization. In September of 1940, the founder experienced the crowning event of his life when he represented Saitama Prefecture at the ceremony commemorating the 2,600th year of the Japanese Empire. The invitation for this ceremony came directly from the emperor. The founder purchased a new kimono for this very special occasion; he is wearing it in the photograph now displayed in branches and practice halls. Later that fall the All Souls' Memorial Tower (Yaoyorozu Mitama Matsuri Tō) was erected at the Sacred Land. All these climactic events in the year 1940, the result of more than a decade of hard work by the founder and his early leaders, indicate that Gedatsu-kai had come of age as a full-fledged religious movement.

From 1940 through the end of World War II in 1945, Gedatsu-kai continued to develop in spite of the war conditions. In 1941 they held the first Three Holy Sites pilgrimage (San Seichi Junpai), with seven members paying their religious respects at Sennyūji (ancestral temple for emperors), Ise Shrine (a complex of Shinto shrines, considered the most sacred in Japan because it is the site of enshrining the Sun Goddess, ancestress of the imperial line), and Kashiwara Shrine (honoring the ancient imperial line). From the next year the pilgrimage to these three holy sites, considered by the founder as "pillars of the nation," was made by Gedatsu-kai members as a body, a custom that has continued to the present. Later in the same year, Gedatsu-kai members erected the Shōtoku Hi to honor the founder on his sixtieth birthday, out of their sincere thanks to him. In 1942 Gedatsu-kai published a definitive summary of the founder's teaching, Shinkō (Sincere Practice). In the same year he received full Buddhist ordination at the temple Sanbōin of the Daigo headquarters.

After 1942, as the war turned against Japan, it became increasingly difficult to carry out regular religious activities. As much as was possible, the founder and his leaders continued the Great Festivals and the pilgrimage to the three holy sites, but materials were scarce and transportation was difficult. The founder's health began to fail, and he was no longer able to visit distant branches as he once had. About the same time, air raids made life in Tokyo impossible. The founder

1. Okano Eizō (Seiken), founder of Gedatsu-kai, in 1940

moved to a residence at Kitamoto near the Sacred Land not long before the Tokyo
Practice Hall was destroyed in an air raid.

After World War II:
Rebuilding the Organization, and Death of the Founder

By the end of World War II, Gedatsu-kai had grown into a fully developed
religious organization, in spite of governmental restrictions and the necessity to
remain a subordinate affiliate of a larger ecclesiastical order. Japan's surrender in
1945 added a spiritual and emotional shock to a nation that had suffered from
several years of economic hardship, and now had to rebuild its factories and cities.
Like other religions, Gedatsu-kai felt that shock, but it also was able to turn some
aspects of the postwar situation to its advantage. In the brief span from 1945 until
his death in 1948, even though his health was not good, the founder helped rebuild
Gedatsu-kai and turn it in a more independent direction. The surrender and failure
of the war brought about a crisis of values that the founder recognized. He called
the leaders of Gedatsu-kai to meet with him at the Sacred Land, where he was
residing at the end of the war, and advised them to counsel the movement's
panicked members. The founder had encouraged people to be loyal and participate
in the war effort, and some were angry because they thought that religious practice
would guarantee that Japan would win the war. The founder told them to remain
true to the values that had brought them through the war. Some people fell away
from the movement, but even those who wanted to participate faced the nationwide problem of food shortages and transportation difficulties.

The founder attempted to continue the traditional ceremonies, although they
were restricted to a very small scale. The first Grand Festival after surrender in
the fall of 1945 was so small that it was held in the hall at the Sacred Land, instead
of in the woods. Until the 1948 Fall Grand Festival, the ceremonies were held
in this hall, as the number of participants gradually increased. People were confused by the radically changing values, and the founder tried to help them adjust
to the new conditions. The Allied forces who occupied Japan saw State Shinto
and the emperor system as causing the war, so the next year the emperor declared
his human (not divine) character, and a new constitution was written. The founder
accepted the new constitution with its emphasis on people's rights, but he did
not change his view of the emperor's traditional historical status.

One aspect of the postwar situation that benefited Gedatsu-kai (and all of the
so-called new religions) was the new constitution's guarantee of complete freedom
of religion, which enabled Gedatsu-kai for the first time to assume a completely
independent form. Under the new Religious Corporations Ordinance,[39] Gedatsu-
kai was able to set itself up as an independent religion, under the name Shūkyō
Kessha Gedatsu Hōon Kansha-kai (Religious Association Liberation Gratitude and
Thanks Society). The founder told people that they had to conform to the Allied
occupation policy and the new constitution, but as human beings these members
had not changed—they had the same personal and religious nature as before the
war.

The founder was able to help with the rebuilding of Gedatsu-kai, counseling
the leaders and members during the difficult economic and spiritual times shortly

after the war. He was able to face and adapt to the dilemmas of occupation and a new constitution, but he maintained the core of his religious values and the ceremonial life that celebrated them. He oversaw the establishment of his movement as a completely independent religion, and he lived to see the rebuilding of the Tokyo Practice Hall. However, as his health failed, he knew that he could not live long, and he made a final request that his remains be interred at Sennyūji. A priest from Sennyūji came to the ailing founder at the Sacred Land, and at first could not grant permission for this request. Later it was granted, and the founder was at peace. He said that all his teaching is contained in the brief work *Shinkō* (Sincere Practice). The founder died on November 1, 1948, at the age of sixty-eight. He was cremated, and a high-ranking Buddhist priest from the Daigo denomination conducted the funeral at the Sacred Land, bestowing on him the posthumous title Gedatsu Kongō. The organization that this man had founded and its members use this honorary title Gedatsu Kongō, or Gedatsu Kongō Sonja (Sonja for "revered one"), or its variants to refer to him today. His ashes remained in Sennyūji for seven years until Gedatsu-kai erected a memorial monument on land next to Sennyūji, as agreed by Sennyūji authorities before the death of the founder.

Okano Eizō as Gedatsu Kongō Sonja: Founder of a Religion and Model for Religious Life

We have now summarized the life of the founder of Gedatsu-kai as recorded in the official biography printed by this religion. There is much more information in this 500-page work than can be mentioned here: our summary omits many of the anecdotes of the founder's counseling, and focuses on the events that helped shape the formation of the new movement. What is of greatest importance for our story is the role that Okano Eizō played in initiating and developing Gedatsu-kai. In so many ways this religion is a personal expression of his life, emerging out of his traditional upbringing and later returning to his native village: from his spiritual crisis during midlife, he reflected on the traditional values of Japan and reassembled them into a dynamic, vital organization. The fact that Okano Seiken was able to overcome both personal and social obstacles and still maintain, and even expand, his organization, is a testimony to his power as a religious leader. This religion that he formed as an expression of his life became for others, such as Mr. Negishi, a model for restructuring their lives—using the example of the founder's career and the pattern of the religious faith and practices he created.[40]

We have not attempted to verify the historical facts of Okano Seiken's life, although there is no reason to doubt their authenticity. In fact, for our purposes of understanding his career as an ideal religious model by virtue of founding Gedatsu-kai, it is equally if not more important to explore the *perception* of this man by members of the religion that he founded. Throughout this treatment of Gedatsu-kai, we will use especially two sets of material to provide a more balanced treatment of the subject at hand. In addition to historical treatment, such as the biography of the founder, and description based on participant observation, particularly for rituals and festivals, we will utilize (1) life histories, such as that of Mr. Negishi already given in the first chapter, and (2) results from a nationwide survey of Gedatsu-kai members. At this point, we select some references to the founder from a number of life histories, and results from one particular question on the nationwide survey referring to the founder.

In all of the life histories of Gedatsu-kai members, the model of Okano as a founder (referred to by such titles as Gedatsu Kongō) is seen as the pattern for religious life generally and the specific clue to resolving the individual's immediate religious dilemma. Indeed, as we have seen in the first chapter, Mr. Negishi explained in his story that "in the teaching of the founder of Gedatsu-kai, and in Buddhism, there is the law of cause and effect. It is destiny. . . . I learned this at school, and thought it had no relationship with religion—but then later I saw it in the founder's teaching!" The founder is invoked as providing the key to unlocking the mystery of life generally and the answer to Mr. Negishi's particular questions about life. Later in his story, Mr. Negishi elaborates on the same theme, giving credit to the founder. And even when he does not credit the founder directly, his ideas and interpretations are obviously taken over from the founder's teachings—especially the notions of indebtedness and gratitude to kami, nature, and ancestors.

The same general crediting of the founder is found in separate testimonies (taiken) of a young woman, Mrs. Saitō, and a young man, Mr. Abe, published in Gedatsu-kai's journals: the examples are taken from *Yangu Gedatsu* (Young Gedatsu), published during the time of my research in 1979. The full account of each testimonial will be given in the next chapter; the following excerpts illustrate members' views of the founder. The testimony of Mrs. Saitō concerns her story of how she happened to marry her husband, a widower with a young child. Her family was opposed to the marriage, partly because she was too young (she met her future husband when she was eighteen) and too inexperienced. Here is Mrs. Saitō's account of her parents' objections and her successful appeal to the founder to overcome their objections: "They said that sympathy [for the widower and his infant] is no basis for marriage, marriage is full of difficulties, and I was too young, I had not known real difficulties. But I told them that this was according to the teaching of Gedatsu Kongō, and persisted, requesting them to give me permission to marry" (*Yangu Gedatsu* 20, no. 11 (1979):46–48). In other words, she is quoting the founder indirectly as saying that one should willingly accept difficulties as self-discipline. In fact, her parents did relent and give permission for her marriage at age twenty, and she had been married for three years at the time of her testimony. She was a happy wife and mother, but in accordance with Gedatsu-kai (and the founder's) teaching, she had her husband purchase both a *kamidana* (Shinto-style altar) and a *butsudan* (Buddhist-style altar for ancestors), and had him renew regular memorial rites for his first wife.

Another testimony from the same issue is the story of a Mr. Abe, who was somewhat lazy at work and suffered swelling in a leg that prevented him from working, causing great concern for him and his parents. Gradually, through religious practices recommended by his parents and Gedatsu-kai, he came to "know that my discipline was insufficient, and that I was lazy. This surely was a warning from the founder [Kongō sama], I know without a doubt" (ibid., pp. 48–49). In this case, the founder provides the physical symptom that brings about self-reflection and leads to religious renewal of the individual.

In a number of life histories, the figure of the founder is not prominent: more attention is paid to the branch leader or other person who introduced the teaching

TABLE 1.
Attitude of Members toward the Founder

	All Data		Females		Males	
As a man of character (*jinkakusha*)	3,939	69.4%	2,572	69.8%	1,367	68.5%
As a spiritualist (*reinōsha*)	3,111	54.8%	2,015	54.7%	1,096	54.9%
As a businessman (*jitsugyōka*)	1,072	18.9%	650	17.6%	422	21.2%
As a man of the world (*ku-rōnin*, one who has seen much of life)	1,329	23.4%	850	23.1%	479	24.0%
As a kami-like man (*kamisama no yō na hito*)	3,946	69.5%	2,634	71.5%	1,312	65.8%
As a thinker (*shisōka*)	289	5.1%	159	4.3%	130	6.5%
Other than the above	77	1.4%	39	1.1%	38	1.9%

and the particular ritual such as the amacha memorial rite or the mediation ritual of gohō shugyō that helped resolve the problem. But implicitly the members recognize the founder as the one who discovered these rituals: as one branch leader reminded us when we were listening to a number of testimonies, the founder discovered the way (such as the mediation ritual of gohō shugyō) of communicating with the spirit world. And when worship in the home was mentioned, even by those who did not refer to the founder prominently in their life histories, all said that they worship the founder.

A founder is a complicated person, and the perception of a founder by members of his religion is also quite complex. When we were conducting our study of Gedatsu-kai, we felt that the founder was perceived as a kami, especially because after his death he became an official object of worship, along with the Buddhist divinity Gochi Nyorai and the Shinto (kami) Tenjin Chigi. To confirm the actual attitude of members toward the founder, we included a specific question in our nationwide questionnaire: "16. How do you consider the founder (Sonja) in terms of the following kinds of persons? Please circle three of the following you feel rather strongly about." Results of this question are given in Table 1.[41]

As the results clearly show, Gedatsu-kai members see their founder primarily as a kami-like man and a man of character, with the category of "spiritualist" following closely, and "man of the world" and "businessman" much lower in importance; the category of "thinker" is very low, and the "other" category is not significant. In this particular question, there is little variation between females and males (and there is little variation among age groups). These results from the nationwide survey confirm the material from the life histories and testimonies that the founder is viewed as a model figure—kami, man of character, spiritualist—whatever categories are used: he resolved his own religious crisis in a dramatic fashion and remains a resource for helping others handle their religious problems. We will see how the founder's model was prominent in the lives of the people who followed him and joined his movement.

3

WHO JOINS GEDATSU-KAI
Life Histories of
Individual Members

Okano Eizō was a powerful personality with strong character and firm religious commitment. But a single person, no matter how forceful and charismatic, does not constitute a religion. Gedatsu Kongō Sonja is more than Okano Eizō as a historical person; his title signifies that he symbolically represents "the revered one," "the founder" for a group of people. Because he was viewed as a religious model by a common group of people, Okano became the founder of a movement with sufficient force to continue after his death. In other words, Okano Eizō was the man, but Gedatsu Kongō Sonja was and is the perception of the man by the ongoing religious community that follows him. In order for a religion to develop out of a founder's revelations and inspiration, a sufficient number of followers must be attracted to his or her person, message, and practices; in turn, the followers must create a momentum that enables the movement to recruit new members and forms the nucleus of a movement with its own ethos.

The relationship between founder and followers is crucial in all "founded" religions, and this is characteristic of most Japanese new religions. In the case of Gedatsu-kai, as seen in the testimony of Mr. Negishi and in the biography of the founder, the life and teachings of Okano constitute a reconfiguration of the Japanese religious tradition which provides an ideal model used by Mr. Negishi to restructure his life and general world view. If Mr. Negishi's life history can be seen as a microcosm of Japanese religion, the template for this miniature version is the personal example and religious way of life of the founder as interpreted by the Gedatsu-kai community. It is the sharing of this "template" or pattern of religious life by members of Gedatsu-kai that constitutes it as a distinctive religious community or tradition.

There are many ways of analyzing the formation and nature of Gedatsu-kai as a new religion, but first we should further familiarize ourselves with the movement in its most undiluted form, by listening to its members speak about their religious experiences and the role the founder and Gedatsu-kai have played in their lives. These "inside" stories (together with the statistical results of a nationwide survey of members to be discussed in the next chapter) must be central in any theoretical attempt to account for the origin and nature of such movements. For the moment we are more concerned with how the parts of the movement fit together—the founder, members, organization, and rituals; we will reserve for the final chapter more comprehensive discussion of the origin and nature of Gedatsu-kai.

We have already heard the story of one member, fifty-one-year-old Mr. Negishi, a university graduate who is on the executive board of Gedatsu-kai. Because eight other life histories will be featured in this chapter, it may be appropriate to indicate the general research plan for collecting and reporting these accounts: this context is crucial for their credibility. In other words, how does the reader know that these life histories reflect a cross-section of Gedatsu-kai, and are not arbitrary or accidental anecdotes? The research plan attempted to insure representativeness by making sure that the life histories "represented" as broad a range of the Ge-datsu-kai community as possible: male and female; young and old; residents of metropolitan Tokyo, suburbs, and rural areas; three levels of followers, including ordinary members, branch leaders, and executive officers. In order not to impose on these people an artificial format that would unduly shape the style or content of their story, the "interview" was requested and conducted as an account of each member's taiken (testimony) or life history. Each member had told and retold this taiken at branch meetings and/or regional meetings, so it was not difficult or artificial for the person to recount this story again. Of course, such stories should be treated as the *remembered* self-interpretations of their lives and experiences, not the actual or verified accounts of their activities.

All life histories were collected at branch meeting places or the Gedatsu-kai headquarters. Our first visit to a local branch was devoted to introductions, learn-ing about the branch, and generally developing rapport. Branch leaders encour-aged members to stay after the regular service and give brief versions of their taiken to the research team. We listened to these short testimonies of a few minutes each, and were able to ask the branch leader to request a more lengthy interview with particular members whose taiken was interesting or whose individual cir-cumstances helped make the sample more "representative."[1] No requests were refused, and branch leaders, who understood our attempt to cover various types of people and various kinds of religious experience, were helpful in suggesting some members. Life histories were given orally on the second visit. All life histories were related in Japanese and recorded on tape; I kept running notes of each story in English, and typed up the notes on the same day or the next day, checking key passages and gaps against the tape. The longer life histories took about two hours to tell and involved considerable repetition; they have been edited here to reduce some repetition.[2]

First the life history is retold or summarized, to convey the firsthand flavor and nuance of the actual experience of the member; second, its content is analyzed and interpreted as a "religious universe," to demonstrate that such stories present a unified set of beliefs and practices for the individual member as well as Gedatsu-kai membership as a whole. Two life histories will be presented at greater length in this alternate fashion of the "raw" taiken and the interpreted religious universe. Then six life histories will be summarized more briefly, followed by a general interpretation of the religious universe or unified world view of Gedatsu-kai based on nine life histories (including Mr. Negishi's account with the eight in this chapter).

The Life History of Mr. Nakajimo:
Renewing Ties with the Ancestors through Gohō Shugyō

One such life history is that of Mr. Nakajimo[3] (a fictitious name), who at the time of interview on October 23, 1979, was sixty-eight years old. This interview took place in a suburb of Tokyo at the "I" Branch of Gedatsu-kai. We had met Mr. Nakajimo at the previous regular meeting of the "I" Branch and had heard an abbreviated version of his story then, when the branch leader asked a number of members to give short accounts of their taiken. The second time we visited this branch, we went for the dual purpose of observing the mediation ritual of gohō shugyō and, after the formal meeting ended, recording several life histories. Therefore, this interview begins, naturally, with a discussion of gohō shugyō, rather than the usual request to relate the member's taiken. In the following format, Q indicates my questions, A Mr. Nakajimo's answers.[4] Brackets are used to explain context, identify terms, or summarize repetitious material.

Q: Have you received the gohō shugyō?

A: My wife and children have, but I haven't very much. Being a Christian, I didn't enter into Gedatsu-kai practice much myself. But my wife was very active. In gohō shugyō she was frequently told that her ancestors had made mistakes, and that she should perform memorial services for them and apologize on their behalf.

Q: And did you receive gohō shugyō yourself?

A: Yes, three or four times. But it wasn't very clear to me—just a lot about ancestors and apologizing and memorial services. That was all.

Q: When did you first receive gohō shugyō?

A: Two or three years ago.

Q: When did your wife first receive it?

A: Ten years ago—maybe longer.

Q: When you first received gohō shugyō, were you going through any particular trouble?

A: What prompted me was illness in the family. My family members, relatives, and acquaintances told me to practice it with all my strength. I really was not that devout, but since another person started doing gohō shugyō for me, I felt that I had to do it, too.

Q: Who was this other person?

A: A friend. At first I just couldn't put much trust in the gohō shugyō, but I was told to try it and see. That's why I did it at first. And things came up that I hadn't expected at all—for example, about my wife's mother's concern with money matters. Because this was inexcusable, I was told to apologize.[5] Through gohō shugyō I was taught things like this that I had no idea of beforehand. This is a different matter, but another person received gohō shugyō for the sake of someone in my family who was sick—they were praying for the sick one. So when I was asked by the person who had done this for us, it seemed only natural [to receive the gohō shugyō and, as advised,] to go to a shrine to apologize to my wife's mother.[6]

Q: A shrine—your tutelary shrine [ujigami]?

A: Yes. I've been going to the shrine since ten or fifteen, maybe more, years ago. My wife's brother died, so at the first of every month she would go to the ujigami, or the memorial stone, or the parish temple. That was her custom. But, as I said, because I was a Christian I thought it just as well not to go to such places. That was what I felt then. Later I changed my mind.

Q: Was that before or after your wife's joining Gedatsu-kai?

A: After.

Q: When was that?

A: That would be fifteen or sixteen years ago. From about ten years ago, we went to the parish temple or memorial stone at the beginning of every month.

Q: At that time had you entered Gedatsu-kai?

A: No, I didn't have anything to pray for at that time. It was just that this was my ujigami and my ancestors, and I had been under the care of this ujigami, so going there was an expression of thanks. The memorial stones and the parish temple were the same: I had received their protection, and going to these places was a form of thanks.

Q: Your family parish temple is what sect?

A: Jōdo Shinshū. Higashi Honganji. And the family in which my mother was born was a temple family.

Q: Were you a Christian from your youth?

A: I became a Christian at age eighteen. I was baptized at age twenty.

Q: What church?

A: Nihon Kirisuto Kyōdan [United Church of Christ in Japan]. There aren't very many of these churches. They are very scholarly in their teaching. I had gone to Sapporo. Most of the people in this church were quite knowledgeable. There were many intellectuals. Hokkaido University is there, and there were many university students in the church.

Q: You were born in Hokkaido?

A: Yes. At that time, so that I could go to school, I was living with a family that happened to be Christian. Until that time I had been just an ordinary, traditional Japanese—though from youth up I didn't have any particular faith. But when I got up in the morning, my mother would say, "Go pay your respects before the [Shinto] household shrine and the Buddhist altar." If I didn't, I wouldn't get anything to eat. That was the way it was. My father and mother were both people of deep faith. Anyway, because this was the way it was, it seemed natural [to us]. It was a [family] custom for us to go to the household shrine and Buddhist altar, then to wash our hands [and eat breakfast]. But when I moved into this other house, there was no household shrine and no Buddhist altar, so I thought it a strange house. Two or three days later I mentioned something [about the absence of traditional altars] to the family, and they said it was because they were Christian. From a child's perspective it appeared as if there were no kami there at all. What a strange house, I thought.

I didn't know much about Christianity, and didn't understand why, with all the fine religions in Japan, they would accept a foreign religion. In their house they had a Bible, and they urged me to read it. I did so earnestly. The head of the family was an elder in this church, so every week missionaries and ministers would visit the house. I didn't really understand why, but there was some kind of rebellion within me. I was reading the Bible diligently. If I asked them [the family members] or the minister about the Bible, they would say, "You haven't read the Bible [enough]. It is good. Just read it." They wouldn't argue with me. Really, when I was young, I didn't think that there was only one true kami. That's how

I felt when I began reading the Bible. And I was encouraged to read it. There must have been some rebellion in me at that time.

Q: How old were you when you moved into that house?

A: Age sixteen.

Q: So you lived there until you were twenty?

A: No, I moved to another house. That was a Christian house, too. But that house belonged to the Holiness tradition—Kiyome Church. The head of that house and I went to different churches. I was twenty when I received baptism, so my parents couldn't object. When I was twenty-four, I was on my own and opened up a business. This was right next to my mother's house. At that time, every day for about half a year, my mother urged me to convert [from Christianity back to Buddhism]. She was born in a temple family, so naturally all of our ancestors were connected with Buddhist temples. She told me not to practice a foreign religion. "Return to Buddhism!" [she said.] But by that time I was rather devout. At the time I converted to Christianity, it [the church] was in the country—of course, it is now a city, but then it was a country church. We gathered together friends who shared the same ideas, and once a month we had a minister come. We had a number of people of the same mind gather, and we talked; even when the minister didn't come, we studied the Bible on our own. That's the kind of church it was.

I was in business, so I became an officer of that church. The minister asked me to be an elder and lead the Bible study. It was just as I was doing this in the church that my mother asked me to change my religion. I was reading the Bible, but didn't want to mention it, so I just said, "Yes, yes" to her so as not to get into an argument. But every day, every day she would come. I was devotedly reading the Bible, because I believed in it. After all, the kami I worshipped was not a small kami or Buddha, but a kami of the entire world, the entire universe. Also, I believed that it was man's duty to do this, so I couldn't change my faith. When I told this to my mother, she was quite annoyed.

After some time had passed, one day I finally said, "Well, our thinking is different, but I don't want to disagree with you. If you dislike Christianity that much, then I'll give it up." She breathed a sigh of relief. "*But*," I said, "there is one condition. I will never enter another religion." Then the expression on my mother's face changed again. At last she said that if I believed that strongly, I should keep my faith, and she would practice Buddhism. She said that if giving up Christianity meant losing all faith, that would be bad. After that she didn't say anything. Afterwards, I had my own house, and since there was no church, we would meet in my house. Then after the war [World War II], I ran the Sunday School. I closed my business [on Sundays] to do this.

At the time I married, my wife was Buddhist. [Later] she was baptized and did practice Christianity for a while. Both my wife and her mother were devout, [especially since] fifteen or sixteen years ago when they got very interested in religion. They looked into various religions, such as Tenrikyō and Seichō no Ie, but with no effect. Then they found Gedatsu-kai and decided that this was genuine religion. I remained a Christian all that time. Finally my mother-in-law said, "There are all kinds of religions, but it would be too bad not to practice Gedatsu-kai. This Gedatsu-kai's teaching is the easiest to understand, and this is the genuine religion, a convincing religion." Well, that was twenty years—twenty years ago, this entering into Gedatsu-kai.

Q: Your wife?

A: My wife's mother. And right after that, my wife entered Gedatsu-kai. I kept it [my interest] to myself, but started asking about Gedatsu-kai. Then my son— I have several sons—he wanted to go to Tokyo, so at age twenty-three my son left our house to go into business. I set him up, but my wife and I were [really] opposed to this, because he was still too young. But he insisted, so he did leave the family, and it didn't go well for him. He gave it up after a year. He was too far in debt and couldn't continue. His business ended in failure. And then a letter came to us. "Really, father, I failed. As you said, father, I am really too young and ignorant of the world. I didn't study matters well enough, and I held a lot of mistaken ideas. Therefore I would like to take up spiritual training for two or three months. I know that you will probably be against this, father, but please let me take part in this spiritual training." So he went to the Gedatsu-kai headquarters.

Q: Headquarters? The Tokyo Practice Hall?

A: No, Tokyo—I mean the practice hall at the Sacred Land in Saitama Prefecture. Two or three months passed, and again a letter came. It said that the original agreement was for two or three months, but that he was a slow learner; he was sorry, but hoped he could continue with this spiritual training for a while. So about two years passed. That was the first case of one of my sons' entering Gedatsu-kai. So I was the very last one. As I told you, I thought that Christianity was right. [It had a long history, but] this Gedatsu-kai wasn't very old. It started about the beginning of the Shōwa period [1926]. So I just couldn't bring myself to trust this religion. I stubbornly stuck to Christianity.

But as I said before, there was sickness in the family, and other people were trying to help us. When we wondered about the reason [for the sickness], my wife and relatives said that it was some offense against the ancestors or the kami. But I was sure that I hadn't offended them, so I didn't want to join Gedatsu-kai. Then in 1964, mother—my wife's mother, [our family's] grandma—unexpectedly said to me, "Your ancestors are in Fukui City, so there ought to be a memorial stone [there]. Go and pay your respects at your ancestors' memorial stone." Well, I was a little resistant and said that since the main house of the family was still there, and many elderly family members, too, there was no need for me to pay a visit. My feeling was that it was enough to pay my respects at the memorial services for my mother, father, and grandparents [in Hokkaido]. I felt that there was no need for other visits. But she said, "You have abandoned your ancestors." It was 1964 when she said this.

The same year my wife, her mother, and I—the three of us—went to Sapporo because my son had sent us tickets for the Olympics [so we were on our way to Tokyo]. At that time mother—my wife's mother—said, "Why don't you go on to Fukui City and pay your respects at your ancestors' memorial stone? Go on to Fukui City." [Fukui City is located on the Japan Sea coast, almost due north of Kyoto.] Well, at that time my mother and father were long dead, and relatives who would have known about these things had died, too. I knew about Fukui City in a general way, and [in Hokkaido] we had an Association of People from

Fukui Prefecture [Fukui Kenjinkai]. My father had been an officer in the association. I visited all the officers of that association, but they couldn't tell me the address of my family in Fukui City. These people were rather old, and their memory was poor—but even the old women from Fukui Prefecture were saying that I should go back. So when these old people told me to go, I just couldn't object and say I wouldn't. I just said that I wasn't sure yet, we didn't have any address at all, maybe my relatives were no longer there. . . . But my wife insisted, "There certainly *are* relatives there. If you go, you will see." She received gohō shugyō at that time, and that's what she was told: "If you go, you will see."
Q: During gohō shugyō?
A: Yes. She said that because we had been told "If you go, you will see," we should go. So I agreed. I still didn't understand, but anyway we went to Fukui City. I really began to think that this gohō shugyō must be something miraculous. We went to Fukui City and began searching from district to district, since neither my wife nor I knew the city. We went to the City Office to search for the Nakajimo name, but it was a Sunday so there was nothing we could do. We got into a taxi—there was no other way to make inquiries around the city—and when the driver asked us where he should take us, I said, "It doesn't make any difference. Straight ahead!" So off we went, completely in the dark [as to where we were going]. On the way we asked people if they knew of any Nakajimos, but no one did, so we just went farther. Finally we got out of the taxi. The next time we asked, we were directed to the house of a Nakajimo family, [and of course we wanted] to see if they were relatives. This person was very kind, but said there were lots of Nakajimos in Fukui City and he didn't know where my ancestors might be from. [So we thanked him and left.]

We didn't know what to do and just walked around quite a while. Finally we decided that anything would be better than this, so we had someone direct us to an old, a very old, Buddhist temple. We wandered into that temple and asked [at the office] if there was a Nakajimo memorial stone here. They said they didn't know about any, but we checked the temple death register all the way back. The family name was not in it, but there was [a name with] the character [read] *jū* or *shige*—and there was such a name in my main family. (I am a second son.) In the [Hokkaido] family I was born in, there is a memorial tablet for a person who died at the beginning of the Meiji period [1868–1912]. [The name on it is] the posthumous Buddhist name. I had copied this name and brought it with me. What I noticed was this same character, shige. The priest wasn't there, but we talked to his wife and tried to find out if the Nakajimo family was in the death register. All I had written down was the Buddhist name, and the Meiji year, month, and day [of death]. Looking at the temple record, [I found the same name, but] there was one month's difference. The priest's wife said, though, that the old calendar and the new differed by a month. So I figured that this shige might be one of my relatives.
Q: Was that a Jōdo Shinshū temple?
A: Yes. I didn't know for sure [that this person was a relative], but said that if they didn't mind, I would take some of the soil from around that memorial stone back to my family's memorial stone in Sapporo. We were just about to leave, when the son of the Nakajimo family we had talked to earlier—a big lumber dealer—came rushing in. He said that his father had returned home [later] and

told him that the Nakajimos who had gone to Hokkaido were from his family, and
that he belonged to the main family. The father has died since, but there is no
doubt that we are of the same family. [About that time] the temple priest came
in, too, and since we had traveled all the way from Hokkaido to locate our ancestors, they ordered in food and gave us a nice meal. [They urged us to stay longer
and visit the memorial stone,] but we had already made arrangements to stay in
Kyoto, so we had to go on. That was the first time [we went to Fukui City]. The
next time was when we learned through gohō shugyō—that is, my wife was told—
that no one was taking care of the memorial stone.

Q: When was this gohō shugyō received?

A: Well. . . .

Q: The first was in 1964?

A: Yes, 1964. It was after that. . . . I'm not really sure.

Q: The next year?

A: Yes, [about] the next year—quite a while after the first. [Anyway,] we had a
main family there [in Fukui City], and they had a very nice Buddhist altar. That
first time we didn't go to the memorial stone. I had thought that the memorial
stone would be taken care of since the main family had such a fine Buddhist altar,
but in gohō shugyō we were told that the memorial stone was not being taken
care of. I thought this was peculiar. Then about three years ago [1976], we suddenly
received a phone call from the house we had visited in Fukui City. They said that
they had found the memorial stone of our family, and they asked us to come. This
was just before the time of Buddhist memorial services for ancestors [in the late
summer]. My father hadn't said too much about his ancestors. There had been a
second marriage in the family four generations ago, and the family was split. This
may be a shameful thing to talk about, but that's the way it was. But the present
Nakajimo family in Fukui City, the main family, put up a very nice memorial
stone. There are many Nakajimo memorial stones, but they are all different. My
family's memorial stone would probably be something like a *muenbotoke* stone
[the stone of a dead person or persons without descendants or whose descendants
do not observe the regular rituals].

Then came this phone call from the house in Fukui City—not the head of the
house, he had died, but the son of the former head, or rather his wife. She said
that they had remembered this visit of a relative from Hokkaido some eight years
ago—he must be a fine person to come all that way to look for his ancestors—
and that [they had learned that] there was a family taking care of the memorial
stone, but it was not a Nakajimo family. This family had been looking after ancestors
for a hundred years or so, but they were about to give it up. In that case the
memorial stone would become a muenbotoke [stone]. Well, we went to Fukui
City, [and it turned out to be] the same main family as ours. The name written
in the death register was not the [posthumous] Buddhist name; it was the family
name. The family name and the [Buddhist] name on the memorial stone did not
agree, but I thought they were [probably] the same. We discussed it with the
temple priest, and [he, too, thought that] this seemed to be our family stone. He
said that we had better take care of it. I thought [it would be good] to have a new
memorial stone put up [in Hokkaido] and have the spirits transferred there. Then
the former memorial stone could be treated as a muenbotoke. But when winter
comes to Fukui, there are times when you just can't move memorial stones [to

the special muenbotoke site]. And also I would have services in Hokkaido. In the
end I told him that I would assume responsibility for it, and then I returned home.

About a year later we wanted to go to that memorial stone in Fukui City [and
see to our responsibilities]. We talked about it, but what with business and all,
we couldn't work it out. We wanted to go at the time of the Buddhist memorial
services for ancestors, but couldn't. So we decided that even if we couldn't go
then, we would go later. At that time my wife received gohō shugyō again. She
was told, "Go to Fukui City!"

Q: From Sapporo?

A: No, by this time we had moved to Tokyo. But why were we supposed to go
to Fukui City? [The answer was the same as before.] "If you go, you will see." I
couldn't understand this at all. Well, we couldn't go the year before last or last
year either, so we went this year. But the old memorial stone that we had thought
was being taken care of by the temple actually was not being looked after. Then
we understood. The memorial stone was *not* being treated as a muenbotoke
[stone]. This was when we first understood what the matter was. [But before going
any further] we wanted to check with the main family [in Hokkaido] to see whether
this memorial stone was really one for our ancestors, because if you make mistakes
with memorial stones, people say that bad things will happen. [We went back to
Hokkaido and checked, but the main family, too,] wondered what the circumstances were. Finally I said that we [all] ought to go to Fukui City, so the main
family said they would go with us to the memorial stone. This time my elder sister
and her son—my nephew—all of us went to Fukui City. Finally we got the
memorial stone taken care of. This was [my wife's and my] third trip, and little
by little we came to understand the situation of our ancestors. So this is the really
important thing that we learned [through gohō shugyō]—something we hadn't
anticipated at all: the fact that the memorial stone had not been taken care of,
had not been offered memorial services.

Q: You requested memorial services at that Jōdo Shinshū temple?

A: Yes, three times.

Q: You've had memorial services performed in Gedatsu-kai, too?

A: Yes. We still do.

Q: In Gedatsu-kai you have memorial services for individuals?

A: Yes.

Q: That is a miraculous tale, isn't it?

A: Yes, it really is miraculous. [My experience] may be a small thing, but after
all, it is not a lie. And there really is such a thing as the link of karma. Of course,
I was studying Christianity all the while, so I wasn't paying visits to shrines and
temples, or performing [acts of] repentance and thanksgiving. That's the way it
was, but Gedatsu-kai got me to studying [,too], and practicing gratitude and thanks
(hōon kansha). Thanks and repentance were really not thoroughgoing in Christianity. Because I was a devout Christian, I was self-confident. I thought that I
didn't need a household shrine because Christianity was a religion of faith. Even
with regard to the memorial stone and my business—I had a watch-and-jewelry
business—I thought I could take care of things myself. I did pay my respects to
kami and ancestors, but from the viewpoint of kami, I was a bad person. From
the viewpoint of the average person, of course, I was a virtuous person. I seemed

to be prosperous and serving the kami. But when I came to study it—for example, the link of karma—I really did not have a feeling of gratitude for this link of karma, for my money, and so on. But after all, the ancestors—well, we are in the same bloodline, of the same blood, and. . . .

Q: Karma link?

A: Yes, we have a karma link, and Gedatsu-kai teaches us to be thankful for this. And if we do something wrong, we are supposed to apologize to the ancestors. Well, I had known about these things in a general sort of way, but to realize that they are actually so! As the branch leader said [in a talk we all had heard earlier that day], there may or may not be repentance in Christianity, but if you're not [sincerely] repentant yourself, it is nothing. Gedatsu-kai taught me this. Even if you think you are doing the right thing, it's not always the case [that you are]. The same [act of] repentance—you may not even notice it yourself if you are just [mechanically] saying and doing things—is nothing. Whether you go ahead and do it or not, you think things are all right. But recently I have come to see that this is not the case; I have come to examine myself more closely.

Q: You mentioned repentance—have you visited the Sacred Land?

A: Yes, we go there often.

Q: At the Sacred Land, do you practice repentance and *ohyakudo* [a form of repentance that involves walking back and forth between two stone pillars a hundred times]?

A: Yes, ohyakudo too.

Q: Was that from two or three years ago?

A: No—well, it wasn't too many times, but I did it while still in Hokkaido.

Q: When was it that you moved to Tokyo?

A: It's been ten years now.

Q: And the time you joined. . . .

A: Gedatsu-kai?

Q: Yes. That was in Sapporo as far as your wife is concerned?

A: Yes, in her case it was in Sapporo.

Q: And it was after the move to Tokyo that you yourself entered Gedatsu-kai?

A: Yes, I really—Gedatsu. . . . Well, my wife was attending, and I attended, too, for a while, but I was in Christianity—still a member of a church. I'm [still] a member of the church. So [at first] I couldn't agree to entering Gedatsu-kai. I thought that if I were to join here, the proper thing would be for me to cut my Christian ties and then enter Gedatsu-kai. That was my idea, but I decided to consult [others] about it. [It is true, though, that] thanks to my study of Christianity when young, I was able to lead an honest life. And then there was my family's finances, and my family itself—since I had received Christianity's protection in these matters. . . .

Q: This was the United Church of Christ in Japan?

A: Yes. In August—no, September, the first of last month—I went to Hokkaido, and it became a big problem. I had received the help of the church, and I was thankful, so why should I have to cut my ties with Christianity? Anyway, I went to Sapporo and consulted with [the minister of] the church there. But the minister had changed since my association with Gedatsu-kai. Before, I had told the former pastor that I was looking into Gedatsu-kai and that we had had this message in gohō shugyō, and he had said just to wait. But now I believed in the gohō shugyō. So this [new] minister said, "If you have gone this far, you may as well go ahead and practice Gedatsu-kai." Did you know that Reverend Kashima [fictitious name], a leader of Gedatsu-kai, is Christian?

Q: Really?

A: Yes, [anyway,] he was formerly a Christian. I have met him many times, and he told me, "Nakajimo, it's all right for you to be a Christian." He said that I had surely been blessed as a Christian. Well, I don't really understand the blessing of Christianity.

Q: That blessing of Christianity—what would that be?

A: Well, I don't know exactly, but as he said, "You surely were blessed." My wife and children told me that Christianity was probably good for me. "Even if you enter Gedatsu-kai, that won't change," they said. If you practice Christianity, there is no such thing as not being blessed. There is no Christian who has not been blessed. So I decided that it was all right to go ahead [and enter Gedatsu-kai]. And even now, receiving gohō shugyō, [I am sure that] gohō shugyō is not false.

Q: How many times have you received gohō shugyō?

A: Three.

Q: During those gohō shugyō, did you receive any special messages?

A: Just small things. Nothing special. My wife's mother—her trouble with money, and the time my brother died [and I was told to perform] memorial services.

Q: Memorial services for your brother?

A: Yes, we still hold them. [Then there was the message about] Batō Kannon, too. It wasn't all that clear, but "Batō Kannon has also been of help to you"—this came out in gohō shugyō. [Batō Kannon is a popular Buddhist deity featuring a horse's head; it is identified in Sanskrit as Hayagrīva.] Both my wife and I denied this, but when we went to Hokkaido—my father had already died, but [when alive], even though poor, he would pay visits to shrines; he and my elder brother, too—I wondered why my father had visited his ujigami so frequently. There was another small shrine he also visited, and when I asked, sure enough, it was a shrine for Batō Kannon.

Another time when our son was sick, my wife received gohō shugyō. [She was told that the sickness] was related to Batō Kannon, and that we should go to Batō Kannon and give thanks. So we paid visits [to Batō Kannon] for that purpose for about twenty days. Even these days—what day of the month is it?—we often pay a visit to express gratitude when we can. So, you see, we thought that we had no connection with Batō Kannon, but my father had prayed to Batō Kannon. It may seem a small thing, but we received this message in gohō shugyō, and when we checked, it turned out to be right.

Q: What about the rest of your family? Your daughters?

A: Well, that's a family matter. Some family members do, and some don't. My daughter, now, goes to the Sapporo Practice Hall. My oldest son, second son, and oldest daughter—my fourth child—they were all telling me to go to Gedatsu-kai. They did so because of their own experience. They had undergone gohō shugyō and received much help. There was only one of my children who didn't urge me to practice [Gedatsu-kai].

Q: Well, that is an interesting story.

A: At first, of course, I was opposed to this. Later, for a long while, I just thought I would keep this [faith in Gedatsu-kai] to myself. But as I said—this overlaps with what I said earlier—Gedatsu-kai teaches the same thing [as Christianity], but it teaches us in a fashion *much* more easily understood. At first I disliked this kind of "faith in answer to prayers," but after all, it teaches us clearly things we [otherwise] don't understand. I was practicing Christianity, and maybe it was because I didn't have [enough] faith, but I didn't experience such things in Christianity.

Q: Is there "faith in answer to prayers" in Christianity, too, sometimes?

A: Well, anything, after all—it is the same in Christianity. Things occur because you have faith. This is the same in Christianity. For example, my children were in a car accident, but weren't injured. Surely this was "faith in answer to prayers." You find this in Christianity, too. But Gedatsu-kai teaches *concretely, concretely.* Since my children were safe in the accident, they gave thanks for this protection. Gedatsu-kai teaches us *concretely* about this protection.

Q: Do you have a Gedatsu-kai traffic safety amulet in your family?

A: Yes, my son has, I think. I don't drive myself. And a "body protector" [*mimamori*]—we all keep a "body protector" next to our skin.

Q: Any other talismans?

A: In addition, [there is a household shrine] in our home for the ujigami—not a formal altar, but one of the kind found in any ordinary house. For example, Gedatsu-kai's Tenjin Chigi—what in Christianity they call the kami of heaven and earth. And then we have a Buddhist altar. It was only after we moved to Tokyo that we first got a Buddhist altar. Our children bought it for us.

Q: Your children?

A: Yes, I had been a Christian and felt I didn't need one. But then I built a new house in Tokyo and had to think about a Buddhist altar. They wanted one very much, so I thought I would buy one—and then they said they had already bought one, so I couldn't object. At any rate, they brought it home and said, "Father, father, you are a Christian, so don't worry—you can even put a cross in it!" (Laughter) But we don't have any memorial tablets for [particular] ancestors of our family. The altar is just for the generations of ancestors [in general].

Q: There are no memorial tablets at all?

A: No, no one in my family has died. All the memorial tablets are with the main family.

Q: And at your home you perform the sweet tea memorial service?

A: Yes, every day. As I said before, it is best for the entire family to worship the same way. In Christianity, too, I thought the same way. My wife felt this way, too. In Christian worship services that's how it is, along with prayers before sleeping. After all, if you take the view that there is something holy, kami exists, so we should pray to kami. I haven't really given up Christianity.

Q: This goes back to your earlier reference to your family, but you were born in Hokkaido, and much earlier had your family come from Fukui City?

A: Yes, four generations earlier—about a hundred years ago. But now there aren't many people who know about those things—about ancestors and the like. And I felt sorry for the ancestors.

The Religious Universe of Mr. Nakajimo:
From Traditional Upbringing to Christianity,
and Return to Ancestral Tradition

Every human being has unique experiences that define him or her as an individual, as well as shared aspects with other humans—depending on the degree of their common heritage. Comparing and contrasting the life histories of Mr. Negishi and Mr. Nakajimo is instructive in probing some general characteristics of Japanese culture and religion, as well as some distinctive features of Gedatsu-kai. It is not to be expected that every member would have identical experiences in joining and participating within Gedatsu-kai, and this is certainly true of these two men. It is only natural that different people will find attractive and emphasize different facets of Gedatsu-kai; the full range of the movement's religious world view will become apparent only after hearing a number of life histories from various people—representing different ages, sexes, geographical areas, and levels of Gedatsu-kai organization.

These two persons share a number of common factors, the most obvious of which is that they are members of Gedatsu-kai, male, and about the same generation in age (although Mr. Nakajimo is seventeen years older than Mr. Negishi). On the other hand, their lives also vary significantly in several respects. They hail from different geographic areas of Japan: Mr. Negishi is a native of Tokyo; Mr. Nakajimo is a native of Hokkaido (whose ancestors came from Fukui) and is now retired in a suburb of Tokyo. Both are relatively well educated, although Mr. Negishi's university degree places him in a higher category of educational attainment than Mr. Nakajimo's high school diploma. Their religious lives are especially interesting, because they share the common world view of Japanese religion in general and Gedatsu-kai in particular, and yet each has a distinctive experience that emphasizes contrasting dimensions of Gedatsu-kai.

If we begin with the general world view of Gedatsu-kai, as first elaborated in the discussion of Mr. Negishi's life history in chapter 1, we find a remarkable similarity. Both men ascribe to a religious system—although they would not use such a formal term—in which kami, ancestors, Buddhas, and founder are central. Karma and repentance, as well as gratitude and thanks, are crucial to the acting out of their religious lives. The tutelary kami shrine (ujigami) and parish Buddhist temple (bodaiji) outside the home are as important for these two men as the household Shinto shrine (kamidana) and Buddhist ancestral altar (butsudan) within the home. Both perform regular Gedatsu-kai rituals in the home, such as the amacha memorial rite; both are devoted to the precedent of the founder, who established such rituals. In fact, these two men's religious values are so closely aligned that if they met, probably they would not be able to see any significant discrepancy. However, there are also considerable differences in the religious careers of the two members.

One of the major disparities between the two lives is the age of entry into Gedatsu-kai: Mr. Negishi came into contact with the new religion as a young man, while Mr. Nakajimo did not learn of it until middle age and did not actually enter until past middle age. Perhaps the single most important contrast is the manner of their entry into this movement: Mr. Negishi flowed into it rather naturally in a smooth transition from the traditional values of his home to a more explicit reformulation of these values in Gedatsu-kai; Mr. Nakajimo underwent a sharp break from his traditional upbringing when he converted to Christianity, and then returned to his ancestral tradition because of the tie that Gedatsu-kai reestablished with his ancestors.[7] Note, for example, that Mr. Negishi always visited the tutelary kami shrine, and appreciated Gedatsu-kai's teaching because it built upon this traditional foundation—entering the movement was not a break from but an elaboration of his traditional values. However, for Mr. Nakajimo, entering Gedatsu-kai meant renewing ties to local tutelary shrines and parish Buddhist temples. The same pattern holds for the household Shinto shrine and Buddhist ancestral altar (butsudan): although both now possess them and practice before them, Mr. Negishi never experienced a gap in this connection, whereas Mr. Nakajimo discarded such traditions in his late teens and did not reestablish them until late in his life—it was his adult children who purchased a butsudan for his home.

The reason for entering also varies considerably for the two. Mr. Negishi says he entered, in effect, because it spelled out a total way of life—what we might call in English a philosophy of life (or might even label an "existential" answer). Mr. Nakajimo entered Gedatsu-kai because it was a kind of reentry into the arena of ancestors and traditional practices that he had abandoned when he converted to Christianity in his late teens.[8] Even the process of recruitment is dissimilar— for Mr. Negishi it was a neighbor who introduced him to Gedatsu-kai, while for Mr. Nakajimo the key persons were his wife and mother-in-law. (Later we will explore the prominent role of women within Gedatsu-kai, and for this purpose it is well to remember that even Mr. Negishi first went to learn about this new religion in the company of his older sister.)

The two life histories are told in contrasting styles: Mr. Negishi's account is more elaborate and rational, while Mr. Nakajimo's is more personal and concrete. Because Mr. Negishi is a college graduate, he is more sophisticated in framing his story, and as an executive of the movement with three decades of membership, he is thoroughly familiar with the whole body of Gedatsu-kai doctrine and practice. Mr. Nakajimo's lower educational attainment, shorter time in the movement, and status as an ordinary member all lead him to give a straightforward account focusing on his personal experience rather than a more comprehensive statement. Even when these two report participation in the same Gedatsu-kai practice of the mediation ritual of gohō shugyō, their experience varies significantly in content, intensity, and permanence. Mr. Negishi's experience was rather mystical and intense, something he recalls vividly today, although the content was mainly a confirmation of his traditional values. Mr. Nakajimo's experience in gohō shugyō was not nearly so dramatic and is something he does not recall vividly—in fact, it is mainly the simple message about ancestors provided him indirectly through his wife and mother-in-law that is important to him.

It is worth noting that as much as the two stories seem to differ, nevertheless they do not contradict each other. Rather, the two careers are complementary in pointing out alternative means of appropriating various aspects of Gedatsu-kai belief and practice. Mr. Negishi and Mr. Nakajimo are two discrete human beings with unique dimensions of their individual lives as well as shared features such as their participation in Gedatsu-kai. It may appear commonplace and unnecessary to state that we should not expect the religious lives of these two members to be identical in key areas such as their reason for and manner of joining, and their experience in the same ritual. However, many Western-language treatments of Japanese new religions have tended to assume a rather uniform reason and behavior when people join a new religion. For the moment, we will profit more by a closer look at the life histories and testimonies of specific individuals; general statements about the world view of Gedatsu-kai members will be saved for the latter part of this chapter, and theoretical issues will be discussed at the end of this book.

The Life History of Mrs. Koshikawa:
Healing and Peace of Mind through Personal
Repentance and Renewal of Family Practices

The lives of two men have been described and analyzed, but this does not mean that male careers are definitive of religious experience within Gedatsu-kai. Indeed, females constitute about two-thirds of the movement's membership, and deserve at least equal treatment. The first example of a life history of a female member of Gedatsu-kai is that of Mrs. Koshikawa. She is a member of the "C" Branch, located in a seaport on the Pacific Ocean coast about two hours from Tokyo by fast train. This branch was chosen for study partly because of its location in a coastal city, outside metropolitan and suburban Tokyo, and partly because it is a dynamic young branch and is recruiting many new members. At the time of interview, December 27, 1979, Mrs. Koshikawa was fifty-two years old and worked in an elementary school. She had joined Gedatsu-kai about a year and a half before the interview. This life history was recorded under some time constraint, because of the convenience of the group and the arrangement for my colleague and me to complete this research trip in one day, with a two-hour train trip to the seaport city and a two-hour return trip. As with other branch interviews, we had made a preliminary visit a month earlier. When we arrived at the branch December 27, 1979, the branch leader and the assistant branch leader had arranged for four women to tell their taiken (testimonies). They were well prepared, and told their stories without pause. Here is Mrs. Koshikawa's story, translated as it was given, in first-person narration; explanations and identifications are provided within brackets.

Last year, 1978, I first came to Gedatsu-kai. In June 1977, my body was weak. I thought that I was strong, but daily work made me tired. About October [1977] my father died. At that time there were a lot of [my personal] mistakes I thought about. I thought I should be concerned with memorial rites at the grave. And in 1978 I felt that I should perform worship there. At that time I thought that the grave was of no [serious] connection [to other matters]. That is, *externally*. But *internally*, things were bad [for me].

I went to the doctor for a careful examination. Apparently my liver and gall bladder were OK. But the doctor could give me no exact diagnosis. As far as my internal organs were concerned, the doctor said there was nothing [wrong]. But in the small of my back I still had trouble, with hot sensations and also pain. Again I went to the doctor, and he said that because I was nervous, he couldn't help me. I felt "scolded." I was angry. I still had a dull pain in the small of my back. But it changed. Especially when I was carrying things it bothered me. I have a small home, but even simple cleaning became difficult. [Mrs. Koshikawa went on to describe her change in personality, too.] I didn't even want to see anyone's face. I stayed in my house, didn't want to see anyone. The doctor prescribed a corset. But nothing helped. Even a bigger corset didn't help. The doctor said it would get better. But the pain in the small of my back got worse. Every day it got worse, both my body and spirit. I was all bent over, like this—[Mrs. Koshikawa gestured with her body, her back curved and head hung down]. Also my face looked very bad. I felt this myself when I looked in the mirror. My own feeling was poor.

In early January 1978, my self-confidence was poor. But I now returned to the primary school where I had been working. I was told by a friend to come along [to Gedatsu-kai], but I didn't care for such "religious beliefs." I just said "yes, yes," so as not to disagree. Then on the evening of March 3 my condition got very bad. And my friend Takahashi said Gedatsu-kai had a good leader, and that I should have this leader take a look at my sickness. Finally I said that I would go. This was when I was talking on the phone, and I said that I had to hang up, I didn't even have the strength to hold on to the phone. [Mrs. Koshikawa gestured how she had put down this heavy receiver.] I hung up, because I didn't even want to talk. Then the next morning I was very bad. It was a very clear day, March 4, and usually the wind is very strong in our city at that time, but it was a very nice day. I had to wear heavy clothing, and felt a little better. [Mrs. Koshikawa implies that on such a fine day she should not have needed so many heavy clothes; i.e., this was the time of spring rejuvenation, but she was still sick and cold.]

Anyway, I didn't want to break my promise, so I came [to Gedatsu-kai]. I met the Gedatsu-kai leader for health consultations. He checked my condition. He said the bones in my lower back were probably slipped out of place. But the pain in my lower back was caused by the suffering of my ancestors. Not just ancestors [in general], but he asked if there weren't in my family some spirits of dead infants that we did not ritually memorialize. I was told to perform the sweet tea memorial, and so I did. But I didn't think that it could possibly be the spirits of dead infants [that were the cause of my suffering]. So I mentioned this to my older brother. And my older brother told me that there were indeed two other infants [in our family] who had died, who in relation to me were elder brothers. One had died six months after birth, and another had died immediately after birth.

I was born about ten kilometers from this city. Now it [my birthplace] is a city, but when I was a child it was a remote area. There our family belonged to a Nichiren temple. This temple was something like a university in ancient times. And university students came there often, for ascetic practices. We were parishioners of the Nichiren sect—that is, my parents' family. One of my family there, named Iitaka, had been the village headman. And in ancient times the family had a lot of money. But now they are in a neighboring village—they made many mistakes, and they are now poor. My ancestors are there. But my family left that village, and moved to another village. But the graves are [still] in the old village. When they moved from the old village to the new village, they would make many trips to honor the graves every year. For the ancestral memorial rites they thought

of moving the gravestones to the new village. But the Nichiren temple said moving
the gravestones would be difficult. And—it is embarrassing to put it this way—
the gravestones are in the middle of the cemetery, and a fine set of gravestones.
So they [the temple] said the gravestones couldn't be moved. [Mrs. Koshikawa
implies that it would leave an empty space in the middle of the cemetery.]

The two elder brothers [who died as infants] were separate from the adults'
grave site, about one kilometer away in the mountains. There was a special grave
site for infants. I went to both of the villages [where my family had lived]. Also
I went to the grave site for infants. I found out about the elder brothers at the
time of my parents' death. I have six siblings. As for the tombstone, I didn't know
which stone it was, but did know about the infants generally. It was a mistake to
move the stones, I thought. Mother was eighty-five, and once a year came to this
village, but she was old, and it was difficult for her.

So from the Gedatsu-kai leader I learned that this was the biggest mistake.
[Mrs. Koshikawa means it was a mistake not to take better care of the family
gravestones.] Last year, May 1, I went to the old village, and not just to the family
graves, but saw there was a big mistake. There was an Inari [stone] that my
ancestors had worshipped.[9] My father, before he went to the new village, had
entrusted the Inari [stone honoring a kami] to neighbors. I checked, and found I
could pay my respects—the neighbors didn't mind. I received [from Gedatsu-kai]
a repentance paper and performed repentance at the local parish Shinto shrine,
and had memorials performed. My elder brothers had died and become *muen*
[ancestors not memorialized by living relatives]. The Gedatsu-kai leader taught
me about that. The grave had been taken care of for thirty years. But on March
first, for the first time I saw that I was mistaken [about the graves]—I must
recognize my own mistakes. I performed memorial rites and repentance. I recognized my own mistakes. Every day I came to this [Gedatsu-kai] meeting place,
I performed the amacha memorial rite here. And, what was remarkable was the
amacha memorial rite. When the memorial rite began, I was not conscious of it,
but I cried. I couldn't stop. Why? Why did I cry? The next day, again, I cried
when the memorial rite started. It was my mistake—this was fundamental. My
own mother was just thinking of formalities. My father had gone to the spirit
world, and was suffering. Actually, it was my father crying. My family had given
up Inari. Their children had become muen. My family forgot the debt owed to
kami. [After all], they had received the power of kami.

All this was miraculous. The Gedatsu-kai leader said to ask kami [i.e., to resolve
the problems]. I didn't know [how to proceed], but I was thankful [for this advice].
I didn't know what to do—what kami was it exactly? There was a stone by the
road [in the old village where my family had lived]. And my family had gone to
that kami. It was Inari. The stone was so old it was hard to read, but I did a
rubbing, by placing my handkerchief over it, and it was Inari. I came back to this
city, and told my family it was Inari.

The first time I practiced the mediation ritual of gohō shugyō was May 29,
1978. And the result [of the mediation ritual] was that it was the Matsuwadayama
Inari. It requested twenty-one days of memorial rites, this was the message [ob-
tained from gohō shugyō]. But it would be difficult to go all the way there [to the
village], so the leader said I could perform the memorial rites here [in the meeting
place]. For twenty-one days I performed special memorial rites. When these rites

were completed, I practiced gohō shugyō again. Again [the result was that] it was Matsuwadayama Inari, so I could trust [gohō shugyō].

This time I practiced the gohō shugyō my eyes were shut, but there was a bright light in my eyes. And it was like a steel bar came down my back. The first time it happened I wrote characters on the floor mats. But the second time—not only was there a "brightness which shone," but also I was told that Matsuwadayama Inari was satisfied with the twenty-one days of memorial rites.

After that, I paid a religious visit to Matsuwadayama Inari at New Year's, the March equinox, in May, at the festival of the dead, at the fall equinox, and at the end of the year. I was completely devoted to Inari. And I did a lot of study under the leader. In July I went to Tokyo. A Gedatsu-kai leader organized things there. He had gravestones set up there, for my old mother who was having difficulty traveling to the distant village. Nichiren priests were there. These memorial tablets I took to the tombstones there. In the mediation ritual of gohō shugyō I learned that it is good to have all gravestones together. After that—I believed in Gedatsu-kai completely.

The Religious Universe of Mrs. Koshikawa:
Correcting Family "Mistakes" Relieves Personal Problems

When we compare and contrast Mrs. Koshikawa's life history with that of the two men, we find similarities and dissimilarities, in both the secular and religious areas. The three share the same generation, with less than twenty years separating their ages. But differences are also prominent, not the least of which is gender. One sharp contrast is geographical; Mrs. Koshikawa resides in a coastal city far from the metropolitan and suburban Tokyo where the two men now live. With just one and a half years' membership in the group, she is a newcomer, in contrast to the two men, who have been members for many years. Because she did not mention schooling in her taiken, I asked her about this after she finished her story, and she said she had attended twelve years of school—the same as Mr. Nakajimo, but less than Mr. Negishi. Her status as a housewife and worker in an elementary school places her economically lower than the independently wealthy Mr. Negishi and the former businessman Mr. Nakajimo; however, she gains some prestige from her husband's position as a superintendent of a school.

In the realm of religion, Mrs. Koshikawa shares with the men the same general world view of Gedatsu-kai, which need not be outlined here once more. However, there are several aspects of her entry into the religion and emphasis of some dimensions of it that are not prominent in the men's stories. The beginning of her story makes clear that she had particular problems, and entered Gedatsu-kai through the successful diagnosis and resolution of these problems. At first she had difficulty relating the several problems—a sense of guilt after her father died, particular physical ailments, and a general fatigue and lack of self-confidence. She was unable to fathom the sense of guilt toward her father, although she felt she should do something; she made repeated visits to a physician, who said she had no physical problems, which made her feel even worse; and generally she seemed to have a loss of energy and direction, not knowing where to turn. Both Mr. Negishi and Mr. Nakajimo grew slowly in the faith and practice of Gedatsu-kai, gradually understanding that a problem existed. On the other hand, Mrs. Ko-shikawa began with specific complaints and problems, and first visited Gedatsu-kai for health consultation (*kenkō shidō* or *kenkō sōdan*), later understanding and taking care of her problems.

She began to practice the amacha memorial rite at the advice of the Gedatsu-kai leader, who diagnosed her back pain as caused by the suffering of her ancestors, but she was still skeptical of his notion that her ancestors were not properly cared for. Reflection convinced her that the ancestors known by her were not really well cared for, and questioning of her family revealed two "family skeletons." She learned for the first time that two older brothers had died as infants; they had been buried in a general burial ground for infants but were not regularly me-morialized. This kind of "discovery" or remembrance of miscarriages, abortions, stillbirths, and infant deaths as later causes of misfortune is a common feature in the stories of female members that is not found in those of male members. The fact that these dead infants are Mrs. Koshikawa's siblings, and not her own chil-dren, does not diminish the misfortune for her family: family mistakes are also Mrs. Koshikawa's mistakes. A hallmark of Japanese religion is this kind of family identity, which is reemphasized in Gedatsu-kai (and is strongest among women, as statistical evidence will show).

Mrs. Koshikawa had a more dramatic "conversion" experience than either of the men. In the process of performing the amacha memorial rite, she cried, and the next day she cried again during the rite: through this ritual she became aware of her own mistakes and realized a change of heart. This sudden realization and drastic change of heart, resulting in the easing of her physical and spiritual com-plaints, is not seen in the accounts of the two men. However, Mrs. Koshikawa's account cannot be simply juxtaposed to those of the two men, because in at least two respects her religious life places her in greater affinity with one man than the other. On the one hand, some of the features of her story, such as the *rediscovery* of both ancestors and forgotten family religious practices, are very similar to the experience of Mr. Nakajimo. On the other hand, in her gohō shugyō experience Mrs. Koshikawa is closer to Mr. Negishi's mystical experience—in fact, she goes beyond his being transported back in time. A truly classic expression of mystical "enlightenment" (Eliade 1965) is found in her statement that while her eyes were closed "a brightness shone," and it felt as if a steel bar came down her back. The fact that Mrs. Koshikawa shares some religious features with the two men shows that religious life in Gedatsu-kai is not totally determined by gender—in fact, the precipitation of her religious activity by a sense of inadequacy after her father's death is similar to Okano Eizō's response to his father's death.

Six Life Histories:
Religion Improves Business and Work, Heals Children,
Aids Artistic Creativity, and Eases Human Relations

Previous life histories have been given in great detail, and as close to the original as possible, in order to preserve some of their concreteness and drama. However, it would require too much space (and it is not necessary) to recall in full every life history the author has recorded. Now that three of them have been presented at some length, we can use six briefer accounts in order to present a wider range of persons and religious experiences. These include accounts of two additional women from "C" Branch and two women from "Ok" Branch in Tokyo, and two taiken of young people—an unmarried man and a recently married woman—as reported in the publication *Yangu Gedatsu*. These stories will provide greater insight into the religious lives of females and young members of Gedatsu-kai. They are given one after another without analysis; later they will be discussed as a group.

Mrs. Kawakami

Mrs. Kawakami is another member of "C" Branch who was interviewed the same day as Mrs. Koshikawa. She was fifty-three years old at the time of the interview; she and her husband run a bread shop. She was a recent member, having joined Gedatsu-kai earlier that year. The following is a summary of her life history.

Mrs. Kawakami first came to Gedatsu-kai in April 1979, through the introduction of a friend. She is affiliated with the Nichiren sect, through marriage to her husband, and there are many gravestones in her family. Her husband is a parish representative (*danka sōdai*) at their Nichiren temple. Before her marriage she was affiliated with a Shingon temple, and she took one of her natal family's gravestones to the Nichiren temple cemetery of her husband. She was active in honoring the muen (those without living relatives to memorialize them) in her family, offering them incense. But it was a mistake to move the gravestone. She had studied the *Lotus Sutra* a lot at the Nichiren temple, but it did not do much for her. By contrast, the teaching of Gedatsu-kai is excellent. She wishes that she would have had the opportunity to study the new religion earlier.

In October 1979 her family opened a bread shop. She studied Gedatsu-kai hard at that time, because there were many difficult problems. Night and day she came to the branch leader and assistant branch leader for advice. (The branch leader is a bank executive, and his wife, the assistant branch leader, is successful in a cosmetics business.) It turned out that her ancestors were suffering, so she made formal apologies (*owabi*) to them, performed memorial rites, and performed the hundredfold repentance (ohyakudo). Her husband, too, had made mistakes, and participated in these religious practices. She could talk a whole day about all these activities.

She asked the branch leader about the meaning of memorial rites. Then she saw her own mistakes. For six months she kept this up. She came to see the connection between a living person and a dead person in the spirit world (*reikai*). She was brought into Gedatsu-kai by a friend. At first she couldn't believe its teaching about the ancestors, tutelary kami, and so on. But there were lots of problems in her business. And there was no one to talk to. Then the branch leader became the financial guarantor for her business, and she began to work out her problems. Mrs. Kawakami said that the most important thing in Gedatsu-kai is improvement of one's fortune (*unmei kaikaku*). In this regard, Gedatsu-kai helped her study. So it is also an improvement of character.

That is the gist of Mrs. Kawakami's taiken, which she recited without interruption. Afterward she provided additional information in response to my direct questions. She was born in this seaport and has lived here her entire life. She completed the ninth grade of school. Before entering Gedatsu-kai, she participated in religion occasionally, such as going to the shrine of the tutelary kami at New Year's. She and her husband had both a Buddhist ancestral altar and a Shinto household shrine, but were not especially devout in making offerings. Her husband's family belonged to the new religion Tenrikyō, but he was not active in it, although he has participated in the Nichiren temple. Now both are active in Gedatsu-kai, and consider it the "real religion" (hontō no shūkyō). For the benefit of their shop, her husband performs the tochikuyō (memorial rite for a locale); I asked her if this was the makikuyō, a rite of pacifying spirits of the dead and purifying the locale by pouring amacha around the premises, and she said that this was what she meant. Her husband takes amacha and "spreads" (maku, maki) it on the ground in front of their shop. She went on to say that the formal apology ritual is great. She performs apologies at the tutelary kami shrine and at the altar of the Gedatsu-kai practice hall. In their shop they have enshrined a "pillar kami" (mihashiragami). They venerate the "pillar kami" and then perform the tochikuyō.

Mrs. Kawakami told how Gedatsu-kai had helped with the difficulties of her daughter-in-law's pregnancy and with an easy delivery. In fact, because the hatsu mairi (first day for a visit to a shrine for a newborn child) was the same day as a celebration at the branch practice hall, they made this ceremonial "first visit" at both the branch practice hall and the shrine of the tutelary kami.

Mrs. Kawakami's final remarks concerned her gratefulness to Gedatsu-kai. Since her entry, she has come to understand human life and spirits. For example, even if a person dies, the spirit lives on. However, we should regard the dead not with fear, but with thankfulness. And Gedatsu-kai is good for improvement of fortune.

Mrs. Miyauji

Mrs. Miyauji was also a member of "C" Branch, interviewed the same day as Mrs. Koshikawa and Mrs. Kawakami. She was forty-four years old at the time, a lifelong resident of this seaport. She graduated from a junior college and teaches in a public school. She had entered Gedatsu-kai about a year and a half prior to the interview. For the following account, Mrs. Miyauji referred to some handwritten notes. Most of the life histories we recorded were related without any such notes, but Mrs. Miyauji's case is a good example of how the taiken (testimony) becomes a formal personal document. Mrs. Miyauji had given us a short version the previous month when we visited "C" Branch, and on the second visit seemed a little nervous in presenting her story to us fully and accurately. Apparently the reason for this nervousness was that she had told her testimony at a monthly meeting of the Tokyo Practice Hall, and she wanted to be sure that the version she told us conformed to the one she had given there. The branch leader had asked her to tell this taiken at the Tokyo Practice Hall because of its interesting, dramatic character. This was borne out on the day of our second visit to "C" Branch, when we recorded the longer version of her story; as we were eating, after the interviews, the assistant branch leader played a tape recording of Mrs. Miyauji's testimony from the Tokyo Practice Hall, and it was so powerful that all conversation and eating stopped, because the participants of the branch meeting wanted to hear her story.[10] The following is a summary of Mrs. Miyauji's life history.

Mrs. Miyauji began by reviewing the brief account of her life history that we had discussed previously. Her daughter had been sick for seven years. A "teacher" (*sensei*) from Gedatsu-kai looked at her daughter. Then the teacher and Mrs. Miyauji looked at her family's memorial tablets. Mrs. Miyauji had never known her biological mother, having been raised by a stepmother. Before she came to study Gedatsu-kai, her daughter's ear was so bad that she could not attend school. Then Mrs. Miyauji studied Gedatsu-kai, received the apology paper (*owabijō*), and for twenty-one days performed apology (owabi). She then understood the wonderful power of Gedatsu-kai. She has a friend who studied at Ochanomizu University a year, and this friend said that the counseling taught there is very much like that of Gedatsu-kai. But the university counseling doesn't go so far as enlightenment (*satori*).

Mrs. Miyauji's stepmother was a member of Risshō Kōsei-kai (a prominent new religion emphasizing worship of ancestors and faith in the *Lotus Sutra*), Mrs. Miyauji had gone to Rissho Kōsei-kai fifteen years before she entered Gedatsu-kai, but she didn't like it. Her fellow workers, too, were involved in Risshō Kōsei-kai, and she read some of its publications. She did not know about Gedatsu-kai at the time, but she was wondering about Risshō Kōsei-kai.

Several years ago, the owner of a photography shop near "C" Branch urged her to attend Gedatsu-kai. She came to this branch and talked to a teacher, who showed her many things, and her personality completely changed. He healed her child completely. Her older sister was suffering from cancer, and her stepmother had practiced Risshō Kōsei-kai for many years. Once when her sister was very sick, Mrs. Miyauji came to "C" Branch at midnight to talk this over, and was told that she could be involved in both Risshō Kōsei-kai and Gedatsu-kai. She came to understand her own mistakes—she "enlightened" (*satotta*) herself; in other words, she is self-enlightened. She learned that we must not be resentful; there is always a cause for suffering. We must perform the amacha memorial rite.

Mrs. Miyauji's child was sick and could not go to school. When she did attend, she was teased by eighteen of the twenty-one students in her class, because she could not hear well, and therefore could not do her work well or even speak clearly. But her school teacher said that there was no point in transferring her, because it would be the same anywhere the child went. Mrs. Miyauji was criticized because she was a teacher and was not able to deal with her own child's problems. But through health consultations (kenkō shidō) this gradually cleared up. For example, from September 1978 through March 1979, when her daughter was in her second year of middle school, she was sick: her homework piled up and they were worried about her, but then her fever went down one month before final exams, and all went well.

Mrs. Miyauji's father had been active in religion. He revered Fudō (a Buddhist deity) at Narita.[11] Her father liked temple people, and a priest often visited their house to perform memorial rites. But Risshō Kōsei-kai hates Inari, so when her stepmother entered Risshō Kōsei-kai, she threw out Inari. And Fudō also was no longer worshipped in the home. So, many years later, Mrs. Miyauji performed apologies (owabi) for twenty-one days, to apologize for dropping these family practices.

Her older sister had cancer, and Mrs. Miyauji was performing "purification" (*kiyome*). (*Kiyome* is the Gedatsu-kai term for a kind of quiet meditation and/or prayer that precedes the mediation ritual of gohō shugyō.) It is "OK"[12] to do this purification anywhere, but she had been performing purification and praying with all her might at the branch practice hall. This was after her stepmother died. And in the midst of her performing purification, there was a telephone call. Her older sister was crying out for her—suffering from the pain of her cancer. Apparently the older sister was involved in Risshō Kōsei-kai; she had received their *mandala* (a sacred object) and had placed it in her Buddhist ancestral altar. The older sister said that she was going to die. So Mrs. Miyauji went to her and recited "Namu Gedatsu Kongō" ("I have faith in Gedatsu Kongō") and also the *Hannya Shingyō* sutra. They did away with the Risshō Kōsei-kai mandala from the sister's family Buddhist ancestral altar. The pain left her sister, who had not been able to eat for some time. She then entered Gedatsu-kai, and has eaten well every day.

Mrs. Miyauji told other aspects of her appreciation of Gedatsu-kai, especially her experiences in the mediation ritual of gohō shugyō and other practices. One time in gohō shugyō she received a message (shirase) about Konpira, considered a tutelary kami (ujigami) in the area where she lived.[13] So she took a fuda (paper talisman) to this shrine, and later discussed this with a person in the Shuhōbu (a special department for counseling on religious matters, which can be translated as "Spiritual Training Division") at the Sacred Land, who confirmed that she had acted properly. As a result of her practice in Gedatsu-kai, she performed memorial rites and even used amacha extract (as an ointment for minor skin problems). At first she thought that she couldn't perform the apology ritual, but she later performed it many times. This is because many things became clear to her through rituals such as gohō shugyō at the branch practice hall.

As a child she went occasionally to the shrine of the tutelary kami, such as during the Shichigosan ("Three-five-seven") festival, but after that she did not go. Then after she joined Gedatsu-kai, she received the "apology paper" (owabijō), and "with Gedatsu Kongō" she made apology to the kami.

In the group context of several interviews the same afternoon at the "C" Branch, especially because the members and the branch leader and the assistant branch leader knew each other so well, it was natural for the leader to chime in with interpretations or for other women to contribute aspects of their life histories that complemented the story being told. At this particular point in the afternoon, as Mrs. Miyauji finished her more formal account of her taiken, we asked some questions of her to get a fuller picture of her life (her lifelong residence in the seaport, her educational record, her exact date of entrance into Gedatsu-kai, etc.). When these questions tapered off, Mrs. Koshikawa gave a brief description of the sickness of her daughter that had been relieved through the help of Gedatsu-kai— both the sickness itself, and the lowering of the physician's price for the recommended treatment.

Mrs. Koshikawa's story of help from Gedatsu-kai prompted Mrs. Miyauji to talk more about help she had received. She used to be very afraid of ghosts—so frightened that she would not even let her children talk about ghosts, and when programs about them were on the television, she made her children turn it off. She was afraid of ghosts, but not of people. She was "OK" during the day, but nights were bad. Now that she is an active member of Gedatsu-kai, she is not afraid of ghosts at all. It used to be so bad that when she was on a trip she could not sleep at all, but now she has no problem sleeping. Mrs. Koshikawa and Mrs. Kawakami joined in this discussion, with comments from the branch leader about how they have all been aided in similar ways, both in physical improvements and in other ways such as not being afraid of the dark.

Mrs. Norikawa

A number of interviews were held at the "Ok" Branch in the heart of Tokyo on December 22, 1979, in a situation very similar to that of the interviews held at "C" Branch on December 27, 1979. We had visited "Ok" Branch two months earlier, on October 22, and had listened to brief taiken by about ten of its members. The táiken of one woman, Mrs. Norikawa, was especially interesting, both because of the nature of her illness that was healed, and because she was a former member of Tenrikyō. Later we arranged for an interview with Mrs. Norikawa after the December branch meeting; the branch leader also had several other women attend this interview session.

Mrs. Norikawa was seventy-four at the time of the interview, a lifelong resident of ¡Tokyo, and a middle-school graduate. She is a widow, and entered Gedatsu-kai ten years before the interview. Mrs. Norikawa seemed somewhat intimidated by the interview process, apparently because of the presence of the branch leader, who has a very strong personality. She tended to give a brief portion of her life story and then wait for questions that prompted more information from her. The following is the gist of her story.

Mrs. Norikawa belonged to Tenrikyō, then entered Gedatsu-kai about ten years ago. She could not understand Tenrikyō explanations. She wanted to be saved (*sukuwaretakatta*), but did not understand. They are a big organization. It started out like Gedatsu-kai, but now it is like a big pyramid. The selfish thoughts of Tenrikyō teachers mingled with the teaching of Tenrikyō, and that is why their teachings are not clear. She wanted to be saved, but could not understand Tenrikyō. She tried as hard as she could, but it was no use, so she wondered if there was good teaching.

When she paused, waiting for a question, I asked her if she had a particular problem (*nayami*) at that time. She said yes, that there had been four persons in her family who had drowned. She was concerned about memorial rites, and that is why she entered Tenrikyō. But it was just as if there were a veil over their teaching. And she was suffering.

Then she talked to a teacher from Gedatsu-kai at "Ok" Branch, and he said that if she entered Gedatsu-kai she would have thirty more years of life (she is already at an advanced age). He assured her that she could be saved in Gedatsu-kai. Later she quit Tenrikyō. Gedatsu-kai said that it was OK if she continued Tenrikyō, but it was her own idea to quit—she thought that having just one religion was best. She formally entered Gedatsu-kai in 1973. Some of her family ancestors had drowned, and because of this her karma (innen) was strong; probably this was the cause of her blood pressure problems. Therefore she performed apologies and memorial rites to purify herself. She worshipped kami and performed apologies, and her blood pressure got better. And the heavenly kami (*ten no kami*) forgave her. This was because of the unnatural death (*henshi*) of the family ancestors who had drowned. The Gedatsu-kai people told her that if she entered Gedatsu-kai, she would understand all this.

She entered Gedatsu-kai, and became quite happy. She did eventually perform gohō shugyō, but first had to be in a pure (shōjin) state. It was six months after she entered Gedatsu-kai that she performed the mediation ritual of gohō shugyō, and received a number of messages (shirase). Most of the messages were from spirits—and spirits who are troubled do not come forth. This year her guardian deity (goshugojin) helped her understand this.[14] Her guardian deity is Benzaiten (the goddess of fortune, Sarasvatī in Sanskrit). It was merit from her regular visits to a local chapel for Benzaiten that resulted in her having Benzaiten as a guardian deity.

Before she entered Gedatsu-kai, she was involved in none of these practices. Of course, when she was a child she venerated kami—there was a household shrine (kamidana) in her childhood home. Her younger sister was very sick, and her relatives were worshipping kami. Mrs. Norikawa learned from her younger sister's experience—her younger sister was healed. But from her youth until about ten years ago, she did not practice religion much. Now she goes every month to a major temple honoring Benzaiten. She considers Fudō her guardian deity, too, because there was a small chapel for Fudō near her birthplace. Both her grandfather and uncle had worshipped the Fudō close to the site where she was born, so her family did, too, and the strength of this faith has passed on protection to her family.

When she was a member of Tenrikyō, she had a Tenrikyō altar, but she returned it. She had no household shrine (kamidana) before entering Gedatsu-kai, but now has one. She is affiliated with the Sōtō denomination of Zen Buddhism and has long had a Buddhist ancestral altar (butsudan) for memorial tablets. She does not have Benzaiten and Fudō enshrined in her home—she goes to temples to pay respects to them. As a Gedatsu-kai member, she has enshrined in her home Tenjin Chigi, Gochi Nyorai, and Gedatsu Kongō.

She was brought into Gedatsu-kai by a female friend. She entered the movement alone, and none of her family has joined. She has brought in one other member, who later moved to Hokkaido. She comes to several monthly branch meetings, especially the monthly purification (kiyome) and the meeting on the twenty-eighth (honoring the founder's birthday), as well as the monthly "thanks day" (kanshabi). She has special observances in her home on the anniversary of death days of her ancestors, studies the founder's teachings, and recites the Hannya Shingyō sutra. She received the paper talisman for the amacha memorial rite, and every morning she performs the rite in her home. In the evening she carries out her "greeting" (aisatsu), as well as thanks (kansha) and repentance (zange). On the third Sunday of every month, she goes to the Sacred Land (Goreichi at Kitamotojuku) with the branch, and they pay respects at all of the sacred sites, starting with the Taiyō Seishin Hi (Sun Spirit Monument) and then visiting each of the other sacred sites; she also performs the hundredfold repentance (ohyakudo). Each summer she goes to the mountain Ōyama and Afuri Shrine (near Tanzawa, where the founder practiced).

The branch leader commented that when Mrs. Norikawa was in Tenrikyō her face was sad, but now it is happy—which somewhat embarrassed her. (One reason we requested her for interview was her joyful, optimistic appearance, in spite of her advanced age.) Mrs. Norikawa said that not only did she become happy, but she also became healthy. She remembered that at one Grand Festival (Taisai at the Sacred Land), there was a talk about being happy even when things are difficult. Once she could not see out of her right eye. Then suddenly she could see out of the right eye, but not out of the left. This was four years ago, and the doctor could not give her a clear diagnosis. A teacher in Gedatsu-kai said that it was because of her husband, who had died in the Pacific war—World War II. She had forgotten him, and that is why she lost her sight. Now that her heart is better, her body is also better. In her daily memorial rite, the four drowned persons are treated separately. Now she has a lot of energy. This makes her friends happy to see her, a single person, so active and happy.

Miss Muro

We had arranged an interview at the regular meeting place of "Ok" Branch on December 22, 1979, specifically to hear Mrs. Norikawa's life history. However, the branch leader had also invited two other women, a young artist, Miss Muro, whose story is given here, and an older woman, a midwife, whose story will be mentioned later. Because most of our time was taken up with the interview with Mrs. Norikawa, and considerable comments by the branch leader, there was little time for the two other women, who gave their stories in abbreviated form.

Miss Muro is a well-known artist, with published books of her art illustrations. She had been featured in a Gedatsu publication released shortly before the time of the interview. The following is the gist of her brief life history.

Miss Muro had an ancestor several hundred years ago who was an artist. Her family came from Nagano Prefecture. In the mediation rite of gohō shugyō, she was told to show life in pictures. It has to do with how one "carries" one's heart. (The branch leader commented at this point that Mrs. Norikawa expresses Gedatsu-kai through her happy life, while Miss Muro expresses Gedatsu-kai through pictures.)

Formerly Miss Muro had been a nurse, and she got involved in Gedatsu-kai more deeply because of problems with "human relations"—matters were very difficult at the hospital. She was extremely critical of doctors who knew the diagnosis of a patient, but still prescribed lots of tests just for the money. She took up art because of the message to do so in gohō shugyō, and finally was persuaded by Gedatsu-kai to give up her hospital job and become a full-time artist. She then had a private showing, and since that time she has had a number of them. Recently a company bought one of her designs for wrapping paper, "making her rich" (according to the laughing branch leader, who teased her about her wealth). For Miss Muro, Gedatsu-kai is what made her art possible. For her, Gedatsu-kai led not only to a change in personality, but also to a change in professions, and opened up a new avenue of artistic creativity.[15]

Mrs. Saitō

Two additional taiken (testimonies) are taken from the November 1979 issue of *Yangu Gedatsu* (Young Gedatsu); these testimonials were quoted briefly at the end of the previous chapter. They were selected for a number of reasons: first, they are of younger people, providing contrast for most of the informants, who were middle-aged and older people; second, they demonstrate that similar taiken were published in an official Gedatsu-kai publication at about the same time that we were collecting oral life histories; third, they are of second-generation members

who credit their parents with guiding them into Gedatsu-kai, an important difference from most of our interviewees, who made their own decisions to join the
movement. A taiken can be given in a few minutes or a few hours—depending
on the time available. These two published accounts are rather brief, and are given
here very close to their printed form, except for translation from Japanese into
English; it seemed best to retain the first-person form of the narratives and,
because these are publicly released documents, to use the real names as given in
the printed articles. The following is a translation of Mrs. Saitō's published taiken,
narrated in first person, with brackets indicating implied or summarized material,
and parentheses for the original Japanese or for translation of Japanese terms.

There were eight people in my family, six children and two parents. We were
so poor that we children always had to look after ourselves, and to help with each
other. We didn't always have enough to eat, and sometimes mother went without
eating, saying she wasn't hungry. At that time I vowed to later help my mother,
and give her lots to eat. I was very thankful (kansha) to mother, and I wanted to
repay this debt (ongaeshi) to her. [Mrs. Saitō went on to quote the teaching of
the founder.]

Well, I first heard about my future husband from a friend when I was eighteen.
My future husband had lost his wife in childbirth, but the baby lived. My future
husband didn't know which way to turn, and was having his family care for the
baby. Then I vowed to raise the child myself and marry him, and bring them to
Gedatsu-kai. The first time I went to his house, I had a relative go with me, and
as soon as we entered the house, the first thing I saw was the memorial tablet of
my future husband's wife.

I told my parents and siblings that I had decided to marry him, but my parents
and siblings were against it. They said that sympathy is no basis for marriage,
marriage is full of difficulties, and I was too young, I had not known real difficulties.
But I told them that this was according to the teaching (mioshie) of Gedatsu Kongō
[to accept difficulties cheerfully], and persisted, requesting them to give me permission to marry. Finally, they said that if I persisted so strongly, then they would
consent. Even my future husband's family had some doubts, because they couldn't
understand why a young woman who had never married would be so willing to
become a second wife.

We were married when I was twenty. As soon as we were married, I talked it
over with my husband, and had him put up a household shrine (kamidana); we
got a newly built small shrine and a Buddhist ancestral altar (butsudan), and had
a goshinzen-hiraki (dedication of a shrine) and a goryō-matsuri (ritual for pacifying
the spirits of ancestors). Then, thinking of the trying difficulties of the first wife
who had left me her child, I had him "renew" her memorial tablet and strictly
observe memorial rites for her.

It is now three years since I married into the Saitō family, and we live happily
together. The fact that this is possible is because of the deep love of both of my
parents and my siblings, because they led me in the teachings of Gedatsu. As a
wife and mother, I am glad to serve the ancestors of the Saitō family. Every month
I continue to have the Gedatsu magazine sent around, so that I can better interpret
this taiken I had.

Mr. Abe

A second taiken in this same issue of *Yangu Gedatsu* is that of Mr. Abe. It is translated into English as it is given in the magazine, in the first person, with brackets indicating implied or summarized material.

When I graduated from high school, I thought I would become a cook, because it seemed to me that the ordinary salary man was dissatisfied. I went to a special school, and when I finished this special school for cooks, I entered a restaurant at Asakusa [a popular entertainment district in Tokyo], through the introduction of my teacher. I thought that it was an ordinary restaurant, but then I learned that this restaurant was actually controlled by Toshiba [a major Japanese company], and that probably in March of the next year I would be transferred to the Toshiba factory—that's why I was hired.

I asked my employer to let me think about it. I went home and discussed it with my father, and since it seemed to be a good thing, I worked with that restaurant. As planned, after the first few months I worked there, I was transferred to the Toshiba company club.

This is what happened toward the end of that year, December 28. Suddenly my body felt weary, and I had a fever—I thought it was because of all the work with year-end parties. And my body just couldn't regain its strength completely. But at New Year's my supervisor said that the Asakusa restaurant would be very busy the first few days of the New Year with all the customers making their traditional first visit of the year to Asakusa, and told me to go help at the Asakusa restaurant for three days. And I wondered why I should have to work through the New Year. [Usually employees are given time off at New Year's.]

This was the year I participated in the coming-of-age ceremony. I gladly received the Gedatsu-kai coming-of-age ceremony at the Sacred Land on the eighth day of the New Year, at the Sacred Land Practice Hall with the North Kantō Block Youth Organization. From then on, I vowed to be self-conscious that I was an adult, and that I must act responsibly.

The Gedatsu-kai coming-of-age ceremony ended without incident, but the next day when I awoke I noticed something strange about my left leg. The muscle behind my knee was stretched, and I couldn't bend it. It didn't hurt, but I had to take off from work. I just rested, but the second day when I woke up it hurt so much I could hardly bear it. The second and third day the calf of my leg hurt so badly that I went to a doctor to have it examined. It hurt so badly that I couldn't stand. But the doctor couldn't diagnose the problem, and had me use an electric massage.

My parents worried about me very much. They said that if it didn't get better after so long, then it must not be only an external cause. They asked me if there was something lacking in my work. My discipline must be lacking, so wasn't there some aspect of my work where I had been lazy? Even if I stayed at home and rested, this would not get better. I should recite the *Hannya Shingyō*[16] [a Buddhist sutra] thirty times before going to sleep.

That night I tried to bear the pain, but then I recited ten times, and thirty times, and while doing so the pain eased up. Then while practicing the *Hannya* sutra, after five days, a week, ten days—I gradually was able to stand and then to walk. Now I know that my discipline was insufficient, and that I was lazy. This surely was a warning from Kongō sama [the founder], I know without a doubt. So this caused my parents and all of my fellow workers to worry greatly about me, and I really want to apologize to them.

The Religious Universe of Gedatsu-kai Members:
The Power of Kami, Buddhas, Ancestors, and Founder
Resolves Human Problems

The above six life histories, although considerably shorter than the first three (those of Mr. Negishi, Mr. Nakajimo, and Mrs. Koshikawa), are sufficiently detailed to indicate the varied background of Gedatsu-kai members, the range of their religious experience, and the prominent features of their religious universe. The interconnections of aspects of Gedatsu-kai belief and practice within one life history, as well as among the nine life histories, are instructive for understanding the overall system or world view of Gedatsu-kai, and provide insight into the dynamics of contemporary Japanese religion.[17]

Previously, in analyzing and interpreting the religious universe of Mr. Negishi, we saw that the general features of his world view included four major objects of worship (kami, Buddhas, ancestors, and founder), distinctive beliefs (such as his feeling of indebtedness for "being allowed" to live and his concern for karmic connections), and involvement in particular study and practice (such as self-reflection and performing gohō shugyō and the amacha rite). Because this general world view of Gedatsu-kai is reflected also in the other eight life histories, the analysis and interpretation of the nine accounts as a whole will focus on more concrete aspects of the lives and experiences of these people. To become a member of Gedatsu-kai (or any Japanese new religion) does not necessarily mean an automatic or blind acceptance of a formal teaching, certainly not in the form of the intellectual conception of a "world view" as has been presented in this analytical treatment. Rather, the general world view is accepted as it fits into the daily lives and particular problems of the individual members.[18] As emphasized in Gedatsu-kai teaching and in the life histories, people must "actually experience" (*jikken suru*) religion in their own lives. By tracing common elements in the concrete experience of these nine members, we can see how Gedatsu-kai's world view operates in their daily activities, work, family, and even creativity.

There are many ways of approaching the system of Gedatsu-kai, but for our purpose of treating these nine life histories, it can be seen as two balanced worlds: on the one hand is the religious power of Gedatsu-kai; on the other hand are human beings and their specific problems and suffering that the power resolves. Individual members hold to the common world view, while selecting from it and emphasizing aspects that help them with their particular concerns. Seen historically, this foundation of power comes from the rich heritage of Japanese religion. Members, of course, look more closely to the mediating rituals and persons making this power available, especially the rituals devised and recommended by the founder, and the present Gedatsu-kai branch leaders and "teachers" (sensei) who carry on the work of the founder.

The basic principle for successfully mediating power is quite simple to state— although not necessarily easy to put into practice—and is roughly the same for any religious system. To make use of the religious power, a person must be in harmony with it and apply it in an appropriate and consistent manner. To be more specific, in Gedatsu-kai, in order to make use of the power of kami, Buddhas, ancestors, and founder, an individual's own life must conform to the general pattern of principles these powers represent. In Gedatsu-kai terminology, this means that the individual realizes his/her life is owed to these powers, and the individual's perception of this indebtedness comes through the transmission of the founder's revelations and idealized practices. For a person to be in harmony with these powers, he/she must have the proper attitude, cultivate this attitude personally through training or discipline, and perform properly the efficacious rituals that actualize the principles in the world and incorporate the principles in the life of the individual. The ideal attitude is spelled out in the term *hōon kansha*, "gratitude (or repayment of indebtedness) and thanks." Discipline is the systematic training of body and mind to perfect one's attitudes and actually implement it: discipline means regular religious devotions as well as hard work and personal character (usually seen in Neo-Confucian terms). Rituals are important because they are the recognized channels for mediating power.

In the system of Gedatsu-kai, the human predicament is interpreted as inextricably linked to the four main powers, and usually it is human neglect or "mistakes" that tend to throw out of balance the world of powers. When people neglect or improperly memorialize ancestors, discontinue traditional religious practices for kami and Buddhas, or do not acknowledge the fact that nature allows them to live, then potential blessing turns into misfortune, sickness, and general personal turmoil. [19]

But when a person recognizes the bounty of nature, he or she is open to receive blessings. When a person renews ties to a kami or Buddhist divinity formerly worshipped in this family—or renews ties to the local tutelary kami and the parish Buddhist temple—the lines are open for their power to flow to that person. And when a person remembers the ancestors and properly memorializes them, misfortune turns to good fortune, illness to health, and personal turmoil to peace of mind. Stated as an ideal system, of course, this is too much of a panacea: but this is true of any ideal presentation of any religious tradition. In actual practice, there is considerable frustration and much effort and reflection before this ideal harmony can even be approximated. The general world view is expressed in the themes and concrete content of the individual testimonies.

All the life histories share the common theme that the best way to realize religious power is to follow the trail blazed by the founder. Generally, the clue to the realization of the first three powers is in the life and teachings of the founder; they become the model for members to emulate. For example, Mrs. Saitō persuaded her parents to allow her to marry a widower by appealing to the founder's teaching about accepting difficulties. More specifically, the rituals the founder invented or recommended are the practical means the members follow to recognize, harmonize with, and utilize the four powers. Even after Mrs. Saitō was married, she continued to follow the founder's teachings, leading her husband into the practice of Gedatsu-kai, and having him restore the traditional practices of the home, to the point of making sure that his first wife's spirit was properly (and regularly) memorialized.

There is a general repertoire of rituals and practices that most members follow, with some more special practices carried out by members with particular problems. All members utilize the amacha memorial rite to pacify the spirits of ancestors and purify the members' hearts. This is an effective means of coming into contact with the spirit world, and generally "getting right" with the four powers. A more specialized technique is the mediation rite of gohō shugyō, which is able to unlock particular problems of illness and suffering. When a person discovers the nature of the mistake or problem, special corrective measures must be taken. In addition to the amacha memorial ritual and gohō shugyō, often the person may be required to perform a set of apologies (owabi, usually a set of prayers before a shrine) or carry out the hundredfold repentance (ohyakudo). An even more specialized ritual is the tochikuyō (memorial rite for a locale) or makikuyō (ladling amacha around the premises as a memorial rite). This rite is performed primarily by people who are troubled by bad spirits (usually not family spirits) around a home, and by people such as Mrs. Kawakami's husband for protection and blessing of a home or business. Gedatsu-kai is concerned with opening and maintaining communication with the divine and spiritual world, but this knowledge is not a self-sufficient gnosis: rather, the knowledge obtained is used to set things right. Usually this means changing one's attitude and developing a regular routine or discipline of religious practice, in such a way that the person can now make use of this power. Regular practice and discipline strengthen one's personal base of power, and not only improve the character and quality of one's life, but also serve as preventive measures against possible misfortune and catastrophe. This is a rough outline of the "power" half of Gedatsu-kai's universe.

The other half of Gedatsu-kai's universe, as seen from the members' life histories, is the dilemmas of human life and the actual problems the power is used to resolve. The preceding nine life histories reveal problems related to occupation, health, human relations, and "being saved" (or peace of mind). Each of these problems can be illustrated by reference to at least several life histories. For example, Mrs. Kawakami's story is mainly about how Gedatsu-kai has helped her and her husband run their bread shop: "the most important thing in Gedatsu-kai is improvement of one's fortune." But she adds that it also was helpful in "improvement of character." And she is grateful to Gedatsu-kai for aid in her daughter-in-law's pregnancy and childbirth. Mrs. Kawakami practiced the main rituals of amacha memorial rites as well as the mediation ritual of gohō shugyō, and formal apologies. This religion helped her to understand the spirit world, and to enter into a peaceful relationship with her ancestors. She and her husband have dedicated their bread shop by enshrining a "pillar kami," and he performs the rite of ladling amacha in front of their shop (makikuyō). In other words, this life history is focused mainly around protection of this husband and wife's business, but it also involves personal character development and health protection for their family.

Mr. Abe's story, too, centers around work, although the situation is much different, in that he is a full generation younger than Mr. and Mrs. Kawakami, and he is an entry-level worker in a large company, whereas the Kawakamis are owners of a small shop. Nevertheless, the rationale of the two stories is similar: Gedatsu-kai teaching encourages the hard work and devotion that are essential for success in occupation or business. A slight variation in the story of Mr. Abe is that he is more concerned with the founder and his own conduct (laziness), and his story is about sickness as a warning from the founder; the Kawakamis are more concerned with ancestors and the preventive measures for misfortune, such as the rite of ladling amacha in front of their shop. The interesting point is that whether one is the proprietor of a small shop or a lowly worker in a large company, Gedatsu-kai provides the clue to hard work and successful business. Robert Bellah in his work *Tokugawa Religion* (1957) has pointed out the pattern of beliefs that supported a work ethic in the development of modern Japan, and most of the values he analyzed are still prominent in the contemporary religion of Gedatsu-kai. At the same time, it should be noted that Mr. Abe's story—a kind of confession of breaking the rules of Gedatsu-kai and a reaffirmation to follow these rules—also points up the network of beliefs and practices that constitute the movement as a living religion. Mr. Abe and his parents recognize a sickness that is difficult to diagnose and does not go away, as a potential religious omen: sickness may be caused by incorrect faith, improper practice, or inadequate work. The "discipline" that Mr. Abe's parents asked him to examine meant both his effort in work and his following of Gedatsu-kai teaching. In other words, he could not be true to the discipline of Gedatsu-kai if he was slack in his work. And the corrective measure is to practice religious discipline—reciting the *Hannya Shingyō*—in order to recover his health and rediscover his work commitment.[20]

There are many unconscious connections within a life history that are not mentioned by the person telling the story, and will not be seen by the person unfamiliar with popular Japanese religion. For example, another connection between religion and occupation is found in Mrs. Miyauji's reference to the message about the popular deity Konpira in her practice of gohō shugyō. Konpira is a complex divinity especially important along the seacoast, for protection on the sea. It is natural that Konpira would be important in the seaport where Mrs. Miyauji has lived all her life—and more likely that Konpira would appear to Mrs. Miyauji than to Mrs. Koshikawa, who had grown up in a rural area and moved to this seaport later. Also significant is the fact that Mrs. Miyauji's father had owned a shipping business before World War II—there is an implicit connection here between the father's maritime occupation and Konpira as one of the divinities especially close to mariners.[21]

The prominence of sickness as a motive and concern in the practice of Gedatsu-kai is obvious, constituting a direct or indirect feature in the three lengthy accounts and the six briefer life histories, except for the artist Miss Muro (and this may be only because interview time was limited and she focused on her artistic inspiration). The sickness may be the individual's or a family member's, of short or long duration, physical or more psychological (such as Mrs. Koshikawa's unexplained fatigue). Some people, such as Mrs. Koshikawa, are so distressed by particular complaints that they come to Gedatsu-kai specifically for health consultation (kenkō shidō). Others enter the movement more for peace of mind and concern for proper religious commitment, and find out indirectly that proper religious practice actually improves health. This was the experience of Mrs. Norikawa, who "wanted to be saved" and wanted to care for her drowned ancestors, and only gradually came to understand that her blood pressure and sight problems could be resolved through religious insight and ritual practice.

The discovery of "mistakes"—whether committed by self or family—is likely to uncover the reason for sickness and misfortune. These mistakes most frequently are neglect or improper memorializing of ancestors, lack of self-reflection and harboring bad thoughts about others, and the breaking of family religious practices (such as a family custom of honoring Inari that has been discontinued). The principle here is that sickness *may* be caused by disharmony between the person (his/her attitude, discipline, ritual practice) and the spirit world. Repeated questioning of individual members, branch leaders, and executives about the causal link between religious powers and personal illness revealed a consistent position on the balance between modern medicine and religious healing: people should follow modern medicine when it is appropriate, and resort to religious healing when there is a special problem that modern medicine cannot handle (because of its genesis in spiritual causes). Gedatsu-kai also goes further today than in its early days in emphasizing that people are responsible for their health, and should eat nutritious food (such as brown rice). It is interesting to note that in the life histories emphasizing specific problems of physical illness, such as Mrs. Kawakami's account, a lengthy course of diagnosis and treatment with a regular physician was followed before turning to religious means of healing.[22]

Some of the rationale for interpreting illness is clear from the explicit explanation within the life histories, and some must be deduced from the implicit understandings. Three explicit principles are that (1) there is a direct or indirect connection between this world and the world of divinities and spirits; (2) this connection is primarily the tie of karma between living persons and the world of divinities, spirits generally, and especially family ancestors; and (3) the connection may be individually based, but more frequently it is tied to the social group of the family— living and dead.[23] A fourth principle, more implicit than explicit in the life histories, is the exact reason, timing, and severity of illness. The three explicit principles are illustrated in most of the nine life histories. The notion of connection between this world and the spirit world is mouthed by each person interviewed, almost as a matter of common sense, but is also backed up by individual experience. The notion of karma (go, innen), too, although phrased in many ways, is a constant in all of the life histories: Mr. Negishi uses the sophisticated analogy of genetics, while most members use the more concrete notions of social (or biological) inheritance from ancestors. And most Japanese people recognize that religious as well as social fortune and misfortune are based on the social group to which one belongs, as well as one's individual effort and attainment.[24]

The fourth principle is more difficult to specify, and involves a certain amount of mystery, even arbitrariness. Usually the preconditions for spiritually caused illness (or misfortune generally) exist for some time, although nothing happens, and then either gradually or suddenly things go bad.[25] It is easier for Gedatsu-kai members to trace the three basic principles than to apply the fourth principle: to specify why *this* person at *this* time has *this* severe ailment or misfortune. The implicit understanding is that there is a kind of running balance between this world and the spirit world, and some slight imbalance can be tolerated, but if one or both sides become too unprincipled or chaotic, then the imbalance becomes so drastic that a sickness or other misfortune is provoked. It is not easy to predict just what, when, where, and to whom this will happen, although it is relatively easy to analyze a past catastrophe, and to avoid a future set of problems through preventive measures.[26]

The standard Gedatsu-kai corrections for such misfortune are to purify the person and pacify the spirits through sincere practice of amacha memorial rites, the mediation ritual of gohō shugyō, special apologies, and repentance such as reciting the *Hannya Shingyō* and performing the hundredfold repentance (ohyaku-do). Concern for sickness is prominent in Gedatsu-kai, as well as in other Japanese new religions, and in Japanese religion as a whole.

In addition to problems of occupation and illness, Gedatsu-kai members are concerned with human relations. The notion of human relations (*ningen kankei*) is a major concern in Japanese society as a whole, which emphasizes the significance of group identity, especially family identity. Usually the ideal is expressed as the subordination of individual wishes and identity to group goals and identity. The founder phrased human relations in Neo-Confucian terms such as loyalty, patriotism, and social harmony. Members are aware of some of the more formal conceptual categories of Neo-Confucianism, especially as reformulated by the founder; however, in their life histories they focus on specific relationships and concrete human problems. In all of this, the fundamental principle is that any attitude or action interfering with social harmony is wrong—a good example of a "mistake," which the person corrects both by altering attitude and behavior and by ritually restoring balance (through apologies and repentance). We have seen how Mr. Abe's "mistake" of laziness and lack of discipline caused the physical ailment with his leg; by restoring his "discipline"—both spiritually and occupationally—his leg was healed and social harmony was restored in his work situation. In Miss Muro's case, troubled human relations were the dilemma from which she sought release through Gedatsu-kai's help. The resolution of her problem was more complex, because it was not a matter of her mistake, but the conflict between her personal honesty and the deception of physicians in the hospital where she worked. But Gedatsu-kai helped her escape this intolerable (and unchangeable) situation by discovering her artistic talent in the mediation ritual of gohō shugyō, which enabled her to leave her compromised nursing career and become an artist.

Mrs. Saitō's life history shows how complicated human relations can be—in this instance, the future Mrs. Saitō was advised by her parents not to enter the ambiguous role of second wife and stepmother. Nevertheless, the young woman reminded her parents, who were Gedatsu-kai members, that the founder encouraged people to face difficulties squarely, relying on his teachings. Her persistence in quoting to her parents the founder's teachings made them acquiesce to her marriage. As mentioned previously, it was Mrs. Saitō's faith in the founder's teaching and personal discipline, coupled with her scrupulous religious practice, that enabled her to harmonize this difficult set of human relations.

These examples of human relations deal with rather dramatic, even traumatic, instances of interpersonal conflict, and these more sensational episodes do stand out in the life histories. Indeed, even when the founder was first learning his counseling technique, he encountered a woman with many interpersonal problems: her dead mother-in-law who had been so cruel, her drinking husband, and her bad children. When the woman followed the founder's advice to offer amacha and have memorial rites performed for her mother-in-law, she came to recognize her past "mistakes"—her mother-in-law had been right to criticize the daughter-in-law's pride. In effect this woman was responsible for her own interpersonal conflict, and once she made her peace with the dead mother-in-law, in the process correcting her wrong attitudes, her relations with her husband and children became better (and her physical complaints disappeared). This illustrates further a basic principle of human relations: if a person has poor attitudes and poor discipline, he or she will have poor relations with other people. A corollary is that a person who has poor relations with the world of divinities and spirits will have poor relations within the world of humans.

However, it is not necessarily the case that human relations must be worked out in such dramatic and traumatic fashion. As Mr. Negishi put it in his life history, going to the shrine of the local tutelary deity "is like saying hello to your mother and father." In other words, everyday practices of religious piety at local shrines and temples or at the household shrine and ancestral altar correspond to the social practices of filial piety and social harmony. Religious piety and filial piety reinforce each other, and there need not be a dramatic crisis for these values to be mutually enhancing.

A fourth area of human problems that Gedatsu-kai members resolve through the power of kami, Buddhas, ancestors, and founder is what can be called loosely "being saved," or more broadly peace of mind. The Japanese new religions have been criticized far and wide for their stress of "this-worldly benefits" or personal wishes, and they certainly do contain this element: this is true of Gedatsu-kai, other new religions, and Japanese religion as a whole. But it should be pointed out once more that the founder disavowed the use of religion for mere personal gain. Okano deliberately replaced crass "belief" (shinkō) with "sincere action" (shinkō): the intention of the founder was to stress self-reflection and sincere action in his religion.

Perhaps the most sophisticated example of a "philosophy of life," reflecting the member's higher educational level, is the account of Mr. Negishi, which features a well-reasoned and comprehensive rationale for all of life, including scientific facts and comparative material from other religions. It is not an exaggeration to label Mr. Negishi's life history an "existential" statement. A similar thrust is found in other life histories, although phrased more concretely and directly. For example, Mrs. Norikawa said that she entered Tenrikyō because she "wanted to be saved," and when she did not achieve religious fulfillment, she entered Gedatsu-kai with the same intention, this time successfully. What does it mean within Gedatsu-kai to "be saved" (sukuwareru)? The life histories do not provide a succinct definition, but we may infer that it means to find the answer to life in such a way that a person can lead a meaningful, happy career. Mrs. Norikawa certainly exhibited this joie de vivre to outsiders such as me and my colleagues, just as much as she did to fellow members and the branch leader. For Mrs. Norikawa it was assurance that she was doing the right thing about her drowned ancestors. And of course, as we have seen, getting right with ancestors enables one to get right with oneself.

This peace of mind is phrased differently in the nine life histories. For Miss Muro it is escape from an impossible set of human relations and development of artistic talent. For Mr. Abe it is restoring his sense of dignity and worth as an adult and good employee. For Mrs. Koshikawa it is a triple resolution of physical complaints, fatigue, and guilt at the time of her father's death. Gedatsu-kai's answer to the question of the meaning of human life and solution of specific problems may be described concretely as "being saved" or peace of mind, or may be interpreted more abstractly as an existential statement or comprehensive philosophy of life.

Life histories are invaluable as personal documents of the lives of people who join a new religion, expressing concretely the way they perceive themselves, the reasons and circumstances for their joining, and how they view the benefits of membership and participation in the movement. These nine examples afford an "inside" view of Gedatsu-kai, with all the drama of frustration, suffering, discovery, realization, and joy that is the stuff of religious experience. These nine stories contain more than distinctive individual experience: they share a common set of religious beliefs and practices, a unified religious world view. Nine such accounts out of several hundred thousand Gedatsu-kai members may seem to be too small a representation to generalize about this movement, but because they display such diversity of personal background and variety of religious experience, they enable us to frame "the religious universe of Gedatsu-kai members."[27] In other words, the general world view of Gedatsu-kai as a living religious system can be constructed (or reconstructed) even from these nine life histories. Two additional accounts, one by a branch leader (in chapter 5) and one by a headquarters executive (in chapter 6) will be given to throw light on the organization of Gedatsu-kai. But now we turn from this intensive, personal view of Gedatsu-kai members, to look at an extensive, quantitative view of these members as reported in a questionnaire survey.

4

THE MEMBERS OF GEDATSU-KAI
Results of a Nationwide Survey

Our view of Gedatsu-kai to this point has been based primarily on the treatment of the lives and experiences of ten persons: first, Mr. Negishi's life history, which reveals his personal religious universe and the context of Gedatsu-kai within Japanese religious history; second, Okano Eizō, whose biography discloses his personal struggles, spiritual crisis, and founding of the new religion; and third, the life histories of eight members of the movement, which express considerable difference in personal backgrounds and individual religious experiences, but nevertheless reveal a common world view. The purpose of presenting these kinds of materials is to provide an intensive, "inside" view of Gedatsu-kai and the dynamics of Japanese religion. The story of the founder, as lovingly remembered by his followers, lays the foundation for this religious movement. The nine testimonies show how members interpret and reshape the details of their lives by following the model of the founder's life and teachings. The members who told their life histories included (or were asked) such facts as their age, occupation, and reason for joining, the person who introduced them to Gedatsu-kai, and the extent of their practice and participation in the movement. Because these facts are directly related to the drama of their actual lives and concrete religious experience, they hold a significance far greater than just nine individual cases.

But however valuable these personal, intensive documents are for providing a close view of actual Gedatsu-kai members, it is also important to obtain rather impersonal information giving quantitative, extensive insight into the membership of the movement as a whole. The main question here is, What are the characteristics of the total population of Gedatsu-kai members, roughly a quarter-million people? In other words, what are the quantitative "facts," both demographically and religiously, for the 250,000 members of Gedatsu-kai, and are there significant correlations between variables such as gender or age and religious practice? If these data were available, it would be possible to explore many theses about members of Japanese new religious movements, such as their reasons for joining, their frequency of religious practice, and how their practice changed after joining. The only way such questions can be pursued by a small research team is to conduct a survey that would sample the total Gedatsu-kai community and would afford quantitative confirmation and elaboration of the dramatic "facts" found in the personal material of life histories.

Our initial plan was to supplement life histories with a questionnaire survey of a few branches in different geographical areas, but when Gedatsu-kai headquarters was receptive to the idea, and in fact gave permission to include all 368 branches that existed in 1979, we expanded the plan to do a nationwide survey. This meant quickly preparing and distributing a research instrument to all 368 branches. As a research team, we sifted through many questionnaires and hundreds of questions in order to draft a rather ambitious questionnaire, which was then discussed with Gedatsu-kai headquarters. Gedatsu-kai officials helped us reduce this ambitious questionnaire to a more manageable size—one they could encourage branches to administer to members and return to the Tokyo headquarters. Because our main research goal was to assess traditional and contemporary religion, we made this the focus of the questionnaire.[1]

Fifty questionnaires for individual branch members were distributed to each branch (shibu) and discussion group (*zadankai*). (Some were hand-delivered to branch representatives at a national meeting held at the Goreichi; the remainder were mailed to branches.) A total of over 18,400 questionnaires were distributed. Thanks to the kind cooperation of Gedatsu-kai headquarters and many branches, 5,707 individual questionnaires were returned to us by the time we tabulated responses. The return rate figured by individual returns is 31%; but these 5,707 returns were submitted by 232 of the 368 branches, a return rate of 63% for branches, assuring a representative sample of branches from across Japan—from Hokkaido to Okinawa.

The present chapter focuses especially on this nationwide survey, selecting some results, providing cross-comparison of certain results, and generally interpreting the significance of the questionnaire for understanding quantitative aspects of who joins Gedatsu-kai. The analysis is broken down into four questions: who are the members of Gedatsu-kai, why do people join Gedatsu-kai, who recruits members into Gedatsu-kai, and what are the religious changes after joining?[2]

Who Are the Members of Gedatsu-kai?

The first question about Gedatsu-kai members is, who are they? The members who returned questionnaires are the sample that provides the picture of the total national membership. This question focuses on membership in terms of gender, age, occupation, historical period, and age at time of entry (into Gedatsu-kai). From the results of this nationwide survey, and from published materials, it is possible to identify the membership of Gedatsu-kai with some general statistics. (Except when other dates are specified, all of the statistics mentioned in this book are for late 1979 or early 1980, when the survey was completed.) Every year the Ministry of Education, Science, and Culture (Monbushō) of the Japanese government publishes a Religion Annual (*Shūkyō Nenkan*) that contains information about religious groups registered with them, as reported by the religious groups (but not checked by any government agency). The 1979 Religion Annual lists for Gedatsu-kai 216,528 adherents and 463 clergy (397 men, 66 women) (Bunkachō 1980).

TABLE 2.
Questionnaire Respondents by Fifteen-Year Intervals
(Age at Time of Questionnaire)

	All Data		Females		Males	
0–15	(16)	.5%	(6)	.2%	(10)	.5%
16–30	(497)	8.8%	(261)	7.1%	(236)	11.8%
31–45	(1,547)	27.2%	(922)	25.0%	(625)	31.3%
46–60	(2,046)	36.0%	(1,401)	38.0%	(645)	32.3%
61–75	(1,274)	22.4%	(898)	24.4%	(376)	18.8%
76–92	(156)	2.7%	(105)	2.9%	(51)	2.6%
No response	(142)	2.5%	(90)	2.4%	(52)	2.6%
Total	(5678)	99.9%	(3683)	100.0%	(1995)	100.0%

Japanese scholars usually consider the membership figures reported by religious groups to the government to be on the generous side, but this gives some indication of the size of Gedatsu-kai.

In comparison with other Japanese new religions, Gedatsu-kai is a medium-size organization—much smaller than Sōka Gakkai and Tenrikyō with millions of members, but much larger than the many movements with tens of thousands of members and only local or regional impact. With 368 local meeting places, from Hokkaido in the north to Okinawa in the south, it is a well-organized movement with a nationwide network of local branches and a well-developed central headquarters.[3] In fact, Gedatsu-kai was active in the United States from before World War II, continued to be active during World War II within internment camps for Japanese, and still has a small but healthy following in California (Opler 1950a, Opler 1950b, Ishii 1983d).

In the nationwide survey, the members are disproportionately female: 3,683 females, or 64.5%, and 1,995 males, or 35.0% (29, or .5%, gave no response on gender). The numerical prominence of women in Japanese new religions is well known; later we will see that women are very important in the dynamics of the movement, especially in recruiting members.[4] This survey also is heavily weighted with older members; this is partly because the questionnaire was distributed at branch meetings, and "young people" (even including married couples with no children) usually attend special youth meetings (seinenkai) rather than branch meetings. However, Gedatsu-kai does appear to have an "older" membership than that of other religious groups in Japan.[5] This age breakdown is shown in table 2 by fifteen-year intervals.

For comparative purposes, we will consider age by four groups, as shown in table 3. These four age groups were selected for analytical purposes because they provide considerable range of age and sufficient number of cases for some cross-tabulation: age 0–30, although relatively small in actual number, does cover the younger generation, with some young families; age 31–50 is the largest of the four groups (for all data), spanning the child-rearing years; age 51–65, although including only fifteen years, is only slightly smaller for all data than the age 31–50 group—and covers the late child-rearing years and middle age; age 66–92 is relatively small in number (although one and a half times the size of the 0–30 age group) and spans retirement years (the oldest person in the questionnaire sample

TABLE 3.
Questionnaire Respondents by Four Age Categories
(Age at Time of Questionnaire)

	All Data		Females		Males	
0–30	(513)	9.0%	(267)	7.2%	(246)	12.3%
31–50	(2,226)	39.2%	(1,365)	37.1%	(861)	43.2%
51–65	(1,972)	34.7%	(1,403)	38.1%	(569)	28.5%
66–92	(825)	14.5%	(558)	15.2%	(267)	13.4%
No response	(142)	2.5%	(90)	2.4%	(52)	2.6%
Total	(5,678)	99.9%	(3,683)	100.0%	(1,995)	100.0%

TABLE 4.
Questionnaire Respondents by Four Age Categories
(Age at Time of Entry Into Gedatsu-kai)

	All Data		Females		Males	
0–30	(1,621)	32.4%	(936)	28.7%	(685)	39.1%
31–50	(2,400)	47.9%	(1,628)	50.0%	(772)	44.1%
51–65	(897)	17.9%	(636)	19.5%	(261)	14.9%
66–92	(91)	1.8%	(57)	1.8%	(34)	1.9%
Total	(5,009)	100%	(3,257)	100%	(1,752)	100%

was ninety-two). As can be seen from the grouped results at fifteen-year intervals in table 2, the largest fifteen-year interval for all data is age 46–60 with 36.0%.

The respondents in this questionnaire sample are predominantly middle-aged, but this reflects the actual age at time of the questionnaire. Another interesting way of looking at age in relationship to Gedatsu-kai is age at time of entry, which was calculated by subtracting the number of years since entry from the absolute age. The two tables showing the four age categories—table 3 by age at time of questionnaire (1979–80), and table 4 by age at time of entry into Gedatsu-kai— provide interesting points of comparison and contrast. The biggest difference between the two is the larger number of members in the age 0–30 group for table 4. As previously explained, the questionnaire sample tends to exclude many "young people" (who attend special youth meetings), so it is not surprising that in table 3, which shows age at time of questionnaire, there are few members age 0–30. However, in the table showing age at time of entry into Gedatsu-kai, the age 0–30 group is much larger. (In table 3, age 0–30 is 9.0% of the questionnaire sample; in table 4, age 0–30 is 32.4% of the questionnaire sample.)[6] This shows that many members do join between ages 0 and 30. The age group 31–50 is largest for each table, although considerably larger in table 4, indicating age at time of entry. The age group 51–65 is almost twice as large in table 3 as in table 4. However, the fact that 17.9% of the total sample joined between the ages of 51 and 65 is evidence of the power of Gedatsu-kai to reach middle-aged people and draw them back into traditional practices; this is a fact that will help us interpret the significance of the movement in relation to traditional Japanese religion. The age group 66–92 is somewhat smaller in the second table, showing age at time of

TABLE 5.
Year of Joining Gedatsu-kai
(Grouped Results by Five-Year Intervals)

	All Data		Females		Males	
1935–1940	(123)	2.2%	(76)	2.1%	(47)	2.4%
1941–1945	(104)	1.8%	(65)	1.8%	(39)	2.0%
1946–1950	(236)	4.2%	(138)	3.7%	(98)	4.9%
1951–1955	(390)	6.9%	(268)	7.3%	(122)	6.1%
1956–1960	(433)	7.6%	(271)	7.4%	(162)	8.1%
1961–1965	(676)	11.9%	(450)	12.2%	(226)	11.3%
1966–1970	(813)	14.3%	(539)	14.6%	(274)	13.7%
1971–1975	(1,071)	18.9%	(708)	19.2%	(363)	18.2%
1976–1980	(1,310)	23.1%	(828)	22.5%	(482)	24.2%
No response	(522)	9.2%	(340)	9.2%	(182)	9.1%

entry—1.8%—and yet it shows the ability of Gedatsu-kai to attract people of advanced age into religious practice.

On the whole, Gedatsu-kai's membership as reflected in the questionnaire sample is relatively "young" when considered in terms of the number of years of membership in the movement, as can be seen in table 5, which indicates the year of joining Gedatsu-kai. These results are grouped in five-year intervals from 1935–1940 to 1975–1980 to show the dramatic growth of the movement in recent years.

The five-year interval with most growth, 1976–1980, which actually includes only the four years 1976–1979 plus the first month of 1980, accounts for 23.1% of all data. As table 5 shows, 68.2% of the questionnaire sample joined Gedatsu-kai between 1961 and 1980. The relatively young religious age—number of years since entering Gedatsu-kai—is all the more significant when considered in the light of the middle-aged character of the sample: we might think that this predominantly middle-aged sample would correspond to many years of membership in Gedatsu-kai. As previously was pointed out, when the questionnaire respondents are grouped by absolute age at time of the questionnaire into fifteen-year intervals, the largest group is age 46–60 with 36.0%. However, even though 36.0% of the questionnaire sample is in the age 46–60 group, a larger percentage of the sample (42.0%) joined between the years 1971 and 1980. These results probably reflect two important interrelated factors: Gedatsu-kai's relatively short developmental history (the three decades 1930–1960 represent the formative years when few members were recruited) and the movement's ability to recruit middle-aged members. Obviously, this pattern may change as Gedatsu-kai becomes more well established. It is likely that as the membership who joined between 1960 and 1980 ages—and draws in "second-generation" members—there will be a different membership pattern (including length of membership) in the next twenty-year interval of 1980–2000.

Another aspect of Gedatsu-kai membership clarified in the nationwide survey is occupational representation by Gedatsu-kai members. Question 5 of the questionnaire requested "occupation" (*shokugyō*) and provided a blank for open-ended response; specific answers were then tabulated as indicated in table 6. (In table 6, percentages are figured by including 818 "no response" answers, amounting to

TABLE 6.
Occupation of Gedatsu-Kai Members

	All Data		Females		Males	
Professional and Technical[a]	(149)	2.6%	(93)	2.5%	(56)	2.8%
Managers and Officials	(66)	1.2%	(16)	.4%	(50)	2.5%
Clerical and Related[b]	(863)	15.2%	(256)	7.0%	(607)	30.4%
Sales[c]	(639)	11.1%	(319)	8.7%	(320)	16.0%
Farmers and Lumbermen[d]	(532)	9.4%	(324)	8.8%	(208)	10.4%
Fishermen	(13)	.2%	(4)	.1%	(9)	.5%
Mining and Quarrying	(0)	0.0%	(0)	0.0%	(0)	0.0%
Transportation and Communication	(53)	.9%	(3)	.1%	(50)	2.5%
Crafts and Production[e]	(403)	7.1%	(78)	2.1%	(325)	16.3%
Protective Service[f]	(3)	.1%	(0)	0.0%	(3)	.2%
Service[g]	(126)	2.2%	(77)	2.1%	(49)	2.5%
Not Classifiable	(6)	.1%	(3)	.1%	(3)	.2%
Female Unemployed (including housewife, helping in the home)	(1,820)	32.0%	(1,812)	49.2%	(8)	.4%
Male Unemployed	(122)	2.1%	(3)	.1%	(119)	6.0%
Student	(68)	1.2%	(25)	.7%	(43)	2.2%
No Response	(815)	14.4%	(670)	18.2%	(145)	7.3%

[a]teacher, nurse, nutritionist, flower arranger, cameraman, key punch operator
[b]"salary man," typist, business personnel
[c]small shops, restaurants, self-employed, real estate
[d]farming, logging, cattle
[e]carpenters, cabinet makers, repairmen, *ofuro* (bath) maker
[f]policeman, guard
[g]maids, barbers, cleaning worker

14.4% of the total; for comparative purposes in table 7, "no response", unemployed, and students are excluded.)

The results give a clear picture of the major occupations of Gedatsu-kai members, with sharp contrast between males and females. Members come mainly from the working class of clerical and sales personnel, and farmers and craftsmen; however, the single largest category is unemployed females. Because of the large number of unemployed females, and the difference between genders by occupation, we will look first at all data, and then results by gender.

For all data, the unemployed category is highest: 1,820 females, or 32.0%, and 122 males, or 2.1% of the total sample. (As we shall see in the discussion of females, this "female unemployed" category is somewhat misleading.) For all data, the highest single "working" category is "clerical and related" (including "salary man") with 863 persons, or 15.2% of the total sample. Following clerical workers are sales workers (including the proprietors of small shops and self-employed) with 639 persons, or 11.1%; farmers and lumbermen with 532 persons, or 9.4%; and craftsmen and production workers with 403 persons, or 7.1%. A low percentage is found in professional and technical workers, with 149 persons, or 2.6%, and in managers and officials, with 66 persons, or 1.2% of the total sample.

As noted above, 3,683 females represent 64.5% of the total sample. Of those females responding to question 5 regarding occupation, there were 1,812, or 49.2% females in the "unemployed" category.[7] This single largest category for either gender is inflated somewhat by the ambiguities of both the research instrument and the nature of female identity within Japanese society. Because the questionnaire provided a blank space for "occupation,"women responded with a variety of answers such as "unemployed," "housewife," or "helping in the home." When tabulating responses, we decided to group all such responses under the category of "unemployed" as the most general rubric. However, it is is likely that a large number of these women might otherwise be included in the "self-employed" or "sales" category, because many of them may participate in family businesses. (It is interesting to point out in this regard that only 8.7% of the female sample are in this "sales" or "self-employed" category, while 16.0% of the male sample fall in this category.) However, even a woman who works regularly in a family business, and yet does not receive a specific salary, may consider herself "unemployed." For the female sample, after the large category of "unemployed," the next-highest categories are agriculture with 324 females, or 8.8%; sales with 319 females, or 8.7%; and clerical (including typist) with 256, or 7.0%. (The large percentage of "no responses," 670 females, or 18.2%, might indicate females with no occupation who did not know how to respond; these females might further swell the category of "female unemployed.")

The occupational character of Gedatsu-kai membership becomes much clearer from the results of the male sample's responses to the occupation question. The highest categories for males are clerical, with 607, or 30.4%; craftsmen and production workers, with 325, or 16.3%; sales workers, with 320, or 16.0%; and farmers and lumbermen, with 208, or 10.4%. Unemployed males are only 119, or 6.0% of the male sample.[8] Figures are rather low for professional and technical workers, 56, or 2.8%; managers and officials, 50, or 2.5%; transportation and communication workers, 50, or 2.5%; and service workers (barbers, cleaning work), 49, or 2.5%.

The occupational profile of Gedatsu-kai can be compared with the occupational profile of the Japanese population as a whole by extracting figures from the *Japan Statistical Yearbook* 1980; because this yearbook does not include students or unemployed, these categories (and also "not classifiable" and "no response") are excluded from the Gedatsu-kai survey.[9] Table 7 reveals some significant differences.

Table 7 shows that Gedatsu-kai membership has representation in all major occupations in the Japanese population, but is significantly higher and considerably lower in particular categories. The three categories of clerical, sales, and farmers-lumbermen-fishermen are much higher for Gedatsu-kai; clerical workers and farmers-lumbermen-fishermen are almost twice the national percentage, with sales workers about one and a half times the national percentage. Other categories are

TABLE 7.
Occupation of Gedatsu-kai Members Compared with the Japanese Population

	Gedatsu-kai	Japanese population
Professional and technical	5.2%	7.8%
Managers and officials	2.3%	4.0%
Clerical and related	30.3%	16.4%
Sales	22.4%	14.3%
Farmers, lumbermen, and fishermen	19.1%	11.0%
Mining and quarrying	0.0%	.1%
Transportation and communication	1.8%	4.4%
Crafts, production, and labor	14.1%	32.6%
Protective service and service	4.5%	9.0%
Total	99.7%	99.6%

all lower than the national percentage, with craftsmen and production workers showing the most dramatic difference at less than half the national percentage. In other words, compared to the national profile, Gedatsu-kai is overrepresented in the "middle" categories of clerical, farmers-lumbermen-fishermen, and sales, while underrepresented in both the "high" categories of managers and officials and professional and technical, and the "low" category of craftsmen and production workers (blue-collar).[10]

The occupational data on Gedatsu-kai members help us better to appreciate aspects of the life of the founder and his teachings, as well as features in life histories. One dimension of the founder's life that is emphasized in Gedatsu-kai's official biography is his hard work, through both business difficulties and business success; this is interpreted and expressed through the founder's heavily Neo-Confucian ethic of hard work and loyalty. And we have seen in life histories of individual members that Gedatsu-kai faith and practice help a person become a good worker (Mr. Abe's testimony of laziness corrected) and a good small-business operator (Mrs. Kawakami's life history about the bread shop she and her husband ran successfully through the help of special rituals such as the veneration of the pillar kami and the use of amacha to purify the premises).

The occupational composition of Gedatsu-kai, with major representation in the working class (especially for males, but also for females), leads us to conclude that the values of its members probably are typical of working-class values—the work ethic of Japan. It is likely that Gedatsu-kai shares these values with Japanese society and religion as a whole, but the sample in this nationwide survey is most directly linked to the working class of clerical workers, farmers and fishermen, and sales workers (and not so directly to blue-collar workers). The large ratio of "unemployed" females (including housewives) in Gedatsu-kai verifies a widely held notion that middle-aged women are the mainstay of new religions, and that new religions are a major outlet for such women. It is not surprising that such women would be attracted to the founder's strong Neo-Confucian rationale for family and social solidarity in general, and that Gedatsu-kai continues to emphasize such values. The major profile of Gedatsu-kai membership, predominantly "un-employed"-housewife females and working-class males, reveals a strong unity across genders, because the Gedatsu-kai version of traditional values links hard work in occupation with filial piety and family solidarity.

The general answer to the question, Who are the members of Gedatsu-kai? is: people who are as old as (for Buddhism) or older than people in other Japanese religions; about two-thirds are females, especially unemployed (for salary) or housewives, with some in farming, clerical work, and sales; one-third are males, primarily in clerical work, and also craft work, sales, and fishing-farming occu-pations; many of the members have joined recently, within the ten years prior to 1980; many joined the group when they were already middle-aged.

Why Do People Join Gedatsu-kai?

One of the most interesting—and ambiguous—questions about new religions is why people join them. The question seems obvious enough, and members of Gedatsu-kai have little trouble discussing their personal motives, as has been seen in the life histories; similarly, academics have offered a number of interpretations of the reasons people join Japanese new religions. It is not surprising that there is considerable variation between these two versions of the rationale for joining—the actual statements of members, and the scholarly interpretations by academics. This question is much more complicated than the previous factors of gender, age, and occupation, and requires more care in discussion.

When members tell in their life histories why they joined Gedatsu-kai, they tend to focus on particular problems in their lives that were resolved through entering and participating in the movement. Mr. Negishi says that this religion provides him with the power to live; Mr. Nakajimo says that it helped renew his contact with family ancestors and protects his family; others say that they were healed, had interpersonal conflict resolved, or achieved peace of mind. In other words, Gedatsu-kai members relate a personal, concrete description of why they joined. However, it would be a mistake to assume that there is one and only one motive or reason given by members for joining: in fact, a feature of the life histories that helps us interpret motive in the questionnaire data is the presence of a number of overlapping motives within one person's experience. For example, Mr. Negishi might say that he joined because Gedatsu-kai gave him the power to live, and yet he is impressed with the fact that his mother's health improved. Mr. Nakajimo says his reason for joining was to be reunited with family ancestors, and yet he feels also that Gedatsu-kai helped alleviate family illness. Mrs. Koshikawa's explicit motive for joining was to cure her physical and spiritual problems, and yet later in the process of entering Gedatsu-kai she discovered and resolved religious dif-ficulties related to her ancestors. The interweaving of a number of motives is apparently the normal pattern for people who join Gedatsu-kai, and even though only one motive is recorded on the questionnaires, this plurality of motives should be taken into account in any assessment of the survey.

Academics, however, are interested more in the "reason behind the reason": What are the major social and psychological factors that determined or influenced (and to what extent) the personal choice to participate in a new religion? Academics are less concerned with the plurality of concrete personal statements of reasons for joining, and are more concerned with sweeping causal factors that are "behind" any personal motives. The most widely used academic interpretation of the ultimate reason why people join Japanese new religions is a combination of sociological and psychological theory, focusing on the rapid social change and breakdown of traditional social and religious structures after the Meiji Restoration of 1868, and especially after World War II, with the attendant personal anxiety and disorientation that stimulated or caused Japanese new religions to form, and people to join them. Later we will discuss these academic interpretations, taking into account their contributions, as well as pointing out some reservations with these interpretations. What is most important here is to recognize the distinction between members' stated motives for joining and scholars' academic interpretations of reasons for joining, in order to clarify the way in which we will eventually relate the two.

The emphasis on personal statements, especially life histories, in our interpretation of Gedatsu-kai is based on the judgment that most of the Western publications on Japanese new religions have been premature in emphasizing the "reason behind the reason" for people to join a new religion without having paid sufficient attention to the motive itself as given by the people. This is understandable, in part, because of the scarcity of firsthand accounts of members telling why they joined a new religion: until recently, few such materials existed in Western-language publications. In this chapter, our major concern is to provide concrete information about how members of Gedatsu-kai view their experience of joining; this information will be helpful for understanding not only the formation and activities of Gedatsu-kai, but possibly other Japanese new religions, as well. Therefore, we will concentrate first on the motives for joining given by members in the nationwide survey, listening as carefully as we can to their primary rationale, before we advance to a secondary rationale.[11]

Question 8 of the questionnaire distributed to Gedatsu-kai members asked for "motive (*dōki*) for joining," supplying a blank space for the response. Results are given in table 8. An advantage of this open-ended kind of question is that it allowed members to answer freely without being confined to predetermined categories; a disadvantage is the large number of "no responses," 3,091, or 54.5% of the total sample. Apparently a majority of the sample either could not, or chose not to, specify a particular motive for joining. Hindsight teaches us that it is not surprising so many Gedatsu-kai members could not fill in a small blank space about their motive for joining. In the first place, as seen previously in the life histories, there are complex reasons for joining a new religion, and probably many members were unable to quickly reduce their entry into Gedatsu-kai to just one particular motive. In the second place, the lack of suggested categories may have confused respondents, who chose to leave this question blank rather than try to supply a category.[12]

However, in spite of the large number of nonrespondents, it was not difficult to tabulate the results for those members who answered this question; categories for tabulation were determined by the research team after each member read more than a hundred individual questionnaires. In establishing tabulation categories, the intention was twofold: to retain as much of the concreteness of the responses as possible, and at the same time to arrange the categories for grouping

TABLE 8.
Motive for Joining, by Specific Categories

	All Data		Females		Males	
Sickness						
sickness (general)	(9)	.2%	(6)	.2%	(3)	.2%
own sickness	(373)	6.6%	(231)	6.3%	(142)	7.1%
family sickness	(344)	6.1%	(249)	6.8%	(95)	4.8%
mental (seishin) sickness	(19)	.3%	(17)	.5%	(2)	.1%
health consultation (kenko sōdan)	(30)	.5%	(21)	.6%	(9)	.5%
other sickness	(21)	.4%	(10)	.3%	(11)	.6%
Growth, Birth, Education						
miscarriage/abortion (ryūzan)	(21)	.4%	(18)	.5%	(3)	.2%
stillbirth (mizugo)	(10)	.2%	(6)	.2%	(4)	.2%
school examinations	(4)	.1%	(3)	.1%	(1)	.1%
work	(2)	.0%	(1)	.0%	(1)	.1%
marriage (joined at time of marriage because spouse was a member)	(69)	1.2%	(56)	1.5%	(13)	.7%
unlucky year (yakudoshi)	(0)	0.0%	(0)	0.0%	(0)	0.0%
death of relative or other person	(71)	1.3%	(53)	1.4%	(18)	.9%
other growth, birth, education	(12)	.2%	(8)	.2%	(4)	.2%
Economic Reasons						
economic problem (individual or family)	(31)	.5%	(18)	.5%	(13)	.7%
business problem	(19)	.3%	(7)	.2%	(12)	.6%
economic, business advice	(8)	.1%	(5)	.1%	(3)	.2%
farm work, marine work	(1)	.0%	(1)	.0%	(0)	0.0%
other economic problem	(5)	.1%	(0)	0.0%	(5)	.3%
Politics						
politics (general)	(0)	0.0%	(0)	0.0%	(0)	0.0%
Human Relations						
human relations (general)	(1)	.0%	(1)	.0%	(0)	0.0%
husband-wife relations (conjugal problems)	(31)	.5%	(30)	.8%	(1)	.1%
daughter-in-law–mother-in-law relations	(10)	.2%	(10)	.3%	(0)	0.0%

TABLE 8. (Cont'd)

	All Data		Females		Males	
parent-child relations	(38)	.7%	(30)	.8%	(8)	.4%
other family relations (trouble)	(102)	1.8%	(71)	1.9%	(31)	1.6%
sexual relations	(8)	.1%	(6)	.2%	(2)	.1%
other human relations	(33)	.6%	(25)	.7%	(8)	.4%
Spiritual, Religious Matters						
spiritual, religious matters (general)	(2)	.0%	(0)	0.0%	(2)	.1%
ancestor worship	(52)	.9%	(37)	1.0%	(15)	.8%
spirits (*rei*) generally	(24)	.4%	(15)	.4%	(9)	.5%
spiritual cultivation (*seishinteki shūyō*)	(73)	1.3%	(49)	1.3%	(24)	1.2%
spiritual problems (*nayami*)	(54)	1.0%	(31)	.8%	(23)	1.2%
other spiritual, religious matters	(9)	.2%	(6)	.2%	(3)	.2%
Preference						
preference (general)	(1)	.0%	(1)	0.0%	(0)	0.0%
sympathy with the teaching	(170)	3.0%	(108)	2.9%	(62)	3.1%
vague preference ("encouraged to join," "joined after talking to member")	(353)	6.2%	(221)	6.0%	(132)	6.6%
second generation	(320)	5.6%	(187)	5.1%	(133)	6.7%
attraction of the members' personalities	(22)	.4%	(10)	.3%	(12)	.6%
other preference	(141)	2.5%	(84)	2.3%	(57)	2.9%
Other						
other reasons ("no special reason," and reentry)	(94)	1.7%	(52)	1.7%	(42)	2.1%
No response	(3,091)	54.5%	(1,999)	54.3%	(1,092)	54.7%

as general areas. The general areas, to be explained more fully later, are: Sickness; Growth, Birth, Education; Economic Reasons; Politics; Human Relations; Spiritual, Religious Matters; Preference; Other; and No Response.

The major motives for joining as given in the questionnaires are similar to those found in the life histories, as discussed above, but the exact breakdown is quite interesting. Analysis of the results for respondents to the question of motive provides many interesting insights into the nature of religious life in Gedatsu-kai. We will look at the motive question from the viewpoint of various factors, but

TABLE 9.
Motive for Joining, by General Categories

	All Data		Females		Males	
No response	(3,091)	54.5%	(1,999)	54.3%	(1,092)	54.7%
Preference	(1,007)	17.7%	(611)	16.6%	(396)	19.8%
Sickness	(796)	14.1%	(534)	14.7%	(262)	13.1%
Human Relations	(223)	3.9%	(173)	4.7%	(50)	2.5%
Spiritual, Religious Matters	(214)	3.8%	(138)	3.7%	(76)	3.8%
Growth, Birth, Education	(189)	3.4%	(145)	3.9%	(44)	2.2%
Other	(94)	1.7%	(52)	1.4%	(42)	2.1%
Economic Reasons	(64)	1.0%	(31)	.8%	(33)	1.7%
Total	(5,678)	100.1%	(3,683)	100.1%	(1,995)	99.9%

first it is important to get an overview of the raw results. A broad picture of the most frequent responses emerges in table 9 from a listing of the general areas in order of numerical responses.

These figures call for some explanation, especially because they are based on the tabulation of open-ended responses. First, there is no sure way of determining the significance of the large number of "no responses," but because "no responses" constitute more than half of the sample, this means that the percentages of the other categories are more than double for those who did specify a motive. In other words, excluding "no response," and considering the total of specific responses as 100%, Preference totals 38.9%, Sickness 30.8%, Human Relations 8.6%, Spiritual, Religious Matters 8.3%, Growth, Birth, Education 7.3%, Other 3.6%, and Economic Reasons 2.4%. Second, these "general areas" must be understood as including several overlapping categories of specific responses. Because of the complexity of these overlapping categories, they are illustrated here in the form of a mathematical tree, and then discussed in greater detail.

The mathematical tree illustrating survey results for motive shows not only the pattern of general areas, but also the breakdown of the general areas into more specific categories, all of which provide interesting insights into aspects of Gedatsu-kai religious life. The major significance of the results of the nationwide survey on this question is that Preference and Sickness are the two most important responses Gedatsu-kai members give as motive for joining Gedatsu-kai. These two general areas deserve closer attention, with breakdown of relative percentages for each area. The general area Preference includes the main categories "vague preference," "second generation," "sympathy with the teaching," and "other preference." The term *preference* was used in tabulating responses for motive that focused on a choice or preference for Gedatsu-kai, expressed concretely as sympathy with Gedatsu-kai teaching, persuasion to join after talking with members, attraction by current members; by contrast, "preference" stands apart from other motives focusing on particular problems to be resolved, especially sickness. The general area of Preference, with 1,007 responses, represents 38.9% of all responses for motive. Treating these 1,007 responses for Preference as 100%, the relative percentages for categories of Preference are as follows. The category "vague preference" (which includes responses such as "encouraged to join," "joined after talking to a member"), with 353 responses, represents 35.1% of all responses for

TABLE 10.
Mathematical Tree of Responses for Motive for Joining

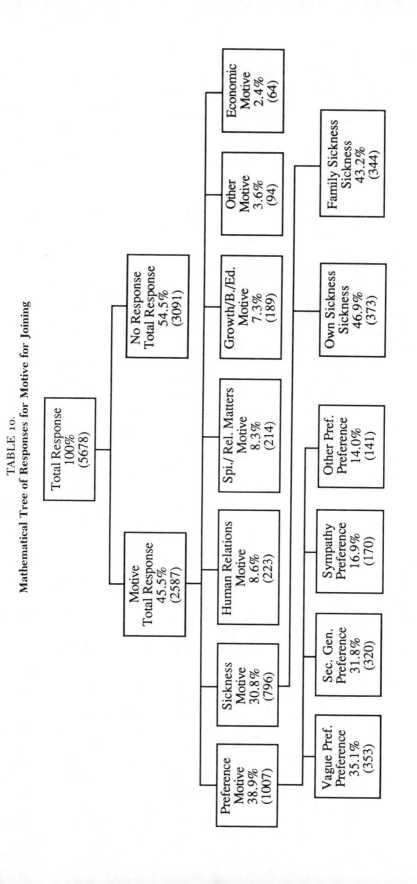

Preference. Other categories under Preference are "second generation," with 320 responses, or 31.8%, "sympathy with the teaching," with 170 responses, or 16.9%, and "other preference," with 141 responses, or 14.0% of all responses for Preference.

This breakdown of results for Preference highlights several facts: the two categories of "vague preference" and "sympathy with the teaching" demonstrate both the persuasiveness of Gedatsu-kai members in recruiting and the attractiveness and power of Gedatsu-kai teaching. On the other hand, the results for "second generation" as motive for joining probably indicate two different aspects about Gedatsu-kai: on the one hand, this would seem to be a rather low percentage when compared with older established religions, and shows that (as of 1979) Gedatsu-kai is a new religion which most people join as first-generation members; on the other hand, this percentage is large enough to indicate that Gedatsu-kai has generational continuity, and in the future (after 1979) more members may join as second-generation followers in a family tradition, rather than as a solution to particular problems.

The general area of Sickness, with 796, or 30.8% of the total responses for motive, is smaller than the general area of Preference. However, Preference includes together several somewhat different categories, and if the category "second generation" is removed, the general area of Preference falls to 687, or 26.6% of total responses. Within the general area of Sickness, the two most frequently mentioned afflictions are "own sickness" and "family sickness." The relative significance of these two categories can be seen by treating the 796 responses for Sickness as 100%; in this case, "own sickness," with 373 responses, represents 46.9% of all responses for Sickness, while "family sickness," with 344 responses, represents 43.2% of all responses for Sickness. We have seen in the life histories that one's own sickness and the sickness of others (especially children) are major reasons for religious reflection, and this is borne out in the responses of Gedatsu-kai members. The relative importance of "own sickness" and "family sickness" is seen also in the fact that each category has a higher number of responses than for "second generation" (with 320 responses). The two general areas of Preference and Sickness have a sufficient number of responses to demonstrate some interesting differences by age, gender, year of entry, and age at time of entry, as will be shown after all general areas are treated.

After Preference and Sickness come three general areas of motive with about the same percentage of frequency in the questionnaire. The area of Human Relations, with 223, or 8.6% of the total responses for motive, includes the category of "other family relations (trouble)" with 102 responses, and several other categories of family relations (especially "husband-wife," "parent-child," and "daughter-in-law–mother-in-law") with fewer responses than "other family relations (trouble)."[13] In other words, this area of Human Relations is so directly concerned with the family that it might be called "Family Relations." The close connection between social harmony—especially family harmony—and religious commitment was emphasized by the founder, as seen in his biography. And good family relations are a prominent feature of many of the life histories, even when other factors, such as sickness and ancestors, are the main concern. However, the religious significance of the family is much greater than can be seen in the rather low percentages of this area of Human Relations. Even in the general area of Sickness, family is a major factor, because "family sickness," with 344 responses, accounts for 13.3% of the total responses for motive. This is a good example of how family is a factor in other general areas of motive for joining.

The general area Spiritual, Religious Matters constitutes 214, or 8.3%, of the total responses for motive. This area includes the categories of "spiritual cultivation (seishinteki shūyō)," with 73 responses; "spiritual problems (nayami)" with 73 responses; and the smaller categories of "ancestor worship" and "spirits (*rei*) generally," with fewer responses. The rather low frequency of Spiritual, Religious Matters is surprising, especially because it includes the specific category of "ancestor worship," with only 52, or 0.9%, of the responses for motive. Given the central role of ancestors in the belief and practice of Gedatsu-kai, it would be logical to assume that "ancestor worship" would be a major category for motive in joining. However, the perception of members apparently focuses on more specific problems, such as the sickness or family problems caused by improper worship of ancestors. The same comment may be appropriate for "spirits (rei) generally": although spirits figure prominently in life histories, apparently members focus more on the problems caused by improper relation to spirits, and do not join "because of" spirits. It is less surprising that the number indicating "spiritual cultivation" is relatively low, because it is probable that motive for joining is more likely to be a specific problem, and "spiritual cultivation" is what a person practices after joining.

The statistics for motive for joining discussed to this point have been presented in the general format of all data, females, and males to highlight the order of importance of the most frequently recorded reasons for entering Gedatsu-kai, without distinguishing the historical period or age of members when they joined; this means that "all responses" includes members who joined Gedatsu-kai from the early stages of its development in the 1930s as well as in the recent stages of its development in the 1970s; "all responses" includes members who when joining were in their teens, as well as members who were in their eighties. Breaking down some of these statistics by time of entry and age at time of entry provides some interesting insights into why people join Gedatsu-kai—people in different historical periods and people in different age groups. First we will look at people who join in different historical periods and see what changes occur in motive through time.

For cross-tabulation purposes, three historical periods of entry into Gedatsu-kai are considered: 1935–1960, 1961–1970, and 1971–1980. All respondents indicating motive, year of entry, and gender have been cross-tabulated to show characteristics specific to each of the three historical periods. It would take too much space to cite all the statistics for these cross-tabulations, but some interesting trends emerge, especially for the two most important general areas of motive— Sickness and Preference. The most significant trends are the steady increase in the relative importance of Sickness as a motive for joining through the three historical periods, and the steady decrease in the relative importance of Preference as a motive for joining.

There are two factors that make this counter-trend surprising. First, some scholars have argued that as a new religion develops and becomes established, specific "this-worldly benefits" as motives for joining and belonging become less important (Watanabe 1968). Clearly this is not true for Gedatsu-kai. Second, the general

TABLE 11.
Preference as Motive for Joining, by Three Historical Periods

	Entered 1935–1960		Entered 1961–1970		Entered 1971–1980	
All data						
Preference (general)	(1)	.3%	(0)	.0	(0)	.0%
Sympathy with the teaching	(37)	11.9%	(49)	16.4%	(78)	23.6%
Vague preference	(82)	26.4%	(108)	36.2%	(144)	43.6%
Second generation	(144)	46.4%	(91)	30.5%	(47)	14.2%
Attraction of the members' personalities	(5)	1.6%	(5)	1.7%	(10)	3.0%
Other preference	(40)	12.9%	(45)	15.1%	(51)	15.5%
Total	(309)	100.2%	(298)	99.9%	(330)	99.9%

area of Preference includes a large percentage of second-generation members, and obviously there could have been relatively few second-generation members in the 1935–1960 period, when Gedatsu-kai was just beginning to organize, and almost all members necessarily were first-generation members. In the periods 1961–1970 and 1971–1980, there were more members of advanced age, who— we might expect—would tend to bring their children into Gedatsu-kai as second-generation members, and this would tend to inflate figures for Preference for these two periods. But this is not the case: the figures for "second generation" as a motive for joining decrease rather than increase. In fact, as the table above demonstrates, when responses for Preference are considered to be 100% (excluding "no response"), "sympathy with the teaching" and "vague preference" increase significantly in importance from 1935–1960 through 1961–1970 and 1971–1980, while "second generation" becomes much less important. These figures show that Gedatsu-kai is still primarily a first-generation movement, and that within the general area of Preference, "sympathy with the teaching" and "vague preference" are two to three times more important than "second generation" as motive for joining during the 1971–1980 historical period. (Because figures are not dramatically different for males and females, they are not listed here.)

It is not possible to deduce from the questionnaire results alone the reasons for the counter-trend of Sickness and Preference, but it is important to keep in mind that the two main areas of motive for joining are not constant through the three historical periods—Sickness increases in importance, while Preference decreases in importance. And the decrease in Preference is due mainly to the decline in "second generation" as a motive.

There are also significant differences in motive for joining by *age at time of entry* (not age at time of questionnaire). The large number of respondents in the two most important general areas of motive, Preference and Sickness, make it possible to arrange some results for motive by age and gender. The results for three categories of Preference and two categories of Sickness respectively have been cross-tabulated by gender and by the four groups of *age at time of entry* to

TABLE 12.
**Vague Preference, Second Generation, and Sympathy
With the Teaching as Motive for Joining**

	0–30		31–50		51–65		66–92	
Vague Preference								
females	(61)	25.8%	(100)	45.9%	(42)	53.2%	(5)	71.4%
males	(47)	26.1%	(54)	45.8%	(17)	47.2%	(6)	85.7%
Second Generation								
females	(110)	46.6%	(31)	14.2%	(3)	3.8%	(0)	0.0%
males	(81)	45.0%	(14)	11.9%	(0)	0.0%	(0)	0.0%
Sympathy with the Teaching								
females	(33)	14.0%	(46)	21.1%	(22)	27.8%	(0)	0.0%
males	(18)	10.0%	(27)	22.8%	(13)	36.1%	(1)	14.3%

indicate gender-specific and age-specific motives. Note that for these tables, the sample is the smaller number of respondents who answered all the questions of motive, gender, age, and year of entry.

In table 12, which compares only "vague preference," "second generation," and "sympathy with the teaching" as motive for joining, percentages are figured from the total of responses who answered the questions of age and sex, and indicated a motive for joining within the area of Preference; these three categories represent about 80% of the responses for each gender. (Results are given by each category, female and male, to simplify gender comparison.) Table 12 makes possible comparison and contrast of both age group and gender for three categories of motive in the general area of Preference. For example, in the first column for "vague preference," 25.8% represents 25.8% of females age 0–30 who chose "vague preference," compared with all females age 0–30 who indicated a motive for joining within the general area of Preference. Similarly, the second figure in the first column, 26.1%, represents 26.1% of males age 0–30 who chose "vague preference," compared with all males age 0–30 who indicated a motive for joining in the general area of Preference. This shows very little variation between males and females in this age group, and the pattern of frequency for females and males is close in all age groups. Reading the rows horizontally, we find significant increase in the percentages as age of entry advances: from age 0–30 to age 66–92, the percentages become about three times higher. Obviously, "vague preference" increases steadily from lower to higher age. (There are relatively few responses for the age 66–92 group, but they support the steady increase from lower to higher age.)

The cross-tabulation is the same for "second generation" figures: columns compare gender, rows compare age groups. Not surprisingly, almost half of the age 0–30 group in the general area of Preference lists "second generation" as motive for joining, but this percentage drops sharply in the age 31–50 group, is inconsequential for the age 51–65 group, and is not recorded for the age 66–92 group. If a person is led to join Gedatsu-kai by a parent, this is most likely to occur before the person is 30 years old. However, Gedatsu-kai does recruit middle-aged people, and middle-aged parents who join may help account for the 14.2% of females and

TABLE 13.
Own Sickness and Family Sickness as Motive for Joining

	0–30		31–50		51–65		66–92	
Own Sickness								
females	(51)	49.0%	(115)	40.3%	(45)	43.7%	(7)	58.3%
males	(38)	62.3%	(64)	47.8%	(31)	62.0%	(4)	80.0%
Family Sickness								
females	(41)	39.4%	(144)	50.5%	(46)	44.7%	(4)	33.3%
males	(18)	29.5%	(57)	42.5%	(15)	30.0%	(0)	0.0%

11.9% of males age 31–50 (for the general area of Preference) who indicated "second generation" as motive for joining. In this category, as in the preceding category, there is no appreciable difference between female and male frequencies.

The figures for "sympathy with the teaching" show a steady increase in percentages from the youngest age group to age 51–65; the fourth category includes only one response and cannot be considered. There is only slight variation by sex, with more females age 0–30 motivated by "sympathy with the teaching," and more males age 31–50 and age 51–65 motivated by "sympathy with the teaching."

In the three specific categories of "vague preference," "second generation," and "sympathy with the teaching," there is considerable difference by age, but very little by sex. For both males and females there is an increase with age for both "vague preference" and "sympathy with the teaching"; there is a sharp decrease with age for "second generation."

Selected results from the general area of Sickness can be arranged in the same manner as the above selected results from the general area of Preference. The two main categories within the general area of Sickness are "own sickness" and "family sickness," representing about 90% of all motives for joining in the area of Sickness. The following table for "own sickness" and "family sickness" shows crosstabulation for each of these specific motives by sex and *age at time of entry* (not age at time of questionnaire). The percentages are for the total number of respondents who answered the questions for age and sex and indicated a motive for joining within the general area of Sickness. Because not all responses fit into the set of two categories "own sickness" and "family sickness," percentages do not total 100% for each gender. (Results are given by each category, female and male, to simplify gender contrast.)

The figures for "own sickness" show that it is the primary motive within the general area of Sickness: it is not lower than 40% for any age group, and ranges well above 50%. (Age 66–92 supports this general tendency, but has too few responses to support conclusive remarks about the higher percentages in this age group.) Although "own sickness" is rather high for all age groups, it is lowest for the age 31–50 group; this is not surprising, since this is the age of focus on the family, and we see just the reverse pattern for the motive of "family sickness." There is a marked difference between females and males in each age group for "own sickness" as motive: males are consistently much more concerned with "own sickness" than females. Males are closest to females for "own sickness" in the age 31–50 group, but in every other cell male frequencies are much higher than female frequencies. The cross-tabulations for "own sickness" present an interesting contrast with the cross-tabulations for "family sickness."

Within the general area of Sickness as motive, "family sickness" is not so high as "own sickness." "Family sickness" reaches 50% in only one age-gender cell, notably for females in the age 31–50 group, but "own sickness" is just below or well above 50% in all cells. The highest frequency for "family sickness" is in the age 31–50 group, and this is the group in which frequencies for females and males are closest. But in every age group, frequencies of "family sickness" for females are considerably higher than for males. (Again, the most advanced age group supports this tendency but has too few responses for conclusive comparison.) This cross-tabulation for "family sickness" shows a reverse pattern from the cross-tabulation for "own sickness." "Family sickness" is highest in age 31–50, "own sickness" is lowest. Males are significantly higher across the board for "own sickness": females are significantly higher across the board for "family sickness."

There are no exactly comparable results from questionnaire surveys of other Japanese new religions, but it is probable that these gender-specific and age-specific characteristics are not distinctive for Gedatsu-kai; rather, they may be features of Japanese society and religious life generally. The Japanese family may not be the central social unit it once was—and may not conform so closely to the Neo-Confucian ideal of Gedatsu-kai's teachings—but it still is a primary social unit that is important for both social identity and religious action: this is borne out by the fact that "*family* sickness" is a significant motive for joining Gedatsu-kai, and by the fact that this motive is highest in the age 31–50 group. The gender-specific characteristic of Gedatsu-kai members in the general area of Sickness—showing higher frequencies of males for "own sickness," and higher frequencies of females for "family sickness"—raises interesting questions both within and outside Japanese society. In contemporary Japan, it is widely recognized that women are primarily concerned with home and family, and men are more concerned with life outside the home and their own personal lives (Lebra 1984:129–37). This is certainly true for Japan, and yet it may be a feature of most urban-industrial societies in which men are preoccupied with economic pursuits outside the home and women are concerned mainly with the bearing and raising of children and the home generally. Ohnuki-Tierney has shown that Japanese women consistently are more directly involved than men with family sickness (1984:12, 143, 180–81, 187). It is probable that these data indicate the dominant role of Japanese women in the home for the family in general, especially for sickness, and also for religious matters.[14] The special role of women in Gedatsu-kai, however it is interpreted, is also clear in the recruiting process for new members.

The general answer to the question, Why do people join Gedatsu-kai? is that, according to their own statements, they join primarily for the reason of their preference for the movement, secondarily for handling sickness, and to a lesser degree for reasons related to human relations, spiritual and religious matters, and growth, birth, and education. Of the two major motives for joining, Preference breaks down into the three specific reasons of "vague preference," "second generation," and "sympathy with the teaching"; Sickness breaks down into "own sickness" and "family sickness," with females consistently higher than males for "family sickness." By historical periods, from the early to the most recent period,

Preference decreases in importance, while Sickness increases; within Preference, "vague preference" and "sympathy with the teaching" increase, while "second generation" decreases. By age at time of joining, from youngest to oldest age, "vague preference" and "sympathy with the teaching" increase, while "second generation" decreases; "own sickness" is lowest and "family sickness" is highest in the 31–50 age group.

Who Recruits Members into Gedatsu-kai?

The preceding section on why people join Gedatsu-kai focused on the motives individual members reported for joining, in order to assess the relative importance of the various reasons. However, we have seen that joining Gedatsu-kai—or any new religion—is more complicated than a single motivating factor: usually there are several interrelated motives that influence a person's joining. And the process is even more complex than a person sorting out one or more possible motives, because joining almost never depends just on the measured decision of a lone individual. Rather, the path to joining Gedatsu-kai usually is opened by a member of the religion who introduces the person to it. The member who introduces or "recruits" a person as a new member is a family member or relative, or an acquaintance—friend, coworker, or neighbor. The purpose of this section is to analyze and interpret "who recruits members into Gedatsu-kai," but first the notion of "recruiting" must be clarified.

In Gedatsu-kai, as in other Japanese new religions, there is a clear notion that a person does not join a movement solely on his or her own initiative. From the viewpoint of the institution, members are expected to lead others into membership by telling them about their experiences, distributing Gedatsu-kai publications, and inviting them to meetings. This process of "recruiting," or "introducing" or "leading in," new members is called michibiku in Gedatsu-kai (and in some other new religions). Standard dictionary definitions of the verb *michibiku* are "to guide, lead, or usher in" (Masuda 1974:1088). In a number of life histories (taiken), Gedatsu-kai members used this verb when talking about how they were introduced, or introduced other people, to the movement. From the viewpoint of new members, there is also a clear notion of the person (or persons) who introduced them to Gedatsu-kai; in fact, there is a specific term for this person, *michibikikata*, literally "introducing-person." Theoretically, every Gedatsu-kai member has at least one michibikikata; the term was used freely by members who told their life histories, or it was immediately recognized when asked, and the "introducing-person" was immediately identified.

In order to avoid misunderstanding, it is best to state explicitly what the verb *michibiku*, "to introduce" or "to recruit," and the noun *michibikikata*, "introducing-person" or "recruiting-person," *are not*. The process of *michibiki*,[15] or recruiting, is not the kind of aggressive, high-pressure tactic of conversion or proselytizing emphasized in Western-language literature on Japanese new religions. The rapid growth of membership in Sōka Gakkai, and its aggressive recruitment tactics in the 1950s and 1960s, attracted particular attention from both Japanese and Western scholars. The important point is that the "introducing" or "recruiting" of michibiku (or michibiki) in Gedatsu-kai is quite different from what has been written about the aggressive recruitment of Japanese new religions.[16]

In Gedatsu-kai, the michibikikata is the essential personal contact that eventually leads an individual to join the movement. The michibiki, recruiting or introducing, is the action by that member—whether it is an accidental conversation or a suggestion initiated by the member—that brings the person into the path leading to membership. A typical recruitment process can be reconstructed from the life histories, which usually emphasize the person and events that brought this individual to Gedatsu-kai. The individual has a problem, such as sickness, human relations, or general malaise, and mentions this problem to a family member, relative, or acquaintance; or he or she may appear so troubled that the other person asks what the matter is. In the ensuing discussion, the Gedatsu-kai member analyzes the problem in terms of the movement's world view of belief and practice (such as the harm that befalls people who do not properly venerate ancestors), and encourages the person to come to a meeting or read some of the religion's literature. In case of a serious problem, the member may introduce the individual to a branch leader or other Gedatsu-kai figure (such as a specialist in health consultation). The michibikikata may have to repeatedly suggest and encourage participation in Gedatsu-kai, and usually takes the person to meetings for the first few times, but there is no attempt to coerce the individual into joining.

Gedatsu-kai in theory and in practice interprets the religious change that occurs when a member joins as taking place within the consciousness of the individual. In theory, as established by the founder and as codified in doctrine, the crucial event is for the individual to reflect on *(hansei suru)* his or her life and realize indebtedness to nature, kami, ancestors, and society. In practice, as told in the many life histories collected from Gedatsu-kai members, the crucial event is the moment of reflection and realization that changes the individual's life and turns him or her to Gedatsu-kai. (Of course, this is an ongoing process of reflection and realization.)

It is important to note this process carefully, especially to avoid misunderstanding of the nature and direction of the religious change. For example, it would be a mistake to translate the verb *michibiku* as "to convert." It is not the case that either a person or the founder or other divinities "convert" an individual. This process of religious change is understood as occurring within the individual, rather than being caused by another human being or divine being. In their life histories, Gedatsu-kai members use the passive tense to say they "were introduced" *(michibikareta)* by a certain person, but it would be wrong to translate *michibikareta* as "were converted." An individual has a problem, is introduced to Gedatsu-kai as a way of solving it, and then solves the problem through reflection and realization—which leads to religious action such as repentance and rites for ancestors.

Question 7 of the questionnaire asked for michibikikata, "person who recruited you," and provided categories of "father," "mother," "elder brother," "younger brother," "elder sister," "younger sister," "husband," "wife," "relative," "friend," "coworker," "neighbor," and "other." In the Japanese phrasing of the question (as in Japanese generally), the number—singular or plural—of "person(s) who recruited you" was not specified. Most responses were for one person, but 384 gave responses of two or more. (Percentages for this question, therefore, total more than 100%.) For tabulation purposes, several categories were combined,

TABLE 14.
Recruiting Person (Michibikikata)

	All Data		Females		Males	
Father	(447)	8.0%	(206)	5.6%	(241)	12.1%
Mother	(882)	15.9%	(567)	15.4%	(315)	15.8%
Elder/younger brother	(217)	3.9%	(107)	2.9%	(110)	5.5%
Elder/younger sister	(410)	7.4%	(291)	7.9%	(119)	6.0%
Husband	(92)	1.5%	(92)	2.5%	(0)	0.0%
Wife	(59)	1.1%	(3)[17]	.1%	(56)	2.8%
Relative	(853)	15.4%	(534)	14.5%	(319)	16.0%
Friend	(1,165)	21.0%	(823)	22.3%	(342)	17.1%
Coworker	(221)	4.0%	(101)	2.7%	(120)	6.0%
Neighbor	(862)	15.5%	(629)	17.1%	(233)	11.7%
Branch leader (or sensei)	(299)	5.4%	(197)	5.3%	(102)	5.1%
Other than above	(51)	.9%	(29)	.8%	(21)	1.1%

and one new category was added. "Elder brother" and "younger brother" were combined as "brother," and "elder sister" and "younger sister" were combined as "sister." Because the category for "other" included many written responses for "branch leader (*shibuchō*)" or "teacher (sensei)"—both referring to semiprofessional leadership from Gedatsu-kai—this was treated as a separate category, labeled "branch leader (or teacher)." The "other" category was renamed "other than above" to indicate other than all previous categories.

The results for question 7 are listed in table 14. In order of highest frequencies, results by specific categories for all data are: "friend," with 1,165, or 21.0%; "mother," with 882, or 15.9%; "neighbor," with 862, or 15.5%; "relative," with 853, or 15.4%; "father," with 447, or 8.0%; "sister," with 410, or 7.4%; "branch leader (or sensei)," with 299, or 5.4%; "coworker," with 221, or 4.0%; "brother," with 217, or 3.9%; "husband," with 92, or 1.5%; "wife," with 59, or 1.1%; and "other than above," with 51, or .9%. These results highlight the most important recruiting persons, with "friend" as the single category with highest frequency, followed closely by the three categories of "mother," "neighbor," and "relative."

These results take on greater significance when they are rearranged into three major classifications: "family and relative," "acquaintance," and "branch leader." The total percentage for recruiting persons for all data in the classification of "family and relative" (including parent, sibling, spouse, and relative) is 53.2%; the percentage in the classification of "acquaintance" (including friend, neighbor, and coworker) is 40.5%; and the percentage for "branch leader" is 5.4%. This classification of recruiting results shows that "family and relative" is the largest group introducing individuals to Gedatsu-kai, followed closely by "acquaintance," with "branch leader" a distant third.

These three classifications of recruiting persons throw light on the nature of Gedatsu-kai, Japanese new religions, and Japanese religion and society generally. As a voluntary organization with many first-generation members, Gedatsu-kai could grow in membership only through a recruitment process. There are some second-generation members who were "born into" Gedatsu-kai, but generally such new religions are part of a situation markedly different from the religious pattern

TABLE 15.
Recruitment by Family Members

	All Data		Females		Males	
Father	(447)	8.0%	(206)	5.6%	(241)	12.1%
Mother	(882)	15.9%	(567)	15.4%	(315)	15.8%
Elder/younger brother	(217)	3.9%	(107)	2.9%	(110)	5.5%
Elder/younger sister	(410)	7.4%	(291)	7.9%	(119)	6.0%
Husband	(92)	1.5%	(92)	2.5%	(0)	0.0%
Wife	(59)	1.1%	(3)	.1%	(56)	2.8%
Total	(2,107)	37.8%	(1,266)	34.4%	(841)	42.2%

of Tokugawa times—in which a person (or family) was affiliated with a local Shinto shrine by residential area and with a parish Buddhist temple by hereditary succession. Until late Tokugawa times, there was no such explicit recruitment: a person participated in religion mainly according to residence and family tradition. With Gedatsu-kai and other voluntary religious organizations, an individual has to make a conscious decision to join, and the range of choices for this decision is circumscribed by the religious movements he/she knows about or is introduced to.

These three classifications of recruitment help us see the kinds of personal contact that lead a person into membership in a voluntary religious organization. These results are limited to Gedatsu-kai, but it is quite likely that they speak for other new religions. Perhaps the most important lesson learned from these results is the overriding importance of family and relatives for introducing a person to Gedatsu-kai. Even though the family tie to a Shinto shrine by residential location and to a Buddhist temple by hereditary affiliation has become weaker, it is still the family and relatives who are the key recruiters into religion. Friends and neighbors are also very important, with single-category percentages ranking quite high; the response for coworkers is rather low by comparison. The fact that "branch leader (or sensei)" is so low in frequency—only 5.4% for all data—simply confirms the fact that Gedatsu-kai (like most Japanese new religions) is primarily a lay movement. In fact, it is more lay-oriented than most Japanese new religions, partly because of its rather recent development and lack of professional leaders on the local level.

The breakdown of the largest classification of "family and relative" also is interesting. The reponse for "relative" is larger than any single family category except "mother," but of course "relative" includes all kin other than immediate family. After this inclusive category, the single kin with highest frequency is mother, followed by father, sister, and brother. In other words, parents come first, followed by siblings, with spouse far behind. However, whether it is parents, siblings, or spouse, females are more active at recruiting than males, and this is the case for both all data and by gender, as seen in tables 14 and 15. (Only results for immediate family are given, with percentages figured from the total of all who responded to gender and at least one category of recruitment: immediate family members represent 2,107 responses, or 37.8% of this total for all data.) These selected results for immediate family only show more conclusively the prominent role of women in Gedatsu-kai, especially by comparison of females and males. For all data, about twice as many were recruited by mother as by father; for females, almost three times as many were recruited by mother as by father; for males, too, more were recruited by mother than by father, although the ratio of differential is not so large. The figures for sister-brother comparison show a similar tendency, with recruitment by female siblings at a higher frequency than that by male siblings across the board: even males show a slightly higher percentage of recruitment by sister than by brother. Recruitment by spouse is a relatively low percentage compared with all other recruiting persons, but here, too, husbands are more likely to be recruited by wives than wives by husbands. The dominant role of women in Gedatsu-kai might be assumed from the larger number of women in the movement—almost two-thirds of the questionnaire sample are females. However, two other general and particular interpretations are equally important. In general, some sociologists hold that in modern societies, women concentrate on "emotional" aspects of society such as child-rearing and spiritual matters, while men concentrate on "instrumental" aspects of society such as occupation and economy.[18] In particular, some specialists in Japanese culture point out the preeminence of women in the home, and the tendency for men to "depend" on women, not only in daily care, but also in spiritual matters.[19]

An interesting sidelight on the role of women in Gedatsu-kai is found in comparing two items from separate parts of the questionnaire. The just-quoted figures for wives and husbands come from question 7, "person who recruited you" (table 14), with 2.5% of women recruited by husband, and a slightly higher 2.8% of men recruited by wife. However, in question 8, "motive for joining," under the subcategory of Growth, Birth, Education (Table 8), there is the specific category "marriage," meaning "joined at time of marriage because spouse was a member." In this case, 1.5% of females joined because husband was a member of Gedatsu-kai, while .7% of males joined because wife was a member. These are rather small percentages, but point up a contrast with gender-specific tendencies for recruitment. Generally in recruitment, females have higher frequencies than the corresponding males (mothers higher than fathers, sisters higher than brothers, wives higher than husbands). Why then should women show lower frequencies in question 8 when "marriage" is a motive for joining? It appears that in formal circumstances such as marriage, women "go along" with their husband's religion, following the general tendency for women to yield to men in a formal setting. (This is the more "instrumental" aspect.) However, in the rather informal setting of who persuades whom to join a new religion—recruitment—women are much more persuasive and dominant. (This is the more "emotional" aspect.)[20]

The percentages from these two results of the questionnaire may not be sufficient, by themselves, to support this generalization, but several aspects of Mr. Nakajimo's life history also lend support to this interpretation. Mr. Nakajimo began his life with traditional religious practices, became a Christian in his late teens, and joined Gedatsu-kai through his wife and mother-in-law much later. In his life history, he mentioned that when he married, his wife became Christian, even though she did not practice Christianity after marriage. (In this case, as with the "marriage" percentages for motive from the questionnaire, in a formal situation, women yield to men.) However, later, when Mr. Nakajimo's wife and mother-in-law joined Gedatsu-kai and had spiritual communication with his own family ancestors, Mr. Nakajimo began to wonder about his ancestors and eventually entered Gedatsu-kai—through the informal introduction of his wife and mother-in-law.

These aspects of Mr. Nakajimo's life history reinforce the interpretation of the questionnaire results that females are more likely to yield to husbands in formal situations, but males are more likely to depend on wives in informal or "spiritual" situations.

The above remarks concerning the relative dominance of female recruiting persons are based on all responses for any (or multiple) recruiting persons, considered by all data, females, and males. However, cross-tabulation of these responses by three historical periods of entering Gedatsu-kai reveals a number of trends from the earliest to the more recent historical period of Gedatsu-kai. Table 16 provides evidence that recruitment patterns have changed sharply from the early period of 1935–1960 through the more recent period of 1961–1970, and again in the most recent period of 1971–1980. Recruitment by parents decreases considerably through this time span, with decrease of recruitment by father remarkable—from 13.1% to 4.1% for all data. Recruitment by mother also decreases, but more moderately—from 19.9% to 12.4% for all data for the same time span. Females and males record the same tendency for decrease of recruitment by parents, although at somewhat different rates.

For recruitment by siblings, recruitment by brother decreases for all data, while recruitment by sister increases. For recruitment by brother, there is a counter-tendency for gender, with slight increase for females and noticeable decrease for males. For recruitment by sister, both females and males report a noticeable increase.

Recruitment by spouse also reflects a counter-tendency through time: recruitment by husband decreases steadily, while recruitment by wife increases steadily. Recruitment by relative is a little higher in the middle historical period (1961–1970), with little difference between all three periods and only slight gender difference.

Recruitment by friend generally increases through time, with slight gender difference. Recruitment by coworker is another case of counter-tendency, with females increasing through time, males decreasing. Recruitment by neighbor also provides mixed results: females are generally constant through time, while males decrease. Recruitment by branch leader shows another counter-tendency for gender, females decreasing slightly through time, males increasing. (Recruitment by "other" figures are minimal.)

One of the most evident recruitment tendencies through the three historical periods is the increase in female percentages. Even when comparing the decrease for the father-mother pair, percentages for father decrease more sharply than those for mother. For siblings, sisters increase while brothers decrease through time; for spouses, wives increase while husbands decrease. (Recruitment by relatives, for whom gender is not known, remains rather constant.) This set of cross-tabulations indicates that not only are the percentages of female recruiting persons higher for all respondents, but also these percentages become higher with the passage of time. The dominant position of female recruiters is also reflected in the analysis by age groups, to be treated next.

The above remarks concerning recruiting person are based on analysis of the questionnaire results for all data, females, and males, but without consideration of age at time of joining. When these results are cross-tabulated by the four age groups, both age-specific and gender-specific characteristics become more ob-

TABLE 16.
Recruiting Person (Michibikikata):
Cross-Tabulation by Three Historical Periods

	Entered 1935–1960	Entered 1961–1970	Entered 1971–1980
Father			
all data	13.1%	8.2%	4.1%
females	10.6%	5.6%	2.7%
males	17.6%	13.4%	6.7%
Mother			
all data	19.9%	16.2%	12.4%
females	19.4%	17.1%	12.0%
males	20.9%	14.2%	13.2%
Brother			
all data	4.5%	3.9%	3.7%
females	2.9%	3.0%	3.1%
males	7.3%	5.8%	4.9%
Sister			
all data	5.8%	7.8%	8.7%
females	7.2%	8.9%	8.8%
males	3.5%	5.6%	8.5%
Husband			
females	4.0%	2.7%	1.9%
Wife			
males	2.0%	2.9%	3.7%
Relative			
all data	14.3%	16.9%	15.5%
females	14.7%	16.1%	14.3%
males	13.6%	18.5%	17.5%
Friend			
all data	18.9%	20.0%	23.8%
females	19.8%	22.3%	25.6%
males	17.4%	15.4%	20.6%
Coworker			
all data	3.9%	3.7%	4.3%
females	2.1%	2.7%	3.5%
males	7.0%	5.8%	5.7%
Neighbor			
all data	16.9%	15.7%	15.6%
females	18.3%	16.6%	18.6%
males	14.5%	14.0%	10.1%
Branch Leader			
all data	5.7%	5.8%	5.6%
females	6.5%	6.0%	5.4%
males	4.2%	5.6%	6.0%
Other			
all data	1.3%	0.8%	0.8%
females	1.1%	0.6%	0.8%
males	1.5%	1.0%	0.9%

TABLE 17.
Recruiting Person (Michibikikata):
Cross-Tabulation by Sex and *Age at Time of Joining*

	0–30		31–50		51–65		66–92	
Father								
females	(129)	14.1%	(23)	1.5%	(2)	.3%	(1)	1.9%
males	(146)	21.8%	(32)	4.3%	(0)	.0%	(1)	3.1%
Mother								
females	(330)	36.0%	(125)	7.9%	(11)	1.8%	(1)	1.9%
males	(192)	28.7%	(52)	6.9%	(5)	2.0%	(0)	0.0%
Brother								
females	(27)	2.9%	(53)	3.4%	(15)	2.5%	(2)	3.7%
males	(36)	5.4%	(48)	6.4%	(13)	5.2%	(1)	3.1%
Sister								
females	(59)	6.4%	(150)	9.5%	(56)	9.2%	(4)	7.4%
males	(27)	4.0%	(50)	6.7%	(27)	10.7%	(3)	9.4%
Husband								
females	(53)	5.8%	(28)	1.8%	(3)	0.5%	(0)	0.0%
Wife								
males	(2)	1.8%	(30)	4.0%	(11)	4.4%	(0)	0.0%
Relative								
females	(131)	14.3%	(230)	14.6%	(99)	16.2%	(7)	13.0%
males	(99)	14.8%	(131)	17.5%	(53)	21.0%	(5)	15.6%
Friend								
females	(89)	9.7%	(436)	27.7%	(200)	32.8%	(16)	29.6%
males	(73)	10.9%	(175)	23.4%	(62)	24.6%	(7)	21.9%
Coworker								
females	(30)	3.3%	(51)	3.2%	(13)	2.1%	(1)	1.9%
males	(56)	8.4%	(41)	5.5%	(7)	2.8%	(2)	6.3%
Neighbor								
females	(93)	10.2%	(338)	21.4%	(127)	20.8%	(12)	22.2%
males	(61)	9.1%	(116)	15.5%	(32)	12.7%	(4)	12.5%
Branch Leader								
females	(37)	4.0%	(106)	6.7%	(35)	5.7%	(7)	13.0%
males	(24)	3.6%	(45)	6.0%	(20)	7.9%	(2)	6.3%

vious. The following table shows percentages by females and males for each of the four age groups, for each of the recruiting persons. These cross-tabulations provide additional insight both into the dynamics of recruitment into Gedatsu-kai, and into Japanese society and religion generally, which for sake of convenience are discussed here in the order of the table.

The results for recruitment by father and by mother show decisively that age 0–30 has the highest frequency for both categories. It is not surprising that this age, the crucial formative and early adult years, would reflect greater parental influence than more advanced ages. However, there is significant difference by gender and age. Fathers recruit a large percentage of both females and males in the age 0–30 group, but this drops to a smaller percentage of males and a very small percentage of females in the age 31–50 group; numbers are too small in the age 51–65 and age 66–92 groups for meaningful comparison. (Of course, when respondents reach the higher ages of 51–65 and 66–92, it is likely that one or both parents may be deceased, so that recruitment by parent is no longer a possibility.) By contrast, mothers not only recruit a much higher percentage of females and males in the age 0–30 group, but also continue to recruit at a greater percentage than fathers for the age 31–50 and age 51–65 groups. (Age 66–92 has too few responses for meaningful comparison.) This is added support for the previous discussion of the tendency for males and females to depend upon females for spiritual guidance. It is possible that the relatively higher percentage of recruitment by father in the age 0–30 group is due to the fact that many respondents attribute joining (for such motives as "second generation") to recruitment by father because he is the *formal* head of the household—even though the mother may informally guide religious life. (Again this raises the question of the relationship between formal and informal leadership—instrumental and emotional roles.)

The results for recruitment by brother and by sister show comparable results for the father-mother pair. For recruitment by brother, the figures are steady from age 0–30 through age 51–65, with too few responses in age 66–92 for meaningful comparison. Results for recruitment by sister are consistently higher than for recruitment by brother. For recruitment by sister, there is a significant increase from age 0–30 to age 31–50, and results remain at about the same level through age 66–92. In the father-mother pair, mothers not only are more influential than fathers in recruitment in the age 0–30 group, but they also continue to exert more influence in the age 31–50 and age 51–65 groups, whereas the father's influence falls more sharply after age 0–30. In the brother-sister pair, sisters not only are more influential in recruitment for the age 0–30 group (except for males recruited by brothers being slightly higher), but they also increase in influence in the age 31–50 group and continue that influence through age 66–92; recruitment by brother is lower than by sister and is steady through the four age groups (with few responses in the fourth age group).

The results for recruitment by husband and by wife again show the increase with age for females' influence on recruitment. For age 0–30, husbands recruit a greater percentage of wives than wives recruit husbands. As was mentioned earlier, it is likely that this "yielding" of women to men, in this case wives to husbands, is part of the pattern of female subordination to formal, institutional structures. However, it is noteworthy that after age 0–30, there is a reversal of recruitment tendencies for husbands and wives. The percentage of wives recruited by husbands falls off sharply in age 31–50 and is minimal for age 51–66; the percentage of husbands recruited by wives increases significantly from age 0–30 to age 31–50, and is constant through age 51–66. (Age 66–92 shows no responses for either gender.) Obviously women exert greater influence in recruitment of men than the reverse, and women exert much greater influence for the above-30 age groups, certainly for ages 31–66, and in some cases (as in recruitment by sister) through the age 66–92 group. It is likely that recruitment by males (especially fathers and husbands) may be somewhat higher in the age 0–30 group because of the tendency in Japanese culture (especially among females) to yield to the male head of the house.

Results for recruitment by relative are rather high, and show no great variation by gender or age. This is the only category of kin where gender is not known—it would be interesting to know whether female relatives such as grandmothers, aunts, and female cousins exert more influence in recruitment than male relatives such as grandfathers, uncles, and male cousins.

Results for recruitment by friend are considerable at age 0–30, but double at age 31–50, and stay steady through age 66–92. Results for recruitment by coworker are higher for males than females, are highest at age 0–30, fall slightly at age 31–50, then fall more sharply at age 51–66, and responses are too few for meaningful comparison at age 66–92. Results for recruitment by neighbor show that more females than males are recruited by neighhors; recruitment by neighbors is significant at age 0–30, but increases considerably at age 31–50 and remains constant through age 66–92. It is not surprising that the results for coworkers and neighbors demonstrate reverse patterns by gender: more men work outside the home than women, and men are more concerned with work matters, and are more likely to be close to and recruited by coworkers; fewer women work outside the home than men, and women are more concerned with neighborhood than work, and more likely to be recruited by neighbors.

Results for recruitment by branch leader show relatively low percentages at age 0–30, with a slight rise at age 31–50 and rather constant percentages through age 66–92 (except for a sharp increase in females age 66–92).

The breakdown of recruitment by the four age groups makes clear some of the particular patterns for age and gender that operate in the process of joining Gedatsu-kai. Recruitment is not a simple matter; in fact, 384 respondents indicated more than one "recruiting person."[21] Recruitment, like motive, involves a number of factors that impinge on a person's life in such a way that he or she is brought to the point of joining Gedatsu-kai.

The general answer to the question, Who recruits members into Gedatsu-kai? is: mainly family and relatives (especially females, with mothers the single largest family category); acquaintances such as friends, neighbors, and coworkers are a close second; and religious leaders of Gedatsu-kai (branch leaders) are a distant third. By historical periods, from the early to the most recent period, females generally and also friends become more significant as recruiting persons. By age at time of joining, from youngest to oldest age, parents decline in significance as recruiting persons, but mothers at a lower rate of decline than fathers; other family and relative categories remain constant or increase slightly as recruiting persons; among acquaintances, friends show the greatest increase as recruiting persons for both genders, while neighbors increase especially among females, and coworkers decline in significance.

What Are the Religious Changes after Joining Gedatsu-kai?

To this point, the members of Gedatsu-kai have been discussed mainly before and in the process of joining—who are the members, why do they join, and who recruits them? Now we turn to some aspects of their religious life after joining. Generally there have been two rather broad and somewhat contradictory theses about the nature of people who join Japanese new religions and what happens to them after joining. The two theses are not always clearly stated, and in fact frequently are not even distinguished; nevertheless, they share the common notion that Japanese new religions are modern versions of traditional Japanese religions.

What distinguishes the two theses is a different view of the kind of people who join a new religion and what happens to them after joining. One thesis holds that the people who join a new religion are "traditional" in their outlook, and that is why they join—in other words, they were traditional before they joined, and do not change their "traditional" outlook after joining a new religion whose beliefs and practices are also "traditional."[22] A second thesis holds that the people who join a new religion are alienated from the "traditional" in their outlook, and that is why they join—in other words, they were nontraditional before they joined, and change their "nontraditional" outlook in the process of joining a new religion that is "traditional." These theses usually are not stated so baldly in the secondary literature; in fact, the same article or book may use each argument separately to explain different aspects of new religions, without recognizing the logical contradiction between the two. Of course, the actual dynamics of joining and participating in a new religion might well be much more complex than these two contrary theses: it may be that members of a new religion demonstrate some aspects of both theses. However, there has been little concrete evidence offered to verify either thesis.

It was this concern for the nature of beliefs and practices of the joining members, and the nature of religious change in their beliefs and practices, that led us to design a set of before-and-after questions on the questionnaire. We wanted to compare and contrast certain "traditional" practices of Gedatsu-kai members before and after joining, which was phrased in question 14: "Please indicate the practices you have followed before joining Gedatsu-kai and after joining Gedatsu-kai." Under the question were a number of traditional practices, with space for indicating practice or no practice before and after, and for some items, relative frequency of practice before and after. "Traditional" practices selected for this question were possession of a picture of the imperial household, worship at kamidana (Shinto-style altar in home), worship at butsudan (Buddhist-style altar for ancestors in home), visits to the local Shinto shrine of the tutelary deity (ujigami), visits to the family Buddhist parish temple (bodaiji), pilgrimage to Ise Shrine, pilgrimage to Yasukuni Shrine, and participation in other new religions. Results for this question are given in table 18.

Analysis of the before-and-after results for each category provides interesting concrete information on the practices of the people who join Gedatsu-kai, and their change in religious behavior after joining. In table 18, results are given in the order of the original questionnaire; in table 19, the results have been rearranged to show degree of change of practice and degree of change in frequency of practice. To calculate the degree of reported change in religious behavior for each category, the percentages of "no practice" before joining were compared with the percentages of "no practice" after joining; similarly, the percentages of "practice" before joining were compared with the percentages of "practice" after joining; for those categories with relative frequencies, the percentages for "occasional practice" before joining were compared with the percentages for "occasional practice" after joining, and similar comparisons were made for "daily practice" and "annual practice."[23] All results are given in table form here, as the basis for discussion of religious behavior before and after joining Gedatsu-kai. (Figures for "no response" are listed in these tables.)

It is easy to make some general comments on all the categories of traditional

TABLE 18.
Frequency of Religious Behavior, Before and After Joining Gedatsu-kai

	All Data		Females		Males	
Picture of the Imperial Household						
before, no picture	(2,326)	46.4%	(1,630)	44.3%	(1,006)	50.4%
before, picture	(1,158)	20.4%	(749)	20.3%	(409)	20.5%
no response	(1,884)	33.2%	(1,304)	35.4%	(580)	29.1%
after joining, no picture	(2,233)	39.3%	(1,401)	38.0%	(832)	41.7%
after joining, picture	(1,364)	24.0%	(831)	22.6%	(533)	26.7%
no response	(2,081)	36.7%	(1,451)	39.4%	(630)	31.6%
Worship at Kamidana (Shinto-style altar in home)						
before, no worship	(1,512)	26.6%	(884)	24.0%	(628)	31.5%
before, worship	(3,128)	55.1%	(2,121)	57.6%	(1,007)	50.5%
no response	(1,038)	18.3%	(678)	18.4%	(360)	18.0%
after, no worship	(58)	1.0%	(32)	.9%	(26)	1.3%
after, worship	(4,875)	85.8%	(3,142)	85.3%	(1,733)	86.9%
no response	(745)	13.1%	(509)	13.8%	(236)	11.8%
Worship at Butsudan (Buddhist-style altar for ancestors in home)						
before, no worship	(960)	16.9%	(522)	14.2%	(438)	22.0%
before, worship	(3,793)	66.8%	(2,578)	70.0%	(1,215)	60.9%
no response	(925)	16.3%	(583)	15.8%	(342)	17.1%
after, no worship	(53)	.9%	(30)	.8%	(23)	1.2%
after, worship	(4,926)	86.8%	(3,181)	86.4%	(1,745)	87.5%
no response	(699)	12.3%	(472)	12.8%	(227)	11.4%
Visits to the Local Shinto Shrine of the Tutelary Deity (Ujigami)						
before, no visit	(1,144)	20.1%	(678)	18.4%	(466)	23.4%
before, occasional visit	(3,369)	59.3%	(2,237)	60.7%	(1,132)	56.7%
before, visited almost daily	(227)	4.0%	(158)	4.3%	(69)	3.5%
no response	(938)	16.5%	(610)	16.6%	(328)	16.4%
after, no visit	(39)	.7%	(20)	.5%	(19)	1.0%
after, occasional visit	(3,786)	66.7%	(2,384)	64.7%	(1,402)	70.3%
after, visit almost daily	(1,235)	21.8%	(862)	23.4%	(373)	18.7%
no response	(618)	10.9%	(417)	11.3%	(201)	10.1%
Visits to the Family Buddhist Parish Temple (Bodaiji)						
before, no visit	(1,089)	19.2%	(613)	16.6%	(476)	23.9%
before, occasional visit	(3,205)	56.4%	(2,157)	58.6%	(1,048)	52.5%
before, visited almost daily	(72)	1.3%	(47)	1.3%	(25)	1.3%
no response	(1,312)	23.1%	(866)	23.5%	(446)	22.4%
after, no visit	(395)	7.0%	(240)	6.5%	(155)	7.8%
after, occasional visit	(4,012)	70.6%	(2,570)	69.8%	(1,442)	72.3%
after, visit almost daily	(185)	3.2%	(130)	3.5%	(55)	2.8%
no response	(1,086)	19.1%	(743)	20.2%	(343)	17.2%
Pilgrimage to Ise Shrine						
before, no pilgrimage	(2,278)	40.1%	(1,437)	39.0%	(841)	42.2%
before, occasional pilgrimage	(1,198)	21.1%	(748)	20.3%	(450)	22.6%

TABLE 18. (Cont'd)

	All Data		Females		Males	
before, pilgrimage every year	(95)	1.7%	(48)	1.3%	(47)	2.4%
no response	(2,107)	37.1%	(1,450)	39.4%	(657)	32.9%
after, no pilgrimage	(1,268)	22.3%	(895)	24.3%	(373)	18.7%
after, occasional pilgrimage	(1,900)	33.5%	(1,167)	31.7%	(733)	36.7%
after, pilgrimage every year	(609)	10.7%	(286)	7.8%	(323)	16.2%
no response	(1,901)	33.5%	(1,335)	36.2%	(566)	28.4%
Pilgrimage to Yasukuni Shrine						
before, no pilgrimage	(2,428)	42.8%	(1,511)	41.0%	(917)	46.0%
before, occasional pilgrimage	(914)	16.1%	(561)	15.2%	(353)	17.7%
before, pilgrimage every year	(85)	1.5%	(52)	1.4%	(33)	1.7%
no response	(2,251)	39.6%	(1,559)	42.3%	(692)	34.7%
after, no pilgrimage	(2,022)	35.6%	(1,309)	35.5%	(713)	35.7%
after, occasional pilgrimage	(1,201)	21.2%	(716)	19.4%	(485)	24.3%
after, pilgrimage every year	(189)	3.3%	(100)	2.7%	(89)	4.5%
no response	(2,266)	39.9%	(1,558)	42.3%	(708)	35.5%

practices before proceeding to particular remarks about each category. Even a quick look through the tables confirms a clear tendency in every comparison of "no practice" and "practice" before and after: every comparison of "no practice" before and "no practice" after shows a *decrease*: in other words, the percentage of people who before joining did not observe a traditional practice is higher than the percentage of people who after joining do not observe a traditional practice. Every comparison of "practice" before and "practice" after shows an *increase*: that is, the percentage of people who before joining observed a traditional practice is lower than the percentage of people who after joining observe a traditional practice. There is also an *increase* of percentage for every comparison of "occasional practice" before and after, and "daily" and "annual" practice before and after. In other words, the percentage of respondents with occasional or more regular traditional practice before joining is lower than the percentage of respondents with occasional or more regular traditional practice after joining. In every category, "no practice" decreases; in every category, "practice," "occasional practice," and "daily/annual practice" increase.

The most sweeping generalization for gender-specific change is that more females tend to observe practices before joining, and do so with greater frequency, and therefore change less after joining; fewer males tend to observe traditional practices before joining, and do so with less frequency, and therefore change more after joining. However, females show a greater increase of percentage for daily practice in the home and nearby shrines and temples, whereas males show a greater increase of percentage for annual pilgrimage to the distant shrines of Ise and Yasukuni. These general remarks can be clarified and qualified for each specific

TABLE 19.
**Change in Religious Behavior,
Before and After Joining Gedatsu-kai**

	All Data	Females	Males
Picture of the Imperial Household			
before, no picture	46.4%	44.3%	50.4%
after, no picture	39.3%	38.0%	41.7%
(decrease from before to after)	7.1% −	6.3% −	8.7% −
before, picture	20.4%	20.3%	20.5%
after, picture	24.0%	22.6%	26.7%
(increase from before to after)	3.6% +	2.3% +	6.2% +
Worship at Kamidana (Shinto-Style Altar in Home)			
before, no worship	26.6%	24.0%	31.5%
after, no worship	1.0%	.9%	1.3%
(decrease from before to after)	25.6% −	23.1% −	30.2% −
before, worship	55.1%	57.6%	50.5%
after, worship	85.8%	85.3%	86.9%
(increase from before to after)	30.7% +	27.7% +	36.4% +
Worship at Butsudan (Buddhist-Style Altar For Ancestors in Home)			
before, no worship	16.9%	14.2%	22.0%
after, no worship	.9%	.8%	1.2%
(decrease from before to after)	16.0% −	13.4% −	20.8% −
before, worship	66.8%	70.0%	60.9%
after, worship	86.8%	86.4%	87.5%
(increase from before to after)	20.0% +	16.4% +	26.6% +
Visits to the Local Shinto Shrine of the Tutelary Deity (Ujigami)			
before, no visit	20.1%	18.4%	23.4%
after, no visit	.7%	.5%	1.0%
(decrease from before to after)	19.4% −	17.9% −	22.4% −
before, occasional visit	59.3%	60.7%	56.7%
after, occasional visit	66.7%	64.7%	70.3%
(increase from before to after)	7.4% +	4.0% +	13.6% +
before, daily visit	4.0%	4.3%	3.5%
after, daily visit	21.8%	23.4%	18.7%
(increase from before to after)	17.8% +	19.1% +	15.2% +
Visits to the Family Buddhist Parish Temple (Bodaiji)			
before, no visit	19.2%	16.6%	23.9%
after, no visit	7.0%	6.5%	7.8%
(decrease from before to after)	12.2% −	10.1% −	16.1% −
before, occasional visit	56.4%	58.6%	52.5%
after, occasional visit	70.6%	69.8%	72.3%
(increase from before to after)	14.2% +	11.2% +	19.8% +
before, daily visit	1.3%	1.3%	1.3%
after, daily visit	3.2%	3.5%	2.8%
(increase from before to after)	1.9% +	2.2% +	1.5% +

TABLE 19. (Cont'd.)

	All Data	Females	Males
Pilgrimage to Ise Shrine			
before, no pilgrimage ·	40.1%	39.0%	42.2%
after, no pilgrimage	22.3%	24.3%	18.7%
(decrease from before to after)	17.8% −	14.7% −	23.5% −
before, occasional pilgrimage	21.1%	20.3%	22.6%
after, occasional pilgrimage	33.5%	31.7%	36.7%
(increase from before to after)	12.4% +	11.4% +	14.1% +
before, annual pilgrimage	1.7%	1.3%	2.4%
after, annual pilgrimage	10.7%	7.8%	16.2%
(increase from before to after)	9.0% +	6.5% +	13.8% +
Pilgrimage to Yasukuni Shrine			
before, no pilgrimage	42.8%	41.0%	46.0%
after, no pilgrimage	35.6%	35.5%	35.7%
(decrease from before to after)	7.2% −	5.5% −	10.3% −
before, occasional pilgrimage	16.1%	15.2%	17.7%
after, occasional pilgrimage	21.2%	19.4%	24.3%
(increase from before to after)	5.1% +	4.2% +	6.6% +
before, annual pilgrimage	1.5%	1.4%	1.7%
after, annual pilgrimage	3.3%	2.7%	4.5%
(increase from before to after)	1.8% +	1.3% +	2.8% +

category. We will treat briefly the "traditional" character of each practice, and its relationship to Gedatsu-kai teaching and practice as an introduction to the statistics for each practice.

The results for "picture of the imperial household" are surprisingly low, both before and after joining Gedatsu-kai. There are two major reasons that would lead us to expect much higher percentages for having a picture of the imperial family, both before joining and especially after joining. In Japanese culture generally, the imperial household has always been important. The imperial line has been a central symbol of the Japanese national and religious identity, especially since the Meiji Restoration of 1868, and this symbol was used by the Japanese government until 1945 as a means of mobilizing and unifying the citizenry.[24] This fact alone would seem to identify respect or reverence for the emperor as a traditional feature of Japanese culture; and displaying a picture of the imperial household in one's home would seem to be an expression of traditional values. Such pictures are readily available, are inexpensive, and require little time or effort to display—much less time and/or expense than all of the following practices.

In addition to the fact that the imperial household has been central to traditional cultural values, Gedatsu-kai has placed special significance in the imperial line. The founder combined Neo-Confucian notions of loyalty and Japanese notions of patriotism in reverence and support for the emperor. He even risked breaking protocol when he insisted that commoners like himself could enter the Kyoto temple Sennyūji and pay respects to past emperors. This reverential attitude toward the imperial line is informally institutionalized in Gedatsu-kai, as seen in the fact that photographs of the imperial household are conspicuously displayed in Gedatsu-kai headquarters, practice halls, and branch meeting places.

Although there is a twofold reason to expect rather high percentages for "picture of the imperial household," both before and after joining Gedatsu-kai, results do not confirm such expectations. The results for all data for "before, no picture" are 46.4%, almost half of the sample—higher than one might expect. ("No response" amounts to 33.2% for this category, but comparisons here are only for specific responses; "no response" figures combine with the specific responses to total 100%.) After joining, the percentage with "no picture" decreases to 39.3%; in other words, 7.1% fewer members do not have pictures after joining than before. The percentage of members who had a picture before joining is 20.4%, and this increases only to 24.0%—an increase of 3.6%. It is rather surprising that the decrease of members with "no picture" is so small, and that the increase of members with "picture" is also small. Differences by gender are not dramatic, and reflect a general trend for males to show both a higher percentage of decrease for "no practice" and a higher percentage of increase for "practice."[25]

The results for "worship at kamidana (Shinto-style altar in home)" are more in line with what might be expected of a "traditional" practice. Especially since Tokugawa times, it has been the custom to have a small kamidana in the home; simple food offerings are made at the kamidana, protective paper talismans (*ofuda*) from local tutelary shrines or from powerful distant shrines are placed on or near it (to enshrine the power of one or more kami), and simple prayers may be said before it. Some Buddhist groups have forbidden their members to have kamidana in their homes, but generally the kamidana has represented the traditional recognition of kami as a source of life, fertility, and blessing in the home. Of course, the agricultural and seasonal basis for appreciating the blessing of kami has diminished with rapid urbanization and industrialization: "color television has long since outshone the gilt and jollity of village festivals," and the television set may have replaced the kamidana (and butsudan) as central to home life (Dore in Robert J. Smith 1978:xi–xii). It is this kind of neglect of traditional respect and reverence for kami that led Gedatsu-kai's founder to attempt to restore "faith" in kami: but he criticized severely "faith" (shinkō) as mere mechanical repetition of customs handed down from the past, and advocated "sincere practice" (shinkō) as one way of restoring personal, social, and national harmony. One of the three objects of worship in Gedatsu-kai altars is Tenjin Chigi, the kami of heaven and earth, which members should enshrine in their home altars. The attitude of members toward kami as a main source of life and blessing has already been documented in the life histories.

It is not surprising, then, that there are rather high percentages for "worship at kamidana" both before and after joining Gedatsu-kai. Only 26.6% of respondents (all data) indicate no worship at kamidana before joining; this corresponds to 46.4% of respondents (all data) indicating no picture of the imperial household before joining. A much larger percentage of Gedatsu-kai members worshipped at kamidana in their homes before joining than displayed pictures of the imperial household before joining. The 26.6% of all data who reported no worship at kamidana before joining sharply decreases to 1.0%—a decline of 25.6%. (The decrease for no picture of the imperial household before and after is only 7.1%.) This shows a marked change in religious behavior for people after joining Gedatsu-kai: a large percentage of members who did not observe worship at kamidana before joining, began to worship after joining. It is also the case that many people who joined Gedatsu-kai did observe worship at kamidana before joining—55.1%. However, after joining, this 55.1% rises to a remarkable 85.8%—an increase of 30.7%. (Comparable figures for "Picture of the imperial household" are: before joining, 20.4%, after joining 24.0%—an increase of only 3.6%.) This demonstrates that Gedatsu-kai attracts a relatively low percentage of people who did not worship at kamidana before joining, but persuades almost all of them to worship at kamidana; Gedatsu-kai attracts a relatively high percentage of people who did worship at kamidana before joining, but this relatively high percentage is even higher for members after joining. Gender differences follow the general pattern for other categories of this question, with males recording both a higher percentage of decrease for "no practice," and a higher percentage of increase for "practice."[26]

The results for "worship at butsudan (Buddhist style altar for ancestors in home)" are comparable to those for "worship at kamidana," in both the general rationale for this worship and the actual percentages reported. The butsudan is equal to if not more imporant than the kamidana as an indicator of traditional practice. Since Tokugawa times it has been the center of the home as the place of enshrining the family ancestors. The main family always had a butsudan because it held the key memorial tablets for the patrilineal ancestors; other (branch) families usually installed a butsudan only after the first death in their immediate family. Regular offerings are made at the butsudan, and ancestors are ritually honored, especially on anniversary dates of their deaths. The teaching of Gedatsu-kai's founder is similar for both kamidana and butsudan: although many people follow the customary routine for honoring the spirits of ancestors, few sincerely reflect on the meaning of ancestors and perform these rituals from the heart. The founder first experimented with having people recite sutras and practice repentance in front of the butsudan, and eventually developed the amacha memorial rite for ancestors in the home.

Gedatsi-kai members observe worship at butsudan more than at kamidana both before and after joining. For all data, only 16.9% of respondents reported "no worship" at butsudan before joining, and this decreased to .9% after joining—a drop of 16.0%. The figures for those who did worship at butsudan before joining is a high 66.8%, which increases to 86.8% after joining—an increase of 20.0%. Gender differences are the same as for kamidana: males show a higher percentage of decrease for "no practice" and a higher percentage of increase for "practice." The general significance of the butsudan question is similar to the import of the kamidana question. Gedatsu-kai attracts a rather low percentage of people who did not worship at butsudan, but this percentage decreases sharply; Gedatsu-kai attracts a rather high percentage of people who did worship at butsudan, and this high percentage increases to a very high level.[27]

Just as kamidana and butsudan represent complementary traditional elements in the home during the past few centuries, so the local tutelary Shinto shrine and the family parish Buddhist temple constitute a key pair of traditional religious sites for the family outside the home.[28] The local Shinto shrine of the tutelary deity (ujigami) has been the tie of the home to the power of kami, while the Buddhist parish temple (bodaiji) has been the tie of the family to the Buddhist power in venerating ancestors. And, just as the percentages and patterns for kamidana and butsudan are similar, this is also the case for the tutelary Shinto shrine and the Buddhist parish temple.

The tutelary Shinto shrine has been the major site for receiving the blessing of kami (known as ujigami) for a small area, hamlet, section of a village, or ward of a city. Ujigami, literally "clan kami," may once have meant the protective kami for an extended family, but usually it is the tutelary kami for the people born and/or living within an area close to the shrine of the ujigami. Actually there are a number of distinctive types of local Shinto shrines with somewhat different histories of formation (Davis 1977:17–21), but in recent and modern times most people have understood the ujigami shrine to be the small shrine near their home where they participated in seasonal festivals. Formerly this was the shrine where infants were taken to be blessed as the "child of the kami" (*ujiko*, a term like "parishioner"). However, along with urbanization and industrialization, social mobility has helped to weaken this sense of a local tutelary Shinto shrine, and rather few Japanese have a clear sense of a tie to such a shrine.

Indeed, this is one of the aspects of modern life that Gedatsu-kai's founder deplored; he attempted to restore this sense of tie to a local tutelary kami by returning to his native village of Kitamoto and paying respects to the ujigami of his family and his childhood experience. The founder encouraged people to pay visits to their respective local tutelary shrines—and if they had no such tie, to form one with a local shrine. Gradually members came to visit the Sacred Land (both at times of the Grand Festival and on other occasions) as a pilgrimage to the founder's village and as a return to the traditional religious world view—which featured the founder's tutelary shrine and village temple.

The results for "visits to the local Shinto shrine of the tutelary deity (ujigami)" demonstrate the significance of this sacred site to people both before and after joining Gedatsu-kai. For all data before joining, a rather low 20.1% reported "no visit," which dropped sharply to .7% after joining, a decrease of 19.4%. Almost all who reported "no visit" before joining indicated a change to "visit" after joining. The percentage decrease of "no visit" for ujigami is close to the percentage decrease of "no practice" at kamidana and butsudan. For tutelary Shinto shrine (ujigami) and all subsequent categories, relative frequencies were requested: for tutelary Shinto shrine and Buddhist parish temple, the two frequencies are "occasional visit" (before and after) and "daily visit" (before and after). For tutelary Shinto shrine, all data results for "occasional visit" before joining are a rather high 59.3%, which becomes even higher after joining, 66.7%—an increase of 7.4%. For "daily visit" to the tutelary Shinto shrine before, figures are very low at 4.0%, but this increases considerably after joining to 21.8%, an increase of 17.8%.

The general pattern here is similar to that for kamidana and butsudan: a low percentage of "no practice" before joining, but most of the "no practice" changes to "practice" after joining. And even though the questionnaire has no frequency category for kamidana and butsudan, there is great similarity between "practice" before and after for kamidana and butsudan, and "occasional practice" before and after for local tutelary shrine: this occasional practice is rather high before joining and becomes even higher after joining. The most remarkable change is in "daily practice," with very low daily practice before joining, and a sharp increase after joining. Gender differences, too, show similarities between local tutelary shrine, and kamidana and butsudan, with males recording greater decrease for "no practice," and greater increase for "occasional practice." Percentages for females' daily practice are higher before, and increase more, than percentages for males.[29]

The family Buddhist parish temple, or bodaiji, plays a role similar to that of the tutelary Shinto shrine: the bodaiji is a connection to the ancestors and butsudan, much as the tutelary Shinto shrine is a connection to the ujigami and kamidana. During Tokugawa times, the government required families to belong to a parish temple and to record family changes such as births, deaths, and changes of address with this temple. This became a hereditary pattern of affiliation which eventually was considered so customary that even after the legal requirement was removed in Meiji times, it continued to exert great influence, down to the present day. People still tend to have funeral and memorial rites for parents and family members in the Buddhist temple with which the male line of the family has been affiliated. This custom is ingrained in Japanese culture, and yet the founder of Gedatsu-kai criticized people on this exact point: many people perform or have others perform rites for the ancestors merely out of custom, as a transmitted procedure that does not spring from the reflection and sincerity of the actors. The founder told people to renew their relationship with both ancestors and the Buddhist parish temple.

The results for "visits to the family Buddhist parish temple (bodaiji)" are quite similar to the results for the tutelary Shinto shrine. For all data before joining, a rather low 19.2% reported "no visit" to Buddhist parish temple, which dropped considerably to 7.0% after joining, a large decrease of 12.2%. The percentage of "no visit" before to after changes dramatically, but not to the extent of change for "tutelary shrine." (Comparable figures for "tutelary Shinto shrine" are "no visit" before, 20.1%; "no visit" after, .7%; a decrease of 19.4%.) For all data, "occasional visit" to Buddhist parish temple, the "before" percentage is rather high at 56.4%, and the "after" percentage is even higher, at 70.6%, an increase of 14.2%. (In this case the percentages for tutelary Shinto shrine and Buddhist parish temple are closer, but there is greater increase for the latter.) The percentages for "daily visit" to Buddhist parish temple are rather low: 1.3% before, 3.2% after, or an increase of 1.9%. Comparable figures for "daily visit" to tutelary Shinto shrine are much higher: 4.0% before, 21.8% after, a 17.8% increase.

However, this difference of percentages for "daily visit" to Buddhist parish temple and tutelary Shinto shrine may be partly due to nonreligious factors: a tutelary Shinto shrine is always close to the home (which may facilitate more *daily* practice), while the hereditary Buddhist parish temple usually is more distant from the home (which may hinder daily practice). Another factor that helps explain this difference is that the ideal for daily devotions in Gedatsu-kai is to perform the amacha memorial rite for ancestors morning and evening in the home; this may take the place of frequent visits to the Buddhist parish temple (whose main significance is enshrining spirits of family ancestors). However, these are relatively small differences between percentages for tutelary Shinto shrine and Buddhist parish temple. Generally the pattern for these two categories is rather close, even to the point of gender characteristics: males record a higher decrease in percentage for "no visit" and a higher increase in percentage for "occasional visit," while females record a higher increase in percentage for "daily visit."[30]

Two examples of traditional practice more distant from the home and more national in character were used in the questionnaire: "pilgrimage to Ise Shrine" and "pilgrimage to Yasukuni Shrine." Today both shrines are conspicuous, in fact, controversial sites symbolizing the close relationship between the Japanese nation and religious values. Both shrines were prominent in the mobilization and unification of the citizenry after the Meiji Restoration of 1868, but actually the tradition of the Ise Shrine is much more venerable. The legendary account of the founding of the Ise Shrine (actually a complex of shrines) dates its origin to ancient times, when Amaterasu Ōmikami (the Sun Goddess, from whom the imperial line descends) was permanently enshrined there. From medieval times it became the custom to make pilgrimages to Ise as an expression of personal piety and loyalty to the way of kami (Shinto, the national tradition of Japan). Before the advent of rapid transportation, this was a lengthy journey on foot and entailed many hardships, but even today many people consider a pleasant "trip" to Ise a pilgrimage as well as sightseeing and recreation. Many families still enshrine in their homes protective paper talismans (ofuda) from Ise.[31] Gedatsu-kai's founder felt a special relationship to Ise Shrine, and although he suffered considerably from government restrictions on religion and even direct persecution, he remained firm to his conviction of patriotic and religious support for national shrines such as Ise (which were part of the government's program to restrict religious freedom). In fact, eventually he institutionalized this support in the Sanseichi Junpai (Three Holy Sites Pilgrimage) to Sennyūji (a temple enshrining spirits of many emperors), Ise Shrine, and Kashiwara Shrine (famous for its legendary connection with Emperor Jinmu and the founding of Japan).

In general, the results for "pilgrimage to Ise Shrine" and "pilgrimage to Yasukuni Shrine" are more comparable to results for "picture of the imperial household" than to the results for kamidana, butsudan, tutelary Shinto shrine, and Buddhist parish temple. Each category of pilgrimage will be treated separately. Starting with "pilgrimage to Ise Shrine," we find the following results. For "no practice," the percentages for all data are: before joining, 40.1%; after joining, 22.3%, a decrease of 17.8%. Other percentages for all data are: before joining, "occasional pilgrimage," 21.1%; after joining, "occasional pilgrimage," 33.5%, an increase of 12.4%. For "annual pilgrimage," the percentages for all data are much lower: before joining, 1.7%; after joining, 10.7%, an increase of 9.0%. In this category of "pilgrimage to Ise Shrine," every "before" percentage indicates that this pilgrimage is not a high priority for Gedatsu-kai members, although there is more change after joining than is the case for the comparable "after joining" figures for "picture of the imperial household." Males show greater change in all three questionnaire items for pilgrimage to Ise: greater decrease of "no pilgrimage," greater increase of "occasional pilgrimage," and greater increase of "annual pilgrimage." It is likely, however, that the higher frequencies for males for pilgrimage to Ise may be due to nonreligious factors: males have more access to leisure and travel, which makes possible pilgrimage to Ise; also, although females constitute two-thirds of Gedatsu-kai membership, males tend to serve as branch representatives more than females in the annual Three Holy Sites Pilgrimage.

Yasukuni Shrine is comparable to Ise Shrine, in the sense of being one of the most important contemporary shrines expressing the identity of national and religious values. However, Yasukuni Shrine's tradition dates back only to late Tokugawa and early Meiji times, when the government founded special shrines for spirits of soldiers and sailors who died in service of the country. Through the Sino-

Japanese War of 1894–1895, the Russo-Japanese War of 1904–1905, and World War II—which for Japan is dated 1937–1945,—a heightened sense of nationalism and militarism pervaded Japanese culture, and Yasukuni Shrine flourished. The religious rationale for enshrining spirits of war dead at Yasukuni is that these men died for their country, and therefore deserve to be enshrined with the spirits of the emperors as the founders and leaders of the country. This is the only historical precedent for the spirits of common people being united with spirits of emperors. Until the end of World War II, Yasukuni Shrine (and other national shrines such as Ise) received government funds, and their priests were considered in the service of the country; after World War II, with the new constitution and complete freedom of religion, such funds have been considered unconstitutional (as illegal governmental support of one particular religion), but there has been a continuing controversy over the status of such shrines. Communists and the left generally have argued against the special national character of such shrines, and against use of national funds to "establish" a particular religion (citing the danger of a rise of ultranationalism and ultramilitarism); conservatives and the right generally have argued for the special national character of such shrines as preserving the ancient ethos of Japan, and for use of national funds to preserve and maintain a national tradition.[32]

This complex problem cannot be resolved here, but the founder's position on such matters was clear before, during, and after World War II, and has been continued in the teaching and practice of Gedatsu-kai. The founder taught that "sincere action" is the basic principle for religious life and for national life. He did not criticize government restrictions on religion, rather emphasizing the need for people to reflect on and restore their sense of indebtedness to kami and nation. The founder was quite active both in pilgrimages to Yasukuni Shrine and in consoling the orphans of soldiers and sailors during World War II, and encouraged pilgrimage to Yasukuni Shrine after the war (when it was no longer so popular). Today Gedatsu-kai continues to teach respect for Yasukuni Shrine, although it does not directly support movements to change the constitution so that this shrine is once more considered a national shrine entitled to national funds.[33] However, there is no institutional practice of Gedatsu-kai focusing specifically on Yasukuni Shrine in the manner that Ise Shrine is included in the Three Holy Sites Pilgrimage.

The results for "pilgrimage to Yasukuni Shrine" are similar to the results for "pilgrimage to Ise," but indicate less practice. For all data, "no pilgrimage" to Yasukuni, the percentages are: before, 42.8%; after, 35.6%, a decrease of 7.2%. For all data, "occasional pilgrimage" to Yasukuni, the percentages are: before, 16.1%; after, 21.2%, an increase of 5.1%. For all data, "annual pilgrimage" to Yasukuni, percentages are rather low: before, 1.5%, after, 3.3%, an increase of 1.8%. As with Ise, gender comparisons for Yasukuni demonstrate that males record greater decrease for "no pilgrimage," and greater increase for "occasional pilgrimage" and "annual pilgrimage." And as with Ise, it is likely that these higher percentages for males may have to do with males' greater access to leisure and travel. Although Ise Shrine and Yasukuni Shrine are comparable traditional institutions with national stature, the percentages of Gedatsu-kai respondents indicate that Ise is much more important. The percentages for "no pilgrimage" before joining are very close: 40.1% for Ise, 42.8% for Yasukuni. However, "no pilgrimage" after joining declines by almost a half to 22.3% for Ise, but declines only to 35.6% for Yasukuni. The percentages and increases for both "occasional pilgrimage" and "annual pilgrimage" are considerably higher for Ise compared to Yasukuni.

It is not possible to explain this difference simply from these questionnaire results, but two hypotheses are worth exploring. One simple fact is that in Gedatsu-kai, Ise is part of the annual Three Holy Sites Pilgrimage, and many Gedatsu-kai members participate in this pilgrimage through the convenience of large chartered buses. A second factor that may help explain Gedatsu-kai members' preference for Ise over Yasukuni is the same factor that apparently makes "picture of the imperial household" less important than home practices such as kamidana and butsudan, and local practices such as tutelary Shinto shrine and Buddhist parish temple. This factor—apparently—is the preference of Gedatsu-kai members for home and local observances, and ancient tradition, rather than the relatively recent (post-Meiji) themes of loyalty to emperor and support of Yasukuni Shrine as a national monument for war dead. While the emperor has always been an important symbol of Japanese national identity, people seem not to be inclined to continue the exaggerated form of loyalty to the emperor that was used by the government to support modernization from Meiji times, and to support militarism from the 1930s through 1945. Similarly, the degree of support for Yasukuni Shrine that grew in Meiji times and crested in World War II seems to have fallen off.[34]

Some general comments on religious change are now in order. This section began with the question, What are the religious changes after joining? Two general theses were offered as providing clues to answering this question: either traditional people join the traditional new religions and stay traditional, or nontraditional people join traditional new religions and become traditional. The results of this questionnaire provide the basis for limited but more precise response to the question of religious change. The first thing that becomes clear is that there is not necessarily a contradiction between the two theses. The truth seems to be that both theses are partly correct, although the situation is more complicated than just either/or or both/and. The "no practice" items before and after show that a significant percentage of people who join Gedatsu-kai do not observe traditional practices before joining, but begin to observe these traditional practices after joining. This supports the second thesis of change from nontraditional practice to traditional practice. The results for "practice" and "occasional practice" show that a larger percentage of people joining Gedatsu-kai (as large or larger a percentage than the population as a whole) already observe traditional practices; however, it is not the case that they simply continue traditional practices at the same frequency—they increase in frequency. And the results for "regular practice" indicate that even the small percentage of Gedatsu-kai members who practice daily (at kamidana and butsudan) or annually (at Ise and Yasukuni) increases considerably. Therefore, it would be more appropriate to modify the first thesis (which holds that joining a new religion is a continuation of traditional practice) to the notion that joining a new religion is likely to increase frequencies for traditional religious practices.

More specific comparisons and contrasts can be made for the relative increases and decreases in practice (and no practice) after joining. For "picture of the imperial household," relatively few members have a picture, with only slight decrease for "no picture" and only slight increase for "have picture." For both "worship at kamidana" and "worship at butsudan," members report rather low "no practice" before, which decreases significantly, and rather high "practice," which increases significantly. For both "visits to tutelary Shinto shrine" and "visits to Buddhist parish temple," a similar pattern prevails: rather low "no practice" before, which decreases significantly, and rather high "practice," which increases significantly. "Occasional" and "daily" practice increase significantly at tutelary Shinto shrine, while "occasional practice" at Buddhist parish temple increases significantly and "daily practice" increases slightly. Pilgrimage to Ise Shrine and Yasukuni Shrine record percentages and increases more similar to those for "picture of the imperial household"; decrease of "no practice," and increase of "practice" and "annual practice," are greater for Ise Shrine. By gender, males show greater decrease of "no practice," and greater increase of "practice," except for pilgrimage to Ise Shrine and Yasukuni Shrine. Males show greater increase for "occasional practice," females for "daily practice." Older members tend to "practice" more than younger members, and those who joined just before and during World War II tend to "practice" more.

The results of this nationwide survey, together with material in previous and following chapters, enable us to reassess various aspects of new religions: in the last chapter of this work, it will be necessary to reconsider both religious change and the nature of religious tradition in contemporary Japan.

5

BRANCH MEETINGS
The Grassroots Basis and Social Activities of Gedatsu-kai

To this point, most of the material about Gedatsu-kai has concerned the life of individuals: the biography of the founder, the life histories of a number of members, and the statistics for the nationwide survey—the combined figures of individual responses provided by thousands of members. This may give the false impression that Gedatsu-kai is mainly a religion focusing on isolated or loosely related individuals, and the gathering together of separate religious aspirations. Quite the reverse is true: Gedatsu-kai is highly social in character, as the previous chapters indirectly demonstrate. If Okano Eizō had not attracted a substantial following, he would not have come to be viewed as a "founder." If these followers had not developed a momentum of their own, they would not have generated the kind of intense life histories already discussed. If this movement had not formed its own permanent structure and continuing ethos, it would not have reflected the clear pattern of renewal of "traditional" practices evidenced in the survey.

The social character of Gedatsu-kai is also demonstrated in the means by which the above material was made available to the author. The chapter on the life of the founder is based on a Japanese-language publication by Gedatsu-kai headquarters, codifying the oral tradition handed down by the movement's members. Just as the Gospels of Christianity were transmitted and later written down by the early church that formed around the person and teachings of Christ, so this biography is Gedatsu-kai's collective memory of its founder, handed down by the early followers and later codified by the established movement. The branch meeting in Gedatsu-kai corresponds to the "church" in early Christianity: the branch meeting in its earliest form as "meeting place" (shūkaijo) was the initial setting for attracting and uniting followers in direct personal contact with the founder; today the branch (shibu) continues as the major means of attracting members and transmitting the beliefs and practices of the founder. The warmth of branch meetings is the context in which life histories were first told to fellow members, and later retold to the author. In this chapter we will look at the nature of the branch meeting, which enables people to resolve their problems and speak so openly, providing the grassroots basis for Gedatsu-kai. First we will describe and interpret the dynamics of collective activities in four branch meetings, and then we will give the life history of one branch leader.

A Branch Meeting in Suburban Tokyo:
"I" Branch

Many current members of Gedatsu-kai had their first formal contact with this movement when they attended a branch meeting with the person who recruited them; and their most important continuing contact with Gedatsu-kai is through regular branch meetings at the local level. Aspects of branch meetings were mentioned indirectly in the life histories, but some general features may be repeated here to provide a firsthand description.

A "member" of Gedatsu-kai is a person who belongs to one of the 368 branches (shibu) or a smaller unit called zadankai (literally "discussion group"). It takes at least thirty families or households to form a discussion group and at least fifty families or households to establish a branch. A branch is headed by a branch leader (shibuchō). Unless the member has moved since joining, this is the branch he or she originally joined and continues to visit. The lay character of Gedatsu-kai is borne out by the fact that there are no professional "clergy": these branch leaders have no special "seminary" training, hold ordinary jobs (or are housewives), and serve as volunteer lay leaders. Most of the meeting places are in homes or businesses owned by branch leaders, although some branches have used locally gathered funds (without headquarters support) to build and maintain special buildings as meeting places. Every branch sets its own monthly schedule of meetings, with some variation in their kinds and numbers; at least several meetings take place every month, and since the late 1950s and 1960s, when branch organization was systematized, the liturgical order is rather uniform.

We focus here on the Kanshabi, the Thanks Day meeting, the most important monthly branch meeting, and reserve mention of other branch meetings for chapter 7, which treats various aspects of Gedatsu-kai ritual life. To cover the range of different branches, permission was sought and gained from Gedatsu-kai headquarters to visit branches in diverse settings: the four selected for fuller description here are located in metropolitan Tokyo, suburban Tokyo, a seaside city, and an inland (farming or "mountain") village. By observing geographically diverse branches, we are able to discover both the common features of branch meetings and some distinctive aspects of local branches. Part of Gedatsu-kai's strength as a national movement is its ability to appeal to metropolitan Tokyoites as well as to rural villagers. Observations of four branches are given before proceeding to analysis and interpretation. The following description is of "I" Branch in suburban Tokyo.[1]

The "I" Branch is in an eastern suburb of Tokyo, about an hour's distance by train from central Tokyo. This branch was visited October 14, 1979, and then again on October 23, when the interview with Mr. Nakajimo took place. The life history of the branch leader of "I" Branch, Mr. Yanagida, throws interesting light on this branch as well as other aspects of Gedatsu-kai; it will be recorded and discussed after the interpretation of the four branch meetings. Some features o the branch leader's life are previewed here because they came up naturally in the course of the visit, which is described here from observations and notes.

"I" Branch is located a short walk from a Japan National Railway station in the old family home of Mr. Yanagida. Mr. Yanagida tried various businesses before turning to a specialty shop featuring hand-made buckwheat noodles (*soba*) served in rooms of the old residence. On October 14 at about noon, we were invited into one of these rooms, where Mr. Yanagida proudly served his delicacies (including *sobazushi*) while he talked about his life and the "I" Branch of which he is leader. He received his faith almost unconsciously from his mother, who had been in Gedatsu-kai from the very beginning. His mother had experienced major problems with his father, who had affair after affair with many women, but she followed the teaching of Gedatsu-kai and did not get a divorce. Instead she frequently performed the practice of apology (*owabi-gyō*) at a nearby tutelary shrine (ujigami) at 5:30 A.M. This was the faith that led Mr. Yanagida into Gedatsu-kai.

Mr. Yanagida talked freely about many aspects of the "I" Branch, which was founded twenty-four years ago and includes over fifty households.[2] He was able to compare and contrast religion in Japan and the United States, because he lived in Los Angeles for two years and was active in Gedatsu-kai work there. He emphasized the importance of the Ise Shrine and Kashiwara Shrine to the Japanese tradition. He was proud that in the recent Fall Grand Festival held at the Sacred Land in Kitamotojuku (in Saitama Prefecture), his branch was well represented by sixty-five people. Most left their suburban city as a group at 7:30 A.M. and after the Grand Festival returned from the Sacred Land at 2:00 P.M. Some went by train; it was a vacation day from school, so many children attended. Also there were many "Mr. and Mrs. couples"—it used to be only the Mrs. who went, but this is changing.

After an enjoyable, relaxed meal, we went to Mr. Yanagida's residence next door for the branch meeting, which was scheduled to start at 1:30. The meeting place is on the second floor of the building next to Mr. Yanagida's soba business; this floor is large enough to serve as living quarters for his family. The actual meeting place is two six-mat rooms, with a smaller four-and-a-half-mat room on the side. (In Japan, rooms are measured by the number of straw mats—*tatami*—on the floor; a tatami is about three feet by six feet. As in most Japanese homes, shoes are left at the entryway, and people walk about the home in stockings; the soft tatami makes comfortable and convenient seating without special furniture.)

At the front of the main room is an altar the width of the room which features the three main Gedatsu-kai objects of worship: in the center is Tenjin Chigi (the "gods of heaven and earth"), on the right is Gedatsu Kongō (the founder), and on the left is Gochi Nyorai (a Buddhist term for "the *tathāgatas* of the five wisdoms" [*Japanese-English Buddhist Dictionary* 1965:78]). In front of the altar at the right side is a wooden bucket for the amacha memorial rite with a five-sided wooden pillar in the center of it; this bucket contains amacha and a dipper for pouring it over the pillar. To the right of the amacha bucket are a number of memorial tablets. This is the standard pattern for all branch meeting places and all practice halls (*dōjō*).[3] The three main objects of worship are recessed from the room slightly, and in front are wooden tables serving as altars for offerings: mandarin oranges (*mikan*), squash, and packages in fancy wrapping.

From our vantage point in the side room, we were able to see both the activities

2. "I" Branch altar

at the altar and the members. As members entered, they talked freely and happily. Some came to the altar and put money on it, bowed, clapped their hands four times, turned and bowed to the amacha bucket and pillar, knelt and poured amacha over the pillar a number of times, turned and bowed to the group, and then took their place with the other members who were seated and talking happily. Some paid respects to the altar and took a seat without pouring amacha. Generally dress and demeanor were very informal, but Mr. Yanagida was called respectfully *shibuchō sensei*. (*Shibuchō* is "branch leader" or "head," and *sensei* is a term of respect for teachers and doctors, which in this case is close to "honorable" or "reverend." *Shibuchō sensei* translates roughly as "reverend branch leader.")

Just after one-thirty, the branch leader said, "Well, it is time," and began the meeting. He lit candles on the altar, bowed, rearranged some items on the altar, and used a flint and stone to strike sparks over the altar three times,[4] and then once over the group. Next the official liturgy (referred to by the generic term *gongyō*) was recited, including the short version of the Buddhist scripture *Hannya Shingyō*. While the *Hannya Shingyō* was recited, amacha was poured over the pillar standing in the middle of the wooden bucket. Then Mr. Yanagida led the group in recitation of 108 "Namu Gedatsu Kongō." (*Namu*, from the Sanskrit *namas*, is the same "I place my faith in" as in the *nembutsu*, or Namu Amida Butsu of Pure Land Buddhism, and the *daimoku*, or Namu Myōhō Renge Kyō of Nichiren Buddhism. Here Namu Gedatsu Kongō means roughly, "I place my faith in Gedatsu Kongō" as the founder of Gedatsu-kai and continuing source of power.) At this point the printed gongyō was put back on the altar, and Mr. Yanagida played a tape recording of the founder's summary of his teaching—from the foundational Grand Festival, May 8, 1934; all sat quietly and listened to it. Then the formal liturgy was closed with a prayer for "the generations of ancestors of every member's household" (*kaiin kakuke senzo daidai*).

This was the essential formal part of the meeting, requiring only about fifteen minutes, after which Mr. Yanagida talked rather informally. He introduced me and the other members of the research team, and I then explained briefly the nature of our research and our wish to listen individually to members' taiken. The branch leader added a story from his experiences in America (Los Angeles). He was in America on Memorial Day, and when he went to a cemetery, he saw a gravestone with his own family name on it. He was praying, reciting the *Hannya Shingyō*: he was surprised to find his ancestor's grave there. It is karma (en). There is no such thing as not having connection of karma. In fact, there must be some connection of karma with Earhart, too.

Next the branch leader had a young woman speak for a few minutes. She had just been to the Fall Grand Festival, and she related a kind of informal taiken. She was married several years ago. Every morning and evening she gives thanks to the kami. The great thing about the Grand Festival is that it was in the middle of nature. From the time she was married, she has received many blessings. She is originally from Nakano Ward in Tokyo. She had trouble with a child, and she went to the Gedatsu-kai branch (shibu). She was told that she has a paradise but doesn't know it. We must be thankful and work hard, and we can do anything. She thanked everyone and sat down.

It was a little past two, and a short break was announced. During the break Mr. Yanagida said that this day was an "independent thanks festival" (*jishu kan-shasai*)—independent because it was run entirely by the branch. Ordinarily a lecturer from the Tokyo headquarters would come, but because everyone had been busy with the Fall Grand Festival, a lecturer could not attend.[5] During the break some smoked, and talking was lively and friendly. Some opened their purses and made offerings at the altar. A male student and a young girl in their school uniforms also made offerings.

The branch leader called an end to the break after about ten minutes, and began talking generally about Gedatsu-kai and the members' experiences as preparation for our research team to hear individual taiken. It was an informal, impromptu talk covering a number of topics, which can be summarized as follows. He began by talking about karma (en), encouraging them to think of it "for Earhart." There are lots of cases of karma—and thanks, too. He said that they might have wanted to quit Gedatsu-kai—this is fine to tell Earhart; they don't just have to say good things—they can include even wanting to quit. This is the religion of liberation (*shūkyō gedatsu*). They should tell their stories in order to spread Gedatsu-kai. The founder (Gedatsu Kongō) will understand. A human being is not just a thing— a human being has a heart, spirit, and culture. Everyone has his or her own aspirations, but in our daily life we must practice religion every day. If today one has an economic problem, one should look for the cause. Ninety percent of people have misfortune. Why are there such problems? We live between heaven and earth [i.e., in an imperfect world].

The branch leader continued his talk, which began to take on the character of a brief sermon. The founder told us to give thanks to society. The ancestors and the spirit world come into our life. There is no religion separate from life. We should practice the amacha memorial rite, and also the mediation rite of gohō shugyō. Amacha is not just for April 8 (the traditional celebration of the Buddha's birthday, when amacha is poured over a statue of the infant Buddha); it should be offered to the ancestors, who will be happy and rejoice. When you pour amacha for the ancestors, you cleanse your own flesh, your own heart. "From our heart"— this is the meaning of "the meeting for thanks and repayment of gratitude" (Hōon Kansha-kai).[6] This is religion in life. This is what the founder taught and practiced for a long time. There are only two months left of this year. Look back over the year. Be thankful for 1979. And whatever problems you have—problems with children—express your thanks to the ancestors (as a way of solving the problems).

The branch leader ended this combination talk and sermonette and led the group in the formal closing of the meeting from the printed gongyō (liturgy) with prayers to Gochi Nyorai, Gedatsu Kongō, the generations of ancestors (senzo daidai), and other spirits. At the end of the meeting, Mr. Yanagida mentioned that one woman (who wore a kimono) was visiting from another branch. He told them to help themselves to the mandarin oranges that had been offered on the altar (in a nicely wrapped package) and to take the remaining oranges home. This ended the formal meeting, after which some people formed a semicircle to tell their taiken to us. At the end of the meeting there were in attendance six men, twelve women, two young people, and three children.

The branch leader spoke briefly about their branch meetings, held on the second Tuesday of every month (as on October 14, 1979); the twenty-third of the month is their meeting for gohō shugyō, and the sixth is for ancestors (senzo). After this short explanation, individuals talked for a few minutes about their own taiken.

The first woman, originally from Hokkaido, had been introduced to Gedatsu-kai by her aunt there. She had been loosely affiliated with her Buddhist parish temple and tutelary Shinto shrine before entering Gedatsu-kai, but subsequently became much more active. Another woman spoke very briefly about her taiken. Before joining Gedatsu-kai, she went to the tutelary Shinto shrine only at New Year's. Since joining, she has visited the tutelary Shinto shrine often. Her mother died in March 1979, and August 1979 was the first festival of the dead (bon) for her mother. Since joining Gedatsu-kai she has visited the tutelary Shinto shrine (ujigami) every day, and has visited the Buddhist parish temple (bodaiji) every day off.[7] Her bodaiji is a Nichiren temple.

The next man was Mr. Nakajimo, whose lengthy taiken is recorded in chapter 3. The shorter version he related in this branch meeting is a good example of how a taiken can be tailored to a few minutes or a few hours, but it presents no new information, and need not be repeated here.

The next person was jokingly referred to by the branch leader as "fresh" to the group. He had come to see what Gedatsu-kai was like. From the time he was a young boy, he had passed a Shinto (Sumiyoshi) shrine every day, and heard Shinto prayers (norito), wedding ceremonies, and the like—and is grateful for having heard them. In fact, he thought about becoming a Shinto priest. Later he attended a Buddhist youth group. He learned the Buddhist sutra Hannya Shingyō. For a while he attended a Christian Sunday School. From the ninth grade he went to a special school, and he entered a study group for Christianity, but he was not baptized. He went to hear Christ's teaching, and didn't like some of it. Hypocrisy in the prayer bothered him. During World War II there was Shinto—but this was a false faith. So he looked for a faith that was not false. His aunt was a fervent Nichiren believer, and said ardent prayers to Saint Nichiren morning and evening. She wouldn't serve food if you didn't first revere Nichiren. It was thanks (*okage*). She was strict but it helped after all. His wife was at this meeting with him. She joined Gedatsu-kai before he did. He had not yet experienced the gohō shugyō.[8]

Another young woman and a young man spoke very briefly about their limited experiences in Gedatsu-kai. She works part-time. He has not participated in the mediation ritual of gohō shugyō. Another woman told about the taiken of her dead sister, who had worried about the neurotic condition of her son. Her sister had had an abortion—no, it was actually a miscarriage. And the sister thought that because it was a miscarriage, not an abortion, that a simple memorial service (kuyō) would make it satisfactory for the miscarried fetus. But this was not correct. Her sister was taught this in the mediation ritual of gohō shugyō. In fact, the miscarried fetus wanted not only kuyō but to be worshipped as an ancestor (*hotoke*). So her sister did this, and then her son's neurotic condition improved so that he was able to work.

The above are most of the taiken told us on October 14, 1979, at "I" Branch. There was a relaxed and free atmosphere during the meeting and the telling of the taiken. Each person offered his or her testimony without hesitation or nervousness. Occasionally the branch leader would jokingly correct or amplify a point made too modestly, to the amusement of the person telling the taiken. When all had finished their accounts, the branch leader talked with them while our research team talked with an official of Gedatsu-kai headquarters. Eventually these members approached the altar one by one, bowed and clapped their hands, gave a final greeting to the branch leader, and left. One woman bowed to the amacha pillar and poured amacha over it before leaving. The time was about 3:40.

The branch leader took care of some details with the members, then joined our conversation with the headquarters official for another hour. An interview with this official will be included in the next chapter, but several points of this conversation are worth mentioning here. We began talking about the very friendly, relaxed atmosphere at the branch meeting, and the official said that there was a deliberate attempt to keep branches small, so that the leader and members would be close, like friends and relatives. If branches became too big, they would be like businesses. If the branch is small, then people feel free to visit the leader and consult about problems or sickness.

A lengthy discussion also arose about ujigami, which is so important in Gedatsu-kai, and yet has had quite different meanings in Japanese history. The official knew of the different historical nuances of ujigami. At one time this meant a kind of "clan" kami, for people related to one another. Another meaning can be all people born within the territory of a certain local shrine. It was obvious that these meanings did not apply to most Gedatsu-kai members; rather, Gedatsu-kai emphasizes the significance of ujigami as a protective kami for all people who live within a certain area (regardless of relation or place of birth). In other words, the ujigami is the local tutelary deity: through it people receive life, and thanks (kansha) should be expressed regularly to the ujigami at the local Shinto shrine close to a person's present residence.

A Branch Meeting in Inner Tokyo:
"Ok" Branch

On October 22, 1979, about a week after our first visit to the "I" Branch, we attended a branch meeting of the "Ok" Branch in inner Tokyo. Many features of the two meetings, especially the standardized liturgy, were quite similar, and need not be repeated here. One obvious difference was the setting—not only the inner-city context but the building itself. "I" Branch is within easy reach of central Tokyo, but is located in a suburb with a slower pace of life and no high-rise buildings. "Ok" Branch is located in a busy section of Tokyo in the midst of high-rise buildings. The atmosphere of the "I" Branch meeting site is of a pleasant, "homey" old Japanese building whose second story has been made over into a meeting place. The "Ok" Branch, by contrast, meets in a specially constructed room on the top floor of a new seven-story building. We might have passed by the impressive building if the wife of the branch leader had not waited in front and ushered us into the building and elevator.

When we got off the elevator at the seventh floor, we entered the apartment of Mr. Sakatori, the leader of "Ok" Branch. Mr. Sakatori had this building erected two years previously (1977) to house several of his businesses—selling noodles and vegetables—and a top-floor apartment with a special large room for branch meetings. By Japanese standards this is a very large room, twenty-four mats in size, not including the altar at one end. The altar is rather formal, with the unpainted wood and elegant style of construction found in many Shinto shrines. I asked Mr. Sakatori about the construction of the elaborate altar, and he said that it was built by a special shrine carpenter (*miya daiku*). The general layout of the meeting room is similar to that at "I" Branch but larger, rectangular in shape with the altar on a short side of the rectangle; the altar features the same three objects of worship and a container for amacha at the right side. In front of the altar were offerings of vegetables and money. In religious terms, the meeting room is very similar to that of "I" Branch, but the view of Shinjuku (a busy section of Tokyo) from the window reminds a person seated there that this is metropolitan Tokyo.

There were about forty people in attendance at the branch meeting; some of the men were introduced to me, mentioned by their trades—kimono store owner, taxi company owner, barber. The liturgy that opened the meeting was the same as for the "I" Branch, after which was a brief taiken by a man who talked mainly about his experiences at the recent Fall Grand Festival. He thanked the branch leader for his help in arranging their trip to the Sacred Land so that they could attend the festival. This man had had a memorial stone for his family erected recently, and he spoke about memorial services at the time of the equinox. He said that we don't always know the connection of karma, and that we are indebted to nature (*daishizen*).

After this taiken, the branch leader gave a forceful talk urging members to serious practice, to "real religion." He started his talk with a review of the recent Grand Festival, as had the branch leader Yanagida in his talk at the "I" Branch a week earlier. Mr. Sakatori went on to lay down a program for practicing religion. He said there are three things that go together: the first two are self-reflection (hansei) and repentance (zange), and the third is thanks (kansha) to spirits. These

3. Amacha bucket at altar of "Ok" Branch

three together make up true prayer. Just revering the kamidana (household Shinto shrine) is not religion. Just receiving something (like a kamidana) as a decoration is not religion. Genuine religion (hontō no shūkyō) is what the founder (Gedatsu Kongō) has taught; it is the religion that is living in each person's heart right now, in contemporary society. In other words, it is the living in each person's family, daily life, place of work—developed broadly in these areas, and bringing great happiness—this is genuine religion. Mr. Sakatori said he could not overemphasize that this is the difference between established religion (kisei shūkyō) and Gedatsu-kai, which is vitally active in present society. Gedatsu-kai is not a "praying for faith" (inori-shinkō), an "asking for faith" (ogami-shinkō).[9] Gedatsu-kai is a "praying heart" (inoru kokoro), an "asking heart" (ogamu kokoro), within daily life, family, society, one's mission in life—to bring about a great transformation. Mr. Sakatori continued this forceful, persuasive talk or sermon, advocating members to purify society and work for world peace. A person uses his or her own power, but also nature (daishizen) and the spirits of all things (banbutsu no rei).[10] For this reason he gives thanks to kami and ancestors, recognizing from the bottom of his heart the connection of karma.

After the branch leader's talk came taiken by three women. One of the women, Mrs. Norikawa, whose interesting story is recorded in full in chapter 3, gave a short and simple taiken centering around her recent participation in the Grand Festival at the Goreichi.

After these taiken, the ceremony ended, and I was asked to talk. The invitation was unexpected; it had been mentioned only when we entered the meeting room, and then was announced to the group at this point in the meeting. The branch leader told me that a "lecture" for as long as forty minutes would be fine—on American religion, Japanese religion, American society, whatever I wanted to talk about, because these people had not heard an American talk (in Japanese) before. I limited my "talk" to about fifteen minutes, explaining my simple rationale for studying Japanese religion, in order to help Americans better understand Japan, generally within the framework of the "study of religion" (shūkyōgaku) and understanding all religions mutually to promote world peace.

This summary of my talk is given in order to provide the context for the rather incisive questions directed to me. The members of "Ok" Branch wanted to know the nature of "American kami," and how people worship. Mrs. Norikawa (whose life history is given in chapter 3) was persistent in asking if it is true that Americans do not worship their ancestors, and if not, why. I explained (in connection with the earlier question about "American kami") that in a monotheistic religion such as Christianity, Americans direct worship to God in somewhat the same fashion as Japanese direct worship to ancestors. There were other difficult questions— whether Americans express thankfulness to animals, and a request for comparing sokushin jōbutsu (attaining enlightenment or Buddhahood in this body) with American religion. In spite of the serious nature of these questions, we quickly entered into a free and joking spirit, and we laughed easily together. The branch leader asked the final question about the good and bad points of American and Japanese youth. I did not know quite how to handle such a controversial question, and did not want to say anything bad about either country's youth. The branch leader was somewhat disappointed, and later told me privately that there was no need to worry about what I said, because in branch meetings there is both frankness and forgiveness.

After my talk and the question-answer session, we had tea, and the branch leader shared some of his ideas with me. He brought up the subject of education, because one of the women present was the wife of an official in the Tokyo school system. The branch leader said that he would like to see religion back in the public schools. We discussed the problem of the plurality of religions and the difficulty of choosing a particular religion to teach in schools. He recognized the plurality of religions in contemporary Japan and admitted that if religion were taught in schools, it could not be *one* specific religion, but he still felt that religious principles should inform people's lives.

It had been agreed beforehand that our research team could conduct brief interviews with members after the meeting. The branch leader served us a nice soba and tempura dinner before the interviews began. Several of the more interesting interviews are summarized here. In the informal discussion during tea earlier, and as we ate, the branch leader talked with pride about this branch, which was founded forty-seven years ago and is one of the oldest branches of Gedatsu-kai. When the meal was over, our research team first asked the branch leader to elaborate on his memories of the founder. Mr. Sakatori said that he knew the founder from prewar times, when he was in elementary school. The founder had been invited to their prewar home, which was very small, to help people solve their problems. The house was full; people were on the stairway and outside. As a young boy, he was curious and wanted to have a look at this great man, so he climbed up on something, and saw the gentle face of the old man. When the founder looked at him, he slipped and fell. Mr. Sakatori's first impression of the founder remains today—even after much learning and practice, he still remembers him as a gentle person. The founder taught that "all are equal, there is no discrimination." "Revere the kami and honor the ancestors, repayment of gratitude and thanks" (*keishin sūso, hōon kansha*) is the backbone of his teaching. This gentle feeling—this is his main teaching. The founder liked tobacco, and when the branch leader was small, he gave the founder some. He left it on his desk, and then later when he saw him, he wondered if the founder was smoking his cigarettes.

After Mr. Sakatori's reminiscences, other members of "Ok" Branch gave brief taiken relating their indebtedness to the teaching and practices of Gedatsu-kai for helping them resolve their problems. A young man and a woman each gave similar praise for Mr. Sakatori as a good branch leader and sensei (teacher or master) who saw their problems before they did.

One young man was eager to tell his taiken; he was intense, and had asked the most direct and difficult questions of me after my talk, especially about comparing enlightenment in Buddhism and American religion. This young man had entered six years ago. He was "saved" by Gedatsu-kai, and chose it for that reason. It was not a matter of the *study* of religion, it was not *scholarship*.[11] Rather, it was a matter of *higi sanpō* (literally, the "mysterious three methods," which we translate here as the "three mysteries"),[12] that power. If you don't experience it yourself, you can't interpret it. The three mysteries, the amacha memorial rite, the purification (kiyome)—these are important. There are many new religions (shinkō shūkyō), but even if you enter them, it is not like Gedatsu-kai where things bear fruit, and it is "right" (*tadashii*). We must realize (*satoru*) our duty (*yakume*). It is hard practice (*tsurai shugyō*). But this makes the person right (tadashii).[13] He is grateful to the generations of ancestors (senzo daidai). He went on to tell about a medical diagnosis and X-ray that was unable to cure his sickness, because it was a problem with an ancestor's grave.

Most of the people who related taiken at "Ok" Branch, as at other branches, spoke of their own experiences, how Gedatsu-kai had helped solve their individual problems. But some people join because of what Gedatsu-kai has done for other members of their family. One man talked about what it had done for his father, who liked *sake* (rice wine) and drank it almost all the time, even during the day. For a half-year his father came to the practice hall of Gedatsu-kai; he would give up drinking from time to time, but then he would go back to sake. However, after he practiced purification (kiyome), he really gave up sake. First he venerated (the Buddhist divinity) Benten, and he went to the Itsukushima Shrine. At that point he gave up sake for a week or so. Finally he gave it up altogether. This is what the young man is thankful for, why he entered Gedatsu-kai.

A number of other people gave taiken about how they happened to enter Gedatsu-kai; some admitted that they were still new to the movement and did not understand it fully, but it had improved their work and quieted their spirit. These people said their understanding has increased gradually. Several admired the founder, although they never knew him personally; others focused on the serious practice and effective counseling of the branch leader.

After each member had related a taiken, the discussion became more free-ranging. There was general consensus that people join Gedatsu-kai in connection with problems of business, family, and concern for the area around one's home.

There was also agreement that the movement's rituals are powerful. For example, if a person would go to a regular temple (*otera*) and asked for a "ten-thousand-fold memorial rite" (manbu kuyō), it would be too much to ask for. But Gedatsu-kai has the amacha memorial rite that anyone can practice, and other effective practices. The younger, intense man answered a question about what was holy at the Sacred Land (Goreichi): it is gohō shugyō that is holy—not the place.

We had been discussing the unclear notion of the shrine of ujigami (tutelary Shinto shrine), and one member said that before entering Gedatsu-kai she had a protective talisman from Ise Shrine in her kamidana, but after entering she put in Tenjin Chigi and Gochi Nyorai. This comment and other members' statements seemed to indicate that their individual kamidana in their respective homes had become more uniform after their joining by the common enshrining of Tenjin Chigi and Gochi Nyorai; however, their Buddhist family altars (butsudan) and Buddhist parish temples remained different (because each family honored mainly its own ancestors). However, when I asked specifically if there was one ujigami for "Ok" Branch, the branch leader was a little impatient in explaining that the ujigami is different for each person. Even paying visits to shrines (omairi) is individual, "between the kami and the person." It has partly to do with the individual's karma, the faith transmitted from ancestors. Several members confirmed that they had learned through the mediation ritual of gohō shugyō the connection of their ancestors with specific shrines, which they then renewed.

There was strong emphasis on the freedom and initiative of individuals in their religious practice, even if they wished to participate in a new religion other than Gedatsu-kai. The same is true for "emperor worship"—which is up to the individual. I asked if this evening of a "circle" of taiken was something prompted by our research request, or if they often had such a "circle." The branch leader said that although they are formal for the liturgy (gongyō) and sit erect, later they drink tea and sit in a relaxed fashion with their legs crossed and have a good time. Mr. Sakatori insisted again that at such times they are frank, and if members confess their wrongs, it is all taken in stride, with no hard feelings.

We asked specifically about the Yasukuni Shrine, a memorial for war dead, which is a delicate political issue in contemporary Japan. The branch leader said that this, too, depends on the individual. When religious groups go to Yasukuni, then Gedatsu-kai sends a representative. But they do not tell their membership to go. He explained that since the spirits at Yasukuni are their forebears, naturally many Gedatsu-kai members may want to go there. The same is true for children, who naturally, gradually grow into the religion—but parents do not force the issue. When asked about the importance of various Gedatsu-kai events, the assistant branch leader said that the Spring and Fall Grand Festivals are the most important. There were 150 members from "Ok" Branch in attendance at the Fall Grand Festival; 10 will go to Nensai, the founder's memorial in Kyoto. Some members go to the Practice Hall in Tokyo for the services on the first and fifteenth of the month. The members said that when people enter Gedatsu-kai, there is a progression of religious practice from the amacha memorial rite to the purification (kiyome) and on to the mediation ritual of gohō shugyō. They explained that kiyome is a general purification (*jōka*) preceding gohō shugyō, but it is unreasonable to push members to practice gohō shugyō too soon, just after a person joins.

The members also talked freely and without hesitation about health consultation (kenkō sodan) and recruiting (michibiki) when we asked for information. They said that some causes of sickness are medical and can be cured by medicine. Kenkō sōdan in Gedatsu-kai deals only with those sicknesses that medicine cannot cure. For example, there is interference by spirits (*rei no sawari*). People become sick because of spirits, and then they need to attend to the spirit in order to get well. One particular sensei in Gedatsu-kai's health consultation, although he is not a medical doctor, still is very effective in curing people (of spiritually caused sickness). This has to do mainly with religious discipline (shugyō) and spiritual (*reikanteki*) matters, but health consultation also involves nutrition and health foods (*shizen shokuhin*). On the matter of recruiting (michibiki), they said that there are too many tales to recount. Many people enter Gedatsu-kai from Risshō Kōsei-kai. Usually the procedure for michibiki is to invite a new person to some branch celebration. It is unreasonable to encourage the person to perform gohō shugyō immediately. The branch leader chimed in that he did not believe in gohō shugyō until he practiced it himself. We left "Ok" Branch at seven-thirty after spending all afternoon observing the liturgy, listening to taiken, and discussing beliefs and practices.

A Branch Meeting in a Seaport City:
"C" Branch

When planning our study, we had the excellent cooperation of Gedatsu-kai officials, who understood our intention of getting a representative view of branches. We wanted to observe not only branches in metropolitan and suburban Tokyo, but also branches as diverse as possible within easy travel time of Tokyo. In the past, Japanese scholars have distinguished between "fishing villages" (*gyoson*) and "farming villages" (*nōson*), and in our discussions Gedatsu-kai officials not only accepted this distinction, but also suggested a branch in a "fishing village" and a branch in a "farming village," both within several hours of Tokyo. In this section the branch in the "fishing village" or seaport city is described; in the next section the branch in the "farming village" is described.

"C" Branch is located in a seaport city on the Pacific Ocean about two hours from Tokyo Station in Tokyo by fast train. It is more than a mere "fishing village," with a population of about 100,000 and another 50,000 just north of the city, but still the ocean dominates the landscape and the atmosphere of the city. We traveled to this seaport city November 12, 1979, with two Gedatsu-kai executives from the Tokyo headquarters, Mr. Kondō and Mr. Inakage, who were scheduled to speak at this regular monthly meeting of "C" Branch. We were met at the train station by the branch leader, Mr. Matsuura. He took us by taxi to two prominent shrines which served as ujigami in this city, where small offerings of money were made and respects were paid by bowing heads and clapping hands. The second of the two shrines was more impressive, on a hilltop with a hundred steps leading to it, and several rusty anchors in the shrine compound. All this took only a few minutes, with the taxi waiting, and from there we drove along the harbor, with many fishing boats on the left and numerous fresh fish markets on the right. We went to a recreation area by a lighthouse and had a nice lunch of seafood before driving to the "C" Branch for the Thanks Day (Kanshabi) ceremony at two.

While driving around the city, and especially during lunch, we had plenty of time to discuss the rapid growth of "C" Branch. Mr. Kondō had previously told us about a remarkable man who was "recruited" (michibikareta) by a Gedatsu magazine. This is an exceptional occurrence; people usually enter Gedatsu-kai through a personal contact. However, Mr. Matsuura was led into Gedatsu-kai rather accidentally when he visited a large Shinto shrine near his Tokyo apartment, and also close to the Tokyo headquarters of the movement. Often Gedatsu-kai distributes its magazines to such shrines, and Mr. Matsuura picked one up and became so interested in the teaching that he visited the movement's nearby head-quarters and eventually joined. But there was no branch in his hometown—the seaport city—and so he attended another branch. Later he started the "C" Branch, which formally opened on January 1, 1978, with 60 households, and at the time of our conversation on November 12, 1979, had 308 households.

I told Mr. Matsuura that this must be a remarkable growth, to which he humbly replied that there are still many defects in his efforts. But Mr. Kondō said I was correct, that this is a remarkable increase in membership in a short time. I asked them how they accounted for this growth, and Mr. Matsuura said there were many factors, but they had been helped a great deal by the central headquarters. And both the branch leader and Mr. Kondō said that in this area the "big catch" (tairyō) faith was strong, and this had some influence (both positive and negative, as is mentioned shortly). They did some recruiting (michibiki) by visiting houses, spreading the teaching of the founder. They agreed that (traditional) "faith" is strong here, but it is "asking for" (onegai) faith. By contrast, Gedatsu-kai holds that it is our own discipline (shugyō) that leads to benefits in this world. The founder taught that you yourself must practice. The people in this city don't even know of the existence of kami and Buddhas (hotoke). Generally the contrast the two men were making is between those who just ask for things mechanically, and those who are sincere.

Mr. Kondō spelled it out: the people who have "asking" faith want to "take" from the sea. But Gedatsu-kai teaches people to [humbly] "receive" (itadaku) from the sea. I asked if there is a harbor festival (minato matsuri) here, because most seaports do have such a festival. They said that yes, it is August 5, although it used to be according to the old (lunar) calendar on the fifteenth day of the sixth month. I asked if the branch participates in the harbor festival, and the branch leader said that they do not take part as a branch, although some members par-ticipate as individuals. I learned later that Mr. Matsuura, a forceful and energetic person, is a banker in the seaport city, an influential board member of the local bank. His wife, the assistant branch leader, is also quite energetic and outgoing. Part of the local lore is that the women in this seaport city are much stronger, because of the fishing economy and the necessity for women to "protect" the home while the men are fishing. The branch leader's wife, who has a successful cosmetics business of her own, is viewed in this light as a strong woman: she draws many people into Gedatsu-kai through her business contacts.

The "C" Branch had been recommended to us by Gedatsu-kai officials not only because it is in a seaport city and close to Tokyo, but also because it is a rather recent branch that has experienced remarkable growth. Some features of its meet-ing are similar enough to those of the previous two meetings not to be repeated here, but it was obvious from the moment we arrived that its meeting place was quite different from the previous two. In contrast to the "I" Branch, which meets in a remodeled area of an old home, and the "Ok" Branch, which meets in a specially built room in a Tokyo high-rise building, the "C" Branch meets in a new structure, about the size of an average Japanese home but constructed specifically for branch meetings. There is a nice new ujigami shrine to the right of the building itself; the ujigami shrine is like a miniature Shinto shrine, about eight feet high, with a ledge on which offerings of vegetables had been placed. This style ujigami shrine is found in front or at the side of all major Gedatsu-kai buildings such as practice halls (dōjō). Respects were paid at this ujigami shrine before entering the building.

The inside of the branch building is like a Japanese home, but consists mainly of one large rectagular room with the altar on the long side. (The other branches visited have the altar on the short side of the rectangle.) On the street side of the building is a small reception room, on the back side is a small kitchen, and a hallway opposite the altar provides a passage so that a person can go from the front to the back of the building without entering the main room. There was a carpet over the straw mats (tatami), so they could not be counted, but the main room seemed to be as large as or larger than the room used for the "Ok" Branch in the high-rise building. The altar at "C" Branch dominates the room more than in the previous branches visited, not only because it occupies the long side of the room, but also because it is constructed in a more elaborate fashion. There is a small Shinto-style shrine about three feet high for Tenjin Chigi in the center of the altar—like a large kamidana; and there are small Buddhist-style "shrines" (*zushi*) about a foot high on each side of the Tenjin Chigi shrine, one for Gochi Nyorai and one for the founder (Gedatsu Kongō). The general pattern of the altar is the same as for the other two branches visited, but the "C" Branch altar is more impressive, and looks more like a professional meeting place. A lectern at the left adds to this "professional" appearance. As at other branches, to the right of the main altar are the amacha receptacle and pillar.

Our lunch at the seaside made us a little late for the 2:00 meeting, but the leader assured us that we would not miss anything, because they would start with okiyome (or kiyome, purification). When we entered, there were more than forty women and four men in attendance, with ten or more in four rows facing the altar. The man leading the ceremony was the adopted son of the branch leader; he was a high school teacher who had visited the United States to study English. The branch leader's wife, the assistant branch leader, was helping a number of people, showing them how to hold the gohihō booklet during the kiyome ceremony. As the Gedatsu-kai executives and the branch leader had told us, and as was obvious from the hesitant actions and puzzled expressions of some of the participants, this was a new branch with many new members who were not yet completely familiar with Gedatsu-kai ceremonies. After the kiyome ceremony, there was the official liturgy (gongyō); most participants had not memorized it, so the small liturgy pamphlets were distributed. During the gongyō, some chanted with their eyes closed, fully familiar with the liturgy; some read from the printed pamphlet, and some sat silently as passive observers. There were minor differences, such as the assistant branch leader using a large drum to beat a cadence, but the liturgy was standard.

There were a half-dozen new people at the meeting who were asked to stand,

and the group warmly greeted them. Later the special guests from the Tokyo headquarters were introduced. Regular features of the liturgy are not repeated here, but an interesting part of the long introduction to the tape recording of the founder's message (probably for the benefit of newcomers) was the explanation of the founder's significance, the praising of his life and work, and the claim that he will take care of problems (nayami) and suffering (kurushimi). The first taiken of the meeting was by a man about sixty years old who told how he and his wife had been "brought into" (michibikareta) Gedatsu-kai, how they had rediscovered (saiken) their faith, and how their various practices within the movement had brought them blessings—for which they were grateful to the founder, the branch leader, and their own ancestors.

Next Mr. Inakage, an executive from the Tokyo headquarters who was originally from this area, gave a talk. After introductory remarks praising the branch leader and local members, the executive entered into his talk explaining the significance of the Grand Festival (Taisai) and the recent Nensai (Death Anniversary) for the founder. He asked how many had participated in the previous Nensai, and only one person raised a hand. He explained the significance of this death anniversary honoring the founder and his work of initiating Gedatsu-kai; he went on to elaborate the meaning of the large memorial tower for the founder (in Kyoto next to the Buddhist temple Sennyūji), where many souls are enshrined. He said that at the recent Nensai when people visited Sennyūji, many were crying. And after the formal memorial rites for the founder at the Buddhist temple, the people actually entered the memorial tower for the founder and came directly in contact with the sacred itself (i.e., the power of the founder).

In Gedatsu-kai, people practice gohō shugyō and worship the spirits of ancestors. There is no point in having people make religious visits (omairi) unless they venerate their ancestors. The memorial tablets (ihai) for ancestors are like souls (tamashii). People think they have not done anything wrong, but later in gohō shugyō they discover the wrong. All have done wrong. People must correct this wrong. It is not just a matter of ritual as formality (matsurigoto). Benefit in this world comes from proper relation to the spirit world. The executive documented this principle by summarizing a member's statement in that month's Gedatsu-kai magazine. On the blackboard he diagrammed the relationship between this world and the spirit world, and elaborated this notion through the standard Buddhist concept of six levels of hell.[14] He went on to show how, through Gedatsu-kai practices, one can purify oneself, correct wrongs, and remove imperfection—just as a person passes through the six levels of hell and achieves realization. This executive was a powerful speaker, and held the attention of his audience. A woman directly in front of me who was distracted during the liturgy was alert and attentive listening to him.

The branch leader followed up on the executive's talk by emphasizing that they have received the "karma" of the founder, and for this they are fortunate. He referred to this executive who had come all the way from Tokyo to talk to them and explain the teachings of Gedatsu-kai. Usually headquarters people come to a branch once every four months, but they have been coming to "C" Branch more frequently (and for this the members should be thankful). The teaching of Gedatsu-kai is not that easy—in fact, it is difficult. It is not just ordinary matters. There will always be blessings (shiawase) (for which they should be thankful). All of the people present that day have become better because they received the "karma" of the founder.

When the branch leader concluded his talk, the end of the formal meeting was near, and he introduced me. I spoke briefly for a few minutes formally greeting them, mentioning the nature of our study, and asking their cooperation with interviews and with the survey questionnaire that would be distributed. After my brief remarks, several new people were introduced individually, all participated in a song, and there was an announcement of the forthcoming celebration of the founder's birthday. The meeting ended, and we had a "circle" interview situation, as in the previous branch meetings. The brief taiken recorded that day are very interesting, and in fact we arranged to come back and record taiken at greater length on December 27, 1979. Because several of these testimonies have been included in chapter 3—those of Mrs. Koshikawa, Mrs. Kawakami, and Mrs. Miyauji—they are not repeated here.

A Branch Meeting in a Farming Village: "K" Branch

From the beginning of our research, we planned to visit a branch in a "farming village," and after consulting with Gedatsu-kai headquarters, we scheduled a trip to a branch about two and a half hours northwest of Tokyo by express train. This particular branch was recommended by the Tokyo headquarters because it was in an old farming area, and its faith was typical of a "farming village," in contrast to the "fishing village" heritage of "C" Branch. (Because of its location in a mountain area, this "farming village" can be called a "mountain village.") In recent times it has become a resort area within easy reach of Tokyo. It was agreed that we would visit "K" Branch on December 11, 1979, when several Gedatsu-kai officials, including the present head (*hossu*) of the movement, planned to visit. Although we could have traveled to and from this branch in one day, the branch leader, who is the owner of a Japanese inn (*ryokan*), encouraged us to attend the late-afternoon banquet and stay overnight at the inn, which we did. We left Ueno Station in Tokyo about 9:30 that morning and arrived in the mountains about noon. This long train trip provided an excellent opportunity to learn more about the organizational structure of branches, divisions (*kyōku*), and central headquarters from Mr. Kondō, a Gedatsu-kai official from the Tokyo headquarters, but this discussion will be treated later. Our party, which included the present hossu of Gedatsu-kai, was greeted at the train station as a light snow fell.

We went by taxi directly to the location of the branch meeting place, an inn above the train station in the foothills of the mountains. The inn was built on a hillside, with many levels, including a large hot-spring bath on a lower level. It is surrounded by gorgeous mountain scenery, and is part of a local resort catering to Tokyoites who want to escape the city. As soon as we arrived, we went to the large room used for branch meetings, where formal respects were paid before the altar. Then people were taken to their individual rooms, and lunch was served in a common dining room.

After lunch and before the formal branch meeting, there was a special dedication ceremony for a Batō Kannon[15] stone at the home of the second son of the inn owner and branch leader. The party went by taxi down into the valley near the train station to the home where this stone had been erected. As we were told by Gedatsu-kai officials before our visit to "K" Branch, and as many told us during the visit, belief in Batō Kannon is especially strong in this area, where until recently horses and oxen were the mainstay of transportation. Batō Kannon is considered the protective deity (shugojin) of "K" Branch. The ceremony itself was quite simple. The branch leader put on a Buddhist surplice (kesa) before he lit candles and incense. The tables serving as altar held an abundance of offerings: carrots, pineapple, sake, canned fruit juice, oranges, and red snapper. Behind the altar was the polished stone commemorating Batō Kannon and describing the particular merits of this Buddhist divinity. A number of local people were waiting, standing in the cold, with the snow still falling lightly, when the service began. There was a brief version of Gedatsu-kai's liturgy, with special mention of Batō Kannon. Afterward everyone lined up and offered three pinches of incense before the stone. The ceremony, including the trip from the inn and back, took only a half-hour.

When we arrived at the inn, people were gathering in the special room for the branch meeting. This rectangular room, with the altar on the short side, was quite similar to the rooms for the "I" Branch and "Ok" Branch. The altar was filled with more offerings, possibly because of the hossu's presence: there were carrots, turnips, cabbage, mushrooms, eggs, boiled rice with red beans, apples, oranges, pineapple, amacha, and sake. There was also a large stack of offerings in envelopes, and decorations of flowers and evergreens. As the people filed in, there were almost as many men as women—before the ceremony started there were twenty-three men and thirty women; most of the men were in suits, and some of the women wore kimono. The liturgy was the same as for other branch meetings. After the introductory part of the liturgy, Mr. Kondō introduced me and explained our research team's wish to interview them. He went on to emphasize that this was the last Thanks Day (Kanshabi) of the year; Batō Kannon was praised, and he encouraged them to study (religion) hard next year.

The assistant branch leader gave highlights of his twenty years' practice of Gedatsu-kai—he had had doubts at first, but finally set up an altar in his home and practiced there. Now he has his family practice morning and night before the altar. He even has had them perform apology (owabi) at the tutelary Shinto shrine (ujigami). He joked with the audience—only too familiar with the partying that goes on in resort inns—that his children performed the hundredfold repentance (ohyakudo) before the ujigami, all the while listening to the merriment of the nearby hot springs and the musical instruments (shamisen). He was grateful for this Thanks Day, and reminded them that next year was the hundredth anniversary of the birth of the founder, and they should study hard next year.

The branch leader, who had worn a Buddhist surplice (kesa) for the dedication of the Batō Kannon stone, did not have it on for the branch meeting. His perfunctory greeting repeated many of the comments of the previous speaker; in talking about the dedication of Batō Kannon, he said that many people other than Gedatsu-kai members visit the stone, but that is fine. He, too, emphasized the significance of the next year as the hundredth anniversary of the founder's birth, and urged the members to work hard, especially in recruiting (michibiki).

Apparently the other talks were kept short so that the hossu would have time to talk. He began by commenting on nature (daishizen), and how surprising the

4. Dedication of Batō Kannon Stone near "K" Branch

5. Altar at "K" Branch during branch meeting

6. Close-up of metal containers for ancestral tablets at "K" Branch

snow was to him when he got off the train; he compared the snow to ritual purification in water (*misogi*). He led into a discussion of the power of Batō Kannon, saying that the vow of Batō Kannon to help them is related to their own experience (taiken). But the ultimate source is the gohō shugyō initiated by the founder. And there should be thanks to the Okano family. Batō Kannon is so powerful that Gedatsu-kai even erected a Batō Kannon monument in America: this is related to the power of Dainichi Nyorai (the so-called Sun Buddha). If you are devout in your prayers, Batō Kannon will protect you. You cannot see it with your eyes, but you receive this protection. The hossu continued his talk, touching on the universal meaning of the Gedatsu-kai liturgy, which is for the nation as a whole. He said that karma (en), too, is universal. And members should pray for ancestors. Other (Japanese) religious groups don't do this. Gedatsu-kai even includes the American people—that is the reason the people are gathered today. Gedatsu-kai wants to have the world practice this—it is not just a local matter.

After the hossu's talk, there was a short break. By this time there were thirty-two men and thirty woman present. Following the break there was a talk by the division head (*kyōkuchō*). He began by quoting the founder at length, then talked about his own six years as division head—first for the prefectures of Nagano and Yamanashi, and later Gunma, too. He invoked the Gedatsu-kai principle of keishin sūso, emphasizing that everyone venerates kami and reveres ancestors: we can do this easily. But this is hard to work out, even for a man and wife, who must cooperate and be thankful. We offer oranges (mikan) to the ancestors and Gochi Nyorai. But don't quarrel about *what* to offer. For example, if the husband brings home oranges for the altar offering, and the wife says, "But I wanted apples"— this is bad. She should say instead, "Oh, thanks for the trouble of going out in the cold." The husband should say, "Well, if you wanted apples, I'll get apples tomorrow." The moral is that in daily life do what you can, and be thankful for what you are able to do and what others do for you.

The division head emphasized the long span of human history, and how the founder said that it takes three generations to correct a past mistake. This is all the more reason that members should be grateful for every day and reflect on life. And when members practice gohō shugyō and learn of former generations of ancestors who are suffering, and the members are told to perform apologies— again the people should be thankful. If members are not thankful when they carry out practices, it is all false. If people carry out apologies mechanically and offer oranges and apples without sincerity, nothing will help. What is important is the phenomenon causing the problem. That is why thanks cannot be put off for the next day—thanks must be offered every day, from the heart.

After the division head's talk and the closing ceremony of the liturgy, the group went to a large hall on the lower level of the inn, where there was a large reception: the owner's son told me later that there had been more than eighty guests in attendance. The reception was laid out on small individual tables for each guest, who sat on the straw matting. We sat with the hossu and other officials, some of whom left early to catch a train back to Tokyo. We stayed and talked with members, although the large reception was not conducive to the kind of "circle" interview we had conducted at other branches. A number of people spoke of their experiences with Batō Kannon. A woman said that in gohō shugyō she learned about an ancestor from four generations ago who was suffering in hell (as a beast or *chikushō*), but praying to Batō Kannon had saved him from suffering. She was also cured of neurosis when she was "brought into" (michibikareta) Gedatsu-kai. The branch leader, too, talked about the spiritual problems in the area around his son's home where the Batō Kannon stone was dedicated. Through gohō shugyō it was revealed that there was a connection of karma with Batō Kannon. I asked about this connection of karma, which the branch leader had difficulty answering, saying that it probably had to do with his grandfather and ancestors using horses to transport things. This is the protective divinity (shugojin) for the area. But Batō Kannon is not venerated in homes—people go to the ujigami or to the Batō Kannon stone to pray. Another man who raises pigs told of his experience with Batō Kannon, who helped heal a sick pig. From this time his faith in Batō Kannon was strong, and he always goes to Batō Kannon, to tell Kannon about the blessing he receives in gohō shugyō, and to give thanks.

In this free-ranging discussion, I asked about specific practices, such as the hundredfold repentance (ohyakudo), because in a recent visit to a branch in Kyoto, we had been told that the Kyoto branch practices ohyakudo monthly at the memorial monument for the founder. This surprised the members, who said that their practice has become "modernized," and few people at "K" Branch perform the hundredfold repentance. They said they do go to the local ujigami, which has the same name as that of the branch (the "K" Shrine). I asked the name of the kami enshrined there (*shintai*), and after some discussion they agreed it was Suwa Daimyōjin. I commented that this is the same as for the ujigami at the Tokyo Practice Hall, which again surprised them: they were familiar with local practices but did not relate them to national patterns of Gedatsu-kai practice.

The evening was spent leisurely over a nice meal with the owners of the inn, and we talked over many aspects of their family, the inn, and Gedatsu-kai. The next morning I took a walk and found the "K" Shrine only about five minutes away. It is a modest old shrine, with the small compound carved out of a hillside; the shrine has an old thatch roof with some plants growing out of it. There was no activity there, but there were two stones honoring Batō Kannon and one honoring Dōsojin.[16]

The Religious Universe of Branch Meetings:
Formal Liturgy, Leaders' Guidance, Members' Personal
Experience and Informal Interaction

Four branch meetings in diverse geographical settings have been described as carefully and quickly as possible without much interpretation, in order to provide the reader with a firsthand view of the dynamics of these meetings. The settings vary from suburban and metropolitan Tokyo to a seaport city and a mountain village; our research team also observed branch meetings in residential areas of Kyoto and Tokyo. The four branches described offer a representative overview of branch life, making it unnecessary to describe in detail the other two branches.

Just as there is a common pattern to the values and experiences in the life histories of chapter 3 that is interpreted as "the religious universe" of Gedatsu-kai members, so there is a general world view presupposed and acted out in branch meetings that can be described as the religious universe of branch meetings. This religious universe can be interpreted in terms of the shared religious values that constitute it, as well as the activities that express and maintain it. In chapter 3 we saw that the religious universe of Gedatsu-kai members can be interpreted through the statement that "the power of nature, kami, Buddhas, and ancestors resolves human problems and suffering." To a large extent, branch meetings are the extension of the personal experience of members, and this statement about the religious universe of members applies equally to the religious universe of branch meetings. This is not to imply that the members' personal experience precedes the social experience of the branch meeting; in fact, the opposite is more accurate, because the branch meeting is the most important single means of initiating newcomers into Gedatsu-kai and "socializing" their individual behavior into a group pattern.

The central religious values of branch meetings are clearly symbolized in the major objects of worship: the three divinities of the altar—Tenjin Chigi, Gochi Nyorai, and Gedatsu Kongō—and the ancestors. A standard feature of every branch is this style of altar, with minor variations that do not contradict the basic religious pattern. Tenjin Chigi is the power of kami, Gochi Nyorai represents the power of Buddhism, Gedatsu Kongō symbolizes the power of the founder, and the ancestors (in the amacha container) stand for the individual families' ancestors and the spirits of ancestors generally. These objects of worship are the source of religious power by which members alleviate their particular problems and resolve their questions about the meaning of their lives, and the meaning of life generally. The rationale for this diffusion of power from the objects of power to the members is expressed directly in the taiken by individual members, the exhortations or sermonettes by branch leaders, and the talks by headquarters representatives. Individual members "testify" that their individual problems have been resolved;

branch leaders praise the founder and Gedatsu-kai teaching as able to handle members' suffering and problems; headquarters representatives give special advice on particular problems and specific explanation and recommendation of Gedatsu-kai techniques and celebrations. The basic premise of this universe is that people owe their lives and existence generally to the beneficence of kami, Buddhas, ancestors, and founder, and should be grateful and give thanks to them; human problems arise when people break a tie of faith, are ungrateful to kami and Buddhas, or neglect ancestors. This calls for repentance and apology, and rituals to correct impurity on the part of the individual (and impurity on the part of the ancestor)—to restore harmony between human beings and the sacred objects of worship. When this harmony is regained, people are grateful and happy, realizing the preciousness of life and harmonizing with family and society. The way to maintain this harmony is to participate in Gedatsu-kai worship in regular home devotions and in branch participation.

Equally important as this set of shared religious values is the set of social practices that express and maintain them. One of the reasons Gedatsu-kai has been relatively successful in transmitting and maintaining the founder's teaching is that it has institutionalized a balance of formal and informal means for communicating and reinforcing such values. The liturgy itself is rather simple, with its invocation of the power of the objects of worship, and reverence directed toward them, but includes other features that strengthen the bond between members. The recitation of the Buddhist scripture *Hannya Shingyō* is a kind of collective repentance, and the amacha memorial rite simultaneously links individual families with their own ancestors, and all members vaguely with spirits of ancestors generally. As several headquarters representatives indicated in their talks, the liturgy is for the nation as a whole; in fact, as the hossu claimed, it is for the entire world. The formal liturgy is effective for bringing people together and holding them together in terms of a rather simple practice that appeals to many Japanese people. A number of people indicated in their taiken that they "liked" the amacha memorial ritual as soon as they participated in it. And those who were not immediately drawn to the ritual were attracted to the teachings and explanation of human problems.

The formal liturgy itself allows for guidance of individual members, especially by the branch leader, but also by the assistant branch leader and occasionally by representatives from Gedatsu-kai headquarters. This complements the formal liturgy with timely and relevant comments that bring the day's liturgy in tune with current events of the world and Gedatsu-kai. In each branch meeting there was a kind of rehash of the immediate past Gedatsu-kai affair, such as the Fall Grand Festival, which some members had attended. In other words, a branch meeting enables the members to "remember" and reinterpret their past experience in a unified fashion. These talks also relate Gedatsu-kai belief and practice to current events: mundane concerns such as juvenile delinquency and divorce, or wider issues such as world peace. The branch meeting looks to the future, urging the members to "study hard next year," as at "K" Branch's December Thanks Day; and members are reminded of the next year as the hundredth anniversary of the birth of the founder. Coming events are announced and previewed, with encouragement of participation.

These more formal aspects of the liturgy itself and guidance by Gedatsu-kai representatives are balanced by informal contact among the membership. Informal contact begins even before the meeting, as people enter the meeting place and exchange greetings. A break about halfway through the meeting affords some relaxation and relief from the formal liturgy, which again encourages friendly chatting among members. The personal taiken are crucial to the life of the meetings, providing a purely lay contribution: this demonstrates that every person has problems and suffering, and that these problems and suffering can be resolved through Gedatsu-kai beliefs and practices. Some of the lengthy taiken quoted in chapter 3 are rather dramatic, and it is not likely that every person has undergone such radical change. In fact, as the brief taiken quoted from branch meetings indicate, some people, such as Mrs. Norikawa, who have had very dramatic experiences may speak in a branch meeting more about thanks for being able to participate in the recent Grand Festival than about a life-changing experience. The strength of the taiken, seen from a social perspective, is its ability to show every member, vicariously, what it means to live according to Gedatsu-kai's values, and how one can act and react in specific human situations.

This informal interaction, especially after the meeting, is a very important time for "letting down" and having heart-to-heart talks with fellow members in a friendly atmosphere. The members were encouraged to tell the researchers anything, even negative things or their doubts about Gedatsu-kai; and, as the branch leader of "Ok" Branch assured me, after meetings they have frank discussions, and even if a person admits to some wrong, everyone forgives that person. Some new religions have structured their meetings around such counseling sessions; for example, Risshō Kōsei-kai has specialized in such meetings, which they call hōza.[17] Gedatsu-kai does not formalize a counseling activity in branch meetings, but prefers to let the counseling occur as a natural process of this friendly branch atmosphere. Some members with a particularly difficult problem may come to the branch leader for advice, or people may talk things over as the subject arises in discussion with other members after a meeting. (It is also possible to receive help from special departments at the Sacred Land, such as Health Consultation and Spiritual Training.)

To this point we have emphasized the common religious universe of beliefs and practices and the common social activities found in all branches. However, there are also different features in these branches, not the least of which is the geographical diversity mentioned previously. It is part of Gedatsu-kai's strength that it is able to appeal to Tokyoites as well as villagers: there is considerable local flavor in each branch, both in individual practice and in branch practice. For example, Mr. Nakajimo of "I" Branch comes from Hokkaido, but his ancestors hail from Fukui Prefecture, and he now is retired in suburban Tokyo. One minor feature of his story is that he reestablished a connection of faith with Batō Kannon, because he found that his father had worshipped this deity in Hokkaido. This is a minor part of his story, an after-effect of the major religious change surrounding his reestablishment of ties with his ancestors in Fukui. But it fits into his personal story and is appreciated as a part of his participation in "I" Branch even though this branch has no particular affinity to Batō Kannon. By contrast, in "K" Branch, Batō Kannon is a central feature of local faith and appears prominently in many taiken; and the branch has a visiting Gedatsu-kai official dedicate a special Batō Kannon stone. Gedatsu-kai shows a remarkable flexibility in allowing each member and individual branch to relate to specific objects of faith and particular local ujigami, while at the same time linking them to a national tradition (and a claim to universal truth, as seen in its prayers for America, and the presence of Batō Kannon in America).

There are other variations on the local scene not limited to religious matters. The first three meetings described were dominated by women, which probably can be explained by their urban locations, men being at work during the day, and women being freer to attend. The fourth meeting, at "K" Branch, actually had more males in attendance by the end of the meeting, which probably can be explained by the more agricultural location and the time of year—there was no agricultural work, and it was the slack season for tourists at local resorts. Gedatsu-kai branch meetings are suitable for either type of group—predominantly females or a mixed group. (As in Japanese society generally, males tend to dominate positions of control—more males are branch leaders, and they tend to be more in the limelight of branch meetings—but the informal role of women in recruiting members is more significant.) A branch meeting is able to handle both the new-comer and the seasoned member. At the "Ok" Branch, one of the oldest of all branches, with many long-term members, printed liturgy books were not nec-essary, and there was strong participation by the group; at the very young "C" Branch, with many recent members and "first-timers," printed liturgies were much in evidence, and participation varied from disinterest to casual interest to enthusiasm. In general, the branch meeting of Gedatsu-kai is comparable to the church of early Christianity: it is the main means of bringing newcomers into the movement, and the main means for expressing and continuing this set of religious values.

The Life History of a Branch Leader: Mr. Yanagida of "I" Branch

In the description of branch meetings and in the interpretation of the religious universe of branch meetings, the central role of the branch leader is evident. Not only is he responsible for the administration of the branch (which will be taken up in the next chapter), but also he leads the branch as a group and counsels members individually. These leaders are lay volunteers, not only giving their time, but in most cases providing a meeting place and partial financial support for the branch. Some of these leaders met the founder when they were young and he was rather old; some knew him only by hearsay and tradition. These leaders are participating in the early stages of the development of Gedatsu-kai: as the na-tionwide survey has shown, most members are first-generation members. If the branch (shibu) can be compared to the church of early Christianity, the branch leaders (shibuchō) are something like the apostles of the early church—lay leaders who followed their own occupation while advancing the cause of religion.

A question that arose early in our research of Gedatsu-kai pertained to the kind of person who becomes a branch leader, and the personal experiences that shape this decision. Therefore, the plan for collecting life histories included provision for interviewing branch leaders. Some brief life stories have already appeared in the accounts of branch meetings: Mr. Matsuura, leader of "C" Branch, and Mr.

Sakatori of "Ok" Branch. The following is a more lengthy life history of Mr. Yanagida, leader of "I" Branch, as told on January 10, 1980.

By the time of interview with Mr. Yanagida, we knew each other very well. We had met accidentally at the Tokyo Practice Hall when our research team was making initial requests to study Gedatsu-kai, and he immediately had suggested a visit to his branch. He had spent two years in America, and is very friendly with Americans. We did visit his "I" Branch twice for lengthy observations, at which time he was very helpful in explaining matters and arranging cooperation for interviews with members. We also met accidentally at the Sacred Land in Kita-motojuku at the time of the Fall Grand Festival, and at the anniversary of the death of the founder in Kyoto. Each time we met, we struck up a friendly conversation. This made the atmosphere very casual for the interview, with some joking on each side.

When I called to arrange for the interview, which he had agreed to long before, he did not want me to make the lengthy trip to his suburban home, so we found a time when each of us had business at the Tokyo Practice Hall, and we met there for the interview. Mr. Yanagida was familiar with our research project and was quite interested and supportive of the work, so I did not need to explain the interview at length. I did indicate that my interview with him was a way of seeing Gedatsu-kai from the inside, from the viewpoint of a branch leader. And for this reason it would be helpful to hear his experiences (*keiken*) in entering the movement and becoming a branch leader. Earlier he had given a brief version of his family's, especially his mother's, involvement in Gedatsu-kai, and I joked that if there was a michibikikata (recruiting person) for him, surely it must be his mother.

Having spent two years in the United States, Mr. Yanagida is quite conscious of cultural differences between America and Japan, and he began by saying that his experience was very "Japanese" (*nihonteki*). By "Japanese" he meant that becoming a branch leader is not a matter of just study (implying by contrast the seminary experience of Christian ministers and priests). Nor was it a case that he *had* to be a part of Gedatsu-kai, and carry on as a branch leader. Of course, his mother had been in Gedatsu-kai for some forty years. But he corrected my wrong impression that he had experienced a steady and continuous involvement in Gedatsu-kai. In fact he had gone to a Christian school, and even had been baptized. But he entered Gedatsu-kai through his mother's faith—that is, her actual practice of religion, not just "asking for" (*ogande*) prayers. His mother did not want just to pass on to him a big fortune of money. Rather, she tried hard to help him, and to bring him up properly. He apologized for raising again the delicate subject of his father, who had had many affairs and had even left home. His mother, however, did not divorce her husband, even though others strongly urged her to. Her reason came from the notion of "cause and effect" (which Mr. Yanagida quoted in English): if she had divorced her husband, then her children, too, might be "caused" to divorce their spouses. So instead, she tried as hard as she could to have her son study (religion). (And he implied that, by not divorcing his father, she had tried to make her life a model for him, and to help him develop proper values.)

Mr. Yanagida started to talk about his early experience in Christianity, but jumped ahead to 1964 (he remembers the year because it was the time of the Tokyo Olympics), when the head of the American Gedatsu-kai group wrote a letter to Mr. Yanagida asking him to come to America and help with the group. He was going to go alone, but ended up going to Los Angeles with his wife for two years in 1965. His reason for going was that he believed the founder's teaching was for everyone—no matter what race or nationality.

Mr. Yanagida jumped ahead in his story to 1964 apparently to show the extent of his own conviction—he was not mechanically following the lead of his mother. Then he returned to the theme of his entry into Gedatsu-kai, which was a "natural matter"; it was solely because of his mother, who did not divorce his father. This made a great impression on him. At the same time, his mother was very devout, and had deep faith that the kami will always answer you. And sure enough, his father returned after seventeen years. I asked when this was, and he said it was about twenty years ago—about 1960.

Mr. Yanagida told more about his personal circumstances. He had been in the auto repair business but had failed. So he owed money to his mother, and this was a strong connection to her. They went to the "N" Branch in Tokyo for advice and were told to sell some property and with the money to search for the father's girlfriend, so that the father would come home (and they would be a family again). This way they could have a family life. His father's absence was problematic, because in the "Japanese way of thinking" (*nihonteki kangaekata*), if parents have a bitter relationship, it will affect the children. It has to do with "jealousy" (mentioned in English). And Mr. Yanagida was saved by his mother's faith (and by correcting an improper family situation).

Because Mr. Yanagida had twice jumped ahead in his story, I asked him about his earliest experiences in Gedatsu-kai. He said that he went to the founder's place with his mother when he was in the second grade, because he had to wear glasses. They went to the founder to ask why Mr. Yanagida's eyes were bad. After all, his parents did not wear glasses, so why should the child's eyes be bad? The founder's response was that it was a matter of the "karma of sexual desire" (*shikijō innen*), which Mr. Yanagida phrased in English simply as "sex."[18] In other words, the father was bad—the child was not bad, but it was a matter for the parents to study. I asked Mr. Yanagida if "the founder's place" that he had visited was the building at Araki No. 6 that is mentioned in Gedatsu-kai publications as the prewar headquarters near Yotsuya in Tokyo, which later became incorporated into the large Tokyo Practice Hall, and he confirmed that this was the place.

When Mr. Yanagida was young, it was very distressing (*kurushii*) for him, because his health was bad. He caught cold easily, and even had trouble eating— he couldn't eat the usual boiled white rice that Japanese eat; he had to have the rice gruel that is cooked for sick people. Once he went to a Grand Festival with his mother, and she was going to give him rice gruel. But the sensei (teacher or reverend) said that it would be OK for him to eat regular boiled white rice. He did, and from that time he was able to eat it instead of rice gruel. He had even been eating rice gruel in his school lunchbox.

This reminded Mr. Yanagida of a similar experience that had happened to a person at the Grand Festival celebrated in Sacramento during the two years that he was in the United States. This person had a stomachache all night just before the Grand Festival. He went to the head of Gedatsu-kai in America, and was told that each individual must be thankful. That day he went to the Grand Festival, and his stomach was better. This person was a student at the University of California, Los Angeles. He is a second-generation Japanese (*nisei*); now he is in Japan, and he always goes to the Sacred Land in Saitama Prefecture.

Mr. Yanagida then responded to my question about his education. He graduated from Aoyama Gakuin (a four-year secondary institution in Tokyo founded by Protestant Christians). He laughed as he asked himself why he was baptized, and answered his own question by saying that he liked English from the time he was young. When World War II ended, there were many GIs in Japan. The Japanese wartime education allowed no English, because Japan was at war with England and America. But his junior high teacher had studied in England, so he taught the class English. The army was opposed to this, and apparently the teacher had difficulties continuing his English lessons. Mr. Yanagida thought it would be good to talk to GIs after the war. There was a church which had an English-language Bible study, and Mr. Yanagida went to this Bible study, and to Sunday worship services. He was baptized when he was in the third year of junior high. I asked him which church it was, if it was the Nihon Kirisuto Kyōdan (United Church of Christ in Japan), and he said no, it was an ordinary church for Americans. At the time Christianity was said to be good for the Japanese. He forgot which branch of (Protestant) Christianity it was. He had no real Christian faith. At Aoyama Gakuin, a course called "Outline of Christianity" was required of all students for general education.

Meanwhile, his mother was suffering. She was in Gedatsu-kai, and he had entered a Christian church. I asked him when he entered Gedatsu-kai, and he said it was during his second year of college, when he began studying the new religion on his own. He had attended Gedatsu-kai meetings much earlier with his mother, but he entered the movement while he was in the university. He became branch leader about twenty years ago. I asked him if there was any particular problem (*mondai*) he had at the time. He said no, there was no special problem. It had to do more with his "own view of life" (*jinseikan*). It had to do with his imperfection (*mikansei*) and his attempt to turn toward perfection (*kansei*). And he was looking for a "way" (*michi*). He studied Gedatsu-kai. This is the founder's teaching: a human being creates a lot of things—and this is what Christ and the Buddha teach, too, so this human creating is the same as for a kami. That is, a person is like a kami. We are allowed to live. We must work hard. The teaching that the founder left us is a blessing, and we must study it.

There was a Gedatsu-kai teacher, now dead, who taught him—this teacher was not at a branch, but at the Tokyo Practice Hall. The teacher advised him to perform the hundredfold repentance (ohyakudo), which he did at the Sacred Land and at his local ujigami shrine (which in his case is a Hachiman shrine). This was before he went to America; he participated in youth activities and studied hard. Because he had not talked about his childhood, I asked if he had been born in the Tokyo suburb where he now lives. He said he was born in Yamanashi Prefecture in 1933 and moved to suburban Tokyo in 1940. (This made Mr. Yanagida forty-six years old at the time of interview.)

I asked specifically about his religious activities when he was young, such as visiting the tutelary Shinto shrine (ujigami) and Buddhist parish temple (bodaiji); he said that he did not go often to these religious sites. He said that what is most important is the local territory (*tochi*) where one lives. "Where you are living is your ujigami." He continued, saying that big shrines (*oyashiro*) and formal visits (omairi) are *not* what is important. Rather, it is one's heart (*kokoro*) and "the attitude of revering the kami" (*keishin no kimochi*) that are important. He first went to the Hachiman shrine that is his ujigami shrine near the "I" Branch with his mother, but not until he entered the university did he go there on his own. He was baptized because he wanted to practice English—that is why he studied Christianity.

His experience in America was a good lesson for him, because he learned *through* the founder's teachings. The language, food, customs, and so on are different, but life is the same. This is something that you don't learn in a book. He had many experiences with Mexicans, and this was a good lesson. People in America always ask why, and he had to answer them before the conversation could continue. But it has to do with daily life. The founder's teaching, once actually practiced, gave all of them good results. Japanese people, if they study, will be healed. This is how Japanese practice. But Americans ask why. Then later they put this into actual practice. Japanese act more in terms of inner feeling (*haragei-teki*).

Mr. Yanagida recalled an interesting view of the Watts riots in 1965. He remembered that August 14, 1965,[19] was on a Saturday, because they were scheduled to have the Los Angeles Thanks Day celebration. The riots started on Thursday and continued through Saturday. There was a curfew, and no one came to the Thanks Day. So they had a small celebration in a grocery store run by a Japanese-American. All the other stores were burned, but not this one. "Brother" was written across the front of the store. I asked if mostly blacks lived in this area, and he said that 90% or more were black in the area. Blacks bought bread and other things at the store. The Japanese-American was performing memorial rites for these blacks. I asked if it was a special memorial rite for customers (a form of memorial practiced in Japan by Gedatsu-kai), and he replied affirmatively. He said that in this case the spirits of the customers' ancestors protected the store. That's why it was not burned down. The Chinese people's stores were all burned. Why was this? "Brother" was written on the Japanese-American's store, so it was not burned. (Mr. Yanagida also recalled vividly his ministry to "Mexicans" in Los Angeles, which is not recounted here.)

I asked Mr. Yanagida about gohō shugyō, partly because it is practiced regularly at his branch, and because it is also practiced in the United States. He first received gohō shugyō at the "N" Branch when he was in the university, but there was no important message (shirase). Then when the letter came from America asking him to help with Gedatsu-kai in America, he received gohō shugyō, and there was the message that it would be a good lesson for him to go to America. He received gohō shugyō while he was in America, and of course he receives it every month at his branch's regular monthly gohō shugyō practice. He became a "translator" (chūkaisha) for gohō shugyō about twenty years ago. This conversation led into a lengthy discussion of gohō shugyō, because Mr. Yanagida mentioned that his mother had practiced it many years ago, but there was a span of time when Gedatsu-kai stopped the practice. Mr. Yanagida could not remember the details of this aspect of Gedatsu-kai history, so he called in another executive, Mr. Akiyoshi, to help recall the dates and facts. After several requests for help from Mr. Akiyoshi, the interview of Mr. Yanagida's life history turned into a discussion of the history of gohō shugyō; this discussion will be included in the chapter on ritual. (Mr. Akiyoshi's life history will be given in the next chapter.)

Because of the lengthy exploration of gohō shugyō, not much time was left in our interview, so I asked Mr. Yanagida about the future—where did he think Gedatsu-kai and the branches (shibu) were headed? Without hesitation, he said that this is the young people's age. From their parents they learn Gedatsu-kai, then they experience it. But they need an outline. It must be theoretically stated. Gedatsu-kai must have a theory in the future. It is not enough for grandparents to say "do it," they must also know *why*. Young people must be able to *understand*. What the founder left as an oral tradition must be made into a system.[20] He said that Gedatsu-kai needed to publish more books, but they also must expand the work of branches. He said that Gedatsu-kai is not Christianity, but Gedatsu-kai must adopt a church system (*kyōkai seido*). The branch is individual—they use a family home. But this presents problems, for one thing, financial problems. They need to have not a family home, but a "church" (*kyōkai*). I asked specifically what he meant by kyōkai, and he answered that he meant a separate building. Gedatsu-kai needs "special ministers" (*senmon minisuta*).

This was a rare opportunity to talk informally with a branch leader and an executive about the future direction of Gedatsu-kai, so I asked them directly about the liabilities of the move to special buildings and a professional ministry. We had discussed several times frankly the warm, friendly, "family" atmosphere of branch meetings, and I asked if there was a danger of losing this atmosphere if the organization became larger. In fact, I quoted Mrs. Norikawa's reason for leaving Tenrikyō: it was too large and impersonal. And I asked them if they wanted to develop a "church" structure, what were the advantages?

Both Mr. Yanagida and Mr. Akiyoshi said that they didn't want to see the friendly family atmosphere of branch meetings change, but the present arrangement posed many problems. For example, homes often are too small for meetings. Also, another practical problem is that since it is a home, you can't really go at any time, with questions, and to study. For example, if a branch leader owns a fish market and is selling fish, he can't wash his hands and go to the "practice hall" in his home (used as a branch meeting place) to discuss a problem just any old time. So the main advantage would be that one could go at any time for consultation and study, not just at the time of the Thanks Day meeting, not just when it was convenient for the branch leader. Both claimed that they will not lose the feeling of friendliness. And they mentioned that many branch leaders are growing old. But, just as when there are many people living in a home, the older ones can't always interpret to the younger ones. Mr. Akiyoshi admitted that the family atmosphere is fine, but there are problems—economically the family may have to support the branch. And also for the branch leaders, there is the question of ability. And again, he said, people who are running a business can't stop and attend to religion. I asked about one branch we had attended in residential Tokyo, a very large branch with a new ferro-concrete building, which seemed to combine traditional faith with a new setting. However, he reminded me that this is one of the few branches that have registered legally as a "religious juridical person" (*shūkyō hōjin*), and this is an exception. At this point we had to close the interview, because Mr. Yanagida had invited us to an evening meal at a friend's restaurant. We spent the evening in more relaxed conversation; however, the matter of the future shape of branches and the organization of Gedatsu-kai is a subject that will come up both in the next chapter and in the concluding chapter.

In his rambling tale of life in Gedatsu-kai, which spans Japan and the United States, Mr. Yanagida gave no specific reason why he became a branch leader. He was more concerned with ruling out reasons that did not account for why and how he become a branch leader. He did *not* become a branch leader automatically (passed on as a heritage); he did *not* qualify as a leader as a result of book learning. Rather, it was his own experience within Gedatsu-kai, which was stimulated by the model of his mother but was developed through his own practice and deepening understanding. He credits not only his mother but also an influential teacher at the Tokyo Practice Hall with leading him into the religion. The early experience with the founder also made an impression, but it was mainly his questioning as a young man that made him "study" Gedatsu-kai more seriously, on his own. And eventually he became committed to the movement so much that he went with his wife to America, to spread the teaching to all people and all races.

This life history may help dispel some of the stereotypes of new religions and the people who enter them. It is often written that new religions are havens for the poorly educated and "alienated" people who use them to escape from a world with which they cannot cope. But Mr. Yanagida is a university graduate, a successful businessman, and has spent two years abroad. He has had some experience in another religion; he has studied the doctrinal outline of Christianity and is able to compare and contrast the two religions, even to the point of their ecclesiastical structures. Not all branch leaders share this personal profile, but this may help counter the stereotype of new religions as recruiting the dissatisfied, unsuccessful members of society. Mr. Yanagida, of course, shares the religious universe that has been sketched for other life histories in chapter 3, the same religious universe that pervades the branch meetings. And he is an effective personal agent for recruiting new members, for counseling current members, and for maintaining the life of the branch by leading regular meetings.

6

BRANCHES, DIVISIONS, AND HEADQUARTERS
How Gedatsu-kai Is Organized

We have looked at Gedatsu-kai from the individual and local level, from the viewpoint of the founder and members as well as branch meetings. But Gedatsu-kai, like any nationwide religious movement, cannot exist without an elaborate administrative system. In previous chapters this structure was treated only indirectly, as part of the religious experience of members and the religious activities of the movement. In this chapter we will look directly at the administrative structure from the perspective of the organizational arrangement that helps make possible religious life, which is our main focus.[1] In other words, our main question here is, How is Gedatsu-kai organized, such that individual members and individual experiences are unified and maintained on all levels from grassroots local branches to centralized national headquarters?

Branches, the grassroots support system of Gedatsu-kai, serve a dual purpose, linking individual members to each other and all members to the total institution: branches help recruit members into the movement and provide the cohesiveness and continuity of the tradition at the local level; at the same time, they link members and the local institution to the central headquarters and national tradition. The crucial character of branches is borne out in a Gedatsu-kai publication, *Shibuchō-kanji no kokoroe* (Guidelines for branch leaders and officers; Gedatsu-kai 1976), which contains instructions about proper organization of branches and proper conduct of branch meetings. The first sentence of this book highlights the pivotal significance of branches: "The salvation of human hearts and the improvement of social life which is the mission of this movement [Gedatsu-kai]—in the final analysis—if it is not centered in and implemented by branches—will not be achieved" (Gedatsu-kai 1976:1).[2]

The *Guidelines* explain Gedatsu-kai's organizational system to members by using an anatomical metaphor: a drawing of a man holding two barbells. The head of the man is labeled "headquarters" (*honbu*), the chest is labeled "division" (kyōku), and the two arms are "branches" (shibu). One barbell has written on it "salvation of human hearts," the other: "improvement of social life" (ibid., p. 15). This is a convenient illustration of Gedatsu-kai's general organizational structure (which of course is much more complex).

The organization of Gedatsu-kai is relatively simple when viewed in its general outline, sketched here in its recent (1979) form. The local strength and base of the movement is its branches, of which there were 368 in 1979. These branches are linked to the national headquarters by divisions (kyōku), which numbered thirty-two in 1979. A division has a number of branches under its supervision, but has no self-supporting activities or rituals. Divisions are supervised by the headquarters (honbu) in Tokyo. The headquarters is located at the original site from which the founder first guided the movement; it has since grown into a larger administrative center and practice hall.

Branches:
Grassroots Organization of Gedatsu-kai

Previous descriptions of branches have been limited to life histories of individual members and the services at branch meetings. The intensity of the individual experiences, the effective balance of formal liturgy and informal personal inter-action, and the strong character of the branch leaders were evident in these descriptions—but the organizational structure that facilitates these experiences, ceremonies, and leadership has not been so obvious. The actual extent and strength of the administrative organization of Gedatsu-kai, starting with the branch orga-nization, can be appreciated by comparing contemporary branches with the situa-tion at the time of the founder. When the founder first began to attract followers, a group would gather at one follower's home; gradually this home came to be considered a "meeting place" (shūkaijo), and from time to time meetings were held there, depending on when the founder could make an appearance. As was indicated in chapter 2, eventually there were so many followers that the founder could not counsel them individually, and there were so many meeting places that he could not personally conduct all the meetings. One event marking the transition from a rather loose and informal movement toward a more formal organization was the 1934 act of becoming an officially recognized religious group; this coincided with the considerable growth of the group. By 1934, when the movement had expanded to a membership of 850 and forty-one meeting places, most in the Tokyo area, the founder began training others to serve as leaders for the meeting places. But even then, he was directly involved in each meeting place, in the sense that he knew personally and appointed each branch leader. In fact, in the early stages of Gedatsu-kai's history, from its founding until about a decade after the founder's death, the movement was highly personalistic: just as the founder appointed local leaders personally, so each local meeting was run personally by this leader (Ge-datsu Shuppanbu 1979:220, 274).

As the movement gathered momentum, it was necessary to formalize the in-stitutional structure. In the early days, the first followers of Okano had a strong personal connection to him, but a weak connection to each other. The increasingly formal organization of Gedatsu-kai served to centralize authority around the found-er and a small headquarters staff, while specifying the relationship of this headquarters to individual members and the relationship of individual members to each other. In the initial stages of the movement, the main tie of members to one another was the michibiki or "recruiting" tie—people affiliated directly with those who had recruited them. By 1933 there was a sufficient number of members to organize them into five blocks, emphasizing the horizontal ties among followers on both the local and higher levels. In 1936 local meetings were called kaigōsho ("assembly places"), and in 1941 they were renamed "branches" (shibu). At the center of authority, in 1937 the founder appointed seven followers as advisors (shidōin); in 1940 he appointed sixteen additional followers as a second group of advisors. These acts helped strengthen the emerging headquarters and branch organization. However, to this day, in spite of the 'efficient centralized headquarters of Gedatsu-kai, there remains a high degree of independence and freedom of belief and practice at the branch level (Ishii 1983b:80–83).

During the early stages of the movement, it was possible to settle matters on a face-to-face basis, but eventually a number of factors brought about the inevitable tendency toward standardization, which led to the present pattern of relative uniformity in teaching and ritual. One factor was the increasing size of the movement, which made personal leadership by the founder more difficult, forcing him to delegate authority to local leaders. A second factor was the death of the founder, removing the charismatic figure who was at the center of the personalistic leadership, requiring replacement of personal authority with institutional authority. A third factor was the tendency for branch members to follow their branch leaders (especially after the death of the founder), and to be oriented around the branch leader rather than central headquarters or Gedatsu-kai as a unified movement: this threatened to fragment the movement. After the death of the founder, his first disciples held Gedatsu-kai together, attempting to be consistent to the principles of the founder, but apparently sensing that if the movement did not provide more uniform supervision and ceremonies, it was likely to fall part. In fact, it was not simply a matter of size that dictated uniformity: if the movement was to cohere and to grow, it had to establish a consistent teaching, ritual, and authority. The power of Okano's original inspiration and the wisdom of his selection of leaders and initial organization are borne out in the fact that the basic framework has not changed since his death, even though the movement experienced phenomenal growth.

As table 20 illustrates, the major growth of Gedatsu-kai occurred after the death of the founder in 1948, starting especially from about a decade after his death. From 1958 through 1964, a total of 128 new branches were started—more than a third of all branches that existed as of 1979. One of the keys to this dramatic expansion was the dynamic leadership of Kishida Eizan after the death of the founder. One of the earliest and most talented followers of the founder, Kishida used his publishing abilities to help Gedatsu-kai set up its first publications for branches. He was one of the "disciples" who helped guide the movement through the crisis of the founder's death; and he was largely responsible for the rapid increase in membership and branches. The branch of which Kishida was leader was the "parent branch" (oyashibu) of most of the new branches (called "child branch," koshibu) during the rapid expansion. Kishida helped bring about this expansion through his own efforts and also helped plan more uniform branch organization and greater centralized control over branches. Therefore, the kind

TABLE 20.
Increase of Branches (Shibu) by Years

Year	Branch increase	Total number of branches	Year	Branch increase	Total number of branches
1929		0	1955	3	149
1930	2	2	1956	4	153
1931	0	2	1957	5	158
1932	0	2	1958	18	176
1933	0	2	1959	12	188
1934	2	4	1960	10	198
1935	6	10	1961	11	209
1936	7	17	1962	11	220
1937	13	30	1963	49	269
1938	6	36	1964	17	286
1939	7	43	1965	2	288
1940	8	51	1966	3	291
1941	9	60	1967	1	292
1942	1	61	1968	6	298
1943	8	69	1969	3	301
1944	5	74	1970	6	307
1945	2	76	1971	2	309
1946	3	79	1972	8	317
1947	6	85	1973	9	326
1948	4	89	1974	6	332
1949	8	97	1975	3	335
1950	14	111	1976	5	340
1951	4	115	1977	7	347
1952	8	123	1978	11	358
1953	8	131	1979	3	361[3]
1954	15	146			

of standardized branch system that is described today, although based on the founder's notion of local meeting places with local leaders, actually dates back only to the late 1950s.

Guidelines for Branch Leaders and Officers

The extent to which branches have become standardized is the result of careful planning by all levels of Gedatsu-kai organization; this planning from the past decades has been codified in the publication "Guidelines for Branch Leaders and Officers" (*Shibuchō-kanji no kokoroe;* Gedatsu-kai 1976), which was cited above for its interpretation of the central role of the branch in ritual activities and administrative structure. This work sets forth the general rationale for the formation of branches in accordance with the founder's intentions, and provides a succinct definition of branches. "Branches are the study centers closest at hand for people to learn about the lay religion Gedatsu-kai's teaching; they are the institutions in most direct contact with people for the purpose of transmitting the spirit of the founder; they are, so to say, 'spiritual practice halls' [*seishin dōjō*] entrusted by the founder" (p. 11). The branch has the mission of being the place of direct "guidance" to cultivate and enlighten people.[4]

Much of the first half of the book continues to express the general rationale of the branch, and common-sense principles are advanced throughout for organizing and running branches. Great emphasis is placed upon the fact that the origin of Gedatsu-kai, even the individual branch, is with the founder, and persons such as branch leaders and officers should never put themselves ahead of the movement. For example, even if the branch "practice hall" (dōjō) is in a person's home, the person should not forget that this is not a personal matter, it is a mission entrusted by the founder to serve society. There is also caution that neither the branch nor the branch members "belong" to the branch leader. The explicit statement is that both branches and the headquarters serve the founder, but implicitly the authority of the headquarters is upheld.

Many of the guidelines to branch leaders and officers are common-sense advice applicable to any social group, and can be summarized very quickly. For example, the branch leaders should greet the members warmly, should not let family matters intrude on the branch, should not be too lofty (but should study alongside members), should be prompt in starting meetings, and should end them when expected. Generally the guidelines encourage a friendly atmosphere based on cooperation, without ostentation (such as overly elaborate meals—partly because they would require some members, especially females, to miss much of the ritual while preparing the meal). Some advice is more specific to new religions such as Gedatsu-kai: there should not be too much scolding of members, and it is better not to dwell on the chains of past karma, but to emphasize the development of good karma in the future (ibid., pp. 17–24, 46–55).

The latter part of the book gives advice on the organization and management of the branch that is much more relevant to the task of analyzing the administrative structure of branches. Basic principles emphasized are effective leadership, recognition of talented members, cultivation of able officers, and cooperation within the branch. It is emphasized that the leader cannot run the branch alone; even if the branch leader can guide members individually when they are few, as their numbers increase he or she must draw on the help of able officers to counsel members and expand the work of the branch. The guidelines predict that able officer prospects will appear "naturally," and it is up to the branch leader to recognize and cultivate members with "ability." In fact, a note of caution is added to this prediction, that as the branch gets larger, if spheres of responsibility among various officers are not well defined, friction will develop. The procedure for appointment of branch leaders is not mentioned in the book, but there is a warning in an early section that although a "second-generation" branch leader is appropriate when the person has a "heart of faith" and ability, if this is not the case, then the second-generation person should not take over. It is explicitly stated that branch leadership is *not* a hereditary system whereby the descendant of the former branch leader automatically becomes the next branch leader (ibid., pp. 21–23, 59–62).

The branch leader is nominated by the division (kyōku) and confirmed by headquarters in Tokyo, but intrabranch organization and appointment of officers are left to the local branch. The branch leader is encouraged to use this local autonomy wisely in appointing able persons in an appropriate number. Officers should be chosen keeping in mind a number of factors. One general rule is to select officers to represent the geographical districts in which members of the branch live; also, people should be selected by their respective abilities in areas such as planning, projects, propagation, education, administration, youth, and women. Persons should not be chosen simply because of their seniority in age or length of membership. Something to watch for is people who have abilities in recruiting (michibiki) and who actually recruit large numbers: these people are effective in being team leaders (*hanchō*) within the branch. However, the appropriate number is crucial, since having too few officers results in overwork, and having too many officers (just for the sake of organizational complexity) is unnecessary. There are a number of appropriate types of teams (*han*), for example, regional teams (within the branch), especially for the purpose of propagation. Another type is recruiting-lineage teams: appointing as officer a person who has recruited many members, and organizing under him team leaders whom that person has recruited, and organizing under the team leaders other group leaders (*kumichō*) recruited by the team leaders. Other ways of organizing teams are as discussion meetings, or by age or by sex. These suggestions cover a wide range of possibilities for even the largest branch, but there is again a note of caution not to proliferate organization such as teams and groups unreasonably. Actual practices are much more important than organization for the sake of organization. Team leaders must have some independence, but should not develop a "sect" consciousness—some competition between/among teams is fine so long as it is in the spirit of cooperation (ibid., pp. 62–70). Four examples of branch organization, from "the simplest form" to a "functional organization," are diagrammed and explained (ibid., pp. 71–72).

The published guidelines pay considerable attention to the formal structure of branch organization, and in fact "officers are the pillars of branch activity" (ibid., p. 74). However, much attention is also paid to informal aspects of branch organization, especially the key role of women in the life of branches. We have seen from the evidence of the nationwide survey that women are much more active than men as "recruiting persons" (michibikikata). The *Guidelines* approach this subject more indirectly, but still give much credit to women for their key roles in recruiting members and setting the "mood" of meetings. This indirect approach praises women as mothers and wives, even citing the founder's statement that a teenager's problems could be traced back to his or her incorrect upbringing since birth. This statement is not meant to reflect badly on the mother, but to show the special female role in giving birth and nurturing life. Even if both husband and wife work, the distinctive role of women is in the home. Women are more closely involved in daily life and have more opportunities for recruiting (michibiki), such as with neighbors, and "therefore we may say that the womb of recruiting is best suited to women" (ibid., p. 89).

This general appraisal of women as more suitable for recruiting is spelled out in specific recommendations for the role of women in branch life. Branches in which recruiting is centered in women are active and bustling: this sets the gentle, warm mood of a mother for the branch as a whole, and this distinctive character of women leads to great results in recruiting. This is one reason why the branch leader's wife is so important—even if she can't explain the teaching like her husband, it is important for her to be present. (The general assumption here, as in Japanese society generally, is that the branch leader, a position of authority, will be male. There are female branch leaders, but they are in the minority.) The explanation borrowed from the theory of the balance of *yin* and *yang* is that in case the branch leader is severe, his wife may balance him by being more mild. It is very important for the branch leader's wife to be at the women's meeting, especially because there are women's problems that only a woman can appreciate. However, in all cases, the branch leader's wife should not become too emotional and should not talk too much—it would be a mistake for her to disregard the branch leader. Above all, she must realize the great influence she has on the branch (ibid., pp. 86–92).[5]

Other aspects of the *Guidelines* are more general, such as the crucial role of second-generation members in the movement, because they are a barometer of its future. For this reason especially, branches should be aware of the generation gap between young and old, making some allowances for changing expressions of the essence of teaching in order to bridge the gap: a comparison is made with clothes and fashions; clothes remain essentially the same, while fashions change (ibid., pp. 108–109, 117–18). This work closes with a section on the significance of the Thanks Day celebration, urging sincerity rather than outward performance, and specifying that an officers' meeting always is held after the Thanks Day celebration, to reflect on their personal development and branch activities (ibid., pp. 146–55).

Divisions and Headquarters:
Intermediate and Central Organization
of Gedatsu-kai

The general plan of the organization of Gedatsu-kai has already been sketched: branches are the grassroots basis, divisions (kyōku) are the intermediate agencies, and headquarters (honbu) is the central administration. The nationwide system of divisions was established in 1958 (Ishii 1983b:82). The divisions are purely administrative, supervising branches but having no specific activities of their own. They serve to channel information from branches to central headquarters, for example, branch problems, and they make recommendations of new branch leaders to central headquarters; divisions also serve to channel information and directives from central headquarters to branches.[6] This sketch provides the structural outline of the overall organizational plan, but does not indicate the working relationship among the three aspects of the organization. For an interpretation of the inner workings of Gedatsu-kai administration, we turn to the explanation of Mr. Kondō, an executive of Gedatsu-kai.

While on the train trip to the "K" Branch on December 11, 1979, we had a great deal of time to talk, and Mr. Kondō obliged our interest in the history and structure of branches and Gedatsu-kai generally. This is the picture he painted. In the old days, the founder appointed branch leaders directly. At present the smallest branch is fifty families; it takes thirty families to be a "discussion group" (zadankai).[7] Nowadays the Tokyo central headquarters names new branch leaders. Mr. Kondō had traveled with us to "C" Branch and used it as an example. Mr. and Mrs. Matsuura, the present branch leader and assistant branch leader of "C"

Branch, had shown their ability and character by recruiting many families—so they became branch leaders on the division (kyōku) recommendation. There is a "parent branch" (oyashibu) and "child branch" (koshibu) connection between an old and a new branch. The application for a new branch goes to the division. If the Propagation Committee (Fukyōshingikai) of the central headquarters OKs the application, then it is confirmed. The official recognition is at the time of the Fall and Spring Grand Festivals. On the day before the Grand Festival, organizational representatives gather at the Sacred Land and decide many of these organizational matters.

The local branch offices are all decided within the branch by its own members. But this is not done by voting. Usually a person is asked to fill an office; that is, he or she is "entrusted" with the office. Matters such as purchase of prayer papers and handling of dues are left up to the officers. I asked specifically about how economics are handled, since Gedatsu-kai is centralized but so much autonomy rests with the branches. At that time in 1979, the monthly dues per household had just gone up to 200 Yen. (In 1979 a U.S. dollar was equivalent to about 230 Yen—at this rate of exchange, 200 Yen was about $.87 U.S.) These dues are automatically handed over to the Tokyo headquarters. Any amount over 200 Yen that a household gives monthly to the branch is retained for branch use. Gedatsu-kai features many special prayer requests and memorial rites; these requests are made through the branch leader, and all money for these purposes, too, goes directly to the Tokyo headquarters. Buildings for branches are totally "individual"—that is, up to each individual branch. But the branch leaders feel that they are "blessed," so they don't mind providing a part of their residences or commercial buildings for monthly services. Most of these leaders are self-employed, and they feel that their involvement in Gedatsu-kai is good for their businesses. Of course, at "C" Branch and similar places, people are able to exclude part of the building from taxation. Previously we had visited the "R" Branch in residential Kyoto, which Mr. Kondō mentioned as one of the rare examples of a branch that had taken the legal steps to become a religious juridical person (shūkyō hōjin)—only a few branches do this, because it is too much trouble, and then there are legal restrictions that the branch building can be used *only* for religion.

I asked how many professional people worked at the central headquarters in Tokyo. Mr. Kondō said that he really didn't know, but it must be around a hundred. One reason it is difficult to count the professionals is that most of the officials, even the division heads (kyōkuchō), have their own work. Most of these people had their occupations before they entered Gedatsu-kai. It is the people who entered when they were young, and had no other work, who became full-time employees. I asked if two people in the publishing department, who seemed to be extremely busy, were full-time employees, and he said that they were. But he added that there are almost no full-time teachers or what might be called "professional religious instructors" (he used the term *sennin kyōshi*). I asked specifically about several of the top executives of the organization who had considerable responsibility; most of these men had had their own business interests before becoming executives. He used as an example Mr. Sakatori of "Ok" Branch, who not only is a branch leader but also serves as instruction chief (*kyōmu shunin*) (of the Instruction Bureau, Kyōmu Kyōku). Most of these people are self-employed, and can spare the time to go around taking care of Gedatsu-kai business.

Mr. Kondō volunteered that there are some salary men in Gedatsu-kai, but not so many in the higher offices, because they couldn't travel around. He said that the present division structure came about "a little more than ten years ago" (prior to 1979), and he outlined the thirty-two divisions. Youth are organized as "blocks" (*burokku*), with seven blocks of about 3,000 members each. They have some of their own activities.

Mr. Kondō went on to explain the procedures for the monthly headquarters officers' meeting (*honbu yakuinkai*), talking freely about the various organizational dimensions of headquarters, which we had discussed a number of times. Because details of headquarters have not been introduced in this work, we leave Mr. Kondō's narrative about the functioning of administration to quote an organizational chart taken from a Gedatsu-kai publication (see table 21).

A monthly headquarters officers' meeting is held on the twenty-seventh of every month, preceding the monthly headquarters propagation study meeting (*honbu fukyō kenshūkai*) held on the twenty-eighth. These two days of meetings are preceded by the Permanent Board of Directors' meeting on the twenty-fourth of the month, and the Propagation Deliberative Assembly on the twenty-fifth. Mr. Kondō explained that the chain of command is for the division heads to take information and decisions back to the branches, working through the division structure, holding branch leaders' and officers' meetings. Then each branch leader holds an officers' meeting for that particular branch.

However, the distribution of the important prayer papers and talismans (ofuda) is handled by the Tokyo Practice Hall. The requests for ofuda go from the branch (via the branch leader) directly to the Tokyo Practice Hall, and the hall sends them back directly, without going through the division (kyōku), which does not deal with money. Directives from headquarters are sent through divisions; but the division has no activities to support it. Headquarters chooses division heads (kyōkuchō) directly—selecting people with proven ability. I asked if there were many cases such as that of Mr. Sakatori of "Ok" Branch, who served both as branch leader and in another office (as division head for Mr. Sakatori), and Mr. Kondō confirmed this.

This inside view of Gedatsu-kai's administrative operations, supplemented by the official "Headquarters Organization Chart" (table 21), gives some idea of the complexity of the organization and the efficiency of its operation.[8] The headquarters is a highly centralized institution with carefully devised bureaus and departments to oversee various aspects of the movement. Most of the officers are lay volunteers, but they help guide and manage this large movement with skill and efficiency. It is likely that they are utilizing some of the same planning-and-management skills that they learned as self-employed businessmen. The amount of supervision, management, and planning that these officers carry out is all the more remarkable because they are almost entirely volunteers. This aspect of Gedatsu-kai was not studied in detail by our research team, but we did have to appear before the Permanent Board of Directors to gain approval for our request to distribute the nationwide survey. The board was impressive in its careful weighing of the merits of the survey, and in its probing questions of the manner of collecting information and the eventual use and publication of results.

The organization of Gedatsu-kai seems to be very thorough, from the branch level up through the central headquarters. And it seems to be a careful balance

Headquarters Organization Chart

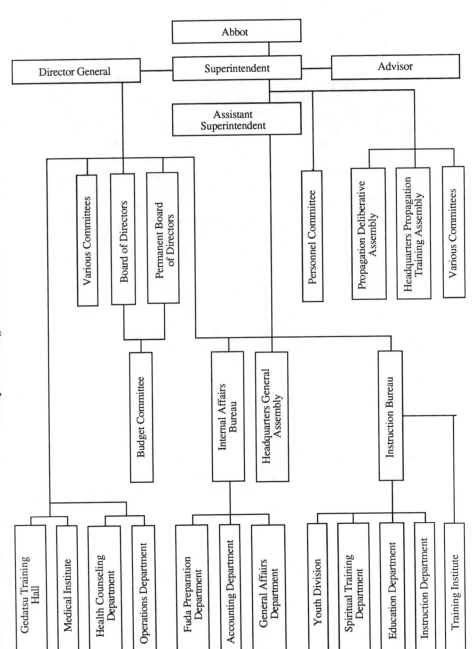

of grassroots support with centralized control. Branches are the local support system; they have considerable autonomy in their affairs but are controlled by the central headquarters through ritual uniformity, economic subordination, and political authority. Central headquarters may have considerable authority, yet headquarters officials are sensitive to the needs and problems of branches, and careful not to offend branch members or stifle grassroots dynamics.

The situation of power and authority in Gedatsu-kai today is quite different from the conditions in the formative period of the movement. In the founder's lifetime, he controlled everything: at the beginning he dealt with every individual, and then with every branch leader, personally visiting every branch. As the movement grew, he came to depend upon the earliest and most talented followers. He accepted Kishida Eizan's suggestion to print a newsletter but turned it into a magazine for all branches. In similar fashion, the first followers—disciples—came to constitute a network of informal advisors, who became more influential in the founder's old age. The founder did not announce a specific plan for the future of the movement, but he expected his closest followers to carry on with his work.

What happened, in essence, is that these disciples gradually developed a more "rationalized" system of governance. The nephew of the founder was named his official successor in 1953, but was too young at the time to exert influence. At present he represents, in Japanese fashion, the indirect hereditary continuity of the founder's presence, and he is an important symbolic figure as well as a member of the Permanent Board of Directors. Of course, in such a highly developed organizational system, the present head (or abbot, hossu) of Gedatsu-kai is not a replica of the founder and does not have the total control of the movement that the founder had. Power within Gedatsu-kai is concentrated in the key offices of the central headquarters, of which the head or abbot is one; other key members are some of the founder's relations and some of the early disciples. Kishida Eizan was one of these officials, holding the title of kyōtō (superintendent) at the time of this study; he died in 1981. The Gedatsu-kai organization may be seen as passing through the last stages of the "age of the disciples"; and it is likely that when there are no living disciples of the founder in the central administration, it may become even more highly "rationalized." In summary, the actual power structure of Gedatsu-kai may be seen as oligarchical, in the sense of a broad sharing of power with a rather complex distribution of power requiring extensive discussion to reach consensus and maintain cooperation. One point that should not be overlooked in this rather bold and impressionistic analysis is that Gedatsu-kai is still a *lay* religion, and that power is still mainly in the hands of lay persons. This is true not only at the branch level, where there is a strong base of power, but also at the central headquarters level.

The Life History of a Headquarters Executive:
Mr. Akiyoshi of the Tokyo Headquarters

From the beginning of our research, we planned life histories as well as the more customary historical and institutional approaches to provide an "inside" view of this movement, and special care was made to collect several life histories of headquarters officials—whom we have labeled more generally as "executives." In fact, Mr. Negishi, whose life history opened this work, is an executive, even though he spoke more about his personal experience (as he was asked to do, focusing on his taiken) than about the organization of Gedatsu-kai. It is well to conclude this chapter on organization by listening to another life history of a headquarters executive; in contrast to Mr. Negishi, who is a lay volunteer, Mr. Akiyoshi is a full-time employee of Gedatsu-kai preparing publications. Mr. Akiyoshi's life history differs from that of Mr. Negishi in more than one respect, and offers a valuable insight into the organization and administration of Gedatsu-kai.

Our research team had worked closely with Mr. Akiyoshi because he supplied us with Gedatsu-kai publications and other information, and he helped coordinate the distribution and return of the nationwide survey. He is a good friend of Mr. Yanagida, branch leader of "I" Branch, and the three of us had talked a number of times not only about Gedatsu-kai, but about everything imaginable—Japan, America, world affairs, the study of religion. Mr. Akiyoshi readily agreed to my request for an interview, and in fact we had scheduled and started an interview once, but it had to be postponed when we were interrupted by business connected with the preparation of the survey questionnaires. The actual interview was re-scheduled and took place on January 18, 1980, at the central headquarters in Tokyo (the administrative offices adjoining the Tokyo Practice Hall).

The interview began with some of my questions about the development of the present Gedatsu-kai organization. Mr. Akiyoshi said that the present board of directors is more recent, but actually it is a continuation of the founder's "first advisors" (*daiichi shidōin*) and "second advisors" (*daini shidōin*). I asked if these were the first disciples (*deshi*), and he confirmed this. In fact, in thinking about this, he commented that Kishida Eizan (referred to as Kishida Kyōtō Sensei, "Reverend Superintendent Kishida") had been one of the "first advisors," and must be one of the few left, most having died. He mentioned some of the "second advisors" still active in the headquarters. Later that day we happened to meet one of these "second advisors" as we came back from lunch, but he politely declined our request for more information on the formation of the board of directors. The big difference between the early "advisor" pattern and the present more rationalized system is that advisors were concerned only with the spread of the faith—it seems hardly proper to call this early stage of informal activity "propagation." In the present highly formalized system—in which the rather abstract term *propagation* is appropriate—the board of directors handles mainly affairs such as finances and management, and "propagation" is handled by another part of the organization.

While we were talking about organization, I asked Mr. Akiyoshi to explain the succession of the founder by the present head (or abbot, hossu) of Gedatsu-kai, the son of the founder's brother. The succession was determined by the founder, who, when his sister-in-law was big with child, mentioned that this unborn child eventually would be his successor. This was stated in front of his major followers, so they all knew it and acceded to his wishes after his death. When this child was in junior high school, there was a formal announcement of his succession, and he became active head of the religion later as an adult. Other administrative matters were not prescribed by the founder, and as Mr. Akiyoshi later mentioned, that led to serious difficulties.

There was no need to explain to Mr. Akiyoshi in detail the purpose of the interview, because he had advised us in every step of our research, and he shared our intellectual concern for interpreting the history and nature of Gedatsu-kai. I told him that it would be very helpful to hear how he had entered the movement, how he had become part of the headquarters, and how he thought we could properly interpret Gedatsu-kai's headquarters.

Mr. Akiyoshi was familiar with most of our research, and he began by saying that his was probably a special case, because he did not enter Gedatsu-kai through faith. His first contact with the movement was occasional and accidental, through his uncle, who has a printing business and who did (and still does) printing for Gedatsu-kai. His uncle was a school teacher who graduated from Waseda University's law department, and who later taught at the Waseda elementary school. Mr. Akiyoshi was born in Fukushima, but he came to Tokyo to go to college and studied in the law department of Chūō University. Occasionally he came into contact with Gedatsu-kai, because his uncle became an adopted son when he married into the family that owned the printing business, and this family home was the site of a branch meeting. From time to time Mr. Akiyoshi went to his uncle's home, but he didn't like religion. He went just to visit his uncle and to pay his respects. They talked, and Mr. Akiyoshi ate with the family, but he did not participate in any of their religious activities.

His uncle did printing especially for the youth department of Gedatsu-kai, and in fact he also wrote articles for the newspaper-format publication that preceded the current *Young Gedatsu* magazine. Because at the time Akiyoshi was a college student, young and bright, he was asked to criticize the uncle's writing for young people. Not only did Mr. Akiyoshi criticize the articles, but he began writing some general articles himself. Mr. Akiyoshi came to the Gedatsu-kai headquarters with his uncle, but he was not a member, and in fact he didn't understand the teaching. He just came along for four or five years, while his uncle took care of the printing business.

After graduating from Chūō University he continued to study in the law department for about four years, helping his uncle part-time in the publishing department of Gedatsu-kai. He agreed to work part-time for one year doing things like writing articles, after which he quit for a year to study for the lawyer's exam. Then he worked for the publishing department every day for another year.

This was about the time that Kishida was coming back to Gedatsu-kai as superintendent—about nineteen years ago. The president (*kaichō*) was Nagata. Mr. Akiyoshi heard that there would be a new organization, and he was asked to work in it. He had no intention of permanently joining, but he continued to work, and then he didn't have time to study. His parents had other children to support, and they encouraged him to take a job instead of "playing around." So he entered the publishing department, even though he was still not keen on Gedatsu-kai as a religion.

Mr. Akiyoshi emphasized that he did not enter through faith; nor did he enter because of a particular problem (nayami). (We had often discussed with Mr. Akiyoshi these patterns of entrance for most Gedatsu-kai members.) In fact, he said that entering Gedatsu-kai did not solve problems for him—it actually *caused* him problems! He was against this kind of faith. After all, he had been in the Zengakuren (a militant student organization during the 1960s), in union movements, and in the student movement. He hated to come to Gedatsu-kai for work. He had no intention of changing personally, but nevertheless he gradually did change.[9] I did not understand his reason for changing, and asked him to explain.

Mr. Akiyoshi answered in an indirect fashion, saying that he always asked questions and didn't accept the answers of Gedatsu-kai's teachers as other people did. He had the reputation of being an outrageous person, because he was always asking questions and was considered rude. This went on for four or five years. But it was partly a change in him personally. He once had a short temper; gradually he changed from a student's argumentative viewpoint, thinking that he had to destroy society. He became more calm and quiet. But it was a personal matter, too. Members asked him questions, expecting that a headquarters official could answer questions about Gedatsu-kai. But he was confused about these teachings himself, not understanding them clearly, and this led him to self-reflection.

As a result he read, not only Gedatsu-kai books, but also books on Buddhism, Shinto, Christianity, Zen, and religion in general. He didn't understand what his own religion was. In his own mind he was asking, "Where is the real thing?" He looked at Gedatsu-kai from the outside, comparing himself to the author and the research team—he did not look at it from the viewpoint of faith, from the inside. But he had been working on the "inside" for ten years; he received many questions and had to answer them. So he had to study Gedatsu-kai in order to answer the questions, answering more from formality, not out of his own conviction.

Mr. Akiyoshi represented a different path for entering Gedatsu-kai, and many young people found it interesting to talk to him because his experience was so different. His own views of life and Gedatsu-kai are mixed—it was very hard for him, but he arrived at it about ten years ago. It was also about ten years ago that he married, and really settled down. The members were pure and devout, but he was not. He was always looking at Gedatsu-kai from the outside. He even recruited people, and formed discussion meetings (zadankai). These people asked him questions, so he studied hard. But the matter that he did not understand was the soul (reikon); he rejected this notion. He could not recognize the existence of a soul and did not understand it. He didn't lie about it, he just told people that he didn't understand it. And the people he recruited were stronger in their faith than he. Problems such as the nature of the soul, spirits (rei), and ancestors (senzo) always arose. Mr. Akiyoshi didn't understand, so he asked his seniors.

Eventually he practiced gohō shugyō, visiting various kami and shrines, and there were many miraculous events. This was not in his head beforehand, not in the books—these were things he did not imagine before he practiced. I asked for an example. He said that people on the third floor of this building (where the interview was taking place) would understand completely what people on the second floor were saying. And there was an old lady who was confused and didn't know what to do, so she asked the kami. This old lady was not in Gedatsu-kai. She went to a shrine, and heard a voice telling her to apologize to her daughter-in-law, whom she was going to drive out of her home. These were the kinds of experiences that impressed him; he began to visit shrines on his own, also going with people he had led into Gedatsu-kai.

Mr. Akiyoshi said that there is still much that he does not understand—not 100 percent. I asked him to clarify this, since he seemed to have settled all his doubts about Gedatsu-kai. He said he is still considering gohō shugyō—he still has doubts about it. For example, there is the important question of the "translator" (chūkaisha) in the gohō shugyō ritual. Before, there was a kind of license (*menkyo*) to become a translator, but now it doesn't exist—any person can become a translator. Mr. Akiyoshi thinks that it would be better to require a license. And it is not just spirits (rei), but also psychology. The conclusion (*handan*) of the translator (told to the person practicing gohō shugyō) is a matter of the actual situation. It has to do with one's personal soul or spirit (tamashii), and if a mistake is made in this conclusion, one's life will be affected. Of course, he hastily pointed out, the change can be for the good, which is fine; but it can also be a change for the worse.

He said the problem is that training is necessary to become a translator. There used to be a lot of possession (kamigakari) in Gedatsu-kai. This is not a mistake, but it is seen as strange when viewed by the common people. There are rather few now, compared to prewar times. Some think that if possession is gone, then what is religion? But some people do not return to their usual, normal selves after such experiences. When they "wake up" (*sameru*) from gohō shugyō, they do not return to normal. I asked, countering his comment, if this would not be considered mental illness (*seishin byōki*). He said no, it was not mental illness. But they would do and see "funny" (*okashii*) things. I asked him if there was no training, even within the Spiritual Training Department (Shuhōbu). He said that the Spiritual Training Department is doing some training, but not generally—anyone can become a translator.[10]

Another doubt he has is about the spiritual problem—running off into the spiritual world. The question is, What does the spiritual world have to do with human existence, life? What is the point of contact between the two worlds? How does human existence go about life? Living (*ikiru*) is first, spirits (rei) are second. It is bad to have spirits (rei) as first priority and life (*jinsei*) as second. I asked him if there were a lot of members who thought as he did, but he said they are rather few. He reminded me that his parents were not in Gedatsu-kai—he came in as a single member. Now his siblings are studying Gedatsu-kai, and his wife is a member. His children follow the ritual, but they are still young.

I turned the interview to organizational matters and the nature of Gedatsu-kai, commenting that many new religions claim to be lay religions (*zaike shūkyō*), but Gedatsu-kai is one of the few that have a right to such a claim, since it has no professional teachers or clergy. He agreed, and said that there are probably only about 200 full-time workers both for the Tokyo headquarters and at the Sacred Land in Kitamotojuku. The division heads and even the officers in the Instruction Bureau and the bureau heads all are self-employed. I mentioned the head of the Spiritual Training Department, whom I had met; from our conversation I knew that he had a very busy schedule of Gedatsu-kai matters. Mr. Akiyoshi estimated that this man spent 80 percent of his time in Gedatsu-kai affairs, and only 20 percent for his own work. But there are occasions when this man's business calls him away from headquarters. Mr. Akiyoshi was illustrating the point that most of the people in headquarters are lay volunteers. Going back in the history of the movement, he said that all of the "first advisors" and "second advisors" in the lifetime of the founder had their own businesses. They got no money at all from Gedatsu-kai. I commented that the voluntary character of their work enhanced their sincerity and enthusiasm for Gedatsu-kai, and he said that there was a tradition of voluntary work. He estimated that in the early 1960s when he began work at headquarters, the headquarters work was still close to one-third voluntary; in the previous system it had been as much as one-half voluntary. In fact, there was a custom of paying for things out of one's own purse. When there was a meeting, these officials would take everyone out to eat and pay for meals out of their own pockets. When they traveled around, they paid for an inn, too, out of their own money. Mr. Akiyoshi feels that this will change—people can no longer do this.

At present the division heads, the Instruction Bureau officers, and various department heads are completely voluntary. These people must work as a family, and have faith as a family. We agreed that the wife's faith and cooperation are important. Mr. Akiyoshi went on to indicate that there should be a change in the direction of a "churchly" (*kyōkaiteki*) organization. There should be full-time teachers (*kyōshi*) or ministers (*bokushi*). He analyzed the problem as a double bind, using an example he had mentioned at the time of Mr. Yanagida's interview. If a branch leader is running a business, say a fish shop, he can't wash his hands and go to the branch's practice hall (*dōjō*) to discuss a member's problems just any old time. And if he does take too much time for branch matters, he neglects his work, and business suffers. So there is an inevitable conflict of work and branch.

I tried to serve as gadfly, commenting that I was impressed with the friendly family atmosphere of the meetings, the dedication of voluntary service, and the relaxed and enthusiastic faith of the group; and I wondered aloud whether Gedatsu-kai might lose this family flavor if it became a "church" with a professional ministry. He said that the family atmosphere should remain, but the advantage of a "church" is that a person could receive guidance at any time. He admitted that it was nice in the old days of the "temple schools" (*terakoya*) when teacher and student were in direct contact.[11] In those days the teacher really had character. Now, with mass education, the teacher's character is low. I had remarked about the sense of unity among the members and even the branch leader, and he agreed that this might diminish if a professional leader were branch leader—which would be a "mass" organization, something he had criticized in "mass" education.

Partly to counter my comments, Mr. Akiyoshi pointed out another problem with the present system. Especially when the branch leaders get old, they lose effectiveness in guidance. I asked if they were branch leaders until they died, and he said this is the case. Also, there is a problem of inheritance—what if the branch leader's child is not active or devout? He said that the child usually succeeds a parent as branch leader, but is not necessarily devout. He compared the situation to a family business—which may succeed or fail in the next generation. Even the founder had laid down principles that a branch is not a private possession, and there is no guarantee that it will be inherited by a family. Ability and faith are the main qualifications for a branch leader. We used the example of Mr. Matsuura, the leader of "C" Branch, who had shown ability in recruiting many members and subsequently became the leader of a new branch.

As the interview was winding down, I asked a delicate question about the early organization of Gedatsu-kai and a group called Minori-kai or Minori-kyō that had split off from the movement; some scholars had told me this, and I had read a brief reference to it in a general description of Gedatsu-kai (Umehara 1978:195). Mr. Akiyoshi did not hesitate to answer, indicating that this had occurred shortly after the founder's death, when Mr. Nagata was head of Gedatsu-kai. Mr. Nagata was a good person, but he used a "one-man" style in running the organization. He got sick but didn't want to quit, so he was forced to. Some had urged him to quit, while others had said for him not to. But Nagata had to quit, so his faction quit also. Nagata was strong in the Kyoto area, and he had some supporters in the Kanto area. He was a man of great character, so his line of supporters and his branch went with him; Mr. Akiyoshi estimated that it has 5,000 to 6,000 members.

I asked if this was the only case of a split (*bunri*, secession), and he said yes. As an afterthought he added that there was another group in Osaka, whose name he had forgotten, that claims respect for Gedatsu-kai's founder as a teacher. Mr. Akiyoshi was surprised to see this mentioned in the other group's writings. Apparently the head of the Osaka group knew Okano Eizō when Okano was first teaching; he took Okano's teaching to heart but did not become a member of Gedatsu-kai, rather developing his own teaching. But later he gave credit to Okano as a good teacher. However, as Mr. Akiyoshi pointed out, this group should not be considered a split or secession from Gedatsu-kai.

He returned to the story of Mr. Nagata when I asked how he had become "president"—kaichō. I recalled reading that the founder had referred to himself as kaichō. Mr. Akiyoshi said that Mr. Nagata had given himself the title. After the founder died, his closest followers selected Mr. Nagata to head the movement. Although the founder had designated his nephew as his successor, apparently he did not appoint someone to head the movement until his nephew could take over. The founder just told his followers to cooperate and get along with each other. The "first advisors" and "second advisors" were this group of early disciples and followers who selected Nagata; his title was *sōmu*, "manager" or "director," and then after a few years he gave himself the title of kaichō.

Actually Kishida might well have become the next head, because he was the major early disciple. But because his printing business failed, he was not financially independent and could not become the head. At about this time, Kishida went to the United States to head the Gedatsu-kai work in America. This was in the early 1950s, shortly after the founder's death in 1948. Mr. Akiyoshi pointed out that Kishida was senior to Nagata in Gedatsu-kai, and it was Kishida who had recruited Nagata. Also, the fact that Kishida was responsible for forming so many new branches led some to expect him to return and take over when Nagata left. But Kishida continued to head the rather small American group of followers, while assuming the key post of kyōtō (superintendent) and returning to Japan regularly to help systematize and organize branches and the central headquarters.[12]

As a final summary question, I asked Mr. Akiyoshi how he thought Gedatsu-kai and the headquarters would change in the future. His response was that although key people in the administration, especially the Board of Directors, would remain voluntary, probably the various departments would employ full-time workers. We had already covered this topic, and he went on to talk about Gedatsu-kai generally. He felt it was important to bring in salary men as members. He indicated that there are some salary men in Gedatsu-kai, but usually they enter through the faith of their parents: the children grow up in a Gedatsu-kai family and then become salary men as adults. But salary men with no previous experience in Gedatsu-kai do not come into the movement directly. I asked him how they would attempt to attract salary men—perhaps through new techniques? He said that they had no special means of recruiting them. But he thought that teaching (*oshie*) is important—that is, not just teaching and practicing religion when there is a personal problem (nayami). Rather, people should be attracted by the teaching itself, apart from personal problems. We had discussed this problem previously, on the taxi ride to a restaurant after Mr. Yanagida's interview; I again brought up the possibility that Gedatsu-kai may be more suited to service workers and self-employed persons. That is, such people may be more apt to grow up in homes with a strong work ethic, and kamidana and butsudan, and therefore move more easily into the founder's values and style of religion. Salary men, who tend to live in large apartment complexes (*danchi*), may have less contact with "traditional" religious practices such as kamidana and butsudan (and have a set of values different from those of service workers and self-employed persons). Mr. Akiyoshi acknowledged this possibility, adding that this is all the more reason why Gedatsu-kai must explain its teaching directly, because many people have not had a "traditional" upbringing.[13]

Mr. Akiyoshi's interview is a fitting conclusion to our discussion of Gedatsu-kai's organization and administration. He is sensitive to the history of the movement, from the personalistic style of the founder to the difficulties of initial organization after the founder's death, and the eventual move to the present system. He also has his eye on the future, thinking that Gedatsu-kai should organize more systematically, with separate "church" buildings and professional religious leaders on the local level, as well as more professional workers at central headquarters. There are several dimensions to this "professionalization" of Gedatsu-kai that are difficult to assess. We must remember that the movement is still in its early stages of development, and it may be inevitable that the informal atmosphere and volunteer leadership will disappear. In other words, even though I served as a gadfly to question the wisdom of this professionalization (and sometimes was asked by headquarters officials to comment on such matters), if Gedatsu-kai maintains or expands its current level of membership and activities, it may enter a new stage of development that—inevitably—includes more professional leadership. On the other hand, there are religious leaders even in the United States who recommend more of the "extended family" style of religious organization that is typical of Gedatsu-kai.[14] This tension between informal and formal styles, lay and professional leadership, is but one of the many problems facing a religious movement—or any social movement—especially during its early development. Ultimately, of course, this is not just an academic matter for discussion, but a crucial aspect of the future existence and development of Gedatsu-kai.

7

RITUAL LIFE
The Round of Religious
Activities in Gedatsu-kai

The present organizational structure of Gedatsu-kai is, in part, an elaborate arrangement for carrying out a very rich ritual life. The various rituals, like the organizational structure of the movement, evolved and became formalized as the founder drew on the background of Japanese religion and developed new forms of religious action. As we saw in chapter 2, Okano's decision to found a new religion was based partially on the revelation to him of new rituals—especially the amacha memorial mass, the okiyome (meditation ritual), and the gohō shugyō (mediation ritual). In the process of working out his own religious problems and helping others to resolve their spiritual dilemmas, he sought more uniform means of practice; the discovery of these rituals enabled him to regularize the techniques by which many people could overcome their personal problems and achieve spiritual fulfillment. By establishing these rituals as the foundation of his religious movement, he made it possible for people—even apart from his personal supervision—to follow the same form of practice and achieve the same beneficial results. These rituals came to be observed by individuals and families in their homes, as well as collectively in the early "meeting places" (shūkaijo) (which, when more formally organized, came to be known as branches, or shibu). Increase in membership was attended by expansion of the number of rituals and greater complexity in their celebration. After the founder's death, especially following the rapid increase in membership of the 1960s, ritual life came to be modified and elaborated into a complete "round" of religious activities. In other words, viewed from its point of historical origins, a rich and effective ritual life is what enabled the development of the organizational structure of Gedatsu-kai; viewed from the present, this organizational structure is what preserves and transmits the ritual tradition. Religious life and social organization are mutually reinforcing, existing in inseparable relationship to each other.

In general, these rituals act out the teachings of Gedatsu-kai and order both individual and corporate life to fit the overall plan of the movement. They actualize the world view of Gedatsu-kai, which has been described previously: by performing or participating in rituals, individuals or groups bring themselves in conformity to this world view, and this blesses them with power and meaning. In the words of Mr. Negishi (cited in chapter 1), "this is what enables us to live." From this religious viewpoint, proper ritual action leads to a satisfying spiritual life. In this chapter, we will describe the major aspects of ritual action in Gedatsu-kai.

The Ritual World of Gedatsu-kai

Ritual is essential to all religious traditions, and although it is difficult to generalize about the entire human heritage of ritual, it may be useful to identify three major characteristics. At the very least, a ritual (1) is a set of prescribed actions, (2) is based on sacred models, and (3) results in a blessing that transforms the participants. Each of the three characteristics deserves brief elaboration. First, ritual is a set of prescribed actions: there are specific procedures which must be followed for it to be efficacious. Rituals cannot be changed arbitrarily; they undergo change, of course, as do all cultural forms, but when they do it must be in conformity to the sacred models on which they are patterned. Second, rituals are based on sacred models: they follow a heavenly blueprint or a revelation or a religious breakthrough that is the source of their power. Sacred models are recognized by a group of people who share the common experience and perception that certain persons, entities, ideas, or forces possess extraordinary power. Third, rituals result in a blessing: the result of performance of or participation in them enables one to receive or enter into the power that is the source of the ritual, and thereby to transform one's life. This transformation may mean resolution of a particular problem; or it may involve moving from a state of powerlessness (or meaninglessness) to a state of power (meaning), or maintaining one's present equilibrium in the face of the threat of disorder and meaninglessness.

These general characteristics of ritual are applicable to Gedatsu-kai as well as any other religious tradition. What is distinctive of Gedatsu-kai is the particular set of prescribed actions, the particular sacred models, and the particular forms of blessings that define its rituals. The particularity of Gedatsu-kai rituals is seen in their indebtedness to the Japanese religious heritage, as well as in the founder's ingenuity in reshaping the previous heritage into new forms.

Viewed in its own context, the ritual world of Gedatsu-kai is a dramatic reconstruction of the religious universe of the founder and his followers: it is the same world of meaning already seen in the life histories of members, branch leaders, and executives. Ritual is a dramatic reconstruction of Gedatsu-kai's religious world view; it enables members to play the role of actors performing dramatic reenactments of this plan of religious fulfillment. The stage for performing this drama is the altar, whose basic pattern is the same for all homes, branches, and other places of worship. Central to this altar are the four main objects of worship: kami, Buddhas, founder, and ancestors. If the altar and its surrounding space constitute the "stage" of this drama, then Gedatsu-kai members are the "actors," and ritual action is the performance. Gedatsu-kai rituals are complex combinations of petition for help in specific human problems, thanks for resolution of specific problems as well as gratitude generally, and celebration of the power and source of all life and meaning. The point of all of them is to draw the person into contact with the four objects of worship in order to bring his or her character and life into conformity with the sacred model, thereby transforming and blessing the person.

Generally such rituals are for petition, thanksgiving, and celebration, but they are also related to a host of more specific actions. For example, the mediation ritual of gohō shugyō is carried out for the special purpose of bringing an individual into direct communication with ancestors or spirits, thereby resolving problems in both the spiritual realm and the present world. An important aspect of the daily ritual in the home, in addition to renewed contact with the four objects of worship, is self-cultivation: improving the individual's character, specifically cultivating time-honored virtues such as filial piety, sincerity, and patriotism. Some annual celebrations follow the customary Japanese practice of marking the seasons— notably for Gedatsu-kai, New Year's, spring, and fall; some are modeled after the life of the founder, honoring his birth and death.

Gedatsu-kai features an entire range of ritual life, from individual or family practice in the home to the collective action of branches, and also a variety of national festivals held at several locations (but centering mainly around the sacred headquarters called Goreichi). Our plan of presentation is to use this overall picture of the ritual world of Gedatsu-kai as an introduction to the description and inter- pretation of specific rituals and ritual contexts. The treatment of specific rituals will proceed from the local and daily level through several intermediate levels to the national and annual level; taken up first is daily ritual in the home, then monthly branch meetings, next monthly regional meetings, and finally annual national festivals. Brief comments on Gedatsu-kai rites of passage close the treat- ment of the round of ritual.

The Home and Daily Ritual:
The Amacha Memorial Mass

After Okano's spiritual crisis but before the formal founding of Gedatsu-kai, he became preoccupied with human problems and spiritual matters, and counseled people who came to him with personal difficulties. These experiences taught him that people with physical complaints frequently had concerns about spirits of the dead, especially family ancestors, and that when these people performed proper memorial rituals, both physical and spiritual troubles were resolved. Okano in- terpreted this solution primarily as a "healing of the heart," and he felt that the best treatment was to combine "teaching" (a way of life) with practice of memorial rites so that people could simultaneously pacify spirits of the dead and "heal" their own hearts. At first he advised troubled people to follow the traditional Buddhist practices such as offering candles or reciting sutras; these practices did bring some results, but they were not completely satisfactory. Continued reflection on the successful resolution of his own spiritual crisis led him to the use of amacha (sweet tea) as a regular means of both purifying one's soul and pacifying family ancestors and other spirits of the dead.

From these humble beginnings developed perhaps the most important of all Gedatsu-kai rituals, the amacha memorial mass. Not only is it the religious activity most frequently observed by members, but it is also the ritual in most direct contact with individuals. Usually members first observe the amacha memorial mass on their initial visit to a branch meeting, and some are attracted immediately to its powerful symbolism of reuniting or harmonizing the living with the spirits of the dead. Mrs. Kawakami, whose life history was cited in chapter 3, emphasized that this was the main attraction of Gedatsu-kai for her: "what was remarkable was the amacha memorial rite." She was so emotionally overcome that she cried, and this experience led her to diagnose and correct her personal and family problems. Part of the "message" she received during the mediation ritual of gohō shugyō was to perform twenty-one days of amacha memorial rites, which she carried out in the meeting place of "C" Branch. Individuals such as Mrs. Kawakami are drawn into Gedatsu-kai through the amacha memorial rite and first practice it in branch meetings, but when they become members they are expected to practice it in the home also.

The most important Gedatsu-kai ritual in the home is the morning and evening amacha memorial rite, which is performed while reciting the *Hannya Shingyō* (Heart Sutra).[1] The ideal is for a family to enshrine the Gedatsu-kai triad of Tenjin Chigi, Gochi Nyorai, and Gedatsu Kongō (the founder) and recite the *Hannya Shingyō* before the triad while pouring amacha over the special family memorial tablets (which rest in a wooden vessel). Thus, the home features the same ritual world of four objects of worship previously seen in branches.

Enshrining of the Gedatsu-kai triad in the life of the member (or family) celebrates the person's formal initiation, a process which provides insight into both the ritual life of the group and the ritual and social tie between individual homes and local branches. Initiation of a person takes place at the local branch of the member who "recruited" the new member (or at the nearest local branch). The name of the person is entered into the branch register, and the membership fee is paid. At that time the person receives a "body protector" (mimamori)[2] and membership badge. Standing in front of the branch altar, he formally acknowledges his own tutelary kami (ujigami) as well as the spirits of his ancestors, announcing his intention to join Gedatsu-kai.

These simple formalities are all that is required at the local branch, but as soon as possible after this initiation, the person is expected to pay a visit to his own tutelary Shinto shrine and perform there a "settling of prayers" (*shingan kaishō*) and apologies. In other words, the person resolves, or makes a kind of "settlement of accounts" for, all the prayers offered up without thanks, or offered up incorrectly, to kami and Buddhas from the time of all his family ancestors down to this person. There is a special Gedatsu-kai paper called shingan kaishō (settling or resolution of prayers) that the person holds between his or her palms while performing this rite at the tutelary Shinto shrine. Then the person apologizes for all aspects of irreverence and disrespect (*fukei fuson*) toward kami and Buddhas committed by him and by his ancestors, and vows that he will become useful to society. The point of the "settlement" and apologies is not directed only at correcting past practice; from this time the new member is committed to avoiding "selfish" prayer requests.

This completes formal initiation into Gedatsu-kai, after which the new member is introduced to branch members at a branch meeting and is expected to participate in the life of the branch. At the same time, the new member enshrines in his or her home the Gedatsu-kai triad (in the form of special papers made and distributed by Gedatsu-kai headquarters through local branches). However, if the person already has a kamidana (Shinto altar) and butsudan (Buddhist altar) in the home before entering Gedatsu-kai, enshrining this triad is managed simply by placing the paper for Tenjin Chigi in the center of the kamidana, Gochi Nyorai in the center of the butsudan with memorial tablets in front of it, and Gedatsu Kongō to the right.[3]

The ease with which a new member can simply enshrine the Gedatsu-kai triad in a home as a miniature Gedatsu-kai altar, "add" the triad to an existing traditional pattern of kamidana and butsudan practice, or (if not in possession of these altars) purchase new ones and then add the Gedatsu-kai triad, testifies to the ability of Gedatsu-kai belief and practice to provide an alternative reconstruction of the traditional practice or to blend with existing practices.[4] Gedatsu-kai does not require the exclusion of other objects of worship or the abandonment of previous practices; in fact, special talismans are printed for "protective kami," similar to traditional talismans, for enshrining in members' homes—kitchen, bathroom, and entrance. (These talismans will be treated later.)

The enshrinement of the sacred triad, along with other protective kami, is the sanctified home setting for the daily liturgy and amacha memorial rite. The term gongyō, "liturgy" or "religious service," usually means reading Buddhist scriptures before the butsudan or in a more formal Buddhist setting. For Gedatsu-kai the gongyō is carried out in the context of the sacred triad, combining kami and Buddhas in the same service. The home service is a simplified version of the formal service in branches, and need not be repeated here. Ideally the individual member (or family) performs the service morning and evening: in the morning pledging thanks and gratitude for the protection of kami and Buddhas, in the evening emphasizing thanks along with reflection and apologies.

As previously seen, the amacha memorial mass is performed by pouring amacha ("sweet tea" or "heavenly tea") over wooden memorial tablets placed in a watertight vessel, while reciting the Hannya Shingyō. The thrust of this rite is simultaneously to pacify the spirits of family ancestors and other spirits related to the family through past practice or through a local connection, and to purify the family practitioners. There is a rather large variety of kuyō fuda, or memorial mass tablets, in Gedatsu-kai; a general presentation of the possibilities for memorial masses in the home illustrates the inclusiveness and flexibility of the movement. These tablets range from those considered mandatory for all members to those optional for persons or families with connection to particular spirits. Kawatō follows Gedatsu-kai practice in arranging mass tablets into four groups: the "five basic" tablets, "standard" tablets, "special" tablets, and "public" tablets.

The "five basic" tablets are considered mandatory for every family because of their deep connection with memorializing family ancestors. Each tablet commemorates family ancestors in a general or special aspect. The first of the five is a general tablet for all "family," in the sense of the generations of ancestors going back to the founder of the family. For Gedatsu-kai, family means the ancestors on both the wife's and husband's sides. This is a departure from the "traditional" family practice of honoring only or primarily the ascendants of the husband's line (Smith 1974:174). The second of the "five basic" tablets memorializes all family ancestors who have become muen, "unrelated" to the family and therefore unable to attain enlightenment or Buddhahood and provide blessings for descendants. In other words, the second category is a general term for all ancestors who have become separated from the line of ancestors in the first category. The third category of the "five basic" tablets comprises family ancestors who have become muen or unrelated for the following specific reasons or karma: financial or materialistic desires, sexual desires, living spirits (specifically those bearing a grudge or hatred), and unnatural death. The fourth category memorializes "seeds" of plants and animals as well as human beings which disappeared without receiving life in this world; in the case of human seeds, this refers to eggs and sperm which did not result in life. The fifth category gives thanks for and memorializes all animals and plants (the tablet specifies birds, animals, insects, fish, trees, shrubs, and grasses) that had to be "sacrificed" in order that the family and its ancestors could live out their lives. The general thrust of all five of these basic amacha memorial tablets is to bring to enlightenment or Buddhahood all the family ancestors and the spirits directly connected to their lives.[5]

The second group of memorial mass tablets is the "standard" tablets; these memorialize spirits with which the person or family develops a relationship through purchase of land or a house, or through business or commerce. Kawatō lists eight separate categories of these "standard" tablets: muen spirits in connection with land the family rents or owns; muen spirits in connection with a house or building the family rents or owns; spirits of families of customers who have helped one's own family (business) prosper; spirits of families of one's employees or subordinates; spirits of fish related to one's business; spirits of birds related to one's business; spirits of trees and shrubs related to one's business; and a blank category to be filled in for spirits related to one's business. Obviously, the first two categories, which deal with real estate, are more common; the next two are general for shop owners and business people, while the last four are for specific businesses (such as fishermen and fish shops, or those who raise and sell chickens).

The third group of memorial mass tablets is "special" tablets, for ancestors who have become muen for a particular reason or karma, one that has been clearly specified, as revealed during gohō shugyō or as advised during special counseling. "Special" tablets are different in that each is for a separate spirit, whereas the tablets for "basic" and "standard" spirits are for unspecified numbers of spirits. Another difference is that the "five basic" tablets are memorialized without time limit, while "special" tablets are memorialized for a specified time, until the particular spirit is pacified. Because a particular wrong (tsumi) has been indicated, a person may also perform apologies (owabi) at a tutelary shrine at the same time that the "special" tablet is memorialized. Kawatō lists eleven forms of "special" tablets: muen because of financial desire, muen because of sexual desire, muen infants, muen through abortion, muen through unnatural death, muen through disappearance, related to living spirits (and grudge or hatred), muen because of enemies, muen because of enemies in relationship to land (one rents or owns), spirits of animals one raises, and a blank tablet for the spirit of a deceased person (name to be filled in).

The fourth group of memorial mass tablets is "public" tablets; unlike the first three groups, which are for muen and spirits of a personal or individual nature, "public" tablets are more for pacifying the spirits of those who died on a broader social or national level—such as in traffic accidents, in natural disasters, or as sacrifices. Kawatō lists six categories for "special" tablets: spirits of members of

Gedatsu-kai previously deceased, muen as enemies in a war, muen as enemies in a battle, the spirits of those lives sacrificed in war damage, the spirits of those who died in earthquakes, and the spirits of lives sacrificed in traffic accidents.[6]

These groups and categories of memorial mass tablets reveal much about the nature of Gedatsu-kai as a religion, as well as highlight the daily activities in the home. The tablets cover a range of ancestors and spirits, from the family in general and its direct ascendants to spirits related through one's locale, business, or work; there are provisions for special karmic connections and the broadest possible "public" spirits, even including fellow countrymen and enemies killed in war. In brief, any possible ancestor or spirit that could conceivably bother or benefit a person is included in this rich variety of memorial mass tablets. This list may appear to be so broad and inclusive that it seems arbitrary, impossible for a single person or family to follow. However, the point is not for any one person or family to practice all of them: the "five basic" tablets are considered mandatory, and added to them are the ones relevant for the particular family. Additional tablets may be obtained in connection with the purchase of a house, or in relationship to one's occupation, or as revealed in gohō shugyō or special counseling. The overall unity of Gedatsu-kai and its memorial mass tablets is similar to the unity of Japanese religion in general, which is not necessarily specified in a written creed or orthodox set of doctrine or sanctified authority, but is the expression of a total world view.

The power of Gedatsu-kai is seen partly in the fact that it enables particular persons and families to unify their lives by daily ritual performance in homes for the sake of most or all of the kami, Buddhas, ancestors, and spirits that have a direct bearing on their welfare. The organizational strength of this movement is borne out again in the manner of requesting, making, and distributing memorial mass tablets. Individual members pay a fee to and request a specific memorial mass tablet from their branch leader, usually at the time of a branch meeting. This request is forwarded by the branch leader directly to the Tokyo headquarters, which has a special area for the construction of tablets and other forms (such as apology papers). This area is the actual site where the founder first guided the budding movement of Gedatsu-kai. In the earliest days of the movement, this is where the founder worked, writing out all the tablets and papers himself. At present, workmen craft the tablets and papers, writing in the proper terms, names of the families, and specific spirits where appropriate.[7] Then, before the tablets and papers are sent out, they are blessed or "perfumed" by being presented together with incense on a special altar in this original section of the headquarters. In other words, the power of Gedatsu-kai and its founder is conveyed with the tablets and papers. Headquarters sends them to branch leaders, who distribute them to members.

When members take these materials to their own homes, not only do they have a miniature altar of the sacred triad patterned after the altars in local, divisional, and headquarters buildings, but they also have concrete means of memorializing ancestors and spirits that have been legitimized and sanctified by the proper religious channels, going back to the founder himself. When members perform the amacha memorial mass, reciting the *Hannya Shingyō* while pouring amacha over these memorial tablets, they are to keep in mind (or meditate on) the names of the spirits they are memorializing. Once or twice a year the tablets are renewed;

7. Workers at Tokyo Headquarters preparing fuda and memorial tablets

old tablets are returned, and new ones are requested. New tablets come from the institutional headquarters in Tokyo, but the old tablets are sent to the Sacred Land at Kitamoto, where they are held until either the Spring or Fall Grand Festival. During this ceremony, the manbu kuyō (all souls' memorial rite) serves as a fitting conclusion to the pacification of spirits the group as a whole has practiced during the preceding year. And because in the making of these tablets they were infused with spiritual life, even after their use in rites this spirit (*mitama*) remains; they are burned in a ritual fire that eliminates their spiritual power.

The significance of the amacha memorial mass can be illustrated by the results of question 13A on the nationwide questionnaire. Individual members were asked, "About how many times a month do you perform the following practices?" Next to part A was a blank in which the member wrote a number indicating the monthly performances of the amacha memorial mass. Figures and percentages for all data, grouped for convenience in frequencies of fifteen times a month, are shown in table 22.

These figures show that out of 5,686 questionnaires, with 20.8% not responding, 25.9% practiced 16–30 times a month, and 35.7% practiced 46–60 times a month. When these figures are adjusted for all persons responding to this particular question (omitting the 1,188 "no responses"), the figures are even more remarkable, as can be seen in table 23.

With "no responses" set aside, almost one-third (32.7%) practiced 16–30 times a month, and almost one-half (45.2%) practiced 46–60 times a month. More than 87% of responding members practice the amacha memorial mass from 16 to more than 60 times a month. Even with some allowance for the fact that respondents

TABLE 22.
Monthly Practice of the Amacha Memorial Mass
(Including No Response)

0 times a month	24	.4%
1–15 times a month	527	9.3%
16–30 times a month	1,470	25.9%
31–45 times a month	137	2.4%
46–60 times a month	2,034	35.7%
61+ times a month	296	5.2%
Occasionally	10	.2%
No response	1,188	20.8%
Total	5,686	99.9%

TABLE 23.
Monthly Practice of the Amacha Memorial Mass
(Excluding No Response)

0 times a month	24	.5%
1–15 times a month	527	11.7%
16–30 times a month	1,470	32.7%
31–45 times a month	137	3.0%
46–60 times a month	2,034	45.2%
61+ times a month	296	6.6%
Occasionally	10	.2%
Total	4,498	99.8%

to the questionnaire (and to this particular question) are likely to be more active members of Gedatsu-kai, this still demonstrates the high frequency of practice of the amacha rite in the home and its great importance for Gedatsu-kai members.

The significance of the amacha memorial mass is much greater than the numerical frequency of its performance: the clue to this central rite is the fact that it is a means of self-cultivation essential to the ethos of Gedatsu-kai. The founder emphasized the need for self-reflection in a "teaching" that focused on such traditional values as filial piety, indebtedness to ancestors, loyalty to country, and hard work. The daily or almost daily repetition of the amacha memorial mass by most members is a means of cultivating and reinforcing these values. This rite is a deliberate form of discipline: it helps a person incorporate and maintain such virtues as filial piety, provides the opportunity for reflection (including repentance of personal failings and corrections of attitude), and enables the individual to resolve physical and spiritual problems.

In general, Gedatsu-kai stresses the religious character of both family and home. The family is a religious corporation joining the living group with the "generations of ancestors" (senzo daidai). The home is a sacred site, sanctified by the more traditional Shinto altar (kamidana) and Buddhist altar (butsudan), as well as by the Gedatsu-kai triad of divinities and the special ancestral tablets used in the amacha rite. Both in life histories and in further discussion, members and executives of Gedatsu-kai repeatedly singled out the kamidana and butsudan as means of cultivating virtue and practicing religion. Mr. Nakajimo's life history in chapter

TABLE 24.
Worship at Kamidana and Butsudan,
Before and After Joining Gedatsu-kai

14. Please indicate the practices you have followed before joining Gedatsu-kai and after joining Gedatsu-kai.

B. Worship at Kamidana (Shinto-style Altar in Home)

(1) before, no worship	(1,512)	26.6%
(2) before, worship	(3,128)	55.1%
no response	(1,038)	18.3%
(total)	(5,678)	100%
(3) after, no worship	(58)	1.0%
(4) after, worship	(4,875)	85.8%
no response	(745)	13.1%
(total)	(5,678)	99.9%

C. Worship at butsudan (Buddhist-style altar for ancestors in home)

(1) before, no worship	(960)	16.9%
(2) before, worship	(3,793)	66.8%
no response	(925)	16.3%
(total)	(5,678)	100%
(3) after, no worship	(53)	.9%
(4) after, worship	(4,926)	86.8%
no response	(699)	12.3%
(total)	(5,678)	100%

3 shows how he abandoned the "traditional" observances of kamidana and butsudan in his teen years when he left his home, and how he returned to these observances after he joined Gedatsu-kai. Mr. Nakajimo's case of renewed practice before kamidana and butsudan is typical of Gedatsu-kai membership, as demonstrated in question 14B and C of the nationwide survey. Results are shown in table 24.

Comparison of the "before joining" and "after joining" categories for both kamidana and butsudan show a dramatic decrease of "no worship" and a dramatic increase of "worship." The incidence of "no worship" goes down from 26.6% to 1.0% for kamidana and from 16.9% to .9% for butsudan. The incidence of "worship" goes up from 55.1% to 85.8% for kamidana and from 66.8% to 86.8% for butsudan. In brief, rather low percentages for "no practice" at these traditional altars in the home fall to negligible figures, while rather high percentages for practice go up to almost 100% (when "no responses" are excluded). These figures demonstrate that Gedatsu-kai members are rather "traditional" in their practice before joining, and become even more "traditional" after joining.

The crucial role the home plays within Gedatsu-kai is also evidenced in the ofuda (talismans) that members can buy through the branch leader; these talismans are similar to those purchased at Shinto shrines and Buddhist temples, but the ones provided by Gedatsu-kai and the relative percentages of purchase by members during one year provide interesting comparison and contrast. On the nationwide questionnaire, members were asked to circle which of fifteen Gedatsu-kai ofuda they had obtained through their branch leader during the previous year. The Gedatsu-kai sacred triad is conspicuous in this group of fifteen talismans: 45.4% obtained the ofuda called Tenjin Chigi Ōgami, 49.3% Gochi Nyorai, and 48.5% Gedatsu Kongō. In other words, just under 50% of the members responding to this question purchased ofuda for the sacred triad during 1979. About the same percentage (49.3%) obtained ofuda called *mihashira daijin* for blessing the main pillar of their residence. An even greater percentage (59.1%) purchased the ofuda called *shihō barai*, literally "four directions purification." The "four directions" talisman is placed in the four corners of the main room of the home. It is worth noting that a greater percentage of members obtained the talismans shihō barai (59.1%) and *muen innen banrei* (58.3%) than any other talismans. (Muen innen banrei is for wandering spirits of the dead, literally "[spirits of the dead with] no relatives-karma-all spirits.") In other words, talismans for blessing and purifying the home are obtained even more frequently than talismans for the sacred triad. This is dramatic evidence of the centrality of the home in Gedatsu-kai as a sacred site.

Branches and Monthly Ritual:
Gohō Shugyō, the Rite of Meditation and Mediation

Among the various rituals and ritual contexts in Gedatsu-kai, a member's home and daily (or almost daily) amacha memorial masses are the most local and frequent. The next level of ritual activity occurs at the branch meeting place and its monthly meetings, which represent an intermediate level between the daily home observances and the national annual festivals. Although in ritual activity the branch may be considered one level above the home, the relationship between the two is close and mutual. In fact, as we have seen in accounts of life histories and branch meetings, a new member's first contact with Gedatsu-kai usually is through a branch: in this sense, branches generate new members and home activity; in turn, the home is sanctified through installation of the sacred triad and performance of the amacha rite, both of which extend Gedatsu-kai values and practices into family life.

The relative independence of Gedatsu-kai branches includes the choice of having the meeting place in a home or business, or constructing a special building; similarly, there is considerable latitude in scheduling the types and the days of monthly meetings. The most important meeting is the Kanshabi, or Thanks Day meeting, which is held once a month at a time convenient to the branch leader and members; this is the form of meeting described in detail in chapter 5, featuring a standardized liturgy with some local variation. In addition, branches may hold a number of other meetings: meetings for okiyome (purification) and ongohō shugyō (the rite of meditation and mediation), meetings for health consultation, youth meetings, and women's meetings. Every branch has a women's meeting (for women with children), which focuses on hobbies and volunteer work. Youth meetings are mainly for the education of second-generation members up to the age of about twenty; smaller branches do not have a sufficient number of young people, and youth activities tend to take place at the regional level. Health consultation is a relatively new aspect, supported by a headquarters department established in the 1970s; it sends out speakers who urge health food and diet along with "natural" healing of illness (especially in connection with spirits that cause illness).[8] Also, depending on the wishes of the local branch leader and members, there may be special days for honoring ancestors, gratitude (hōon), and celebration of the branch protective kami, as well as annual celebrations important in the locale.

We selected for special study the meeting for gohō shugyō (or ongohō shugyō) because this rite of meditation and mediation figured prominently in life histories, and seems to rank next in importance to the Thanks Day meeting. This rite centers around use of the five "mystic letters" revealed to the founder and later confirmed by their presence on the stone stupa on the grounds of the founder's parish temple at Kitamotojuku. A revelation to the founder specified that holding the written characters between one's hands clasped in prayer is a means of communicating with kami. The founder first tested this rite when he was unable to heal a waitress by rubbing her with his hands, as has been described in chapter 2.

Gohō shugyō quickly became a powerful practice in Gedatsu-kai meetings, and has enjoyed a popular but controversial role down to the present. This rite was very important in attracting members, as was the case with the important disciple Kishida Eizan. Other life histories demonstrate its crucial role in diagnosing the cause and cure of personal problems; in some cases, as with Mr. Negishi in chapter 1, gohō shugyō is an "actual experience" (jikken) of the spiritual world that verifies the reality of Gedatsu-kai beliefs and practices.

In spite of gohō shugyō's obvious power and ability to attract members, the rite is so controversial that for a number of years it was formally discontinued. Gedatsu-kai executives explained that while some people were drawn to its otherworldly power, others were offended by its magical character. And before ritual became more standardized, there was some personal abuse of it: it was used for personal gain rather than religious realization. An example was given that insincere people wanted to practice gohō shugyō for divination in order to make money at gambling. The authenticity of the rite depended not only on the sincerity of the individual member but also on the talent and character of the person who served as interpreter (chūkaisha). An inexperienced or unqualified interpreter could easily lead a member astray during the rite or when counseling afterward. Because the rite got out of control, it was discontinued for a while; it was reinstituted in 1950. At present it is rather closely controlled by the Shuhōbu (Spiritual Training Department), which gives some training to interpreters; a printed pamphlet formalizes some of the hand signals by members during their "trance," or altered state of awareness. Even though there is considerable control of this rite, some Gedatsu-kai members and executives still favor the ethical side of the founder's teaching and self-cultivation, and look with disfavor on this spiritualist or magical rite as detracting from the true meaning of Gedatsu-kai. One executive feels that if gohō shugyō is continued, the interpreters should receive professional training in psychology or counseling.

After our research team visited a gohō shugyō meeting, some concerned staff members of the Tokyo headquarters spoke to us, politely but firmly insisting that gohō shugyō is not the heart of Gedatsu-kai; rather, the gist of the founder's teaching is his emphasis on self-reflecton (hansei). This tension between ethical cultivation and "mystical" or spiritual communication is potentially both a divisive and a unifying factor in Gedatsu-kai practice. If members should insist exclusively on only ethical cultivation or only spiritual cultivation, then it is possible that the movement could lose members or suffer schism. However, up to the present, Gedatsu-kai seems to have been able to combine a "both/and" approach: using gohō shugyō as a diagnostic technique for discovering the cause of physical and spiritual problems, and other techniques (such as the amacha memorial rite, ascetic practices, or forms of repentance) to cure such problems. The basic practice seems to be for all members of Gedatsu-kai to engage in some form of self-cultivation; those who also wish to participate in gohō shugyō may do so. But there is no option for members to practice *only* gohō shugyō and not observe self-cultivation. So long as Gedatsu-kai maintains the fundamental character of the amacha memorial rite and its daily (or almost daily) self-cultivation, with the option of occasionally practicing gohō shugyō when there is need to communicate with the other world, it may be possible to hold together both ethical and spiritual techniques.[9]

There appears to be considerable variety in the practice of gohō shugyō from branch to branch, and from occasion to occasion. The following is a description of two observations of this ritual, supplemented by another scholar's more intensive study of it. Our research team observed gohō shugyō once at a branch meeting and once at Goreichi (the Sacred Land). When we observed the monthly Thanks Day meeting of "I" Branch on October 14, 1979 (described in chapter 5) we made arrangements to come back for the dual purpose of observing their monthly gohō shugyō meeting and recording life histories. October 24 marked our second visit to "I" Branch, and we felt quite at home during and after the meeting. When we arrived at 1:25 P.M. at the home of the branch leader, which serves as a meeting place, there were ten people present: one man, Mr. Nakajimo (whose life history is given in chapter 2), and nine women. Mr. Nakajimo and his wife entered, poured amacha over the five-sided pillar while reciting the *Hannya Shingyō*, and then sat with the others waiting for the meeting to begin. The general setting of the meeting, with the sacred triad and ancestral tablets, is the same as described for "I" Branch in chapter 5, and need not be described again. As a thanks for their hospitality at the October 14 meeting, we brought a large package of mandarin oranges (mikan), which was placed on the altar. The oranges were not distributed that day, but cookies which others had brought and offered at the altar were passed around during the tea session. The meeting was scheduled to begin at 1:30 P.M., and as stragglers kept coming in one by one, by 1:35 the group had grown to twenty people (including the branch leader and his wife).

At 1:40 the branch leader opened the meeting the same way as he had the monthly Thanks Day (Kanshabi) meeting: by striking sparks toward the altar and over the people, and then there was joint chanting of the names of the major deities. This is a kind of invocation, preliminary to the gohō shugyō session, which is divided into the preparatory kiyome (or okiyome), "purification," and the actual mediation rite.

After the opening ceremony of invocation, there was a brief consultation (concerning the number of members to participate in the first session) between the branch leader and the woman who was to serve as interpreter (chūkaisha). As a result of the discussion, the participants were divided into two groups: ten lined up in two rows of five across the front of the meeting room, kneeling (with both legs folded under the body) in formal posture, while the others lounged quietly at the back of the room awaiting their turn. The kiyome was begun by the male branch leader and the female interpreter, but later the branch leader was called out (to attend to his business), and the interpreter continued the ceremony by herself. She took from the altar a tray with purple booklets (called *gohihō*, literally "sacred secret formula") and distributed them to the ten people at the front of the room. Each member placed a booklet between his or her palms and held it in front of the body about chest or chin high, in a posture of prayer. There was silence while the people held the booklets, with eyes closed. The leader and interpreter stood at the front of the room, then moved about; the interpreter leafed through a notebook. The leader and interpreter watched the ten closely, while members at the back of the room relaxed and chatted quietly. After about ten minutes of silent kiyome, the interpreter had them repeat to themselves seven times "Gedatsu Kongō," asked them to open their eyes, said "We are purified" (*Kiyomemasu*), and took back the booklets from them, placing them in the tray. Then they said a simple prayer of thanks, bowed to the leader, and went to the back of the room. (This kiyome, which precedes all gohō shugyō proper, actually appears to be a form of meditation, and because gohō shugyō is preceded by kiyome, I have translated gohō shugyō as "meditation and mediation.")

The preceding account of kiyome shows how simple this combination of purification and meditation is when there is no spiritual activity (*ugoki*, literally "movement"). As the first group of ten exchanged places with the other members at the back of the meeting place, the branch leader asked us if this was the first time we had seen kiyome, and explained the purpose of both kiyome and gohō shugyō. He said that kiyome can be carried out anywhere, even in one's home. Its purpose is to perform repentance (zange), remove all ill feelings (*urami*), become purified (jōka), and conduct self-reflection (hansei). After this preliminary process, people are able to go on to the mediation rite of gohō shugyō, during which "things not visible become visible." He went on to explain that although kiyome is preparatory purification for gohō shugyō, one can do kiyome without proceeding to gohō shugyō. (But one does not practice gohō shugyō without first being "purified" in kiyome.) He said that gohō shugyō is not for divination (*uranai*), but for the benefit of suffering ancestors. Such spiritual activity (*reiteki ugoki*) is truly great—it may seem nonsense to many in our present society, but this is actually the case. The result is the perfection of the person's character.[10]

While the branch leader was talking to our research team, the second group of members had assembled at the front of the meeting room, again seated in two rows of five, with the leader's wife in back of the ten. They were in the midst of their kiyome, following the same practice as the first group, and were not bothered by the branch leader's talking to us. They completed their "meditation" of about ten or fifteen minutes, the same as the first group.

The first practice of gohō shugyō followed. The female leader lit incense and placed it on the altar; she and a young woman (who had participated in okiyome) paid their respects to the altar. The young woman placed between her hands the gohō booklet containing the five "mystic letters" (gohō) originally discovered by the founder as an aid in communicating with kami. She raised the booklet above her head, speaking in a low voice to the interpreter but not loud enough for our research team to hear well. The young woman was in a kneeling position with her legs folded under her; she leaned forward, with the gohō booklet still between her hands, and moving her joined hands across the straw mat (tatami), she "wrote" Sino-Japanese characters.

The interpreter could not "read" the characters and asked the young woman to write more clearly. Still unable to decipher the characters, she asked the young woman what she had written, with specific alternatives: "faith-related" (shinkō kankei)? "disrespect" (fukei no koto)? The interpreter still had difficulty under-standing, and told the young woman that if there was something she wanted to convey, she should write the character (by tracing its form on the straw mat). Again the young woman traced characters, scratching the mat audibly with her fingernails. The interpreter still was not sure and asked if it was Kōbō Daishi (founder of the Shingon sect of Japanese Buddhism). Finally there was an affir-mative answer. The interpreter then asked if it was about faith in Kōbō Daishi, and what it was about this faith. The young woman continued to write characters on the mat in a rhythmic fashion, without answering the interpreter directly.

Apparently as a last resort, the interpreter turned to the mother of the young woman, who was sitting about six feet behind her, and asked if their temple affiliation was Shingon. The mother answered yes. The interpreter turned to the young woman and told her that Kōbō Daishi's teaching had been received a long time ago, and then tried to elicit the exact nature of the young woman's concern with Kōbō Daishi. After a brief exchange between the interpreter and the young woman about kami and Buddhas (kamihotoke), memorial rites (kuyō), and proper thanks, the interpreter asked for a conclusion to the ceremony: she said that if this was fine, the young woman should put her hands down. The young woman acknowledged the end of the formal gohō shugyō by placing her hands on the straw mat. The interpreter told her to obtain an apology paper (owabijō) and perform memorial rites, and "when you return home, honor the kami frequently."

This fifteen-minute gohō shugyō ceremony ended with the interpreter and young woman paying formal respects at the altar and placing the booklet on the altar. There followed a brief consultation between the interpreter, and the young woman and her mother. At this point the young woman was wide awake, returning to normal conversation. The interpreter explained about Kōbō Daishi, disrespect (fukei), and irreverence (fuson). The mother said that formerly the young woman had been in Reiyū-kai. The interpreter told her that in Gedatsu-kai, people come from parish temples (bodaiji) of various denominational affiliations of Buddhism; she should obtain an apology paper (owabijō). Kōbō Daishi teaches much to people who are devoted to him. The interpreter, the young woman, and her mother bowed to each other, and this ended the consultation of gohō shugyō.

A second woman, about age thirty, came forward to perform gohō shugyō with the interpreter; they formally bowed to each other and paid respects at the altar, and the woman placed the gohō booklet between her hands in front of her body. When after about five minutes there was no change, the interpreter asked the branch leader's wife to pour amacha over the pillar in the bucket. When about five more minutes passed and there was no change, the interpreter told the branch leader's wife that she could stop pouring tea. The interpreter signaled for silence to women talking in the rear of the meeting room. All this time, the practitioner

8. Gohō shugyō ritual at "I" Branch

was breathing quietly, with no expression on her face, her hands holding the gohō booklet in front of her. (When there is spiritual activity, the hands should be raised.) About ten minutes passed without activity, so the rite formally ended, with the interpreter telling the practitioner to worship the kami and perform memorial rites (kuyō). Then the gohō booklet was returned to the altar, and after formal respects at the altar, the interpreter briefly counseled the woman to pray about the matter and perform memorial rites.

It was about 2:50, and the interpreter said there was time for only one more person to participate in gohō shugyō; the branch leader's wife eagerly came forward. After the usual formalities that begin gohō shugyō, the leader's wife showed her lengthy experience with the rite. She handled the gohō booklet deftly and confidently, raising it above her head and down to her chest quickly twice, and used the booklet to "write" Sino-Japanese characters vigorously on the straw mat. The discussion between the interpreter and the branch leader's wife was about a grave, even the address of the temple where the grave was, with the leader's wife writing answers on the straw mat. The final recommendation from the interpreter was for the leader's wife to practice memorial rites with all her might. The leader's wife concluded with a flourish, rubbing the gohō booklet against various parts of her body. At 3:10 the formal practice of gohō shugyō ended, the branch leader (who had gone downstairs, apparently for business) was called, and the meeting closed with the same pattern as the regular monthly meeting (including the recitation of the *Hannya Shingyō* and the pouring of amacha). At 3:20 the monthly kiyome and gohō shugyō meeting was over, and the group enjoyed tea and also cookies (which had been offered on the altar).

Usually at these monthly meetings, the members chat over refreshments and then go home. On this particular day they stayed (as requested on October 14) to give life histories to our research team. After the stories were recorded and the members had left, we lingered and talked informally with the branch leader about various subjects, including gohō shugyō. Because there were no young people present, we asked about youth in "I" Branch. The branch leader said there were twenty-five or twenty-six young people in the *seinenbu* (youth section). He estimated that about 40 percent of them have participated in gohō shugyō. When asked why other youths did not practice this rite, he said that it is not until after middle school that they recognize their problems (and have need for gohō shugyō). Young people were not present at this meeting because they usually attend the meetings at the Tokyo Practice Hall on the first Sunday of the month. He also commented freely on the preponderance of women in the branch: he thought that about 65–70 percent of members are women (about the same percentage as our national sample), and explained the female majority as being due to two factors—men don't like to tell their problems, and women have more time for meetings.

This was the only planned observation of gohō shugyō by our research team; on one other occasion while visiting various centers at Goreichi (the Sacred Land), we happened to view a much more animated example of the rite. This was not a branch setting; a woman had come to Goreichi with her husband for counseling. We entered a large meeting room from the rear when the gohō shugyō session was already in progress; the woman was quite agitated, crying out and slapping her hand on the straw mat as she emphasized her points. This case was much more dramatic than the three we had observed at "I" Branch; this woman was distraught during the actual gohō shugyō, and her calm demeanor after the rite seemed to indicate a purging of her emotional condition.

The rite of gohō shugyō appears to vary considerably from branch to branch and from person to person, such that it is difficult to generalize from these four examples. Indeed, the four cases present striking differences. The first woman at "I" Branch was rather nervous and apparently unfamiliar with the rite, making communication between her and the interpreter difficult. The second woman experienced no "spiritual activity." The branch leader's wife was a veteran who carried out the rite with a flourish. Only the fourth woman, at Goreichi, appeared to experience an emotional breakthrough or purgation. The most obvious common aspect in the four cases is the preliminary performance of kiyome that precedes gohō shugyō. From limited observation, it is difficult to analyze the kind and degree of "trance" or altered state of awareness of persons participating in this rite.

The importance of okiyome and gohō shugyō can be verified by their frequency of performance as reported on the nationwide survey. The same question was asked for frequency of these rites as for the amacha memorial mass. Tables 25 and 26 give the figures and percentages for all data, grouped for convenience in close intervals.

The frequency of practice for these two rituals is revealing for the religious life and activity within Gedatsu-kai. Out of 5,678 responses for okiyome, 60.8% practice from one to more than five times a month; when the large number of "no response" is excluded, this percentage is 96.5%. Out of 5,678 responses for gohō shugyō, 33.7% practice from one to more than four times a month; when the large number of "no response" is excluded, this percentage is 89.9%. Several overall comparisons and contrasts between frequencies for okiyome and gohō shugyō make

TABLE 25.
Monthly Practice of Okiyome

	Grouped results, including no response		Grouped results, excluding no response
0 times a month	91	1.6%	2.5%
1 time a month	1,448	25.5%	40.4%
2 times a month	746	13.1%	20.8%
3–4 times a month	537	9.4%	15.0%
5+ times a month	729	12.8%	20.3%
Occasionally	32	.6%	.9%
No response	2,095	36.9%	
Total	5,678	99.9%	99.9%

TABLE 26.
Monthly Practice of Gohō Shugyō

	Grouped results, including no response		Grouped results, excluding no response
0 times a month	193	3.4%	9.1%
1 time a month	1,418	25.0%	66.7%
2 times a month	327	5.8%	15.4%
3 times a month	93	1.6%	4.4%
4+ times a month	73	1.3%	3.4%
Occasionally	21	.4%	1.0%
No response	3,553	62.6%	
Total	5,678	100.1%	100%

clear some obvious similarities and differences. We find that the frequency of practice with greatest percentages is one time a month. It is likely that this rather large, almost identical percentage (when including "no response") represents *attendance* at a monthly gohō shugyō meeting, and participating in the preliminary okiyome, but not necessarily participating in the formal gohō shugyō ritual. There is a sharp contrast for practice of two times or more a month: for okiyome, 35.3% practice from two times a month to more than five times a month (56.1% excluding "no response"); for gohō shugyō, only 8.7% practice from two times a month to more than four times a month (23.2% excluding "no response"). The difference may be accounted for by the fact that okiyome may easily be practiced in the home, while gohō shugyō requires an interpreter (chūkaisha) and the formal setting of a branch or official building. This seems to indicate that okiyome is often practiced at home, as well as at branch meetings. As Mrs. Miyauji indicated in her life history (in chapter 3), she was performing okiyome at the time her sister was suffering from cancer; she explained that it is OK to perform okiyome anywhere, but she went to the branch practice hall, and was performing okiyome and praying with all her might. Mrs. Miyauji also practiced gohō shugyō and received specific messages.

A look at "no response" for the three categories of amacha, okiyome, and gohō shugyō is quite instructive. For amacha, 1,188 answered "no response," for kiyome 2,095, and for gohō shugyō 3,553; in other words, using amacha practice as the point of comparison, almost twice as many gave no response for kiyome, and three times as many gave no response for gohō shugyō. This seems to indicate a relative weighting of the three rites, with amacha obviously the most important in terms of regular practice, and okiyome and gohō shugyō less important. However, regularity or numerical frequency alone cannot measure importance, and it may be best to say that okiyome is next to amacha in frequency and importance as a means of self-cultivation; gohō shugyō is practiced less frequently, being reserved for major, even critical, problems. On the other hand, although gohō shugyō is practiced less frequently, it may provide the key to a spiritual problem that is resolved through regular self-cultivation in the amacha ritual. This is the case with Mr. Nakajimo, who rediscovered a vital connection with his ancestors through gohō shugyō. In fact, it was mainly the gohō shugyō experience of his wife and mother-in-law that restored his connection to ancestors and traditional religion; his own few experiences with the rite were uneventful. But it was this rediscovery that led to his participation in traditional rites involving kami, Buddhas, and ancestors—and also the amacha rite.

For a more comprehensive interpretation, we turn to the work of a scholar who has focused especially on gohō shugyō. Takie Sugiyama Lebra, on the basis of intensive field work observing gohō shugyō during the summers of 1970 and 1971, has discussed this Gedatsu-kai rite under the category of "Self-reconstruction in Japanese Religious Psychotherapy" (1982).[11] Lebra views gohō shugyō as a "possession ritual," conducted by a "mediator" (apparently chūkaisha, translated above as "intepreter") and a "host" (the participant). Emphasizing the psychotherapeutic or healing aspects of the rite, Lebra places this activity within the dynamics of "the Japanese moral system" and Japanese forms of healing. She finds in Gedatsu-kai counseling and practice of gohō shugyō a dominant theme of the person (usually a woman) being expected to "blame herself for whatever plight she is experiencing. This pressure for self-accusation is deeply embedded in the Japanese moral system." She goes on to reason that "the Japanese in general are socialized to reflect upon themselves (hansei) instead of accusing someone else suspected to be the source of frustration. A weekly hour of hansei used to be part of the school curriculum. Hansei is supposed to lead to guilt consciousness, remorsefulness, and apology" (ibid., p. 272).[12]

According to Lebra's analysis, gohō shugyō is part of a personal self-reconstruction, the first step being recognition that one's suffering is caused by the person herself (or himself). She notes that "self-accusation is sometimes displayed in the possession ritual," and that this is found in other healing rites of Japanese new religions such as Tenrikyō (ibid., p. 273).[13] The purpose of the ritual is to shift attention from self to other, from ego to alter ("allocentric commitment"). Lebra recognizes that "there appears to be a logical contradiction between self-accusation and allocentric attribution in that one involves interiorization and the other exteriorization of the cause of illness," but for Gedatsu-kai members the two factors are consistent and complementary because of the lack of clear demarcation between self and other, or between self and spirits of ancestors—"identity interchange" (ibid., p. 275). A person's own sins (tsumi) are redeemed through rites such as apology (owabi), usually implemented by an apology paper (obtained from Gedatsu-kai through the branch leader).

Lebra interprets this self-reconstruction as moving from self-accusation, allocentric attribution, and identity interchange to the final treatment of expurgation through okiyome. She treats the "expurgatory ritual" of okiyome as the meditation required to empty the self and achieve the purification essential for gohō shugyō. Similarly, amacha is viewed as a rite of expurgation that eliminates physical pollution and purifies both persons and spirits (ibid., pp. 278–79). Lebra has made a strong case for interpreting the psychotherapeutic dynamics of gohō shugyō through the four aspects of self-reconstruction: self-accusation, allocentric attribution, identity interchange, and expurgation; and has shown these aspects to be central to other Japanese therapeutic practices.

What Lebra has interpreted in psychological categories, the branch leader explained to us in religious terms; the three mysteries or treasures (higi sanpō) of Gedatsu-kai are okiyome, gohō shugyō, and amacha kuyō (the sweet tea memorial mass). As we have seen in the life histories, these are the three sacred means by which people obtain religious power and transform and maintain their lives. Amacha kuyō is highly praised as a regular, daily ritual and form of self-cultivation, while gohō shugyō is singled out by those who have experienced dramatic transformation. Okiyome is not mentioned so frequently, but results of the nationwide survey show that it is practiced more often than gohō shugyō; it appears that okiyome and gohō shugyō are generally considered as part of the same monthly meeting, except when a person has a severe problem and requests an individual gohō shugyō rite.

The significance of gohō shugyō is much greater than might be indicated by mere numerical frequency, as was seen in the opening of Mr. Nakajimo's life history (in chapter 3). His account shows that a dramatic transformation of one's life and values can occur without a specific "breakthrough" or "conversion experience" in a cathartic gohō shugyō. For Mr. Nakajimo, the major results of gohō shugyō are vicarious, especially on the part of his wife, mother-in-law, and children, as well as other unnamed friends who received the rite for the sake of his family members who were sick.

Lebra speculates on "a link between the Gedatsu-inspired self-reconstruction and womanhood. It seems that female dispositions and/or expectations are played up in self-accusation, allocentric attribution, and identity interchange. Women are expected to be less self-assertive, less autonomous, more passive, and their identity more 'relational' " (ibid., p. 280). The leader of "I" Branch has phrased this more compactly: men don't like to tell their problems, and women have more time for meetings. He also implied that women do like to tell their problems (and perhaps the problems of their family). Mr. Nakajimo's life history is a good example of how gohō shugyō by a female family member can resolve a male family member's ambiguity about relations with ancestors. Mr. Nakajimo's vague comments about his experiences in gohō shugyō—"it wasn't very clear to me"—show that the few instances of this ritual in which he has participated might be categorized as involving no spiritual activity or mild activity.

In general, it seems that women are more likely to participate in Gedatsu-kai and to receive gohō shugyō, but variations are not limited to gender differences. There is also a considerable range in the degree of activity within gohō shugyō. Mr. Nakajimo and the second woman observed at "I" Branch on October 24, 1979, experienced little or no spiritual activity. By contrast, Mr. Negishi (whose life history is given in chapter 1) and Mrs. Koshikawa of "C" Branch had highly dramatic experiences that may be called "mystical." The result of gohō shugyō for Miss Muro of "Ok" Branch was that she was told to show life in pictures, and she subsequently became a professional artist. The experience itself ranges from the matter-of-fact to the mystical, and the result can be a sudden and radical transformation or a slow and gradual shift in a person's life. The general thrust of gohō shugyō as a distinctive Gedatsu-kai ritual is to come into contact with the spirits, kami, and ancestors that enable one to transform one's life and shape one's career to correspond to Gedatsu-kai's world view. Some Gedatsu-kai members participate directly and dramatically in gohō shugyō, while others prefer to remain spectators and benefit indirectly from the rite. And there are some members, and even staff members, who prefer the more "rational" and "ethical" path of trans-formation through self-reflection (hansei).

The combined rites of okiyome and gohō shugyō observed in the context of a monthly branch meeting share some of the informal aspects of a monthly Thanks Day meeting at a branch. There is the same opening and closing ceremony, which links the people in common faith and practice, and there is the informal greeting before the meeting as well as the conversation afterward. Therefore, even if a person does not formally receive gohō shugyō during the meeting, the shared problems and experiences after the meeting are informal means of preparing an individual for participation in the ritual. The ability of Gedatsu-kai to draw people together into local groups of voluntary organizations where this sharing can take place is a key to its success as a new religious movement. Monthly branch meet-ings, both the Thanks Day meeting and the gohō shugyō meeting, play vital roles in this voluntary organization.

Regional Monthly Meetings:
Thanks Day and Gratitude Day and
Youth Block Meetings

The next level of ritual activity for members (in terms of proximity to homes and frequency of attendance) after the daily or almost daily amacha rites in the home and the various monthly meetings in branches, is monthly attendance at regional practice halls, or *dōjō*. (*Dōjō* is used to refer to the meeting place for both local branches and regional centers.) There are six practice halls or regional dōjō, located at the Sacred Land (Goreichi), Tokyo, Kyoto, Nagoya, Odawara, and Sapporo. Each has two monthly services: a Kanshabi, or Thanks Day, and a Hōonbi, or Gratitude Day, identical except for the different name. For example, the Tokyo Practice Hall has a Thanks Day on the first of the month and a Gratitude Day on the fifteenth. Our research team attended a number of such biweekly meetings at the Tokyo Practice Hall, and visited both the Goreichi and the Kansai (Kyoto) practice halls. The regional practice halls are also the sites of various other meetings, such as division assemblies, cultural festivals, pacification-of-spirits fes-tivals, social-service meetings, and youth group meetings;[14] our research team observed one youth group meeting at the Kansai (Kyoto) Practice Hall. In general the biweekly Thanks Day and Gratitude Day meetings, as well as the youth group meetings, have the same sacred space and ritual pattern as the Thanks Day meeting for branches, except on a more elaborate pattern; therefore, the description of regional meetings is abbreviated.

The practice halls at Tokyo and Goreichi, being located at the organization headquarters and pilgrimage center, are larger and more elaborate than the Kansai Practice Hall in Kyoto, but all feature the same pattern as at branches: the sacred triad for the altar, and the pail for amacha memorial rites in front of the altar. The Tokyo and Goreichi practice halls can accommodate 500 or more persons seated on straw mats, while the Kansai Practice Hall seats about 200. The liturgy (gongyō), too, is basically the same as for Thanks Day meetings at branches, except for some embellishments such as piano accompaniment for a hymn. Although the general pattern of sacred space and liturgy for the regional practice halls is almost the same as for branches, the size of the buildings and scale of the altar help establish an atmosphere that distinguishes regional meetings from branch meetings. Whereas the branch meetings are rather informal and "homey," the regional meetings are more formal and official. For branch meetings, members travel shorter distances, gather with people they know, and meet in rooms that are larger than in their homes but still on the scale of homes; for regional meetings, members travel greater distances, gather with hundreds of people they do not know, and meet in impressive rooms far beyond the scale of ordinary homes. The prestige of the Tokyo Practice Hall is exceptional because it is also the original site from which the founder guided the growth of Gedatsu-kai.

The official character of the regional practice halls is enhanced by the presence of representatives of Gedatsu-kai headquarters. At the Tokyo Practice Hall, the current head (hossu) of the movement is present at most services; a special seat is reserved for him, and people bow to him before participating in the service (such as presenting their taiken). High-ranking officers of Gedatsu-kai speak at all such meetings, and tend to raise larger issues. The first meeting I attended at the Tokyo Practice Hall was June 1, 1969, when Kishida Eizan, the superintendent (kyōtō), spoke not only on general religious subjects such as Gedatsu-kai teaching and Hinayana and Mahayana Buddhism, but also on controversial subjects. Kishida said that their religious practice was not just for the individual, but for the whole of society and all of Japan, in fact, for the whole world. Everyone needs a sense of gratitude (hōon), and he criticized the Zengakuren (student movement), which was then protesting against and clashing with the police. Another example he used to show how gratitude is essential, even in time of war, was reference to the Vietnam War then raging—he said it is difficult to end the war, but it calls for a spiritual solution. Kishida defended the actions of the Japanese police against the Zengakuren because the police, after all, were protecting the nation, and he said that it is the duty of every individual, too, to protect the nation.

This particular regional meeting had been declared "Okinawa Day," and a delegation of Gedatsu-kai members from Okinawa were honored by Kishida; at this time negotiations were still not complete for the official return of Okinawa from U.S. control to Japan (from the time of the Allied occupation of Japan after World War II). Kishida urged the peaceful resolution of this issue, with the return of Okinawa to Japan. After touching on a number of key anecdotes from the founder's life and teaching, he turned to the subject of Yasukuni Shrine; this shrine was officially and financially supported by the government until the end of World War II in 1945, when the new constitution (and its provision for separation of state and religion) made this national shrine for the war dead a private religious body not eligible for state funds. Some conservative citizens and politicians in the late 1960s sought the reestablishment of both Yasukuni Shrine and Ise Shrine as national monuments eligible for state funds.[15] Kishida reviewed this issue carefully, noting the constitutional question, and said Gedatsu-kai is against this kind of reestablishment of Yasukuni Shrine—but for reasons different from most arguments. Gedatsu-kai is against legal requirements for participation in religion (such as religion was before and during World War II). Rather, religion should be a part of the people, and people should take responsibility for the nation and for Yasukuni Shrine as dedicated individuals. Kishida went on to make similar arguments for individuals to freely support Ise Shrine and Kashiwara Shrine, which, like Yasukuni, are closely linked to Japan's sense of national destiny. Kishida Eizan was a powerful speaker, and he held the attention of the 500 or so in attendance that day, utilizing a nice balance of central Gedatsu-kai teachings with careful treatment of controversial issues.

This paraphrase of Kishida's talk may capture some of the dynamism of the larger regional meetings, which lack the "homey" character of branch meetings, but make up for it with their power in numbers and impressive speakers. Regional meetings help members realize the numerical size and geographical scope of their religious movement as a voluntary organization that is based on grassroots branches but also encompasses national and international issues. In general, regional meetings are more carefully planned and executed. For example, testimonies there are longer and more dramatic. The basic themes of how Gedatsu-kai helped transform members' lives are the same as at branch meetings, but the transformations reported at regional meetings go far beyond the matter-of-fact, mundane testimonies given at branches. Many branch testimonies are simple thanks to the narrators' leaders and fellow members and to the founder for helping them participate in Gedatsu-kai and improve their lives. Testimonies at regional meetings seem to be the much more dramatic life-changes or healings that were first reported at branches and were then selected for repetition at regional meetings. When our team visited "C" Branch and collected life histories, the branch leader insisted on playing a tape recording of Mrs. Miyauji's testimony which had been presented at the Tokyo Practice Hall; it was so powerful that everyone stopped talking in order to listen to it.

One of the major differences between branch meetings and regional meetings is that women completely dominate attendance at the former, while the latter attract a more even proportion of men and women. Lebra reports that "the attendance at branch meetings was in the ratio of about one to five in favor of female members; furthermore, in smaller, sub-branch gatherings and informal activities women were even more predominant," while lecturers and the counseling staff were almost all male. She further notes that "the meeting at the headquarters which I observed, was attended by about 500 people with a ratio of one male to four females: the greater male representation here than at the local ward branches reflects the likelihood that more leaders attended the headquarters meetings" (1982:271). Our research team confirms the dominant attendance pattern for women at branches, but the regional meetings we attended had a greater proportion of men than Lebra's ratio of one male to four females. Question 10 B on the nationwide questionnaire states, "Please circle the activities of the headquar-

TABLE 27.
**Participation in Regional Activities
in Month Prior to Questionnaire**

	All Data		Females		Males	
Gratitude Day (Hōonbi, first of the month)	(724)	12.8%	(451)	12.2%	(273)	13.7%
Thanks Day (Kanshabi, fifteenth of the month)	(1,792)	31.6%	(1,228)	33.3%	(564)	28.3%
Youth meeting (*seinen kōza*)	(332)	5.8%	(113)	3.1%	(219)	11.0%
Women's meeting (*fujin kōza*)	(486)	8.6%	(446)	12.1%	(40)	2.0%
Other study meetings	(432)	7.6%	(227)	6.2%	(205)	10.3%
Other regional meetings	(20)	.4%	(13)	.4%	(7)	.4%

ters, regional centers, and branch in which you participated." Results for regional activities are given in table 27.

A comparison of the absolute numbers shows that female attendance is roughly twice that of male attendance on both Gratitude Day and Thanks Day at regional practice halls. We go along with Lebra's conclusion that "women are more predominant and active at a local level, in informal activities, or in the capacity of the rank and file; whereas their preponderance decreases at the center of the cult, in more formal, public activities, and is totally replaced by male predominance in central administration and teaching roles" (ibid., p. 271). To this we add only the speculation that greater participation of males at regional meetings may be partly due to the fact that men (especially self-employed men) may have greater freedom to travel the longer distances to regional meetings, being less tied to children and home than women. Except for this gender difference in attendance, monthly regional meetings do not depart from the general pattern of branch meetings.

When our research team attended branch and regional meetings, young people were conspicuous by their absence. For this reason we were glad to be able to attend a monthly youth meeting (*seinen kōza*) at the Kansai (Kyoto) Practice Hall on November 4, 1979. Several of our team had traveled to Kyoto on November 2 for the Gedatsu-kai annual celebration of the death of the founder, and were invited to stay over for the youth meeting, in which several of the Tokyo executives would participate. Because the basic Gedatsu-kai model of sacred space and liturgy is essentially the same for this service, it need not be described; a slight variation for the youth meeting is the group recitation of a special "youth oath" expressing commitment to Gedatsu-kai values. The primary difference, of course, is the audience of "young people" (seinen), which for Gedatsu-kai means youths of both sexes from about age fifteen to thirty, including married couples without children. When married couples have their first child, they then attend their local branch, and the wives also attend the women's meeting (*fujinkai*). There is no special provision for children under the age of fifteen, who come to various meetings with their parents. Young people do not participate regularly in branch meetings, but are organized in "block" (burokku) fashion around regional practice halls and hold meetings there on the first Sunday of the month.

9. Youth meeting at Kansai Dōjō (Kyoto) during formal ceremony

The youth meeting at the Kansai Practice Hall on November 4, 1979, began at 9:30 A.M. and lasted until shortly after noon. Young people from the Kansai area (around Kyoto) regularly attend this meeting, and on this particular day there was a group visiting from the island of Shikoku. There were about 150–200 in attendance, about equally male and female, some of whom had stayed overnight; the practice hall has a kitchen and extra rooms so that it can double as accommodations for dormitory-style sleeping arrangements. Two young men and two young women conducted the opening ceremony of the liturgy for the first twenty minutes, until the official greetings by the representative from Tokyo headquarters, who congratulated the four on their handling of the ceremony. Several speakers praised the young people for their hard work, faith, and spirit, especially for the fact that 180 of their block had participated in the just-concluded service honoring the founder's death.

The first testimony was by a young woman in her mid-twenties, from a branch in Shikoku. After entering Gedatsu-kai, she went to the Goreichi for spiritual training (*kenshū*), and there for the first time practiced the hundredfold repentance (ohyakudo)—she recited the praise to the founder while practicing ohyakudo. At first she just imitated her friends in their practice, but later she apologized to the generations of ancestors. After her "training" at Goreichi, she went to the Tokyo headquarters of Gedatsu-kai; she was impressed with the teaching there, too, and wanted to learn and practice more. She publicly apologized to her mother, who gave birth to her and gave her this life. Also she mentioned her obligation to her teachers, and especially to the branch leader who guided (or recruited) her soul. The branch leader helped her see that she should be thankful for the whole of creation, and youth should be grateful to their branch leaders.

The next person to give a testimony was a young woman about twenty, who also had gone for "training" (kenshū) at Goreichi, and in spite of personal difficulties and wanting to go home, stayed for the whole training session. As the young woman recalled her training at Goreichi, she began to cry, and from that point she alternated between talking and crying. She was crying so hard that she tried to wipe the tears from her face with her hand; a woman from the front row gave her a handkerchief. The testimony ended with the comment that through the training she was able to find her own purpose: she became a better person, and wanted to participate again in this training.

It was just before eleven, and a brief break was called with the suggestion that everyone should turn around and talk to his or her neighbor. The meeting had been rather formal up to this point, even though one older person early on had called out in a loud voice for the young people to relax. This break provided a much needed relief, and the young people chatted amicably, with much joking and laughter. During the break, one of the Tokyo officials told us that there are four annual training sessions at Goreichi: during March and July for young people (age 15–30), and during April and September for adults. Featured in the training sessions are lectures by the head (hossu) of Gedatsu-kai and other top officials.

After the break, there was a talk by the leader of this youth group, a man who had been raised in the faith of Gedatsu-kai by his parents, and had many memories of participation in his branch and in youth activities. As the youth leader spoke, the young people again assumed a very formal sitting posture, and for the second time in the meeting, an older man in the back shouted out forcefully, "Relax!" The sudden outburst made all the young people laugh, and the youth leader, surprised by the outburst and the laughter, became flustered, and confessed to losing his train of thought—which caused more goodhearted laughter.

By eleven-thirty his talk was over, and the final speaker for the morning was the official from Tokyo headquarters, who was much more polished and smooth with his delivery. He drew them into the talk first by leading them through some simple calisthenics and then once more praised the young people who had conducted the opening ceremony; he summarized the earlier talks and testimonies through the Gedatsu-kai notion that "we are allowed to live" (ikasarete iru), and said that the abundance of tears was very good (indicating sincerity). The theme of this month's meeting (mentioned by several previous speakers) was peace in one's heart, and it was the main subject of the official's talk. He used various examples to contrast scientific progress with the condition of the human "heart." He said that automobiles and electricity make things convenient, but do they make people happy? He doubted that progress in the human heart had accompanied scientific progress. One very effective anecdote he used was the old saying that a woman's upbringing could be summed up with the syllables *sa, shi, su, se,* and *so: sa* for *saihō* (sewing), *shi* for *shitsuke* (training), *su* for *suiji* (cooking), *se* for *sentaku* (laundry), and *so* for *sōji* (cleaning). The official did not borrow this old saying literally, but used it as a foil, joking about old household tools and how hard things used to be. He had the young people laughing with him, but his point was that the problems of life stay the same, with or without such conveniences— what matters is one's actual life, and one's heart. This led him to emphasize the five traditional virtues of Gedatsu-kai and the teaching of the founder. He encouraged them to participate in the Three Holy Sites Pilgrimage (Sanseichi Junpai) and also the hundredth anniversary of the founder's birth during the next year.

It was shortly before noon when the official ended his talk, and the closing cere-mony and a few announcements marked the close of the youth meeting shortly after noon.

These episodes from one regional youth meeting illustrate the dynamics of young people within Gedatsu-kai. At this particular meeting, young people were adept at carrying out the liturgy and expressing the rationale of the movement. There was alternation of serious attention for the formal liturgy with candid confession and casual joking in the informal parts of the meeting, much as at branch meetings. Obviously the monthly youth meetings at regional practice halls are effective means for giving young people their own special occasion, and at the same time giving them experience in participation and leadership. However, youth organi-zation is one aspect of Gedatsu-kai's present arrangement that concerns some branch leaders and executives, who feel that young people are not adequately brought into the life of individual branches, and that the regional monthly meetings are too infrequent and too distant to maintain a good youth program. Perhaps in the future there will be a somewhat different youth organization and youth meeting style.

Both the biweekly Thanks Day and Gratitude Day services and the monthly youth meetings at regional practice halls are good examples of how Gedatsu-kai rituals bind together members on a larger scale. The familiar altar and common liturgy are standard, but both the broader membership and headquarters officials add a new dimension to regional meetings not found in branch meetings or the home. It is impressive to see adult members of the Tokyo area worshipping with and being concerned for visiting members from Okinawa; it is equally impressive to see young people of the Kansai (Kyoto) area sharing their faith and experiences with young people from the island of Shikoku. Members of a branch are com-fortable with one another and can talk easily, but for the same reason, testimonies can become worn thin. To associate with distant members enables sharing of faith on a larger scale and makes available new people with fresh testimonies. Just as interaction with distant members brings new life, headquarters officials bring new ideas to the local group. Gedatsu-kai representatives are skillful speakers who explain and illustrate the movement's teachings through old-fashioned sayings as well as contemporary political issues. Such regional meetings help link home and branches to Gedatsu-kai as a national movement.

Annual Festivals:
Celebration of Seasons, Founder, and Nation

Discussion of Gedatsu-kai ritual to this point has proceeded from the home to the branch and on to the regional practice hall. The next level of ritual activity, in terms of proximity to home and frequency of attendance, is national celebrations held on an annual basis. Gedatsu-kai has constructed a complete annual cycle or "round" of festivals which complement the daily round in the home and the monthly round at branches and regional practice halls. Most religious traditions have some annual calendar or liturgical year; in Japan every region has its "annual celebrations" (nenjū gyōji), and it is customary for every new religion to have its specific way of celebrating the annual cycle.[16] Gedatsu-kai's ritual calendar, in abbreviated form, comprises:

1. New Year's (January 1, celebrated at Goreichi)
2. Taiyō Seishin Hi Matsuri (Sun Spirit Monument Festival, February 11, celebrated at Goreichi)
3. Sanseichi Junpai (Three Sacred Sites Pilgrimage April 1–3, celebrated in the Kansai area in and around Kyoto; repeated in August for general members and young people)
4. Spring Taisai (Grand Festival, May 8, celebrated at Goreichi)
5. Fall Taisai (Grand Festival, October 10, celebrated at Goreichi)
6. Nensai (Death Anniversary of the founder, November 2, celebrated at the temple Sennyūji in Kyoto)
7. Amacha Shūkaku Kanshasai (Sweet Tea Harvest Thanks Festival, November 20, celebrated at Gedatsu-kai's amacha farm in Nagano Prefecture)
8. Goseitan (Birth Anniversary of the founder, November 28, celebrated at Goreichi)

Early in our research planning, we discussed these festivals with Gedatsu-kai officials. We observed most of them firsthand, except for the Three Sacred Sites Pilgrimage (which was viewed in a lengthy 16 mm documentary film produced by Gedatsu-kai) and the Sun Spirit Monument Festival. Gedatsu-kai's celebrations are a skillful blend of traditional seasonal festivals (New Year's, spring, and fall festivals), recognition of the founder (the anniversaries of his birth and death), and honoring of sites sacred for the nation (the Sanseichi Junpai, or Three Sacred Sites Pilgrimage). These complex annual ritual gatherings are for all members throughout Japan (and some members from the United States); they are significantly different from the three previous levels of home, branch, and regional meetings, because they are major celebrations attracting many members to sites sacred within Gedatsu-kai, and because they take on the air of a pilgrimage. Each of these festivals returns the participant to one or more key aspects of the traditional world view: to harmony with seasonal rhythms, to contact with the person of the founder (embodying ethical virtue and holy power), and to union with the foundation of the nation.

The Gedatsu-kai round of annual festivals is not a clear progression such as is found in the Roman Catholic liturgy with a logical movement from advent to Christmas and on to Lent, Easter, and Epiphany. Rather, it is a reformulation of traditional festivals and the diffuse world view they presuppose, blended with the life and teachings of the founder, and expanded to some specific celebrations (such as the Three Sacred Sites Pilgrimage and the Amacha Harvest Thanks Festival). Because there is no sequential progression, and complete description of each rite would consume too much space (and be repetitive), we will focus on the most important rites, and for sake of convenience we will discuss several rites together.

In the Footsteps of the Founder:
The Grand Festival (Taisai) of Spring and Fall

We begin with perhaps the most important of all Gedatsu-kai festivals, the Grand Festival (Taisai), which the founder established early in the life of the movement. As the founder attracted more followers, he not only spoke with them directly in various meetings, but also took them with him on his monthly religious visits (omairi) to his native village of Kitamoto, where they followed him on his customary pilgrimage route: first the tutelary kami shrine, next the old stupa in front of the parish Buddhist temple, then the memorial stones of his ancestors in the cemetery next to the temple, and finally the small Shinto shrine of the "great kami" (Ōgami). This early tradition of an informal visit to the founder's home village and local religious sites was the background for the first formally organized Taisai on May 8, 1931. The festival officially commemorated the revelation of the five mystic letters ongohō (or gohō) on May 8 two years earlier, but it also falls close to the time of spring festivals important throughout Japan. At the first Grand Festival, fifty people were led on this pilgrimage around the sacred sites of the village.

The first celebration of this festival was called simply the Grand Festival, and it was held on May 8 from 1931 through 1933; but after 1933 the festival was also held on October 10, and since then the two celebrations have been distinguished as the Spring Grand Festival (Haru Taisai) and the Fall Grand Festival (Aki Taisai). Seasonal festivals have been extremely important within traditional Japanese religion. Most Shinto shrines observe a spring festival celebrating the spring and new vegetative life (for example, rice-transplanting festivals) and a fall festival associated with the harvest as a thanksgiving celebration. Spring and fall are also the time of many folk festivals and customs; the Japanese people recognize implicitly the religious significance of marking the two seasons: blessing of the crop with prayers for abundance, and thanks for the harvest that is taken in. Neither the founder nor Gedatsu-kai writings generally have focused on the Spring and Fall Grand Festivals as fitting within the pattern of traditional Japanese religion; rather, the rationale for these celebrations is a combination of following the precedent of the founder and his teachings, and recognizing the bounty of nature. Gedatsu-kai has adopted spring and fall as the time of two of its major festivals, utilizing the traditional themes of blessing/thanksgiving while adapting the celebrations to its own distinctive beliefs and practices.[17]

Much of the significance of the celebration of both Grand Festivals is their observance at Goreichi, where most of Gedatsu-kai's annual celebrations are held. Goreichi, the Sacred Land, as the site of the home where the founder was born and raised and the location of his key revelations and major religious monuments, is a kind of "mecca" in its own right. Any trip there by a member of Gedatsu-kai is a form of pilgrimage because it is a return to the birthplace (and death place) of the founder; traveling to Goreichi takes the member back to the origin of Gedatsu-kai by bringing him or her in contact with so many aspects of the founder's life and teaching. Members pay respects at the founder's old family home, his family's parish Buddhist temple and parish Shinto shrine, and the various monuments sacred to Gedatsu-kai. This mixture of pilgrimage to the center of Gedatsu-kai tradition and "returning home" is part of all trips to Goreichi, and is a major feature of most of the movement's national and annual festivals. Members—by placing themselves at the same sacred sites where the founder was, at the same time made sacred by events and actions in his life, and performing the same sacred rites he instituted or which honor his life and message—are able to "go back" to the power of the beginning of the founder's movement and to the heart of the Japanese tradition. In other words, such pilgrimage is a kind of transformation, a psychological renewal or spiritual rebirth.

Pilgrimage is a central feature of the Grand Festival, and for this reason it is best seen as a process or movement beginning in the home or branch, reaching its pilgrimage goal at Goreichi, and then retracing its path back to home and branch. The tradition of pilgrimage in Japan dates from the Middle Ages, when people walked long distances to national centers such as Ise, or followed a set course of practice sites such as the Shikoku pilgrimage honoring eighty-eight sites sacred to Kōbō Daishi (the founder of Shingon Buddhism in Japan).[18] Gedatsu-kai's pilgrimage pattern is more recent and more closely tied to modern forms of transportation. As seen in chapter 2, the founder was one of the businessmen who helped to plan the construction of a railroad station at Kitamoto, and in the first Grand Festivals the major means of travel was by train from Ueno Station in Tokyo to Kitamoto; Gedatsu-kai even reserved special train cars because of the large number of members attending the Grand Festival.

I first attended a Grand Festival on May 8, 1969, and was able to be part of the travel to Goreichi. Gedatsu-kai officials gladly gave me permission to view the festival, and told me to take an early morning train to Kitamoto from Ueno Station. When I arrived at Ueno Station on the morning of the eighth, a number of Gedatsu-kai guides were stationed in front of the ticket gates leading to the trains; they were holding a large Gedatsu-kai banner, ready to greet members and direct them to trains. When I asked for directions to the platform for the train to Kitamoto, they called another guide on the other side of the gate, and he showed me to the track where a train was waiting. This young man had a Gedatsu-kai band around his arm; a woman, apparently a Gedatsu-kai member, saw this armband and followed along. Most of the seats on the train were taken, but people kept filing in, many of them led by the guides. As greetings were exchanged, the joviality lent an atmosphere of excursion. Members of the movement were identifiable not only by their greetings to one another, but also by their Gedatsu-kai pins, banners, and reading material. On the forty-five minute trip from Tokyo to Kitamoto, some younger members read from issues of *Yangu Gedatsu* (Young Gedatsu). When the train stopped at Kitamoto, a rather small city on this line, most of the people on the train got off; the train station and then the streets were filled with Gedatsu-kai members, who were guided by police and Gedatsu-kai helpers to the site of the festival.

My second participation in a Grand Festival was with our research team on October 10, 1979, a decade after my first trip. As before, Gedatsu-kai officials advised me to leave from Ueno Station in Tokyo about 9:00 A.M. Much to my surprise, this time there were no Gedatsu-kai banners or guides at the station or on the platform. Some people on the train could be identified as Gedatsu-kai members by lapel pins or reading material, but they were traveling as individuals rather than as part of groups. This surprised me and prompted questioning of Gedatsu-kai officials, who said that since the highway system was developed, more people were coming by bus. This change in transportation was evident when we entered the Gedatsu-kai grounds, where numerous deluxe charter buses were parked. Apparently many branches travel to the Grand Festival in these buses. Probably the sense of camaraderie lost on the public trains is more than made up for on the privately chartered buses.[19]

The mode of transportation may have shifted in the decade from 1969 to 1979, but the general character of the pilgrimage and its rituals are basically the same. Viewed in its simplest form, the Grand Festival features three major parts: informal preliminaries for the formal ceremony, the formal ceremony itself, and postceremony activities and departure. There is a preliminary period of several hours when members arrive at Goreichi, and as individuals or groups (some as branches guided by branch leaders) leisurely follow the traditional pilgrimage route and make particular requests, pay special devotions, perform certain practices, or receive specific advice. By a specified time, all members are expected to end their "religious visits" (sanpai) and take their places for the elaborate ceremony. The ceremony itself is just over an hour of elaborate pageantry and talks by high officials of Gedatsu-kai and elected public figures, all woven into the standard liturgy, with some added features. After the ceremony, some people carry out additional sanpai and gradually leave for their train or bus ride home. The following is a summary of the Fall Grand Festival on October 10, 1979.

The preliminary part of the Grand Festival is an informal "religious visit" around the grounds of Goreichi by the members; they may be led by a branch leader or walk from one sacred site to another without following any prescribed order. The "Abbreviated Guide Map to Goreichi" provided by Gedatsu-kai in one of its publications shows the relationship of these sacred sites.

In October 1979 our group left the Kitamoto Station before 10:00 A.M. and walked south with an executive of Gedatsu-kai and many members. The general outline of our "religious visits" within Goreichi roughly paralleled the precedent of pilgrimage set by the founder in his original monthly trips to his home village— even though many sacred sites have been added. We entered the grounds of Goreichi at the site of the Sun Spirit Monument (Taiyō Seishin Hi), a large stone monument with the symbol of the rising sun on it. This is the stone erected by the founder in 1940, in response to his dead father's earlier revelation, as a commemoration of the spirit of the sun (a symbol of the Japanese nation) as man's fundamental spirit. Many offerings were on altars in front of the Sun Monument, and members stood before it with heads bowed and prayed silently.

Activities along this pilgrimage path were brief and individual, with no prescribed course or procedures. From the Sun Monument members walked to Tenman Jinja, the parish Shinto shrine of the Okano family, and paid respects in front of it. They then proceeded to Tamonji, the parish Buddhist temple of the Okano family; some entered, while others lit incense and offered it in front of a statue of Kōbō Daishi to the right of the entrance. Around this temple, the nearby stone stupa (Hōkyōin Tō, where the five mystic letters of gohō were revealed), and the cemetery for Okano's family, the smoke from incense was so thick that it was difficult to take photographs. People purchased incense and offered it at several locations in this area, including the memorial stones for the Okano family. As at many local parish temples, there are various statues and chapels for particular Buddhist divinities around Tamonji.

The next stop on the pilgrimage course was the founder's old family home and birthplace, across the street from Tamonji. This old farm house with thatch roof is both a memorial site for the founder and a meeting place for the Kitamoto branch of Gedatsu-kai. It contains memorabilia of the founder and features a standard Gedatsu-kai altar with the sacred triad and pail for amacha rites. The house was too small to accommodate all visitors, but Gedatsu-kai officials provided tea and refreshments from temporary structures, and many members relaxed there, milling about and talking with friends.

御霊地案内略図

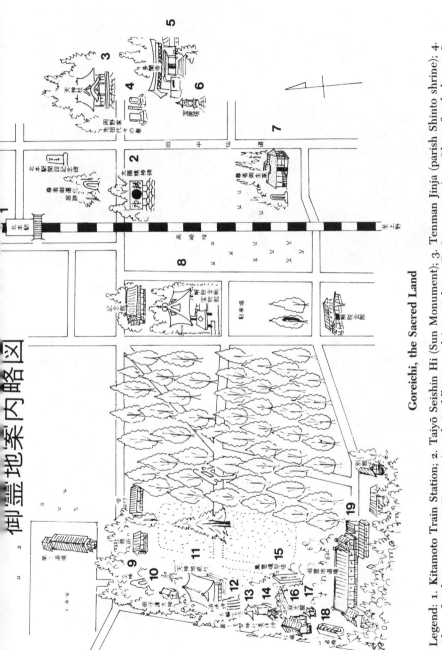

Goreichi, the Sacred Land

Legend: 1. Kitamoto Train Station; 2. Taiyō Seishin Hi (Sun Monument); 3. Tenman Jinja (parish Shinto shrine); 4. Okano family cemetery; 5. Tamonji (parish Buddhist temple); 6. Hōkyōin Tō (stone stupa); 7. Okano family home; 8. Gedatsu Kongō Museum; 9. Tengoshiki (heavenly kami); 10. Goshugo Daijin (protective kami); 11. Tenjin Chigisha (Shinto shrine); 12. Shōtoku Hi (Encomium, or memorial monument for founder); 13. Gedatsu Kongō Monument; 14. Fuji Sengen Shrine; 15. Yaoyorozu Mitama Matsuri Tō (All Souls' Memorial Tower); 16. Kyōzō (Sutra Treasury); 17. Gochi Nyorai Hall; 18. Roku Jizō; 19. Goreichi Dōjō

10. Founder's home at the Sacred Land (Kitamoto) during a Grand Festival

11. Tenjin Chigisha at the Sacred Land

Because we had agreed to meet at the Goreichi Practice Hall, we left the old home area and passed through the tunnel under the railroad, proceeding to the hall. A little more than a half-hour had passed from the time we left the Kitamoto Station. Other pilgrims who left the founder's home visited various sacred sites before the formal ceremony. Among the many monuments and shrines on the west side of the railroad tracks, three of the most important are the ones mirroring the sacred triad of Gedatsu-kai's altar: the Shinto shrine for Tenjin Chigi, the statue of Gochi Nyorai, and two monuments for the founder (Gedatsu Kongō). The Tenjin Chigi Shrine is a recently built Shinto shrine on the site of the small shrine for Tenchi no Ōgami, where the founder received crucial revelations for the founding of Gedatsu-kai. The Kyōzō, literally "sutra treasury" (or depository), symbolizes the resting place of all the spirits of the dead who have received the benefit of Gedatsu-kai's all souls' memorial rite. Nearby is a small building housing a statue of Gochi Nyorai. Several monuments honor the founder—the Shōtoku Hi, a memorial monument erected on his sixtieth birthday, and the Gorin Hōtō, a Buddhist form of memorial tower erected on the thirteenth anniversary of his death (and honoring his virtuous character).

Another key monument is the tower honoring all the spirits of the dead (Yaoyo-rozu Mitama Matsuri Tō), which Gedatsu-kai translates as "All Souls' Memorial Tower." Near this tower is a temporary structure with a large five-sided pillar and amacha for pouring over the pillar. Members line up and wait for their turn to pour amacha. There are also smaller shrines for protective kami and even a miniature Mount Fuji and Fuji Sengen Shrine—because the founder's family had long provided leaders for pilgrimages to Fuji. To the south of these sites, close to the Goreichi Practice Hall, are six statues of Jizō (patron saint of the dead), which receive many offerings.

Members are free to move about and make offerings where and when they wish both before and after the formal ceremony. In a survey of branch leaders, we found that many of them (and apparently their members) take a somewhat different pilgrimage route from the one we took: proceeding from the parking lot north of the Tenjin Chigi Shrine and visiting various sites between the parking lot and the six Jizō, some entering the Goreichi Practice Hall, and from that point traversing the tunnel under the railroad to the founder's home, to Tamonji and Tenman Jinja, concluding with the Sun Monument. Gedatsu-kai officials say that all of this is a matter of "custom," and there is no "proper" order of pilgrimage. (It is possible that some of these patterns reflect the difference between members' coming by train and by bus.)[20]

While members were paying their respects at various sites, our research team entered the Goreichi Practice Hall, where two groups of young people were practicing for the formal ceremony. Four young men were practicing carrying a black lacquered palanquin or "chest" for the souls of the dead (omitama hitsu). Each of the four men wore the Shinto-style "mask" under his nose to prevent his breath from defiling the sacred objects they were carrying. A number of young women dressed in elaborate kimono were going through devotions in front of the altar, in preparation for their role of offering amacha and flowers in the formal ceremony. At eleven o'clock we were given red flowers designating us as guests, and we were asked to go to the special section of folding chairs for guests. As we entered the large area east of the Tenjin Chigi Shrine and other sacred sites, the

12. Gedatsu Kongō Monument (and Fuji Sengen Shrine) at the Sacred Land

13. Yaoyorozu Mitama Matsuri Tō (All Souls' Memorial Tower) at the Sacred Land

14. Pouring amacha over the All Souls' Pillar at the Sacred Land during a Grand Festival

15. Close-up of the All Souls' Pillar

16. Young men carrying chest with memorial fuda in procession during a
Grand Festival at the Sacred Land

loudspeakers announced that it was time for people to end their "religious visits"
(sanpai); branches were asked to gather their members. Most of the people had
already taken their places on straw mats within roped-off sections, their shoes
placed outside the matting. Families and branch members were sitting together
talking and eating lunches they had brought with them; they finished their meals
before the ceremony began.

The formal ceremony began shortly before eleven-thirty and lasted until shortly
after twelve-thirty. It was in effect an expanded and more elaborate branch meeting, with much more pageantry. There was formal seating of the dignitaries on
the program, followed by a parade featuring a Western-style band and majorettes,
with flag bearers for the headquarters, youth division, and branches. After this
showy opening, all participated in the essential features of the Gedatsu-kai liturgy
honoring various divinities, and listening to the tape recording of the founder's
message from an earlier Grand Festival.

The distinctive feature of the Grand Festival was the all souls' memorial rite
(manbu kuyō), which featured a separate entrance for the young men with the
palanquin or "chest" for the souls of the dead, and the young women who offered
flowers and amacha. Special offerings were made before the Gorin Hōtō (Buddhist
memorial) for the founder, recognizing his significance as the founder of Gedatsu-
kai and developer of the rite. The effect of the all souls' memorial rite is to act
out twice a year a grand conclusion to the daily amacha memorial mass performed
in homes, and yet raise the activity to a higher level—in terms of both the ritual
principle and the scope of the participants. "All souls" here means the souls of
all humans (whether in the state of being properly memorialized or in the state
of muen, without a memorial relationship) from time immemorial and the spirits

of all beings. Although the daily memorial mass pacifies ancestors and spirits, performance of the all souls' rite raises the status of such spirits and ensures their proper protection of descendants. In other words, the rite has the power of transforming these ancestors and spirits into protective spirits (*shugorei*). Those who wish to participate directly in the all souls' memorial rite apply through their local branch before the Spring or Fall Grand Festival. Special certificates (*honshō*) for this purpose are made at the Tokyo headquarters, with the names of the spirit to be memorialized filled in.[21] These are offered up at the altar of the Goreichi Practice Hall at the time of the Spring and Fall Grand Festivals and are carried from the altar to the site of the ritual in a special "chest."

The "chest" was carried by the four young men to the special amacha offering site with its five-sided pillar, and amacha was poured over the pillar as the formal act of memorializing the spirits whose names are on the "certificates." The announcer explained the significance of the rite as being due to the mercy of Gochi Nyorai, whose merits brought about the release of all spirits of the dead from all sins and enmity, causing them to never wander again and to be at peace eternally. Later the announcer said that this wonderful rite bequeathed by the founder, pouring amacha over special ancestral tablets, enables people to purify the spiritual character of all things, and to "liberate" (*gedatsu*) all people from suffering.

The certificates for the all souls' memorial rite are preserved indefinitely in the building called the kyōzō (scripture treasury or depository), which contains a statue of Gochi Nyorai. In other words, all the spirits who have been memorialized in this fashion from the beginning of Gedatsu-kai are permanently enshrined in this building as pacified spirits. Because these certificates remain at the Goreichi, in their place papers verifying performance of the all souls' rite are distributed from headquarters to members through branches; members place these papers in their respective butsudan in their homes.[22]

After the all soul's memorial rite, there were formal greetings from the head (hossu) of Gedatsu-kai and other officials, as well as some political leaders. The hossu thanked the people for coming to this celebration, which was not just for the sake of those present but also for the ancestors, for *furusato* (one's native place or spiritual home), for this sacred place (goreichi), for the love of human beings eternally. He encouraged members to follow the founder's spirit, worship the sun, be one nation and one people. He said people should be thankful to society, but especially to the country (*kokudo*), because without the country people can do nothing. Similarly, if there were no society, there would be no life. And people should be grateful to creation, for without creation we cannot exist. People should support the state and peace. People should believe in the founder deeply in their hearts—this anyone can do.

Other Gedatsu-kai executives also presented their greetings, and the mayor of Kitamoto gave an interesting talk. After the brief closing of the formal ceremony, similar to the closing of branch meetings, executives and invited guests (including a prominent politician) went to a large room in the Training Center (Kenshū Senta) for an elaborate reception with fancy *hors d'oeuvres* and a variety of drinks. When we left the Training Center at 3:00 and walked to the Goreichi Practice Hall, we passed the almost deserted area that just a few hours ago had been packed with thousands of people. Over the loudspeaker came an announcement for several people to come to their chartered bus, which was ready to depart. The Gedatsu-kai official commented that all these people come for this Grand Festival of a few hours and go home. The few people who remained were continuing to pay their religious respects at the various sacred sites, and some were performing ohyakudo (the hundredfold repentance) in front of the Tenjin Chigi Shrine.

The Fall Grand Festival of 1979 is a prime example of how the founder's early precedents have been preserved and yet expanded into an elaborate celebration. The "origin" of the festival is the founder's simple monthly omairi, paying respects, to the sacred sites of his home and native village; through the years, as Gedatsu-kai grew in numbers and organizational strength, numerous buildings and special shrines were added, especially those commemorating the founder's revelations and teachings. In the earliest days of omairi, the founder and a few followers made the trip by train and returned to Tokyo the same day; this was the pattern for the first Grand Festival, when fifty followers made the one-day excursion. Later, as more distant members made the trip, they stayed in homes in the Kitamoto area. Today many people still use the train for a one-day trip from their homes to Goreichi and back, while more are utilizing the services of charter buses. Those from greater distances stay in the dormitory facilities at the large Training Center (Kenshū Senta).

What was once simply the Grand Festival became the Spring Grand Festival and Fall Grand Festival. In fact, the number of participants has increased to such an extent that two identical festivals are held on successive days for each spring and fall celebration—in 1979 the Fall Grand Festival was held on October 9 and repeated with minor changes on October 10. Gedatsu-kai officials estimated 10,000 in attendance on the second day. This is one indication of how the celebration has become formalized. What was once a rather informal gathering has become a carefully planned and coordinated event. Our research team was given the mimeographed script for the Fall Grand Festival, complete with stage directions and timing for the entire service.

All these changes and formal arrangements for the Grand Festival are the natural consequences of a larger religious organization with its necessary logistical planning. However, the general rationale of the festival has not changed: even today, this celebration is a repetition of the founder's precedent of a religious visit to the sacred sites of his home and native village. The added features make Goreichi truly a "Sacred Land," a mecca for Gedatsu-kai members. Traveling here is returning to the origins of Gedatsu-kai and the source of their religious lives. This occasion incorporates the liturgy found in home, branch, and regional centers, but performs it at the holy of holies, the actual sites where the founding revelations took place. Members act out their devotions and repentance here, renewing their spiritual lives, but the pilgrimage does not end until they have completed the circle and arrived home. Indeed, the influence of such pilgrimage lasts for a long time. Our research team visited a number of branch meetings during the fall of 1979, and a recurrent theme of members' taiken during the meetings was their spiritual growth during the previous Grand Festival and their thankfulness for having been able to attend it.

Honoring Seasons: New Year's and the Amacha Harvest Thanks Festival

The celebration of New Year's and the Amacha Harvest Thanks Festival are two more Gedatsu-kai annual celebrations which, like the Grand Festivals of spring and fall, mark the seasons and at the same time incorporate Gedatsu-kai theory and practice. New Year's is celebrated at Goreichi and is similar to the Grand Festival in its emphasis on pilgrimage to the Sacred Land. The Amacha Harvest Festival is a more recent and remote celebration.

New Year's is an important traditional festival in Japan, marking the end of the pollution and decline of the previous year and the ushering in of a fresh and propitious year. Before the Meiji Restoration of 1868, it was celebrated according to the lunar calendar, and although lunar observances still linger, the primary celebration is now on New Year's Eve and New Year's Day according to January 1 of the Western or Gregorian (solar) calendar. In recent Japan, a widespread custom is for people to pay visits to temples and shrines on New Year's Eve or New Year's Day for the double purpose of sending off the old year and bringing in the new; usually they remove the old talismans from the home and purchase new ones at shrines or temples.

Gedatsu-kai has adopted New Year's as one of its major festivals, utilizing the traditional theme of ending/beginning while adapting the celebration to its own distinctive beliefs and practices. This festival is especially significant to Gedatsu-kai, because it was on New Year's Day 1929 that Okano received the revelation to establish a religion—while he and a religious specialist stood before a shrine near his parents' home, the future site of the Sacred Land. For Gedatsu-kai, much of the significance of the New Year's celebration is its observance at Goreichi, the Sacred Land and pilgrimage center of this religion.

For the 1980 New Year's celebration, Gedatsu-kai officials suggested that we come to Goreichi late on the evening of December 31 and stay overnight, so that we could see both the late evening and early morning practices. On December 31, 1979, we left Ueno Station in Tokyo shortly after 10 P.M. and arrived at Kitamoto about 11 P.M., walking the short distance from the Kitamoto train station to the nearby Goreichi. We did not go directly to the Goreichi Practice Hall, but followed the route traced by Gedatsu-kai members as part of their New Year's pilgrimage, basically the same as for the Grand Festival pilgrimage. The first monument most members visit is the Sun Spirit Monument (Taiyō Seishin Hi). On this night the monument and many offerings in front of it were illuminated by a spotlight; Gedatsu-kai volunteers were in attendance around the stone, feeding a fire to stay warm. From there we walked to the Shinto shrine Tenman Jinja, which was selling the usual Shinto-style talismans; neither the shrine nor the nearby vendors (found in and around all shrine precincts during festivals) were doing much business. Next to the Tenman Jinja is the Buddhist temple Tamonji, which was closed; there were no activities around the temple, at the nearby cemetery with stones of the Okano family, or at the stupa where Okano discovered the five mystic syllables. From the temple we walked to the old Okano home, where some Gedatsu-kai members were coming out of the lane toward the Goreichi grounds proper on the other side of the railroad tracks.

After visiting the old home, we went directly to the Goreichi Practice Hall, where we had agreed to meet Gedatsu-kai officials, and arranged for our night's lodging. We talked with the official about Gedatsu-kai matters until 11:40, when we left for the area in front of the Tenjin Chigi Shrine, the site of the main festivities for the Grand Festival. A short while before, this area had been quiet, but now people were arriving and activities began to pick up. We had been told that there would be sake after the formal ceremony; such sake blessed and served at religious celebrations is called *omiki*. A stand was set up for the sake by the six Jizō, and several other stands were selling the same goods found at most shrines and temples on these occasions. They were selling items such as *ema* (votive tablets) with the animal of the year (according to the Chinese calendar for 1980, a monkey), with the Gedatsu-kai name on them. Most Japanese people who visit a shrine or temple on New Year's buy some such ema or a talisman, as a casual wish for good luck in the coming year. Some people were making purchases, while others were paying respects at sacred sites, pouring amacha over the five-sided pillar, and returning the previous year's kuyō fuda (memorial mass talismans) for burning. It was quite cold and getting colder; to keep warm, people huddled around wood fires burning in five-gallon cans. More elaborate raised open braziers had been prepared, but because of high winds they were not lit. In spite of the cold, a few members were performing the hundredfold repentance (ohyakudo) in front of the Tenjin Chigi Shrine.

The formal ceremony started just before midnight at the Tenjin Chigi Shrine. The gist of the brief ceremony was a Shinto-style service led by a Gedatsu-kai member dressed in formal Shinto attire, although he was not a Shinto priest (*kannushi*). There was a formal announcement of the New Year, and the "priest" blessed the crowd in the customary Shinto fashion by waving a *gohei* over the crowd. (A gohei is a long stick with paper streamers on it, used at Shinto shrines for the purpose of purification and blessing.) The head (hossu) of Gedatsu-kai played a central role in the ceremony, slowly mounting the shrine steps one by one, receiving a formal written prayer from the "priest," and reading it to the crowd over the loudspeaker system. After a brief greeting from the superintendent (kyōtō) of Gedatsu-kai, a brief version of the usual Gedatsu-kai liturgy was recited in front of several nearby monuments, ending at the All Souls' Monument. At that point people were told to pay their religious respects (omairi) individually. They stopped at the stand for some sake (served cold) and vegetables and then practiced their devotions at various monuments; some poured amacha while reciting the *Hannya Shingyō*, as at other Gedatsu-kai services.

We estimated about 1,000 people in attendance for the formal New Year's ceremony, and Gedatsu-kai officials guessed there would be about 10,000 people visiting Goreichi over the three-day period of celebration from New Year's Day through the third. On this night the parking lot by the museum had only one bus, but numerous cars. Officials said that many would come by bus on New Year's Day, with the crowd peaking about noon. After the formal ceremony, we retraced our steps from the main ritual area in front of the Tenjin Chigi Shrine, going through the tunnel to the old Okano home, the cemetery, the Buddhist temple Tamonji, the Shinto shrine Tenman Jinja, and the Sun Monument. Some people were paying respects in the old Okano home, and we were served tea by the woman in charge. She said that many, but not all, members who come to Goreichi for New Year's stop by the home. The cemetery, Tamonji, and Tenman Jinja had no visitors, but one couple paying respects at the Sun Monument had parked their car nearby and got into it as we approached the monument. From the Sun Monument we returned to the area in front of the Tenjin Chigi Shrine, where more people were performing the hundredfold repentance and paying respects at various sites. By this time—about 2:00 A.M.—the Goreichi was rather deserted, so we went to our lodging provided by Gedatsu-kai, and slept until 7:00

A.M. Even at that early hour, people were making their religious visits. A stand was selling hot noodles, and souvenir stands were open.

We left Goreichi abut 11:00 A.M. New Year's Day, before the arrival of most chartered buses, but we learned about general New Year's practices from officials. The general term in Japanese for a person's first visit of the New Year to a shrine or temple is *hatsumōde*, and Gedatsu-kai uses the same term. Months before at the Kyoto Practice Hall I had seen a poster reading "Hatsumōde begins at Goreichi," and the same posters were displayed at Goreichi on New Year's Day. Officials told us that with improved transportation, few people stay overnight when making their hatsumōde to Goreichi. People who live too far away make their "first visit" at a regional practice hall or at a branch.

New Year's at Goreichi shares many of the features of New Year's renewal celebrated at most Shinto shrines and Buddhist temples: making one's "first visit," depositing old talismans and buying new talismans or souvenirs, perhaps having a drink of sake, and paying respects at sacred sites. Gedatsu-kai has blended these seasonal customs with its own tradition of pilgrimage and self-cultivation. Observing New Year's at Goreichi is much the same as attending the Spring or Fall Grand Festival: coming in contact with the founder and the concentrated power of Gedatsu-kai. The self-cultivation practiced during New Year's at Goreichi imparts a special significance to this celebration, a more "serious" form of dedication (or rededication). The joyous New Year's atmosphere at Shinto shrines and Buddhist temples is not missing at the Goreichi New Year's festivities, but the devotions at monuments and the hundredfold repentance lend an air of solemnity and self-dedication not found at the usual New Year's "first visits." Gedatsu-kai is able to combine all these features—seasonal renewal, pilgrimage, and self-cultivation—in one elaborate set of festivities.

The New Year's festival has been compared to the Spring and Fall Grand Festivals; the three annual events are quite similar, but several contrasts are obvious. A primary difference is that the distinctive ritual of the Grand Festival, the all souls' memorial rite, is not performed at New Year's. Also, the space and time of the New Year's festival are somewhat different from those of the Grand Festival. The space of the Grand Festival encompasses the entire pilgrimage route, with many practices around the Buddhist temple Tamonji and the cemetery; this may be partly a result of the emphasis of the Grand Festival (and traditional Japanese spring and fall rituals) on honoring spirits of the dead. The space for the New Year's festival is more concentrated around the area in front of the Tenjin Chigi Shrine, spilling over to the founder's old home. A person can bypass the parish shrine Tenman Jinja and the parish temple Tamonji, and not miss any of the New Year's event. The time for the Grand Festival is rather condensed, concentrating on the time just before, during, and after the formal ceremony. By contrast, rather few people attend the midnight New Year's ceremony at Goreichi, and many more make their "first visit" to Goreichi during the three-day celebration of New Year's.

The Amacha Harvest Thanks Festival (Amacha Shūkaku Kanshasai) is an annual seasonal celebration quite different from the two Grand Festivals and the New Year's festivities, which are held at Goreichi and involve large crowds. In simple terms, the Amacha Harvest Festival is a thanksgiving ceremony, but a very special thanksgiving for the single crop of amacha at Gedatsu-kai's amacha farm in Nagano Prefecture. Held on November 20 in a processing shed for amacha, the 1979

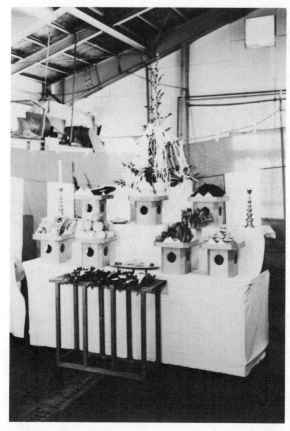

17. Altar for the Amacha Harvest Festival at Kurohime

festival was attended by only 75–100 people including some officials from Gedatsu-kai headquarters. To view the festival, I left Ueno Station in Tokyo at 6:30 A.M. with a Gedatsu-kai official, and we arrived at Kurohime in Nagano Prefecture about 10:40 A.M. The amacha farm is some distance by car from Kurohime Station, making it quite remote from Gedatsu-kai headquarters as well as from the general membership. In the processing shed, a simple Shinto-style altar was decorated with *sakaki* (a tree sacred to Shinto) and bottles of sake, flanked on both sides with gohei (a long stick with paper streamers on it). I had met our research team at Kurohime Station, and we were a little late for the opening prayer by a man dressed in the style of a Shinto priest. Most of the people in attendance were local workers on the amacha farm. Several officials from Gedatsu-kai gave formal thanks to the workers for their hard labor, and spoke generally about thankfulness. At the end of the brief ceremony, there was the usual blessing of the audience by the "priest" (by waving the gohei over the people), followed by a celebration feast with drinks and singing, as is customary at such "parties" marking the end of a season or the completion of a project.

Our research team left the party early to see the amacha fields before we had to leave on our early train back to Tokyo. Unfortunately, the fields were empty, because in harvesting amacha the plant is cut back to the roots; the perennial plant sprouts anew from the roots in spring. In the fields we saw a small shrine for Kurohime Benzaiten: according to local legend, centuries ago, when these mountain fields were first tilled, a large white snake appeared, and the deity Benzaiten protected them from the snake. This shrine serves as a protective deity for the amacha fields. Before Gedatsu-kai had its own source of amacha, supplies were bought from the patent medicine company Jintan (which makes, among other things, a popular lozenge). Gedatsu-kai acquired this land in 1969, and they now need to grow forty tons of amacha just for the movement's own use. The farm is an impressive agricultural establishment, with a number of buildings, special mechanized equipment, and a large crop. But this is more than just a "farm." Before we left the grounds, we were given popular pamphlets on the curative powers of amacha and were shown the special prayer read over the amacha when it is stored; the prayer features the "healing Buddha" Yakushi Nyorai[23] as well as the usual triad of Gedatsu-kai divinities. The 1979 Harvest Festival was the eleventh annual celebration.

As a fall thanksgiving ceremony, the amacha festival fits generally within the Japanese pattern of rites marking the end of the vegetative season, although it comes later than most harvest festivities. Within the round of Gedatsu-kai ritual, this celebration may be described as a festival *for* rather than by Gedatsu-kai members, in the sense that it is a remote thanksgiving ceremony to celebrate the new crop of amacha for Gedatsu-kai use. Members do not have direct contact with the celebration, although the blessed product is mentioned in other festivals: in the previous Fall Grand Festival there was reference to the Nagano farm when the young kimono-clad maidens offered amacha as part of the all souls' memorial rite. If amacha were not central to the regular ritual life of Gedatsu-kai, this remote harvest festival with such a small number of participants might be considered insignificant; but because it celebrates and blesses the harvest of the crucial ritual substance, it constitutes an important seasonal festival for the sake of all members.

Honoring the Founder: Goseitan (Birth Anniversary) and Nensai (Death Anniversary)

Gedatsu Kongō as the founder of Gedatsu-kai is prominent in all the rituals and annual festivals of this religion, but two special annual events dedicated solely to him honor his birth and his death. The Goseitan, or Birth Anniversary, held at Goreichi, shares many features with other rites held there; the Nensai, or Death Anniversary, is held at Kyoto and includes features not seen in previous festivals. The timing of these festivals, linked to the actual birth and death days of the founder, places them both in November. Because the Birth Anniversary is most like previous celebrations at Goreichi, it will be treated first. The Birth Anniversary has been held annually since the erection of the Shōtoku Hi (Encomium) in 1941.

Our research team attended the Goseitan (Birth Anniversary) of Gedatsu Kongō on November 28, 1979; I left Tokyo early in the morning and arrived in Kitamoto before 8:30 AM. While changing trains on the way, I happened to meet the branch leader of "Ok" Branch, and we sat together for the remainder of the trip. As soon as we left the train at Kitamoto, this branch leader was busy greeting people. We walked with others to Goreichi, visiting first the Sun Monument, then the Shinto

Shrine Tenman Jinja, the Buddhist temple Tamonji, memorial stones of the Okano family, the six Jizō and other sacred sites, and finally the old Okano home. The Birth Anniversary celebration included both a memorial mass in the small Okano home and a larger service in the ritual area in front of monuments south of the Tenjin Chigi Shrine.

When we arrived at the Okano home, people were milling about, drinking tea provided by Gedatsu-kai, as during the Grand Festival. General members remained outside the home while branch leaders and officials entered. The ceremony in the Okano home was a rather simple memorial service conducted by the Buddhist priest of Tamonji, because this is the parish Buddhist temple (bodaiji) of the Okano family. Respects were paid to the generations of ancestors of the Okano family line, followed by reciting of Buddhist scriptures by the priest. It is customary at such services to offer three pinches of incense in a brazier; first the head (hossu) of Gedatsu-kai and other officials offered incense, and then boxes of it were passed through the audience for each person to offer three pinches. After the formal memorial mass, the Gedatsu-kai liturgy was recited. There were greetings by the superintendent (kyōtō) of Gedatsu-kai, who patiently explained the meaning of the mass for the founder, to whom Gedatsu-kai members are eternally grateful for founding this religion. And, he said, without the generations of ancestors of the Okano family, the founder would not have been born. He also explained the presence of the priest from Tamonji, the parish temple of the Okano family. A representative of the family replied with formal thanks.

We left the Okano home for the next part of the ceremony, passing through the tunnel under the railroad. Members were paying respects at various sites and performing the hundredfold repentance. Soon the second part of the ceremony began in the large area south of the Tenjin Chigi Shrine. It was a simple variation on the regular Gedatsu-kai liturgy, with recitation of homage to various divinities, and listening to the recording of the founder's voice. There was a special "birthday" (seitan) song, which had been mimeographed and distributed so all could sing it. There were offerings of flowers and congratulatory addresses to the founder. At the end of the service, general members went their way, continuing their devotions, and performing the hundredfold repentance and pouring amacha.

The Birth Anniversary, like all celebrations at Goreichi, is a form of pilgrimage, with the same general pattern of devotions as during the Grand Festival, and allows for individual practices. Its distinctive feature is the Buddhist memorial rite in the old Okano home, for the sake of the Okano family as well as the founder. This festival is much smaller in scale than the Grand Festival: for the Grand Festival two days were required to accommodate the crowds, and even then ropes were used to separate the crowds from the actual performers. For the Birth Anniversary there were no ropes, and a small group of people closed in around the performers. It may be safe to say that the Birth Anniversary is a minor festival honoring the founder.

The Nensai (Death Anniversary) is held November 3 in and around the temple Sennyūji in Kyoto, and is a much larger affair than the Birth Anniversary. I traveled by train with a group of Gedatsu-kai executives November 2, 1979, and we stayed at a Kyoto hotel that night, rising the next morning to go first to the Kansai Practice Hall to pay respects at the altar there. This practice hall is close to Sennyūji, an old temple famous for enshrining the ashes of many members of the imperial family. The story of how the founder in 1939 insisted on the right of "commoners" to enter Sennyūji and pay respects to the emperors—as an act of filial piety—has been told in chapter 2. The close tie of Okano to the temple, and especially his support of it after World War II when it was financially hard pressed, led to Sennyūji's permission for Okano to have his ashes enshrined in a memorial next to the temple grounds.

Kyoto is famous for its old shrines and temples, and the area surrounding Sennyūji, too, is dotted with many sacred sites. When we left the Kansai Practice Hall, we walked with a Gedatsu-kai official to some of these sites surrounding Sennyūji. Many Gedatsu-kai members were paying their respects at these places while waiting for the formal ceremony; in fact, we met the wife of the branch leader from "Ok" Branch in Tokyo. In response to our question, the executive with us said that, as at Goreichi, people are on their own in paying respects at various sacred sites—there is no set pilgrimage order when participating in the Death Anniversary at Sennyūji.

The formal ceremony of the Death Anniversary, somewhat like the Birth Anniversary, features both a formal Buddhist memorial rite and a less formal Gedatsu-kai rite. We returned to Sennyūji before noon, where a large number of Gedatsu-kai members had entered the temple grounds. Inside the temple gate, Gedatsu-kai representatives offered amacha as a hot drink to members, and most people had a glass before participating in the ceremony. General members sat on straw mats in the large courtyard of the temple, while major officials and guests sat within the main temple building. For this ceremony the Gedatsu-kai executives wore a Buddhist-style surplice (kesa) around their necks. There were also about a hundred people inside the temple who played a special role in both parts of the ceremony, because they had paid for requests to have memorialized the spirits of family members who had died during the previous year.

The lengthy memorial service within Sennyūji was the most lavish of any Gedatsu-kai ceremony that I witnessed: there were dozens of Buddhist priests in attendance wearing colorful robes, the temple itself was an old and impressive building with historical significance, and the ceremony was elaborate. The gist of the service was a memorial to the founder, much like the memorial rite for him held in the old Okano home during the Birth Anniversary, but the Sennyūji affair was much more extensive. A procession of priests entered the temple to mark the beginning of the ceremony, followed by Gedatsu-kai's offering of amacha and flowers on the altar. The head (hossu) of Gedatsu-kai gave formal remarks announcing this as the thirty-first memorial to the founder, and giving thanks. The priests then performed a lengthy memorial, reading sutras, ringing a bell, and scattering flowers. After a half-hour the formal offering of incense began, with many dignitaries advancing individually to the central altar to offer three pinches.

At 1:00 P.M. the memorial service for Gedatsu Kongō ended, and then began the *saishi shōryō hōyō*, the memorial for spirits of the dead the first year after their death. For this part of the ceremony, portable incense containers were passed among the guests (as had been done in the Okano home for the Birth Festival), and every person offered up three pinches. At about 1:20 a brief part of the Gedatsu-kai liturgy was recited—the first direct participation by the large crowd of members in the courtyard. Then the head of the movement gave an informal talk thanking the members for coming from throughout the whole country. He

18. Executives carrying memorial tablets from Sennyūji to the Gedatsu
Kongō Memorial Monument

said that many people had made requests for individual memorial rites; he also
recalled how the founder early in his career had been a pilgrim to these sacred
places, and later his spirit was enshrined in the nearby tower. He said that today
the founder's spirit received their memorial mass, and he rejoices in the spirit
world (reikai); these people are the disciples of the founder, and so his spirit lives
on. Another Gedatsu-kai executive spoke, and then the head priest of Sennyūji
thanked all the people and praised the founder; these families would benefit by
following the founder.

About two the ceremony within Sennyūji ended, and after a formal recession
of priests and dignitaries, the Gedatsu-kai officials and members walked the short
distance to the large stone memorial tower for the founder. This second part of
the ceremony was conducted completely by and for Gedatsu-kai. The members
gathered in front of the tower for offering of incense and enshrining the spirits of
the dead previously memorialized in Sennyūji. Two Gedatsu-kai officials carried
trays of the papers bearing the names of the memorialized persons into the lower
part of the tower; they wore the same Shinto-style "masks" (to prevent their breath
from polluting the papers) as were worn by the four men carrying the chest of
papers for souls of the dead in the all souls' memorial rite during the Grand
Festival. First the head and leading officials of the movement offered incense,
and there was a brief part of the Gedatsu-kai liturgy, which included mention of
the saishi shōryō (rites for spirits of the dead). Then all members entered the
tower from the left, going into the dark interior; they offered incense quickly,
exiting from the right. This ended the second part of the Death Anniversary.
Afterward people were free to pay respects at various sites, and executives went
to a special meal in an annex to Sennyūji.

In essence, the Death Anniversary is an elaborate memorial rite, but its significance goes far beyond this ritual. When members make their pilgrimage to Goreichi, they are "returning home" in the sense of going back to the founder's roots, retracing the founder's religious visit to his home village and local sacred sites. By contrast, when members go to Sennyūji, they are coming in contact with the ancient heritage of Japan and the imperial line, returning to the heart of the Japanese tradition. Walking through the inner area of Sennyūji, people can see the rooms where many emperors stayed when they visited the temple. Until the end of World War II, commoners were not even allowed inside the gates of this temple, but now Gedatsu-kai members are almost in direct touch with the imperial house. The connection of the founder (especially his memorial tower) and Gedatsu-kai with Sennyūji enhances its prestige as preserver of the Japanese tradition. In the memorial service, first the founder is brought in touch with the imperial line, and then the spirits being memorialized for the first time are brought into contact with the founder and the imperial line. Gedatsu-kai's own service at the memorial tower solidifies the connection between the founder and members by enshrining them within the same tower: all are linked to the eternal spirit of Gedatsu Kongō.

If the Birth Anniversary is a relatively minor annual celebration, the Death Anniversary should be considered a major festival. Many more people attend the Death Anniversary (in a number of chartered buses); also, the memorial rite is much more elaborate, and Sennyūji is especially holy and prestigious because of its link to the imperial line. Seen together, these two annual ceremonies honor the birth and death of the religion's founder. It is not unusual in founded religions (such as Christianity and Buddhism) to honor founders on their birth- and death days; in Japan the significance of ancestors has made death days (in other words, memorial days) more important than birthdays. The memorializing of members' relatives in the founder's Death Anniversary makes it all the more important. Throughout all of Gedatsu-kai's religious life, the founder is recognized as the ideal religious model to be followed; the celebrations of the Birth and Death Anniversary officially acknowledge and reestablish Gedatsu Kongō as the originator of this religion and its continuing source of power.

Honoring the Nation: The Sanseichi Junpai and Taiyō Seishin Hi Matsuri

The Sanseichi Junpai (Three Holy Sites Pilgrimage) and the Taiyō Seishin Hi Matsuri (Sun Spirit Monument Festival) are treated together because they share the common theme of religious support for the nation. As was seen in chapter 2, each of these patriotic festivals is tied to key events in the founder's career. The three holy sites are Ise Jingū, Kashiwara Jingū, and Sennyūji, each with its own sacred national significance. Ise is venerable for its association with the enshrining of the Sun Goddess (ancestress of the imperial line and generally the protector of grain and fertility for the nation). Kashiwara Jingū traditionally is associated with Emperor Jinmu, the first emperor of Japan, and is thus linked to the foundation of the nation. Sennyūji is the temple noted for enshrining the spirits of the imperial line. As an expression of his religious piety and patriotic fervor, in 1941 the founder led members on their first Three Holy Sites Pilgrimage to these religious centers. Continuing through World War II and down to the present, this tradition has been maintained; members also visit the temple Sanbōin within the grounds of

Daigoji (in Kyoto), the Buddhist establishment where Okano underwent formal Buddhist training.

The pilgrimage itself is from April 1 to 3: on the first day they arrive at Ise, on the second day they make their formal pilgrimage to Ise Jingū and Kashiwara Jingū, and on the third day they proceed to Sennyūji and Sanbōin. The pilgrimage numbers are limited to about a thousand people, each branch sending a branch leader or representative and two general members. Ceremonies at the three holy sites consist of shortened versions of the Gedatsu-kai religious service, with special recognition of the kami and spirits enshrined at each. Part of the ceremonies at Sennyūji is a brief side trip to the tomb of the founder.[24]

From 1967 a second form of the Three Holy Sites Pilgrimage was opened to members at large, especially young people. Held in August, this general pilgrimage has drawn more than 8,000 participants. Our research team viewed a film of the general pilgrimage which had been made three years earlier (1976). This film is a high-quality 16mm production; many copies are in use at branch and other meetings. The copy we viewed had been shown so many times it was rather scratchy. The film opened with a quick preview of the subject of the film, the three holy sites, by presenting footage of each site and explaining briefly its significance. Then it went back to each sacred site for closer individual treatment. The general rationale of the pilgrimage is that it was established by the founder to honor the country (kokudo) and for world peace. Ise Jingū is shown in its two main divisions, Naikū and Gekū: the Naikū is for the Sun Goddess (Amaterasu), representing the "great shrine of the Japanese people" (nihon kokumin no ōmiya); the Gekū provides food for the Ise Shrine (and Amaterasu). Kashiwara Shrine is related to the founding of the country by Emperor Jinmu. The temple Sennyūji has three Buddhist divinities—Shaka, Amida, and Miroku—and is noted for the emperors enshrined there.

The film showed highlights of young people on pilgrimage to each of the three holy sites while providing background information. Every year since 1966, young Gedatsu-kai members have made this journey. They are clothed in white, from shoes to caps; the stated purpose of the pilgrimage is world peace. In 1977, 7,200 young people made the pilgrimage. (We were told later that officials were not eager to increase the numbers beyond 8,000, because of the extensive planning and logistics required.) Before the shrines, the pilgrims perform the Gedatsu-kai style of reverence with four hand claps; at Ise, as is customary for many visitors to this shrine, they purify themselves with water from the Isuzu River.

By no means is this a somber affair: featured in parades to the shrine grounds are the kind of marching band and baton twirlers seen in the celebration of the Grand Festival. (One song the band played was the tune of "I've Been Working on the Railroad.") The narrator of the film said that this pilgrimage is for the traditional spirit of the Japanese people, and one of the banners carried in a Kyoto street parade proclaimed "the [Japanese] people's tradition and contemporary life"—implying that people can be true to their traditional roots and yet fit into contemporary life. Because of the size of the group, they must travel in chartered buses and enter the sacred sites in groups. The film showed young people in the buses, some singing while others slept. The last site of the pilgrimage is the memorial tower for Gedatsu Kongō next to Sennyūji; here some people are shown crying with emotion. The narrator urges people to protect these three holy sites,

19. Youth group at Kashiwara Jingū during the Three Sacred Sites Pilgrimage

which are all connected: gratitude and thanks help people realize world peace. After the film, I asked the person showing it what pilgrims receive when they visit these sites: he said that they receive talismans from Ise and Kashiwara Shrines, and a protective amulet (*mamori*) from Sennyūji.

This pilgrimage has its roots in the practice of the founder, but its present form as a youth festival is rather recent. Obviously this is the major annual event for young people; when we attended a youth meeting in the Kansai Dōjō, some of the young people in their testimonies talked emotionally about how they appreciated the experience of this pilgrimage. Its theme, to honor the religious roots of the country, is a direct extension of Gedatsu-kai's teaching: it is educational for newcomers, and a reinforcement of traditional values for repeat participants.

The Taiyō Seishin Hi Matsuri, or Sun Spirit Monument Festival, is a commemoration of the founder's dedication of the Sun Spirit Monument at the Go-reichi on February 11, 1940, celebrated annually on this date. The monument itself is a large stone with a large red sun in the middle, flanked by two characters composing the word *seishin*, or "spirit." The significance of the date in 1940 was the traditionally reckoned 2,600th year of the Japanese Empire as founded by Emperor Jinmu; until the end of World War II, February 11 was Kigensetsu, "Empire Day," or "Anniversary of the Emperor Jinmu's Accession."[25] Today Gedatsu-kai teaches that this memorial is a symbol of the "heart" or "spirit" of the "selfless great love" of the sun which brings about the whole of creation and naturally causes people to have thoughts of gratitude and thanks. Of course, this monument clearly is a symbol of the Japanese flag, the *hi no maru*, represented by a red circle (against a white background), commemorating the traditional founding of the Japanese Empire, as is clear from the festival.

The Sun Spirit Monument Festival is divided into two segments. In the morning at ten o'clock branch leaders and executives gather in front of the Sun Spirit

20. Taiyō Seishin Hi (Sun Spirit Monument) at the Sacred Land

Monument. They worship as a group, and the hossu (head) reads a formal pro-
clamation, after which they follow the standard Gedatsu-kai liturgy (gongyō). The
ceremony for general members starts at eleven o'clock in the large open space of
the Sacred Land where the Grand Festivals and other ceremonies are held. For
this celebration, a wooden fence is installed to which is affixed an oversize Japanese
flag, and the celebration takes place facing the flag. In addition to standard features
of Gedatsu-kai liturgy, the participants sing the national anthem ("Kimigayo") and
a song honoring the Sun Spirit Monument, closing with three "banzai."[26]

The Sun Spirit Monument Festival is a direct continuation of the precedent set
by the founder in 1940, and in the spirit of those times recalls the ancient, divine
heritage of the Japanese nation. Although Kigensetsu (Empire Day) was officially
removed from calendars after World War II (replaced in 1967 with Kenkoku Kinen
no Hi, or National Foundation Day), it lives on in the memory and ritual action
of Gedatsu-kai. The Sun Spirit Monument and Kashiwara Shrine both honor Emperor Jinmu, at Ise the Sun Goddess (Amaterasu Omikami) is enshrined, and the
ancestral spirits of the imperial line are memorialized at the Buddhist temple
Sennyūji. Founder, imperial ancestors, the divine ancestress of the nation, and
the living members and officials of Gedatsu-kai are joined together in ritual action.

The Round of Ritual Life in Gedatsu-kai

All the preceding rituals form a "round," or complete cycle, of religious activities
in the sense of covering so many possibilities and situations for so many people.
Most rituals are for adults generally, and children are spectators; other meetings
are for young people, and a separate Three Sacred Sites Pilgrimage is a special
event for them. The home is the most "local" ritual scene, with the branch an
important grassroots meeting place, and regional practice halls serving as effective

"joiners" of branches into the larger organization; the Sacred Land, or Goreichi, is the single most holy site of Gedatsu-kai, constituting a mecca or pilgrimage site. Other sacred sites are the founder's memorial tower in Kyoto and the "three sacred sites" in that area. Gedatsu-kai offers the more mundane amacha rite as a daily means of ethical reflection and self-cultivation, but also provides the possibility of meditation in okiyome and the more "mystical" possibility of mediation with spirits of the other world in gohō shugyō. The religious significance of seasons is marked in the Spring and Fall Grand Festivals, as well as at New Year's and at the Amacha Harvest Festival. The founder is honored at all festivals, but especially at the Birth and Death Anniversaries. Religious support for the nation is provided in the Three Sacred Sites Pilgrimage and the Sun Monument Festival. One's own ancestors are memorialized regularly, and the spirits of all people are pacified in the Spring and Fall Grand Festivals. For almost any special religious request, there are specific memorial or apology "papers" which can be obtained through a branch leader.

These rituals seem to cover almost every religious possibility, but one category of rituals conspicuous by their absence is rites of passage. "Modern" countries such as the United States and Japan tend to limit rites of passage to the three standard transitional life phases of birth, marriage, and death, but Gedatsu-kai does not include even these. Usually Gedatsu-kai encourages people to participate in the traditional Shinto rites of birth—presenting an infant to the nearby parish shrine—and to participate in the traditional Buddhist funeral and memorial rites at a parish temple. However, it is apparent that in actual practice there is some overlap between the traditional observance of these three rites and their recognition within Gedatsu-kai. Officials said that after a birth or a wedding, members usually come to the branch meeting place for formal thanks. In fact, as mentioned in Mrs. Koshikawa's life history in chapter 3, because the hatsu mairi (first visit to a shrine for a newborn child) was the same day as a celebration at the branch practice hall, they made this ceremonial "first visit" at both the branch practice hall and the shrine of the tutelary kami. This is just one concrete example of how new rites of passage may develop on the popular level and/or be promoted from national headquarters.

The rite of passage most clearly emphasized by Gedatsu-kai is the memorial mass, which through the amacha rite has become a vital focus of daily devotions. Indeed, as seen above in the section on home and daily ritual, many people who join Gedatsu-kai then go out and buy a kamidana (Shinto altar) and a butsudan (Buddhist altar). Traditionally just the main family had a butsudan with many ancestral tablets, and other branches of a family purchased one only after they experienced death in their immediate family. However, Gedatsu-kai encourages every family to install a butsudan (and to enshrine ancestors on both the husband's and wife's sides of the family). In this sense, although Gedatsu-kai seems to be outside the official ritual blessing of birth, marriage, and death, it is actually a stimulus in two directions: for renewed participation in traditional rites, and for extension and enlargement of these rites (particularly in the home).[27]

In general, puberty rites in contemporary Japan have fallen into disuse, but the life history of Mr. Abe in chapter 3 indicates how Gedatsu-kai is able to infuse new life into old forms. What precipitated Mr. Abe's crisis at work was his participation in the coming-of-age ceremony at Goreichi on the eighth day of the

New Year, when he pledged to be a responsible adult. On the next day he began to experience his leg problems, and eventually he resolved his physical and spiritual problems by recognizing that he was lazy at work—and not living up to his pledge at Goreichi. Our research team did not observe this particular ritual, but it is worth mentioning as a Gedatsu-kai innovation in connection with rites of passage. It is also likely that youth meetings and the Three Holy Sites Pilgrimage may serve as initiatory experiences, and that in these contexts some young people may experience "conversion," just as some adults may undergo "conversion" or similar cathartic experiences at branch meetings (especially during okiyome and gohō shugyō). In this way, Gedatsu-kai is providing a kind of alternative to rites of passage such as puberty rites or "secret societies." It is also quite likely that the movement may expand its round of ritual in the future by developing its own birth, marriage, and death rituals—even if it continues to encourage participation in Shinto and Buddhist rituals. If Gedatsu-kai establishes independent meeting places (apart from home and business) and creates a professional clergy, it would seem natural also to adopt its own birth-marriage-death rituals. At present, Gedatsu-kai emphasizes most the monthly branch and regional meetings and the annual cycle of national celebrations, especially at the Sacred Land.

8

RETURNING TO THE CENTER
Gedatsu-kai, New Religions,
and Contemporary Japan

The major thrust of this book has been to describe, analyze, and interpret Gedatsu-kai belief and practice as a new religious movement. Theoretical questions about the origin and nature of Gedatsu-kai, while kept in mind, have been subordinated to the task of presenting a coherent picture of this new religion. Now that this overall treatment is complete, it is fitting to turn to some of the more theoretical questions. Actually, in gathering and assembling all this information, many more questions were raised than the author can hope to answer; one reason for presenting such a complete description of so many aspects of Gedatsu-kai is the hope that others will take up some of the unanswered questions and develop broader interpretations of the material. However, to bring this work to a conclusion, it seems appropriate to deal with two questions that have plagued Western-language treatments of Japanese new religions: How are we to account for the rise of new religions such as Gedatsu-kai? What is the significance of new religions such as Gedatsu-kai? Discussion of these two questions provides the basis for our concluding view of Gedatsu-kai as a "returning to the center."

Old Religion, New Religion;
Old Tradition, New Tradition[1]

Western journalists and scholars have been fascinated with the rise of Japanese new religions and have not been reticent about providing explanations of their origin. For more than two decades I have followed much of this literature (Earhart 1970a, 1983), but I generally have been disappointed with the nature of these explanations. One reason scholars have been attracted to Japanese new religions is their interest in how the movements happened to come into existence—the suspicion being that there is a kind of causal relationship between certain social conditions and the rise of the new religions. Put in its simplest form, the prevailing explanation is that they arose in response to—or "because of"—social disruption and personal anxiety. This notion, obviously, is an application of previously developed theories of the relationship between social change and religion. It should be emphasized that this notion of causal relationship was advanced mainly as an application of previously developed theoretical discussions, and did not develop out of an adequate analysis of the historical formation and concrete life of Japanese new religions. It seems fair to state that most scholars approached the Japanese new religions with these ready-made theories—rather than studying them thoroughly in order to discover theoretical questions they pose and exploring theoretical solutions.

My own study of Japanese new religions and similar "new religious movements" in other cultures brought me to disagree with this notion of simple causal relationship, and I wrote a number of articles criticizing it (Earhart 1969, 1970c, 1971, 1974a, 1976). However, it proved difficult to offer a positive theory of the formation of the new religions in place of the one I rejected. There were many new religions, and the circumstances of their formation seemed too complex to be interpreted by one grand theory. This is the immediate background of my decision to make a thorough study of one Japanese new religion, in order to resolve some of the questions about these movements.

Gedatsu-kai was selected because of a number of favorable factors: it had developed in part out of the religious tradition of Shugendō, which I had studied (Earhart 1970b); I had made contact with the group in 1969, and was assured of easy access; Gedatsu-kai's beliefs and practices seemed to be typical for Japanese religion generally, making it a good representative case; its membership of a quarter-million meant it was large enough to be a significant, nationwide movement but not so large as to complicate the study. I wanted this study to be as broad as possible with a small research team, utilizing the standard historical approach of placing the movement in its context of development, together with the participant-observation approach of viewing rituals and practices, but also making use of the approach of intensive, "inside" life histories and the approach of extensive survey questionnaires. The results of this comprehensive study form the content of previous chapters; my thesis is that interpretation of the formation of Gedatsu-kai may throw light on the "origin" of Japanese new religions, and also serve as a model for the study of similar movements. The main thrust of this section is to present a positive theory of the formation of new religious movements in Japan, but at the outset it may be useful to provide a critique of prevailing Western interpretation.[2] The works of two widely quoted authors may be taken as typical of this Western scholarship.

Most Western interpretations are based on the premise that " 'religious developments may best be understood as responses to fundamental changes in their social environment' " (McFarland 1967:13). Following this basic approach, the same author concludes that "the New Religions of Japan are variously dated products of or responses to the endemic, recurrently intensified social crisis that has been the burden of the Japanese people for approximately the last three and a half centuries" (ibid., p. 54). The gist of this approach is rather simple: scholars have adopted a view that sees religion as a response to social change, and this forms the basis of the view of Japanese new religions as products of or response to endemic social change.

This view is echoed by another scholar:

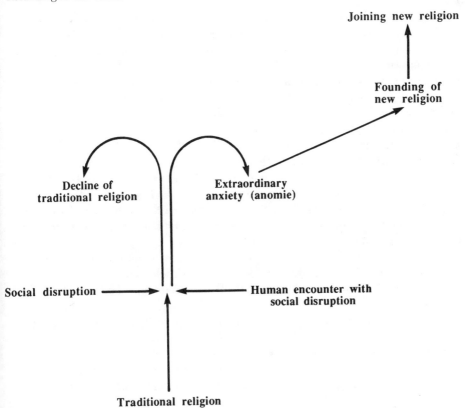

Figure 1. The Anomie Theory of the Formation of Japanese New Religions

> Significant cultural influences are closely related to the individual motivations that predisposed many Japanese to new religious movements and to the changed structures that were brought about by industrialization and warfare. On the one hand, the effect of the simultaneous influence of urban migration, war, defeat, and occupation had been a great increase in anomie—normlessness. The sense of a shared cultural system of values is difficult to maintain in these circumstances. On the other hand, the new religions offer themselves as antidotes to anomie. (Yinger 1970:170)

As this scholar reiterates, Japanese new religions "can serve as pressure chambers for the socially disadvantaged, faced with problems of adjustment to a new environment" (ibid., 273).

The prevailing interpretation of Japanese new religions can be summed up as follows: New religions arise because traditional religion and society are disrupted by radical social change; this creates extraordinary anxiety (or normlessness, anomie), which prompts the formation of new religions and stimulates people to join them. Without discussing the argument further, let me attempt to diagram the argument so that its major points are more distinct (see fig. 1).

This diagram is read from the bottom up. Traditional religion continues until it is interrupted by radical social change or social disruption, as a result of which it declines. At the same time, humans encounter social disorder, in turn experiencing personal disorder, and because traditional religion has declined and cannot be depended on, they are plagued with extraordinary anxiety. It is this extraordinary anxiety that stimulates founders to initiate new religions and ordinary people to join them.

At this point it is best to comment only briefly on several deficiencies in this theoretical position. It would be inappropriate to claim that this theory is completely "wrong," for it is incontrovertible that various kinds of social change are closely related to the formation of such new religions and the entry of members into them. However, there seem to be at least three ways in which the social factor has been misinterpreted in the treatment of such movements.

The first misinterpretation is placing excessive importance on social conditions, to the extent that they practically amount to the *single* causative factor in the emergence of new religions. Equally important are the influence of the prior historical tradition and the innovative decisions of founders and organizers. This is a major point of our argument, as will be spelled out in concrete detail later in the analysis of the formation of Gedatsu-kai. For the moment it is enough to insist that any account of the formation of new religions should include at least all three factors of social conditions, influence of religious tradition, and innovative decisions of founders.

The second misinterpretation of social conditions, such as anomie, is a logical fallacy. There is the vague notion that if "endemic crisis" or anomie occurred sometime before, and new religions arose sometime after, then anomie *caused* the emergence of new religions. This is the logical mistake of assuming that an antecedent is necessarily a causal factor: *post hoc, ergo propter hoc* (it rained this morning, and I came to the office; therefore, I came to the office because it rained this morning). Pointing out this logical fallacy may appear to be an unkind criticism, but it seems that most of the explanations of the origin of the new religions stop short of documenting the fact of prior endemic crisis, and assume that mere mention of prior crisis is sufficient evidence to establish a causal link. And yet, this is not the point—even if there was prior endemic crisis, one must go beyond the mere demonstration of prior occurrence of anomie to show reasonable proof for causal connection between anomie and new religions. These interpretations have not even discussed what would constitute reasonable proof for claiming causal connection between certain antecedents (anomie, normlessness) and other postcedents (new religious movements). Obviously, many social facts precede other social facts, without *necessarily* constituting a cause-and-effect relationship.

The third misinterpretation is the assumption that anomie can *only* result in new religious movements. At least two other possible results of anomie are renewed strength for traditional religion (as might be the case for religion in London during the "crisis" and "anxiety" of the World War II blitz), and the pursuit of secular means of resolving personal anxiety (as seen in sensitivity training in the midst of the relative "normlessness" of recent American society).[3] Because changed social conditions may be directly related to at least these three possibilities (development of new religions, strengthening of traditional religions, or pursuit of secular activities), it is all the more reason why theorists and historians should be more specific about the direct causal relationship between anomie and new religions.[4]

In fairness to the scholars whose writings have been characterized by this diagram, it should be conceded that they may wish to raise objections with this characterization. The preceding "simplification" of the prevailing Western theory of the origin of Japanese new religions, because it emphasizes the unicausal aspect of this theory, undoubtedly will be seen by its proponents as an "oversimplification" as well as an overemphasis on the unicausal nature of this explanation. If I have missed features of complexity and multicausal explanation in the earlier literature on Japanese new religions, this was unintentional; if other scholars raise these points of complexity and multicausal explanation in their theories, the present "oversimplification" will have served some of its purpose in furthering the discussion of the origin of Japanese (and other) new religions. However, for the purposes of this work, we continue the criticism of the prevailing theory on the basis of this simplified characterization.

One of the confusing aspects of the whole discussion of anomie and its relationship to religion is whether the concept of anomie is supposed to explain the origin of all religion or only the emergence of new religions; this is a problem of the general theory that cannot be treated here. One scholar who has questioned the relevance of the anomie theory for interpreting Japanese new religions is Eimi Watanabe Rajana. Among other points, she suggests that membership in a new religion, representing affiliation to an "intermediate organization," probably indicates that such people are not anomic (suffering from extreme anxiety or normlessness); and that for this and other reasons, "data based on such personality tests are unreliable as indicators of whether anomic individuals are attracted to Soka Gakkai or not" (1975:194). Helen Hardacre has used her own documentation of the Japanese new religion Reiyū-kai to criticize the "crisis" interpretation of Japanese new religions. She argues that "while a crisis may explain (in some weak sense of that word) why groups form at a particular time, it does not account for their persistence once the time of crisis has passed. . . . To say of Reiyukai that it represents a reaction to crisis would ignore its positive attempts to address the problems of Japanese society and also its inheritance of concepts, beliefs, and rites of Japanese Buddhism" (1984:10). These two scholars point out some of the limitations in the current Western literature on Japanese new religions.

Rather than criticizing this literature further or discussing theoretical models as such, I prefer to illustrate a more balanced approach to the formation of Gedatsu-kai, which may serve as the prototype for a theory of the formation of Japanese new religions. On the basis of the preceding description, analysis, and interpretation of Gedatsu-kai, we can construct a more comprehensive model of the formation of Japanese new religions. For the sake of brevity, the model will be given in diagram form and discussed in terms of the diagram. By transposing all the complexities of Gedatsu-kai's formation to a diagram, it is possible to isolate the crucial factors and to illustrate their relationships (see fig. 2).

This diagram is a graphic analysis of Japanese history and religion viewed in terms of the formation of Gedatsu-kai. Its basic principle is the interaction of three factors through time. These three factors, considered to be most important for the formation of the movement, are the social environment, prior religious influences, and innovations of the founder and his followers. (In the format of the diagram, the social environment is on the left, religious influences are at the bottom and innovative forces are on the right.) Of course, each of these three factors has internal subfactors of interaction—such as social, political, and eco-

Innovative factor of founder,

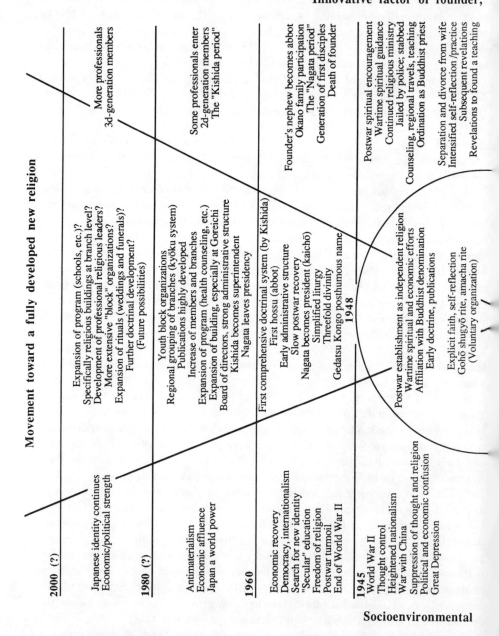

Movement toward a fully developed new religion

Socioenvironmental

2000 (?)
Japanese identity continues
Economic/political strength

More professionals
3d-generation members

1980 (?)
Antimaterialism
Economic affluence
Japan a world power

Some professionals enter
2d-generation members
The "Kishida period"

Expansion of program (schools, etc.)?
Specifically religious buildings at branch level?
Development of professional religious leaders?
More extensive "block" organizations?
Expansion of rituals (weddings and funerals)?
Further doctrinal development?
(Future possibilities)

Youth block organizations
Regional grouping of branches (kyōku system)
Publications highly developed
Increase of members and branches
Expansion of program (health counseling, etc.)
Expansion of building, especially at Goreichi
Board of directors, strong administrative structure
Kishida becomes superintendent
Nagata leaves presidency

1960
Economic recovery
Democracy, internationalism
Search for new identity
"Secular" education
Freedom of religion
Postwar turmoil
End of World War II

First comprehensive doctrinal system (by Kishida)
First hossu (abbot)
Early administrative structure
Slow postwar recovery
Nagata becomes president (kaichō)
Simplified liturgy
Threefold divinity
Gedatsu Kongō posthumous name

1948

Founder's nephew becomes abbot
Okano family participation
The "Nagata period"
Generation of first disciples
Death of founder

Postwar spiritual encouragement
Wartime spiritual guidance
Continued religious ministry
Jailed by police; stabbed
Counseling, regional travels, teaching
Ordination as Buddhist priest

Separation and divorce from wife
Intensified self-reflection/practice
Subsequent revelations
Revelations to found a teaching

Postwar establishment as independent religion
Wartime spiritual and economic efforts
Affiliation with Buddhist denomination
Early doctrine, publications

Explicit faith, self-reflection
Gohō shugyō rite, amacha rite
(Voluntary organization)

1945
World War II
Thought control
Heightened nationalism
War with China
Suppression of thought and religion
Political and economic confusion
Great Depression

nomic subfactors in the social environment—as well as Buddhist, Shinto, and Confucian subfactors in the sector of religious influences. But viewed broadly, it is these three elements that come together to constitute the formation of Gedatsu-kai. These factors (and their subfactors) are always mutually influencing each other, but from the perspective of the formation of this movement they form a crucial intersection during the life of the founder, Okano Eizō. This intersection, depicted

followers, organizers

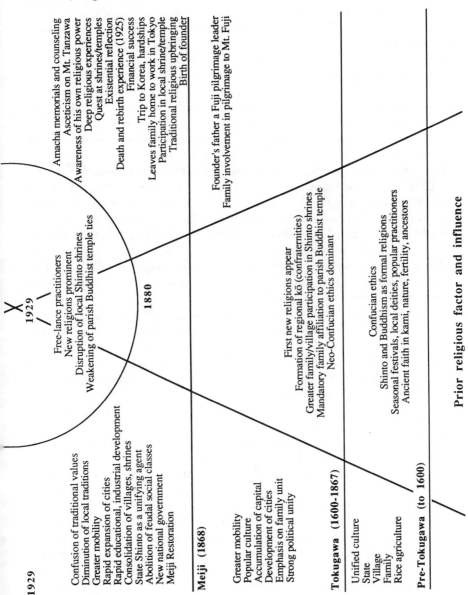

Figure 2. Social, Religious, and Innovative Factors in the Development of Gedatsu-kai

factor and influence

in the diagram as a circle where the three factors meet, is the nucleus of the formation of Gedatsu-kai.

In order to grasp an overview of the dynamics of the diagram, it is convenient to consider it as a lower half and an upper half, bisecting the nuclear circle. The lower half includes all the forces that converge to bring Gedatsu-kai into existence. The center of the circle, where social, religious, and innovative factors meet, is the beginning point of Gedatsu-kai. The upper half includes all the forces that shape the growth and development of Gedatsu-kai into a new religious movement. In this sense of vertical division, the lower half is the prehistory of Gedatsu-kai, while the upper half is the actual history of development; but, as any historian might remind us, the weight of prehistory is always felt by subsequent history. For example, the traditional emphasis on the importance of venerating ancestors (in the lower half of the diagram) has a lasting influence on the central rite of amacha memorials (in the upper half of the diagram). Of course, the same historical process viewed retroactively (i.e., from the upper half of the diagram toward the lower half) can be seen more in terms of discontinuity, for example, Gedatsu-kai's innovations in modifying traditional memorial rites.

The diagram is designed to show the funneling of traditional religious practices into Gedatsu-kai (the funnel represented by the triangle of prior religious factors in the lower half), and the development of Gedatsu-kai as a religious movement (the development represented by the triangle in the upper half labeled "Movement toward a fully developed new religion"). Obviously, prior religious factors continue to influence Gedatsu-kai within the upper half of the diagram; the only reason such traditions as Buddhism and Shinto are not listed there is that this is a limited graphic illustration of Japanese religious history viewed from the vantage point of the formation of one new religion.

Figure 2 affords us a systematic framework for discussing the formation of Gedatsu-kai, enabling us to balance the three factors simultaneously while tracing their advance through time. The chronological aspect of the diagram is a particular application of the periodization of Japanese religious history used in my other writings and need not be repeated here (Earhart 1983:x-xi; Earhart 1969; Earhart 1974a). However, to give an overall view of the chronological development of Gedatsu-kai, a simplified version of figure 2, showing only historical periods and developmental stages, is provided as figure 3.

Figure 3 features the same interaction of three constitutive factors through Japanese history, but adds seven developmental stages for both the prehistory and actual historical development of Gedatsu-kai. Stage 1, distant background (from prehistory to about 1600), indicates the basic features of Japanese culture and religion that were the most general context out of which the movement emerged. Stage 2, the immediate background (from 1600 to 1868 [beginning of the Meiji period] or 1880 [birth of the founder]), includes the particular developments of the distant background that helped give rise to many new religions. Stage 3, the personal background (from 1880 to 1929), marks the contact of the founder with current social and religious forces up to the point of his founding of Gedatsu-kai in 1929.

Stage 4, period of the founder (from 1929 to 1948), is the time when the founder inaugurated Gedatsu-kai and shaped its course through his spiritual experiences and his assessment of the social and religious situation. Stage 5, the postfounder period (from 1948 to about 1960 or 1962), is the time just after the founder's death when the first disciples of the young new religion attempted to regularize its rituals and organization. Stage 6, the period of definitive organizational structure (from about 1960 or 1962 to 1980 or shortly thereafter), is the time when success was achieved in developing such organizational goals as larger membership, a nationwide network of branches, and a centralized headquarters. The hypothetical

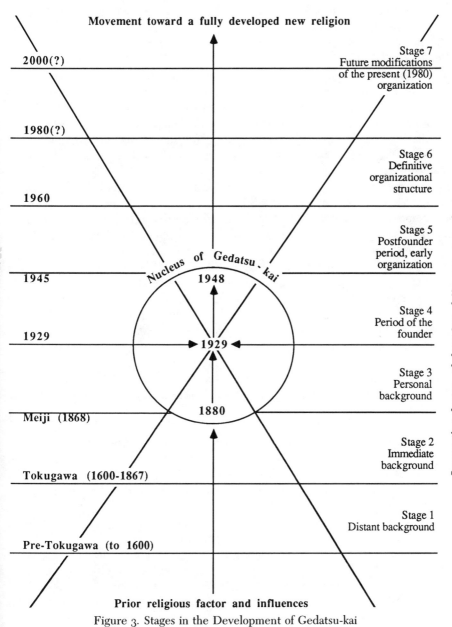

Figure 3. Stages in the Development of Gedatsu-kai

stage 7, future modifications of the organization (beginning somewhere between 1980 and 2000), is posited on the assumption that Gedatsu-kai will probably change significantly from its present lay organization to a more formally and professionally developed structure.

On the basis of figures 2 and 3, I will now interpret the formation of Gedatsu-kai, treating the three factors as interacting forces within each of the stages. Stage 1, the distant background, covers the bulk of the prehistory of Gedatsu-kai, including the basic social and religious factors that lie "behind" the movement. Looking at figure 2 and reading from the bottom, left to right, we recognize that this is the time when a unified Japanese culture took shape around such elements as rice agriculture, family and village structures, and a centralized state. In the religious sector, the ancient practices related to kami, nature, fertility, and ancestors developed more formally into Shinto at the same time that Buddhism and Confucianism entered Japan. The personal or innovative factor cannot be traced clearly in this first stage.

The second stage, the immediate background, covers the Tokugawa period (and a dozen years thereafter), which was so important for solidifying the framework of premodern Japan. Looking at figure 2, we note that this is the time when, in the social sector, there was stronger political unity (with the expulsion of Westerners and unification of the country under the Tokugawa family line). There was also greater emphasis on the family as a social unit. Cities began to develop on a larger scale, accumulation of capital was remarkable, greater mobility of the population was noticeable, and generally popular culture developed in such forms as wood-block prints and novels. In the religious sector, this is the time when Neo-Confucian ethics helped support the rationale of the state and penetrated social institutions generally; families were required to belong to parish Buddhist temples (bodaiji), and local Shinto shrines became more influential on the local level. In terms of religious mobility, pilgrimage associations such as kō (confraternities) became more influential, and individual religious practitioners began to form new religions during the nineteenth century. In the personal or innovative sector, it is difficult to trace the roots of Gedatsu-kai precisely, but the Okano family had a tradition of being leaders (sendatsu) of a pilgrimage confraternity (kō) to Mount Fuji; it is probable that Gedatsu-kai's traditional values of religious devotion, social values of filial piety, and national values of patriotism (much of which is expressed in hōon kansha, or repayment of gratitude) are related to this family heritage of pilgrimage leadership.

Stage 3, the personal background, corresponds to the time span from the birth of the founder to his decision to found a new religion. Starting from the left side of figure 2 with the social sector, we see that this is just after the climactic Meiji Restoration, when the Tokugawa military dictator was replaced with a new national government and the emperor was made the symbol of the new national government, with State Shinto becoming the "nonreligious" rationale of the state. This was a time of rapid educational and industrial development. The old feudal system of four social classes was abolished, and there was much greater mobility of the population, in terms of both upward social mobility (through education) and emigration from the countryside to urban settings.

In the religious sector, too, changes were rapid and far-reaching. The Meiji

Restoration period marked the end of the government requirement for families to belong to parish Buddhist temples, but families still continue to practice memorial rites for ancestors performed by Buddhist priests.[5] The "nationalization" of State Shinto, along with the amalgamation of local shrines, tended to push Shinto into the national orbit and deemphasize participation in it as a local tradition. In short, the earlier system of a family participating in a Buddhist temple by family bloodline and in a local Shinto shrine by territorial residence began to weaken, partly because of greater mobility of the population, partly because of the changed situation of Buddhism and Shinto in the minds of the people. During the late nineteenth and early twentieth centuries, some of the first new religions greatly expanded their membership, and more new religions appeared.

In the personal or innovative sector, this is the time when Okano Eizō was growing up and becoming acculturated through a traditional upbringing which included participation in the local Shinto shrine and Buddhist temple. He moved out of his village setting to Tokyo, experiencing many hardships and even making an unsuccessful business trip to Korea. Toward the end of this stage, when he experienced his spiritual death and rebirth, he began to explore traditional faith more closely, and he was dissatisfied with the current religious scene. He felt that State Shinto was out of touch with the people, and many of the traditional religious practices, such as prayers before the Shinto altar (kamidana) and Buddhist altar (butsudan) in the home, were continued more out of a mechanical sense of formality than as an inner expression of sincerity and genuine piety. Through a series of revelations, especially a crucial revelation on New Year's Day 1929, he was led to found a new religion that would bring people to self-reflection on the meaning of their own lives and a renewal of traditional values.

Stage 4, the period of the founder, marks the earliest steps of Gedatsu-kai as a religious organization guided by Okano. Looking at figure 2 again, from left to right, we see that the social sector was full of important developments. Although Japan had flourished economically from the time of World War I, it floundered during the Great Depression, and politically the tide turned away from liberalism and democracy toward greater state control; this even meant suppression of political and religious movements. Nationalism swept the country as it moved into World War II. The religious sector was characterized by further expansion of new religious movements, in spite of increased government suppression. State Shinto ideology was made a part of the public educational system, and generally all religious organizations, including Buddhism and Shinto, enthusiastically supported nationalism and the war effort.

Looking at the specific development of Gedatsu-kai from the center of the circle where the three sectors intersect, we find that this is where the movement emerged as a voluntary organization apart from Shinto and Buddhism, with its modification of traditional practices, forming a separate socioreligious organization with its own distinctive religious set of beliefs and practices. This is when the amacha memorial rite in homes (for ancestors and other spirits) and the ritual communication with the other world (gohō shugyō) were established as key rituals. Basic to the rationale of this new movement was the notion of self-reflection (hansei) on one's own conduct and sincere cultivation of traditional virtues found in the notion of hōon kansha. This teaching was serialized in a monthly magazine and eventually published as a booklet of doctrine. Membership increased, branches were established, and Okano secured formal affiliation with a recognized Buddhist denomination in order to avoid government persecution.

In the personal or innovative sector, this is the time when Okano received his key revelations and put them into practice. First was the revelation to found a "teaching," followed by other revelations, such as the rite of communing with the other world and the order to establish religious monuments at the Goreichi (Sacred Land) in Saitama Prefecture near his birthplace. He deepened his religious devotions and began counseling people more regularly. These devotions tended to separate him from his wife, which led to their divorce; but he continued and was ordained a Buddhist priest. His growing fame as a religious teacher was not without its perils, for he was jailed by the police, who tried to turn him away from religion, and he was stabbed by a deranged person, narrowly escaping with his life. Nevertheless, he continued with his preaching and regional travels in opening up new branches; he was also active in patriotic activities, such as gathering contributions for the war effort and helping to distribute scarce goods. After World War II, Okano was able to withdraw Gedatsu-kai from the Buddhist denomination it had been pressured into joining, and formed an independent movement.

Stage 5, the postfounder or early organizational period, is when Gedatsu-kai began to take shape as a more formally constituted voluntary organization. Viewing figure 2 from left to right, we see that this was the difficult postwar period for Japan. World War II ended in 1945, at the same time signaling the elimination of government suppression and soon ushering in complete religious freedom. There was considerable confusion, with the sudden elimination of wartime controls and the search for stability and a new identity. The trend was toward democracy and internationalism and, from the early 1950s, a great economic recovery. In the religious sector, viewed here as an extension of Gedatsu-kai's earlier development, the movement assumed greater organizational strength.

The details of Gedatsu-kai's religious and social organization cannot be fully explained here, but it was at this time that they attained more complete form. For example, after Okano's death, he was granted the posthumous title Gedatsu Kongō by the Buddhist denomination with which Gedatsu-kai had been formally affiliated; under this title, the founder became one of the three "divinities" worshipped in the sacred triad found at the headquarters, local branches, and (ideally) every Gedatsu-kai member's home. In other words, the objects of worship assumed a set pattern. Similarly, the liturgy was simplified and standardized. With the demise of Okano, a manager (sōmu) was selected by the leading disciples, and the first head (hossu), a young nephew Okano had designated as successor, was formally named. By the late 1950s, a detailed chart of the doctrine taught by Okano and amplified by one of his first disciples was printed. In the personal or innovative sector, this is primarily the generation of the first disciples. As in any founded religion, the time after the founder's death was a delicate period of transferring authority to the subsequent leaders. Fortunately, Okano had designated important disciples who had the right to select the next leader. The Okano family line was to be continued in the symbolic head, but the founder's nephew was too young to participate actively at this time. Other Okano family members also filled important posts in the organization.

During stage 6, the period of definitive organizational structure, Gedatsu-kai took on its present organizational pattern. Again, looking at figure 2 from left to right, it was at this time that Japan was more fully recovering from World War II, achieving greater economic affluence, and rapidly becoming a world political power. At the same time, there was questioning of social values (as seen in the student riots of the late 1960s) and a growing criticism of materialism. In the religious sector, or Gedatsu-kai's development, in 1962 there was an important shift in the movement's administrative structure. The first postfounder president, a man named Nagata who reportedly ran a "one-man" show, was eased out of office by a newly formed board of directors. Nagata did not leave Gedatsu-kai, although some of the faction supporting his continued leadership did separate and form another new religion (called Minori-kai). The office of president (kaichō) was not filled; rather, the new post of superintendent (kyōtō) was created, which was filled by Kishida Eizan, one of the first disciples of Okano. Kishida, a dynamic developer of many new branches, later went to the United States to lead Gedatsu-kai there. He was called back to become superintendent, although he still spent much time in the United States. This new administration was guided by the board of directors, Kishida, and the hossu, who by this time was of more mature age.

As a result of these changes, a more elaborate administrative structure was developed. The network of local branches was strengthened, especially in relationship to the headquarters, with the number of branches and members increasing dramatically. The program expanded, with publications rising in number and quality, and new ventures, such as health counseling, were launched. The number of branches became so great that they were grouped into large divisions (kyōku); youth were organized into block systems. In the personal or innovative sector, leadership now began to shift to second-generation disciples—people who had never met the founder or who had known him when they were very young. Also, some professionals began to appear in the headquarters structure, that is, those who became a part of headquarters more because of expertise than longevity in the faith. The "aging" of the membership has also become an important consideration. As children of Gedatsu-kai members go beyond junior high, they tend to join the youth organization, which operates as a block system composed of the youth from a number of branches (and meeting at regional practice centers). As more second- and third-generation members appear, it is likely that the nature of Gedatsu-kai as a lay religion will change significantly. Perhaps this is enough of a glimpse into the future, stage 7, which may see the movement developing special "church" buildings and a professional clergy.

We have offered this model of the development of Gedatsu-kai to provide an interpretation of the formation of Japanese new religions that is more balanced in terms of the social conditions, religious history, and personal innovation which seem to be the key constitutive factors. My thesis is that any treatment of the formation of new religions must take into account at least these three factors. Theories which depend on just one or two factors, while not "wrong," are inadequate. We disagree with simple statements that Japanese new religions are products of or responses to endemic social change ("antidotes to anomie"), not because they are completely false, but because they are only partially true. And it is the half-truth that belies their accuracy. For example, if we turn to figure 2 once more, we note that the presence of disruptive social conditions and personal anxiety is an important factor in the emergence of new religions: in another theoretical article I have called this a "precipitating" factor (Earhart 1969:244–45). In other words, the precipitating factor is a necessary but not a sufficient condition, helping "trigger" the timing of a new religion's emergence but not providing the inspiration essential for beginning a movement or determining its content.[6]

Similarly, even if we move across the diagram and include the religious factor (or the influence of religious history), these two factors together are insufficient to bring about the formation of a new religion. To be sure, the weakening of the traditional religious pattern, particularly the diminution of local shrines and Buddhist temples, is also important for the development of new movements: if such institutions were strong and participation in them was active, there would be no thrust for forming and joining new religions. At the same time, vital elements in the religious heritage constitute the content out of which new movements develop. In previous articles, this is what I have called the "enabling" factor (ibid., pp. 243–44). But note that by itself, or even in combination with the social factor, it is insufficient to account for the development of a new religion. Again, we have a necessary but not sufficient condition.

According to this model of interpretation, it takes all three factors to account for the rise of new religions. For, as the analysis of Gedatsu-kai's formation demonstrates, the innovative decisions of the founder cannot be completely subsumed by either social factors or the influence of prior religious factors—or by both in combination. Social conditions did help precipitate new religious movements such as Gedatsu-kai. Also, the shift away from Buddhism and Shinto did assist founders in initiating new groups; and the permanent features of Japanese religion (such as veneration of ancestors) did enable the formation of a new religion by "defining a general context of religious practices which constitute the substratum of the new religions" (ibid., p. 244).[7] But it seems inconceivable for anyone to demonstrate that social and religious factors "caused" Okano to "produce" such new elements as the amacha memorial mass and the gohō shugyō rite. Without this innovative factor of Okano and the subsequent organizers of the movement, one cannot account for the emergence of Gedatsu-kai.

My critics may want to reverse the argument used above against the "crisis-anomie" theory, to the tune that a new religion will not arise solely as a consequence of the presence of a person with innovative ideas. This point should be conceded: a person will become a founder not simply because of innovative ideas and practices, but also only if the time and conditions are right—in other words, only if the social situation helps precipitate and the religious history tends to enable such a movement. This example applies not only to the actual founding, but also to the continuing life of the movement. For example, Okano decided to found a new teaching, but it was, at least in part, social and political conditions that pushed him to become affiliated with an offically recognized denomination (in order to escape government persecution); and it was, at least in part, the complicated pattern of his involvement in Shingon Buddhism and the existence of a compatible Shingon denomination that enabled him to make this affiliation quite easily. In other words, any time we cut across the diagram horizontally, we find that innovative decisions are always related to the social circumstances and prior religious influence.

We have provided this model of the formation of Gedatsu-kai to show that the origin of new religious movements is a complex affair involving *at least* the three factors of social conditions, prior religious tradition, and personal innovative decisions. This model should provide an alternative to the prevailing Western interpretation of Japanese new religions as "responses to fundamental changes in their social environment": they are indeed partly responses to social change, but also much more. The above model attempts to recognize the weight of social conditions in the formation of new religions, balancing this factor with the historical momentum of the religious heritage and the creative work of the founder (and his followers).

This model seems to have a number of advantages over the "crisis" theory of response to anomie. One of its distinct advantages is the ability to handle diachronic as well as synchronic factors. Most Western-language treatments of Japanese new religions discuss events immediately surrounding the rise of those religions—synchronic factors—as if the force of certain social conditions alone is sufficient to "cause" the creation of a new religion and to "cause" people to join it. Such treatments overestimate the role of synchronic socioenvironmental factors, and underestimate the role of diachronic factors, especially the prior religious heritage. An advantage of this model is its ability to relate new religions to the prior religious tradition, showing both continuity and discontinuity.

For example, this model helps us to take into account the various factors involved in Gedatsu-kai's preoccupation with ancestors and the amacha ritual. The historical factor, which "enables" the movement's focus on ancestors, is the long tradition of concern for ancestors in Japanese religion, which was heightened by developments in the Tokugawa era. The socioeconomic factor, which helped "precipitate" Gedatsu-kai's formation, is weakened family ties (and/or the perceived threat to "traditional" family and religious values) by industrialization, urbanization, and geographical mobility. The personal-innovative factor, which gave rise to Gedatsu-kai, is the creation of distinctively new ritual forms such as the amacha rite. What is "traditional" about this is religious concern for ancestors; what is innovative is the development of a new ritual (and new customs such as enshrining a Buddhist altar in every home and memorializing both male and female lines). This theory can account easily for the old and the new in Gedatsu-kai.

Previous Western interpretations have become involved in a double bind: on the one hand, the crisis-anomie argument claims that disruption of tradition is the causative factor that produces new religions; on the other hand, the same argument must acknowledge that much of the religious content of the new religions (such as ancestor worship) is "traditional." In other words, this theory claims that what causes the development of new religious movements is the breakdown of tradition, but at the same time claims that the new movements are "traditional" in their content. But if the new religions are "traditional," then how could the tradition have broken down, in the first place, as a precondition to their formation? This double bind has forced many advocates of the crisis-anomie theory to claim that the new religions are not really "new."

These are some of the dilemmas posed by the study of Japanese new religions. There are clearly some differences between old religions and new religions: the formation of voluntary organizations certainly is one of the hallmarks of such new movements. But the more we study a new religion such as Gedatsu-kai in depth, the more we realize that the faith and practice resemble "old" religion. The organization and delivery system may be different, but much of the religious content (kami, Buddhas, ancestors, and holy persons) is continuous from old religion to new. Perhaps the best characterization of Gedatsu-kai as a new religion is that it is a contemporary transformation of the Japanese religious tradition. (As a banner carried in the Three Holy Sites Pilgrimage proclaimed, "the [Japanese] people's tradition and contemporary life.")

When I was first studying Japanese new religions in the mid-1960s, and even when I was conducting this research on Gedatsu-kai, there seemed to be no suitable idiom for expressing their simultaneous continuity and discontinuity of tradition. The recent book *Tradition* by Edward Shils captures much of what I was trying to convey in previous articles, even though he does not mention new religions explicitly. Shils has argued effectively that there has been too sharp a disjuncture between the categories "traditional" and "modern," and that tradition has been unfairly maligned as only a detriment to progress and not recognized also as a necessary component of every culture (Shils 1981). In effect, to borrow and adapt from Shils's work, the new religion that is Gedatsu-kai is what the old Japanese tradition once was, has undergone transformation, has been handed down to the present moment, and is being transmitted to future generations. The old tradition has become the new tradition—a process that has occurred, and will reoccur, so long as there is something handed down that can be identified as a Japanese religious heritage. In other words, old tradition has become new tradition, old religion has become new religion. This statement is so obvious that there should be no need to present and defend it, and yet most Western treatments of Japanese new religions neglect or overlook this fact.

Returning to the Center:
Gedatsu-kai, New Religions, and Contemporary Japan

The preceding theoretical discussion dealt with the origin of Gedatsu-kai (and similar new religions); this concluding section will take up the nature and significance of Gedatsu-kai as an example of Japanese new religions. The main Western view of the nature of Japanese new religions, as quoted previously, is that they "serve as pressure chambers for the socially disadvantaged" (Yinger 1970:273). There is a tendency to use new religious movements as examples of theories which explain religion as the result of social, psychological, or even economic conditions.[8] As mentioned in the previous section, such theories are not necessarily "wrong," for they do tell part of the truth about new religions, which—like all religions—are related to social, psychological, and economic conditions. But it is the half-truth that ultimately is deceiving, since it does not tell the other half, especially what is "religious" about new religions.

There are two important ways of viewing the other part of the half-truth: one is the applicability of such theories to all religions, the other is the religious *as well as* the social, psychological, and economic character of new religions. Concerning the applicability of such theories to all religions, it should be pointed out that, to the extent that such theories are successful, they must take into account all religious traditions. If a theory is worth its salt, it should not be limited to just exotic foreign traditions and recent developments, but should apply to the familiar and established traditions as well. Furthermore, it is gratuitous to say that the founders and members of "other" traditions are responding to social change and that their religions serve as a pressure cooker, unless the same can be said about all founders and all members of every religious tradition. Are the founders of the "great religions"—Christianity, Buddhism, and Islam—that different from the founders of Japanese new religions? Are the members of Japanese new religions so unlike the participants in contemporary churches, synagogues, and mosques? The major difference, perhaps, is that these once-new religions have succeeded and become old religions, and as such they have become established and respectable. Therefore, few scholars refer to these established traditions as "pressure chambers for the socially disadvantaged." This is one way of looking at the other side of the half-truth—that too often scholars apply theories to new religions when they are not willing to apply the same theories to established traditions.

Another way of looking at the other part of the half-truth is to focus positively on the nature of new religions, for their generic character as religious movements. Ironically, most treatments of Japanese new religions have glossed over their religious dimension, seeing them primarily as deviant responses to abnormal conditions. If a new religion such as Gedatsu-kai is viewed in terms of its religious features, what we see is a miniature version of the contemporary Japanese religious tradition. As a contemporary expression of Japanese religion, Gedatsu-kai enables its members to return to the center of their tradition.

Gedatsu-kai belief and practice renew or reinforce a contemporary version of the general Japanese pantheon of kami, Buddhas, ancestors, and holy persons. Gedatsu-kai encourages services in the home before the Shinto-style altar (kamidana) and before the Buddhist-style altar (butsudan). Also urged are attendance at both the parish Shinto shrine (ujigami) and the parish Buddhist temple (bodaiji). Belief and practice incorporate ethical values of self-reflection (hansei), social values of the family (filial piety), national values of patriotism, and gratitude to nature. As one executive told us, Gedatsu-kai can be summed up in the combined phrases *keishin sūso hōon kansha*: revere the kami and worship the ancestors, gratitude and thanks. The daily amacha rite provides for self-cultivation, while the occasional okiyome and gohō shugyō make possible contact with spirits and the other world. There are many talismans (ofuda) and apology papers (owabijō) to take care of almost any particular religious requirement. All of the preceding objects of worship, sacred sites, beliefs, and practices are "traditional" elements whose modification and incorporation within the larger context of Gedatsu-kai enable members to "go back" into their old tradition and at the same time to "go forward" into the new tradition they are creating and transmitting.

The Grand Festival is a good example of this return to the center of the Japanese tradition. By making this pilgrimage to the founder's native village, they are returning to the Goreichi, the Sacred Land, and in fact the center of the Japanese religious world as viewed by Gedatsu-kai members. They are going back to the heart of their tradition, where the founder received his foundational revelations, which brought to life once more the religious significance of kami, Buddhas, ancestors, and holy persons. The founder, and the members, felt that there was too much mechanical performance and too little sincere commitment and reflection—he contrasted shinkō as mechanical "faith" with shinkō as sincere action.

The Goreichi offers a good vantage point for a concluding look at Gedatsu-kai: from this angle, Gedatsu-kai is the village writ large. Of course, here "village" should be understood as the contemporary memory of an idealized way of life that existed in part in the past, and lives on in the memory of many people today as a complex symbolism of how they hope to live meaningful lives in the present and pass on a heritage to future generations.[9] In other words, Gedatsu-kai attempts to parlay traditional beliefs and practices into the contemporary situation. In his talk at the Fall Grand Festival of 1979, the head of Gedatsu-kai referred to the ideals of furusato, and there was a painted sign reading "furusato" on one of the trees nearby. Furusato is a vague notion of the old village or old home place, and this is a good term to describe the way in which Gedatsu-kai members perceive themselves—as remaining true to the best values of the Japanese tradition.[10] In many ways Gedatsu-kai does preserve these old values, and of course in other ways it represents important innovations.

If Gedatsu-kai can be seen as a microcosm or transformation of "traditional" Japanese religion, then much the same can be said for most other Japanese new religions. This begs the question of what distinguishes the various Japanese new religions one from another. This is a huge question, because it encompasses a dozen "large" new religions, another dozen or two "medium"-size new religions, and a very large number—hundreds—of "small" new religions. The present study, focused mainly on just one new movement, does not afford a comprehensive view of all Japanese new religions—that would require a much more ambitious study. However, some general outlines of the common and distinctive features of these new religious movements can be hazarded.

What draws all these movements together as a common phenomenon is the fact that they are contemporary transformations of earlier Japanese religion. Their common features are what they share with each other and with the Japanese religious world view in general. The distinctive feature of each new religion is found in the particular selection, emphasis, and organization of the elements of this world view. This can be demonstrated briefly in terms of religious objects of worship, because the Japanese religious world view has a host of objects of worship, especially kami, Buddhas, ancestors, and holy persons; the common and distinctive features of new religions can be assessed partly by how they select, emphasize, and organize their objects of worship.

Gedatsu-kai is very close to the popular world view because it embraces all of these objects of worship. Some new religions, especially the thirteen movements which formerly were considered part of "Sect Shinto," have a decidedly Shinto character, and focus primarily on Shinto objects of worship. Other new religions are more clearly Buddhist in character, notably the movements focusing on Nichiren, the *Lotus Sutra*, and ancestors—such as Reiyū-kai, Risshō Kōsei-kai, and Sōka Gakkai. These "Buddhist" movements tend to deemphasize kami and emphasize instead Buddhist divinities.

Ancestors are venerated in most of the new religions, but they are emphasized more by the predominantly Buddhist movements. Gedatsu-kai shares this preoccupation with ancestors. All the Japanese new religions have their holy persons, but there is a wide range of variation, from actual object of worship (as a kami or Buddha) to respected religious leader. Most of the predominantly Shinto movements view their founders as kami; during their lifetimes some were known as living kami, and this mantle is passed on to family successors, usually to the first son. Gedatsu-kai displays considerable Buddhist influence, but still views its founder as a kami. Sōka Gakkai views its founder (if Makiguchi Tsunesaburō can be so designated) as a respected figure who helped rediscover the message of the *Lotus Sutra*; but it is this Buddhist scripture that receives veneration rather than Makiguchi.

The preceding sketch of objects of worship in some new religions gives an indication of how these movements share a general world view and yet form distinctive religious paths by their particular selection and emphasis of elements. The same can be said of organization of these elements. For example, the more "Shinto" new religions arrange their ceremonies and even build their structures along Shinto lines; Buddhist groups tend to incorporate many modern features of architecture, but their altars are more Buddhist in character. And we have seen how Gedatsu-kai incorporates a triad of Buddhist divinity, kami, and holy person (founder) in its worship.

The range of Japanese new religions is as wide as Japanese religion itself. All groups tend to feature a deep personal experience often linked to healing; some emphasize radically the "magical" and "miraculous," while others focus more on the ethical dimension. We have seen that there is a tension within Gedatsu-kai between the "spiritual" and "ethical" character of the founder's message. It seems that there is a similar tension within other movements, and individual members may choose within the range of possibilities in that movement.

It is difficult to balance all of these possibilities of selection, emphasis, and organization within the Japanese new religions, and the above sketch is but a small sample of the range of possibilities. Even in drawing a contrast between "Shinto"-type and "Buddhist"-type new religions, there is the danger of compartmentalizing too sharply. In actual fact, the individual members of new religions seem to hold to many values which they consider to be "traditional"—the linking of worship of religious objects with family stability and national prosperity. This raises the question of the relation of Japanese new religions to Japanese society at present and in the future.

Movements such as Gedatsu-kai harbor a wealth of consciously stated and unconsciously held values. These "traditional" values include not only the village as remembered from the past and idealized for the present and future, but also such perennial values as family unity, national loyalty, hard work, and sincerity. Of course, the contemporary family is much different from the family of earlier ages, more a nuclear unit than an extended group. Indeed, the tendency for the extended family to give way to the nuclear family—and equally important, the perception of the threat to family unity—is an important contributing factor to the formation of new religions such as Gedatsu-kai, whose members combine rededication to religious commitment with strengthening of the family unit.

It should be emphasized that the new family unit strengthened by participation in Gedatsu-kai is somewhat different from the previous extended family (such as is idealized in the Okano family home of the village setting at Kitamoto), as is indicated by the very practice of Gedatsu-kai in the home. Whereas at one time ancestors memorialized in the butsudan were primarily (theoretically, exclusively) of the male line, Gedatsu-kai, like some other new religions, emphasizes memorializing the lines of both the mother and the father. This is a trend that Robert J. Smith noted in his census of memorial tablets in butsudan. "I suggest that the practice of placing Nonlineal tablets in the household altar may be a fairly recent and increasingly common one. When we recall that the great majority of households surveyed were conjugal families, and that wife's kin occurred far more frequently among the tablets for Nonlineals than did mother's or yōshi's kin, we realize that here we may have the opening wedge of *family*-centered as opposed to *household*-centered ancestor worship" (1974:174).

In other words, Smith is documenting the transition from the former extended family (*ie* or household) to the more recent nuclear family, as expressed in different forms of memorializing ancestors. Most scholars writing on Japanese new religions have focused on the reactive character of new religions—reacting to the changed social, economic, and political conditions. It should also be emphasized, as Hardacre has pointed out in her study of Reiyū-kai (1984), that new religions are creative and effective in organizing and meeting the needs of their members—one might say "proactive" as well as reactive. Gedatsu-kai, through the founder Okano and subsequent leadership, has exercised considerable creativity in originating, developing, maintaining, and modifying "new" religious techniques such as the amacha ritual within varying social conditions.

Just as the conditions and ideals of village harmony and family unity have changed considerably during the life of Gedatsu-kai as a religious movement, so have the "traditional" values of national loyalty, hard work, and sincerity. As has been seen in the before-and-after figures for religious practice in chapter 4, Gedatsu-kai members are much less active in "national" values such as possession of an imperial portrait and pilgrimage to the shrines of Ise and Yasukuni than in "local" values such as visits to the local tutelary shrine (ujigami) and parish Buddhist temple (bodaiji). Although the image of the emperor and loyalty to the state are still part of the fabric of Gedatsu-kai, a new national identity is emerging. Indeed, as a nationwide (and international) voluntary organization, Gedatsu-kai itself is a new form of national religious identity. Officials and members place much emphasis on the celebration of the all souls' memorial rite during the Fall and Spring Grand Festivals: individual members are linked not only to the spirits of all deceased Gedatsu-kai members, but also to the spirits of all people and all animals of the entire creation. Like other new religions, Gedatsu-kai has expanded and elaborated national values into international values. Hard work, which once meant (especially for the first son) following in the footsteps of the father and maintaining the family farm or family business, in contemporary Gedatsu-kai means an internalized work ethic (such as for Mr. Abe) in whatever occupation one assumes.

Gedatsu-kai is typical of attempts to preserve "traditional" Japanese values. As such, it is not for all Japanese people. Since the rise of cities several centuries ago, many people have become indifferent to religion. The same is true today, with people often mechanically performing "customary" rites such as funerals and memorials. But Gedatsu-kai shows the power of tradition to preserve latent religious values and practices, and when Japanese people do reawaken to their tradition, it is usually to the kind of beliefs and practices held by Gedatsu-kai.

There are many questions raised by this study which are left unanswered. One of the foremost is the ambiguous character of "traditional" religion, be it old or new, especially its close tie with and "legitimation" of Japanese society in general.[11] Some people have praised the Japanese educational and cultural tradition for its nurturing of self-discipline and hard work—especially those in Western countries who admire Japan's great technological success. Others, who remember the absolute loyalty of wartime Japan, and who lament the social cost of technological achievement, are not so eager to adopt the Japanese model. But such is the ambiguity of the Japanese—or any—religious tradition, and its relationship to the social, economic, and political order. The point of this book is not to persuade Western readers that Japan has all the answers, but to help Westerners understand how Japan is attempting to find its own answer. Gedatsu-kai is one particular way of phrasing the Japanese answer to identity in the contemporary world. For in many ways Gedatsu-kai represents a microcosm of the Japanese religious world today.[12]

NOTES

1. An Inside Approach to Japanese Religion

1. Edo times, the Tokugawa period, 1600–1867.

2. Heian period, 794–1185.

3. Connection, *en*, which is also a Buddhist term meaning a contributory cause (rather than a direct cause); here it is used in a popular Japanese sense of connection of *karma*.

4. Local tutelary deity, *ujigami*; the nature of this Shinto deity (*kami* in Japanese) will be treated in subsequent chapters.

5. Generations of family ancestors, *senzo daidai*, a key term that will be treated in later sections.

6. Formal religious visit, *omairi*; the term can refer to a distant pilgrimage or to any visit to a Buddhist temple or Shinto shrine for the purpose of worship.

7. The Ise Shrine is especially sacred for the Japanese national heritage, since it enshrines the Sun Goddess (Amaterasu) from whom the imperial line descended; Shrine Shinto (*jinja shinto*) was closely tied to developing nationalism from the Meiji period (1868–1912) through the end of World War II in 1945.

8. Emperor Ōjin, who according to tradition was the fifteenth emperor and reigned A.D. 270–310. Technically all Japanese emperors are manifest deities or kami, but some have been singled out as specific objects of worship. Emperor Ōjin is identified with Hachiman, a composite object of worship with both Shinto and Buddhist features.

9. Karma of cause and effect is a translation of Mr. Negishi's laconic and emphatic statement "en, innen." *En* is the karmic "connection" that he frequently mentioned; *innen* is a term popularly used in the sense of "karma" or "fate." It is also a formal term in Buddhist doctrine meaning both "inner and direct cause" (*in*) and "external and indirect cause" (*en*). See *Innen* in the *Japanese-English Buddhist Dictionary*, 1965:129–30. In this work we are more concerned with the popular usage of terms such as *innen*, than with their formal definition in Buddhist doctrine. In this particular case, we have translated *innen* as "cause and effect" because Mr. Negishi is drawing a parallel between evolutionary cause and effect in science, and hereditary cause and effect in religious lives. The nature of this belief will become more obvious in the light of other life histories and the teachings of Gedatsu-kai. For comparative material, see O'Flaherty 1980 and Keyes and Daniel 1983. See note 13 in this chapter for a brief treatment of Gedatsu-kai in the context of this discussion of the formal and informal aspects of karma and Buddhism.

10. Gohō shugyō is a ritual technique combining meditation and mediation with spirits of the other world, especially spirits of ancestors. It will be prominent in the life histories of chapter 3 and will be treated in detail in chapter 5.

11. Kantō Plains, the lowland area surrounding Tokyo in central Honshu.

12. Such sayings, usually attributed to Buddhist notions of karma, can be found in many Asian contexts. For example, Keyes, after quoting a classical Buddhist text on karma, notes that "the formula is often made simpler still, as in this Thai saying: do good, receive good; do evil, receive evil . . . " (Keyes 1983b:263).

13. Buddhism in Japan, as in South, Southeast, and East Asia, can be seen in a variety of fashions. It can be viewed, on the one hand, as a formal system codified in written texts and commentaries and doctrinal statements, usually preserved and transmitted by religious specialists (such as priests and monks); and, on the other hand, as an informal system or world view implicit in the beliefs and practices of lay people. Especially in the scholarship on Buddhism in South and Southeast Asia, there has been heated debate on whether the "real" Buddhism is the formal codified system or the informal popular world view—or a combination of the two. For three recent discussions, see O'Flaherty 1980, Keyes and Daniel 1983, and Southwold 1983. In our study of Gedatsu-kai, we are in sympathy with

Keyes (reformulating Tambiah): "the authority for particular dogmas within local commu-
nities of South and Southeast Asia—indeed, of any civilization—may derive from texts,
but only insofar as these texts have been brought to life in the ritual process and other
modes wherein meaning is socially communicated" (1983a:9). Gedatsu-kai is a complex
mode of religion featuring powerful rituals for bringing to (new) life the traditional Japanese
notions of karma and enlightenment (gedatsu). Obeyesekere (1980) has argued that "rebirth
eschatology" predates the three great religious traditions of South Asia—Hinduism, Jainism,
and Buddhism—and the contribution of these organized religions is their "transformation"
of the preexisting rebirth eschatology. It would be difficult to apply Obeyesekere's argument
directly to the Japanese situation (to the effect that Buddhism is the transformation of
preexisting Japanese notions of rebirth), but it does clarify the possibility of more mutual
interaction between Buddhism and Japanese religion in the formation of new religions such
as Gedatsu-kai.

14. Lebra has traced Gedatsu-kai's emphasis on causative verb forms, which she treats
in terms of passivity. "Passivity is exaggerated in causative-passive-polite-grateful forms, as
such expressions inundate the members' speech and writings. 'Ikiru' (live) becomes 'ikasasete itadaku' (am caused to live by [gods'] benevolence). One would be told: 'Don't think
you are living (ikiru) by yourself, but be grateful for ikasasete itadaku.' One of the auto-
biographical reports, picked up by chance, happens to use this grammatical form 28 times
within four pages" (1982:274).

15. Readers may find a more comprehensive treatment of Japanese religion in standard
surveys (Anesaki 1930, Earhart 1982, Kitagawa 1966). For a quick overview of Japanese
religious history, see "Table of Japanese Religious History, with Chronological Periods and
Corresponding Cultural Features" in Earhart 1982:xiv–xv .

16. Bellah (1957) has argued that religious values, especially Buddhist values spread by
popular teachers, provided important motivation for the development of modern Japan.
Ooms (1985) has emphasized that a broader religious base, especially the alloying of Shinto
with Confucianism by influential scholars, provided not only the Tokugawa government
but also subsequent Japanese society and culture in general with a useful ideology. The
present work, in part, is a documentation of the Tokugawa heritage of religion and ideology
on the popular level in contemporary Japan—as seen in the beliefs and practices of Gedatsu-
kai and in the lives of members such as Mr. Negishi.

2. Okano Eizō

1. A brief treatment of Okano's life can be found in Kishida 1969:11–22; see also Kiyota
1982:41–48.

2. For a detailed treatment of the historical context of Kitamotojuku and the leading
role of the Okanos as a rather wealthy farm family in this village, see Fujii Takeshi 1983:2–
11. Japanese scholars view the accumulation of wealth by rich farmers as an important
economic development linked to social movements and even to the fostering of innovations
such as new religious movements. Ishii places the Okano family in the relatively wealthy,
but not "rich farmer" (gōnō), category. Okano's grandfather was conservative, and unlike
some "rich farmers," he did not join in the Jiyūminken Undō (the Movement for Freedom
and Popular Rights). For an English-language treatment of this movement, see Bowen
1980:107–115. See also Fujii Takeshi 1983:11–16.

3. Pilgrimage associations such as Fujikō were active also in spreading popular teachings
or "peasant ethics" among the people. Although *Gedatsu Kongō den* does not mention
these ethical teachings, it is highly probable that Okano's father received part of his moral
and religious notions from his participation in this Fujikō and passed these on to his family.
For the information on the Okano family's participation in the Ise pilgrimage (which is not
mentioned in *Gedatsu Kongō den*), see Fujii Takeshi 1983:47. As Fujii points out, both
Okano's family and Okano himself, up to the time he founded Gedatsu-kai, participated in
religion as part of the corporate village life, but did not initiate independent religious
practices. Okano's father probably led pilgrims to Fuji in connection with his position as
a village leader.

4. Gluck comments on "the advent of Japan's first 'modern' recessions" of 1890, 1900–

1901, and 1907–1908 and notes that between 1895 and 1915 there was a "sharp rise in the relative percentage of factory production to household or cottage industry"; all of these economic and industrial shifts were perceived by the people generally as moments of change and conflict that threatened their personal lives (1985:30–32). Okano's perceptions of these changes and their threat to Japanese social order and well-being are similar to those reported by Gluck.

5. Fujii reports from one of Okano's letters at the time of his trip to Korea, which expresses a heightened sense of realization of the greatness of the emperor and Japan due to his experience abroad. See Fujii Takeshi 1983:24.

6. As Gluck (1985:159–61) has pointed out, many people (some of whom she calls *minkan,* "among the people" ideologues) criticized the young people who during Meiji times left the villages and ancestral occupations (especially farming) for life and occupations in cities such as Tokyo. This social malady was seen as one of a number of fevers: "city fever," "enterprise fever," or "success fever." Okano's sense of guilt is remarkable because as a second son he would not inherit the family farm and because his father willingly apprenticed him to a Tokyo shop; in Okano's case the guilt seems to be double—first for having left the ancestral farming occupation, second for having failed in his new business ventures. See also Thomas C. Smith 1959:15–16.

7. The notion of *on,* a kind of blessing, and *ongaeshi* or *hōon* as indebtedness or return for such blessings, was first systematically presented to Western readers by Bellah in his work *Tokugawa Religion* (1957). Bellah was concerned especially with the political aspects of these terms: "The political authority has the obligation of bestowing blessings (*on*) on the people subject to it." "Coordinate with the concept of *on* is the concept of *hoon* or the return of *on.* This involves the general obligation to respect and comply with the orders of the political authority" (1957:20–21). These notions are central to Bellah's thesis of "the values of pre-industrial Japan" as "a functional analogue to the Protestant ethic in Japanese religion" (pp. 2–3). *On* and ideas of repayment of gratitude are still very important in Japanese society today. (Because the Japanese term *on*—gratitude—is difficult to distinguish from the English *on,* the Japanese term is underlined throughout the book.) Other treatments of *on* in English are Benedict 1946, Takie Sugiyama Lebra 1974, Rohlen 1974:37, 43, 48, 86, 125, Robert J. Smith 1983: 71, 124, Dore 1958:320–24, 356, 371, 374–75, Stevens 1986:56, 58, and Unno 1985.

8. *Giri ninjō* is a key term of traditional social values. As interpreted by Robert J. Smith 1983:45–46, "It is clear that in Japan the use of law as guarantor of rights and duties is little resorted to directly." Instead, the mechanism for reinforcing and maintaining the social order "is to be found in the highly flexible and difficult to systematize domain of reciprocal obligations and human feelings called *giri-ninjō.*" The ideal is for human interaction to find a balance between the two aspects: "*Giri* is a duty or obligation of a person to behave in certain loosely prescribed ways toward another, to whom the person is indebted," while the expectation of the person being repaid "must be tempered with compassion—*ninjō.*"

9. Many of the details of Okano's personal struggle—from his brief early apprenticeship and various business failures through his unusual apprenticeship at a more advanced age, and eventual success—have been recounted here, because they reveal an important Gedatsu-kai perception of the founder. Even though there is little explicitly religious content in this period of Okano's life, it is highly valued by Gedatsu-kai because it expresses a lifestyle that the movement prizes: his penchant for hard work, his ability to face hardship and even momentary defeats, and through self-reflection, devotion, and filial piety his rise above all obstacles. In many ways Okano represents a model of the filial piety and Neo-Confucian values which he set forth in the formal petition for the official recognition of Gedatsu-kai, translated in part in this chapter. It is worth noting that the bulk of Gedatsu-kai members are in service occupations or are self-employed owners of small businesses, and this tale of hard work and frugality is tailored for their appreciation.

10. "Allowed to live," *ikasarete iru,* which can mean here that his life was spared or that he was revived. See also note 14 in chapter 1 concerning the use of causative and passive verb forms in Gedatsu-kai.

11. It is worth noting, as Fujii Takeshi points out, that until his great spiritual crisis

Okano had known only the "general" religious belief and practice of his village; he had these mystical experiences for the first time in his forties. By contrast, some founders of Japanese new religions had frequent mystical experiences from childhood (1983:48).

12. For the Peace Preservation Law, see Mitchell 1976:39–68; for the impact of the Peace Preservation Law on Japanese religion, see Murakami 1980:78, 82.

13. The term for particular requests (Gedatsu Shuppanbu 1979:156) is *goriyaku*, a general category in Japanese religion usually translated as "this-worldly benefits."

14. The man is referred to both as a person of spiritual power, *reinōsha*, literally "spiritualist," and as *ogamiya*, a healer, comparable to the *yamabushi*, mountain ascetics.

15. *Gedatsu*, while not a common term in Japanese religion, does appear in several other contexts. Two examples I have run across are use of *Gedatsu* in the name of a religious practitioner and in the name of a religious group. The religious figure Gedatsu Shōnin (1155–1213), also known as Jōkyo, is mentioned in the *Warongo* (Katō 1917:58, 62–64). *Shōnin* is a title of veneration that can be translated as "saint." Gedatsu-kō is a group registered in 1950 under that name as a religious juridical person. According to a reference work, this group utilizes various religious scriptures (especially Buddhist but also Shinto and Christian) to enable a person to "enter the ultimate truth of gedatsu." This group writes *gedatsu* with the *hiragana* syllabary instead of the Sino-Japanese *kanji* (Umeda 1966:408).

16. *Kongō* is a key Buddhist term that has been used in the "Buddhist" name of various figures. For example, Kūkai (774–835), the founder of Shingon Buddhism, also known by his honorific posthumous title Kōbō Daishi, is venerated by pilgrims who visit eighty-eight sites on the island of Shikoku sacred to him; in the course of their pilgrimage they recite "Namu Daishi Henjō Kongō" (Statler 1983:28).

17. The standard *Kenkyusha's New Japanese-English Dictionary* (Masuda 1974:22) translates *amacha* (as a drink) as "tea of heaven" and "hydrangea tea." For botanical treatments, including reference to use of this hydrangea in folk medicine in various parts of the world, see Rehder 1954:288 and Stern 1974:293.

18. "Seeds," *shuji* in Japanese, *bīja* in Sanskrit, are the sources in consciousness of the manifestation of earthly appearances. For a technical Buddhist treatment, see *shuji* in the *Japanese-English Buddhist Dictionary* (1965:301).

19. Fujii Takeshi notes that Okano had been involved with a religious practitioner (Ishii Iwakichi), an ascetic (*gyōja*) or spiritualist (reinōsha) who performed healing by having people place between their hands a talisman (*fuda*) on which he had written characters. Fujii suggests that this is a precedent for Okano's particular form of practicing gohō shugyō (1983:52).

20. The Shōtoku Hi was unveiled November 28, 1941, the sixtieth birthday of Gedatsu Kongō. Gedatsu-kai translates *Shōtoku Hi* as "Encomium" in its English-language materials.

21. The Hōkyōin Tō (also known simply as Hōkyō Tō) is named for the Hōkyōin darani. According to the *Japanese-English Buddhist Dictionary* (1965:113), the Hōkyōin darani is the *karanda-mudrā-dhāranī*: "The dhāranī mentioned in the *Pao-ch'ieh-yin-t'o-lo-ni-ching* (Hōkyōin-darani-kyō). It is composed of forty incantations. The *sūtra* states that if one invokes this *dhāranī* one can bring a person up to paradise even from hell, and also can prolong the lives of the sick and give much wealth to the poor. In the *Shingon* and *Tendai* Schools, this is counted as one of the three *dhāranīs* and is chanted every day."

22. Fujii Takeshi cites the local reputation of the tower and its frequent visitors as a significant factor in the development of the Goreichi or Sacred Land as a holy site; it is noteworthy, as we will see later, that the first "Grand Festival" held here was dedicated to this tower (1983:53).

23. For thought control, see Mitchell 1976; for government persecution of religion during this time, see Murakami 1980.

24. Fujii Takeshi notes that the arrest of Okano and the attempted suppression of Gedatsu-kai were due to suspicions about "spiritual healing"; this is different from the suppression of some new religions such as Oomoto, because of conflict with the imperial tradition and fascism (1983:65).

25. Fujii Takeshi calls Kurosawa the "pipe" or conduit for Shingon influence upon Okano (1983:52).

26. In explaining the meaning of *kang* (cord), Fung is referring to the formulation of

Tung Chung-shu (ca. 179–ca. 104 B.C.). Fung goes on to say that "the compound word *kang-ch'ang* meant, in olden times, morality or moral laws in general." These formulas— with many variations—were current in later China and eventually in Japan. For use of this term by Kōbō Daishi (Kūkai 774–835), see Hakeda 1972:158–59. From Tokugawa times (1600–1867), many Japanese Neo-Confucianists disseminated versions of these teachings, and in early Meiji times (1868–1912) the Japanese government officially propagated these values. See Warren W. Smith, Jr. 1959:46. Okano learned these values in his early schooling and in the setting of his traditional home; as mentioned previously, his father probably received considerable Confucian influence through his participation in a Fuji pilgrimage association (Fujikō). Fujii Takeshi has traced the more immediate influence of Dōtoku Kagaku upon Okano. Dōtoku Kagaku, literally "ethics science" but translated by this group as "Moralogy," was founded as an ethical movement in 1928 by Hiroike Chikurō. See Murakami 1980:91; for English-language publications by Dōtoku Kagaku, see Earhart 1983:71 (items 297–300). Fujii Takeshi has documented the influence of Hiroike's emphasis on self-negation and a selfless heart as the "highest ethic" upon Okano, who transformed this Confucian ethical teaching into his religious message of self-reflection (*jiko hansei*) (1983:55–57).

27. Ooms (1985:209, 260) cites the use of the "three fundamental bonds and five cardinal principles" (which he refers to as Three Bonds and Five Constants) in Tokugawa ideology, specifically in the writings of Yamazaki Ansai (1618–1682).

28. Four-character compounds such as *shinkei sūso* are frequently used in Japanese as condensed formulas with encompassing significance. The same four characters, slightly rearranged as *keishin sūso*, were also important in government attempts to unify the people: "The Home Ministry bureaucrats who headed the Shrine Bureau between 1904 and 1921 . . . promoted the ideological function of the shrines in unifying the sentiments of the people in the spirit of 'reverence for the gods and respect for the ancestors' (*keishin sūso*)" (Gluck 1985:141).

29. *Gyō* and *kō* are different pronunciations of the same Sino-Japanese character, also pronounced *iku* (*yuku*) or *okonau*.

30. The criticism of religious practice as mere mechanical repetition which requires correction by sincere motivation is, of course, a charge heard within most religious traditions at one time or another. In Japan this accusation was made not only of religious practice but also about national and social values in general. Gluck quotes three such criticisms of mechanical repetition of the Rescript on Education from the early 1900s (1985:154).

31. The two terms for "with relatives" and "without relatives" are *uen* and *muen*; the common term for spirits of the dead who are not memoralized by living relatives (and therefore may haunt or plague the living) is *muenbotoke*.

32. The founder's fears of social problems were also a major theme in the turbulent times of social change from the beginning of Meiji (1868) through 1945, and to some extent still remain today; for documentation of such fears, especially in Meiji and Taishō (1912–1926) times, see Gluck 1985:10, 28, 34, 239, 273. For a recent Japanese expression of such fears, see Matsushita 1976. See also Robertson 1979 for similar comments in relation to the late Tokugawa movement of Shingaku.

33. *Tenjin Chigi* is a general term for "the gods of heaven and earth"; see Masuda 1974:1781 under *tenjin*. The *ten* of Tenjin and the *chi* of Chigi are the same characters for writing *Tenchi* in *Tenchi Ōgami*. The idea of heaven has complex philosophical and religious nuances in Japan. For the philosophical (and political and social) nuances, see Matsumoto 1978. Fujii Takeshi has traced the immediate precedent for Tenjin Chigi to the influence of the new religion Amatsukyō upon Okano; in fact, Fujii attributes much of the "Shinto" influence and elements within Gedatsu-kai to Amatsukyō. Amatsukyō was founded in 1924 by Takeuchi Kiyomaro, a former ascetic (*gyōja*) in the movement Ontakekyō; Amatsukyō emphasized a tradition of great antiquity, predating the traditionally revered founder of the Japanese imperial line, Jinmu, to the effect that the Japanese emperors ruled over the whole world. Okano was briefly active in Amatsukyō and visited their headquarters before beginning his own movement. Fujii sees Amatsukyō with its emphasis on the national tradition of Shinto (especially Tenjin Chigi) and the emperor as a means of expressing the renewed respect for country and emperor that Okano had realized after his short sojourn in Korea. See Fujii 1983:59–62.

34. For En no Gyōja, see Earhart 1965 and 1970b:16–21; for a general treatment of Shugendō, see Earhart 1970b. For Shugendō influence on Gedatsu-kai see Miyake 1987.

35. It is difficult to assess the degree of freedom and coercion in Okano's institutional actions prior to and during World War II (which for Japan began in 1937 with warfare in China). Fujii Takeshi makes a convincing case for the perseverance of Okano's original intentions even through the influence of other traditions such as Dōtoku Kagaku (Moralogy, with its Confucian influence), Amatsukyō (with its Shinto influence), and esoteric Buddhism (Mikkyō) and Shugendō (with broad Buddhist influence); Okano blended all of these elements to fit his own "religion" of spiritual self-reflection and ritual practices. Fujii concludes that Okano did not necessarily compromise his basic teaching while conforming to government pressures. (1983:68–70).

36. As Robert J. Smith has pointed out, the Meiji government deliberately used Confucianism to "instill the virtues of imperial loyalty and filial piety" through the newly established national system of compulsory education, converting "filial piety from a private duty into a civic virtue." The Meiji oligarchs used "the universally observed practice of ancestor worship" to support the emperor, arguing "that inasmuch as all Japanese are descended from the imperial house, all are related," and all Japanese should worship the imperial line as an expression of repaying their debt of gratitude to their ancestors. "And lest there should be any remaining, nagging doubt about the conflation of imperial loyalty and filial piety, the subjects of the emperor were said to be his children" (1983:31–32). Okano was simply making a logical (but radical and unexpected) conclusion from the premises laid down by the Meiji government. Morioka has documented carefully what he calls "family-state ideology and 'ancestor religion' ": he cites the statement of the emperor at his 1928 accession: " 'the Imperial Ancestors who built up the country treated the people like their children and made the whole country the same as a household.' This is none other than 'family-state ideology,' and ancestor religion had, by definition, a close connection with it" (1977:188). Morioka shows that Okano could quote official government statements for his argument that people are the children of the emperor.

37. Two aspects of the founder's innovation of commoners' entering Sennyūji are worthy of special notice. First, Okano's following of popular Neo-Confucian teachings did not necessarily mean blind acceptance of the status quo or strict conformity to authority; in this case, Okano broke new ground in changing the status quo and challenging authority to allow commoners to directly worship their "parent" emperors. He was trying to change the status quo (exclusion of commoners at Sennyūji) by appealing to higher authority (all Japanese, as children of the emperor, can and should directly honor their imperial ancestors). Second, in Japanese religion generally there has been a tendency for "dilution" of the participation at major shrines from imperial and elite groups to lesser and finally common groups. Davis (1983–1984:203–204) has traced briefly a similar pattern of the transition of worship at the Ise Shrines. Okano's innovation, then, can be seen as another example of the "leveling" of religious participation in Japan, but its radical shift is no less dramatic because of its sudden and independent (rather than gradual and collective) challenge of the practice at the time.

38. "In 1940, the Religious Organizations (Shūkyō Dantai) Law, which had as its objective the control of religion and mobilization of religion for the war effort, was enacted" (Murakami 1980:95).

39. The significance of the Religious Corporations Ordinance is the shift from prewar suppression and oppression of religion (especially under the Religious Organizations Law) to freedom of religion. For legal questions about "Japanese Religion in the Modern Century," see Murakami 1980. "The Allied Occupation of Japan and Japanese Religions" has been covered by Woodard: "The Shinto Directive was issued by SCAP [Supreme Commander for the Allied Powers] on December 15, 1945, and the Religious Corporations Ordinance was promulgated by the Japanese government on December 28" (1972:27). "The Religious Juridical Persons Law, so named to distinguish it clearly from the Religious Corporations Ordinance which it replaced on April 3, 1951, was the only legislation *enacted by the Diet* during the Occupation" (ibid., p. 93).

40. The comparison and contrast of Okano's career with that of other founders of Japanese new religions would lead us too far astray from our more limited topic of interpreting Gedatsu-kai. For comparative materials, see Earhart 1983, especially "Founders," in the

topical index; a fascinating autobiography of one founder (in English translation) is Niwano 1978. For the life of another founder, see Araki 1982; for the general notion of "the living kami idea in the new religions of Japan," see Shimazono 1979.

41. Because each respondent was asked to circle three answers, the number of responses is more than the number of respondents, and the percentages total more than 100%.

3. Who Joins Gedatsu-kai

1. For example, Mrs. Norikawa of "Ok" Branch was selected because of a number of factors: she was an elderly widow, had experienced a dramatic cure of eye problems, and was a former member of Tenrikyō.

2. The idea of using life histories to get "inside" a new religion developed after reading the dissertation of Guthrie (1976). Guthrie's published version of his dissertation (1988) was not available for use during the preparation of this book. Three anthropologists encouraged and assisted me in thinking through this possibility and applying it to the Japanese situation of new religions: Alan H. Jacobs of Western Michigan University, David W. Plath of the University of Illinois, and Robert J. Smith of Cornell University. Their kind help is readily acknowledged, but of course, responsibility for the recording, analysis, and interpretation of the life histories rests solely with the author. A number of works were read in preparation for the collecting of life histories: Beattie 1959, Beattie 1964, Dollard 1949, Geertz 1983, Kluckhohn 1945, Pelto and Pelto 1978, Turner 1967, and Van Velsen 1967. A more recent work is the anthology of Dunaway and Baum (1984); in this large work, see especially Mintz 1984.

3. In a previous article (Earhart 1980a), I used the fictitious name Nakajiba for this person, but I have changed it to Nakajimo in this book.

4. In this interview, Mr. Nakajimo was slow to move into his own account of his experience—he had given a brief rendition of his taiken at our previous meeting, and seemed not to know where to begin his story. I asked leading questions until his story began to flow naturally. In other interviews, members moved more quickly and naturally into their stories as soon as they were asked to tell their taiken.

5. What is implied here is that Mr. Nakajimo should have given money to his financially troubled mother-in-law. Since he did not, he should now apologize.

6. The act of apologizing to a living person or to the spirit of a dead person is at the same time an act of repentance.

7. In an article focusing on this life history (Earhart 1980a), I have interpreted Mr. Nakajimo's life as having three phases: traditional, nontraditional, and neotraditional.

8. Entry into a new religion in connection with renewed relations to ancestors (or spirits of family members) seems to be a common theme in Japan. See Dore 1958:319–20 and Hardacre 1984. The reasons (or motives) for joining Gedatsu-kai will be treated in considerable detail in chapter 4, as part of the discussion of results of a nationwide survey of Gedatsu-kai members.

9. Throughout Japan, it has been the custom to erect stones, usually along the side of a road or near a temple or shrine, with a simple inscription honoring a particular kami or Buddhist divinity; Inari is one such popular kami, usually represented by the form of a fox. For a general treatment on Inari in English, see Buchanan 1935.

10. The ability of Gedatsu-kai members to "reconstruct" their lives through taiken is an important point that will be discussed later.

11. There is a large independent pilgrimage center for Fudō at Narita, near the new Narita International Airport in Chiba Prefecture; it is also rather close to the seaport where "C" Branch is located. Fudō is a popular Buddhist deity with a menacing visage, usually holding a sword; the full name is Fudō Myōō, in Sanskrit Acala.

12. The American slang "OK" has been adopted in everyday Japanese, and is retained in the summary of life histories.

13. The significance of Konpira, a popular divinity along the seacoast, will be discussed in the next section.

14. Gedatsu-kai members who practice for a long time may have a particular deity specified as a guardian deity.

15. Another example of an artist being "inspired" by Gedatsu-kai values and especially by the founder is the Japanese-American haiku poet and translator Kenneth Yasuda. See Yasuda 1957:v, xi. De Vos in his intensive psychological study of achievement among Japanese writes, "I find a more complex configuration of internalized values motivating individual Japanese. This configuration is common to Japanese artists, scientists, scholars, government officials, and soldiers, as well as to businessmen and entrepreneurs" (1973:183). The case of Miss Muro and the other life histories provide religious evidence for the fact that people in various occupations share a similar set of "internalized values motivating" them.

16. For information on the *Hannya Shingyō*, see n. 1 in chapter 7.

17. Testimonies are the lifeblood of Japanese new religions, but also figure prominently in other social contexts. Rohlen describes oral testimonies of bank workers "in which company values are confirmed" and printed testimonies in the monthly bank magazine which recall "the trials and sacrifices of previous generations" (of bank workers) (1974:55, 43, 56). Testimonies and miniature life histories of Risshō Kōsei-kai members are printed in the monthly English-language magazine *Dharma World*; for example, see Ichihashi 1986. Similar testimonies can be found in the English-language publications of other Japanese new religions. Yamada's dissertation (1984) is an interesting account of "narratives of the religious experience of Japanese-American and Caucasian members of the Church of World Messianity, Los Angeles, California."

18. Hardacre, in criticizing the earlier "crisis theory" interpretations of the origins of Japanese new religions, emphasizes that her study of Reiyū-kai reveals much more than "reaction and response. The following account . . . emphasizes the founders' positive initiative in formulating a creed and their purposeful transformation of traditional elements to match new circumstances" (1984:10). This double issue of accounting for the complex origins of new religions and the equally complex "conversion" experiences of new members, will be treated at greater length in the final chapter.

19. As Robert J. Smith (1974:124) perceptively pointed out in his thorough study of ancestor worship, "I think it is fair to say that to the extent that most Japanese attribute misfortune and illness to the ancestors at all, it will be said that the cause lies in the neglect of the collectivity of the ancestors rather than in the malign disposition of any single forbear." In other words, neglect is the main cause of misfortune/illness, and not the inherent malevolence of a spirit of the dead. In Gedatsu-kai there are abundant cases of individual spirits of the dead causing misfortune or illness, but once pacified they are either neutralized or turned into benevolent benefactors; spirits are not permanently malevolent. The connection between sickness and ancestors is by no means unique to Gedatsu-kai or Japanese religion. "Medical anthropology is replete with accounts of folk systems where illness is embedded in a network of social relations including those with ancestral spirits" (Early 1982:1492). For another comparative treatment of theories of illness, see Murdock 1980.

20. Dore's summary of an interview with a section chief in a Tokyo cosmetics firm in the 1950s reveals a similar combination of work ethic with familial, political, educational, and religious values, as well as concern for health. See Dore 1958:211. For an article treating Mr. Abe's story as an example illustrating "Buddhism as Power," see Earhart 1987.

21. Konpira is the name for a deity protecting seafarers; the name is derived from the Indian deity Kumbhīra.

22. I did not read Ohnuki-Tierney's work *Illness and Culture in Contemporary Japan* (1984) until after my materials were gathered, analyzed, and interpreted, but her synthetic work provides a valuable wider context in which the Gedatsu-kai views and actions concerning illness and healing can be better understood.

23. The term *spirit* in English tends to call up playful images of "spiritual" seances or simply contrasts the "spiritual" realm with the material. But in Japanese, the notion of spirit (rei) is an extremely important aspect of the human makeup and religious experience in general. For example, one of the themes of the eleventh-century *The Tale of Genji* is that the spirits of wronged women may possess other people and cause sickness or even death. This theme is echoed in Enchi Fumiko's modern novel *Masks*, in which the characters discuss spirit possession in *The Tale of Genji*. A number of principles related to spirits in *The Tale of Genji* are very similar to current notions of spirits such as are found in Gedatsu-kai. Spirits of wronged persons, both living and dead, may possess related or even unrelated

persons, but attack persons who have some close connection with the wrong which is the cause of enmity or malice; this may result in personal anxiety or mental imbalance, sickness, or even death. The condition of possession by a malign spirit is treated by rites exorcising the malign spirit and rites strengthening the victim; however, the condition can be permanently cured only by purifying and pacifying the attacking spirit. See Murasaki 1977:168–69, 620 and Enchi 1983:46–52. For an incisive treatment of the theme of karma in Japanese literature, see LaFleur 1983; see also Robert J. Smith 1974:40, 69–114 (especially p. 70 for "a paradigm of the interactive worlds of the living and the dead").

24. As Robert J. Smith (1974:54) has pointed out, "In this connection the question of karma and the cycle of rebirth arises once again. I am firmly convinced that the Japanese never fully assimilated these central concepts of Buddhism" (which Smith here refers to as classical Indian notions of karma and the cycle of rebirth). Obeyesekere, discussing South Asian religions, has argued that most "primitive" peoples have some form of "rebirth eschatology," and that Buddhism introduced the "single causal variable" of "ethicization" which "transforms the simple rebirth theory into the karmic eschatology" (1980:140). Gedatsu-kai certainly has its own form of "ethicization," although it is not solely Buddhist, relying also (as does Japanese religion generally) upon Neo-Confucian and indigenous notions. Obeyesekere's model of "a simple rebirth eschatology" and its transformation is an interesting construction for anyone wishing to develop a more formal model of Japanese patterns of rebirth. My impression is that Obeyesekere's discussion (and the bulk of the materials in the two volumes on karma, O'Flaherty 1980 and Keyes and Daniel 1983) is more concerned with how previous karma affects the rebirth situation of individuals—this may be a distinctive feature of South and Southeast Asian Buddhism. But Gedatsu-kai is more concerned with the (positive and negative) effect of karma upon the lives of individuals and family groups—this may be a distinctive feature of Japanese Buddhism and Japanese religion.

25. O'Flaherty notes the same difficulty in predicting from cause to effect in the understanding of karma in classical India, quoting Lewis Carroll's *Alice in Wonderland* to the same tune: " 'if you drink much from a bottle marked ' "poison," ' it is almost certain to disagree with you sooner or later,' the 'sooner or later' perhaps corresponding to the karmic escape clause" (1980:xxii).

26. Ohnuki-Tierney in her comprehensive work *Illness and Culture in Contemporary Japan* says, "Even more frequently, the Japanese seek etiological explanations for ordinary illnesses in: (1) atmospheric factors such as chill or winds; (2) various physiological factors, such as the inborn constitutions (*taishitsu*), *shinkei* (nerves), and 'blood types'; or (3) quasi-physiological agents such as an aborted fetus" (1984:75), and includes an interesting section "Aborted fetus as an etiological agent" (pp. 75–81). Generally, my field work on Gedatsu-kai (conducted 1979–80, about the same time as Ohnuki-Tierney's) yielded material on illness and religion quite similar to hers, especially the close connection between women's experience of abortion and problems such as illness.

However, some significant differences of fact and interpretation should be noted. Ohnuki-Tierney holds that it is the "freshly dead" that for Japanese are the main source of pollution and sin, and that "some also say that if the living do not take proper care of the dead, then the dead may harm them. In practice, however, this belief is not very strong . . . and ancestors in Japan seldom punish their own relatives" (1984:70, 80). Material in Gedatsu-kai life histories provides ample evidence to the contrary for three points: (1) not just the "freshly dead," but ancestors, even several generations removed, do harm people, especially when memorial rites are neglected or improperly performed; (2) such beliefs are very strong in Gedatsu-kai (as in most Japanese new religions); and (3) ancestors, such as aborted fetuses, especially afflict their own families.

A fourth difference, partly a matter of interpretation, is also important: Ohnuki-Tierney relates aborted fetuses to illness through the notion of their being outside the "network of human relationships": "Although an aborted fetus is quasi-matter, the vital point is that it has never entered the network of human relationships. Ascribing suffering to the aborted fetus therefore avoids the involvement of interpersonal relationships in the sufferings of an individual" (1984:81). However, Gedatsu-kai members were quite specific that the aborted fetus had entered the human realm, and in fact the neglect of such fetuses caused misfortune or illness for the very reason that the family had neglected part of its unit. In fact, during an afternoon of interviewing female members of Gedatsu-kai, I asked if they did not make a religious distinction between a "natural" miscarriage and an artificially or medically performed abortion. They responded that the same repentance and ritual procedures are required in both cases. The reason is that once a life is begun (that is, a fetus begins to grow), it should fully develop, be born, and live to old age. But the rupture of this natural process—whether by miscarriage, abortion, stillbirth, or death shortly after birth—interrupts this natural cycle, and therefore repentance and ritual are required to restore the balance between the living family and the dead ancestors. For other works viewing the fetus as part of the human world in Japanese experience, see Sievers 1983:184, Coleman 1983:66–67, and Steinhoff and Diamond 1977:47, 86, 131.

It seems to me that a crucial clue to illness and healing in Japan is the maintaining of a proper balance between the living family and dead ancestors (and local spirits). Illness may occur when there is disharmony between the living and dead (for example, the mistake of thinking that miscarried or aborted fetuses, and stilborn infants, are *not* part of the ongoing family unit); healing takes place when the rift between the living and the dead is repaired (through repentance which corrects the person's mistake, and through rituals such as the amacha rite which simultaneously purify the living and the dead). Ohnuki-Tierny mentions the notion of imbalance rather than (pathogenic) causation as the perceived source of illness (1984:33), and I think that our overall interpretations, because they depend on this central notion of imbalance, are quite compatible, even though she does not deal directly with ancestors.

27. The basis for this claim, of course, rests not simply on the content and extent of these nine life histories, but also on the manner in which they were collected and the context of this entire study of Gedatsu-kai. About fifty life histories were collected, and they support the interpretation of the world view given above, but there is not sufficient space to cite all of them.

4. The Members of Gedatsu-kai

1. The main questionnaire, the subject of this chapter, was addressed to individual members. Two other questionnaires, one addressed to branch leaders and one to branch officers, were also distributed. The Japanese-language originals for all three can be found in Earhart and Miyake 1983:425–30. An English translation of the individual questionnaire, with tabulation categories and simple results, was included as an appendix in a preliminary version of this work, but because of space limitations it had to be excluded.

2. The data for the statistical analysis were gathered as part of our joint study. I returned from Japan with data sheets for the surveys and had the information typed into our mainframe computer at Western Michigan University, developing categories and approaches for arranging the statistics—such as age groups and historical periods of membership for purposes of cross-tabulations. On a trip to Japan in 1981, I provided Japanese colleagues with a computer tape and printout of the initial results, some of which were used in the analysis and writing of articles for the Japanese-language volume on Gedatsu-kai (Earhart and Miyake 1983). However, these colleagues used the original data and the computer information from Western Michigan University along with computer information from Gunma University to develop some of their own categories and approaches for arranging the data, especially in a detailed chapter featuring many charts and graphs (Ishii 1983c). Therefore, the figures and percentages in this book and in the Japanese-language volume do not always coincide, because of slightly different ways of handling the arrangement of statistics, but there is no substantial disagreement. The Japanese-language volume goes into much greater detail on statistical analysis of several questionnaires of Gedatsu-kai members and officials, and raises interesting comparisons with other surveys of religious awareness and practice in Japan. Some of the results of the Japanese-language article on statistics have been utilized in this chapter. In this book the maximum number of respondents is based on 3,683 females and 1,995 males (excluding no response for gender).

3. The nature of this organization is the subject of the next chapter; for understanding the membership, all we need to know for the moment is that these members participate in local branches that are part of a nationwide movement. Those who do not read Japanese

and are interested in comparable figures for other new religions may find helpful the Statistical Tables in Hori 1972:233–63. In this 1972 English-language publication, Gedatsu-kai is listed on p. 251 as having 484 meeting places, 430 clergy, and 176,532 adherents. Similar figures are listed for other new religions. More recent membership figures are provided in Murakami 1980:168–71; the figure of 455,000 for Gedatsu-kai is a misprint.

4. Even in pre-World War II Suye Mura, Smith and Wiswell report that women dominated lectures by a visiting Buddhist priest (1982:48).

5. Ishii (1983c:231) has compared Gedatsu-kai membership with membership of other religious groups in Japan by ten-year intervals from ages 16–25 through 56+. The figures from the two top age categories, 46–55 and 56+, show that Gedatsu-kai membership is similar to Buddhist but considerably "older" than the memberships of Shinto, Christianity, and Sōka Gakkai.

	Age 46–55	Age 56+	(Percentages of
Gedatsu-kai	24.6%	38.5%	total membership)
Buddhism	23.1%	37.7%	
Shinto	19.6%	29.8%	
Christianity	12.5%	16.5%	
Sōka Gakkai	18.3%	22.5%	

6. Of the 32.4% in table 4 who join between ages 0 and 30, only 4.7% of the total sample join between the ages of 0 and 15, and 27.7% between the ages of 16 and 30.

7. In the previous paragraph, the number of unemployed females was given as 1,820; the discrepancy between 1,820 and 1,812 unemployed females is either respondent error in completing the questionnaire, or (more probably) coding error in marking data sheets (or keying data sheets into the computer). As can be seen in table 6 ("female unemployed"), the three columns indicate 1,820 for all data, 1,812 females, and 8 males. This logical impossibility of 8 female unemployed who are male, representing only .2% of the female sample of 3,683, is recorded here as in the simple results of the questionnaire. For both simple results and cross-tabulations, a small percentage—from 0.0% to 0.4%—of invalid responses were included in "no response."

8. The discrepancy between 122 male unemployed in the previous paragraph and 119 male unemployed here is a recording of simple results, including the logical impossibility of 3 male unemployed who are female. See the preceding note for explanation of treatment of these figures.

9. Figures for the Japanese population are from *Japan Statistical Yearbook* 1980 (Statistics Bureau, Prime Minister's Office [Japan], 1981:51), for the year 1979, the same time frame as the Gedatsu-kai survey.

10. Ishii (1983c:233) has compared the occupations of Gedatsu-kai membership (including housewives, students, and male unemployed) with the occupations of the memberships of Buddhism, Shinto, Christianity, and Sōka Gakkai. In this comparison, Gedatsu-kai has the largest percentage of housewives, at 37.4%; however, as Ishii points out, the percentage of the combined groups of housewives, students, and male unemployed remains rather consistent at about 40% for all religions except Christianity, which is just under 50%. Excluding the three categories of housewives, students, and male unemployed, we find Buddhism and Shinto closest to the national percentages for occupation. Christianity is very high in young females and higher than the national percentages in sales workers, skilled and technical workers, and managers and officials (i.e., white-collar); Christianity is like Gedatsu-kai in that it has not penetrated blue-collar workers. Christianity and Sōka Gakkai are similar in that they have not penetrated farmers, lumbermen, and fishermen. Sōka Gakkai is strongest among self-employed, sales, service workers, and manufacturing and generally blue-collar workers. As has already been seen in comparison with the Japanese population as a whole, in comparison with other religious groups, too, Gedatsu-kai's distinctive occupational feature is housewives, farmers-lumbermen-fishermen, and clerical workers (Ishii 1983c:232–34). For comparative material on Sōka Gakkai, see White 1970:70, 72. For an analysis and interpretation of "Japan's Changing Occupational Structure and Its Significance," see Cole and Tominaga 1976.

11. The notions of "inside" information and "outside" interpretation may be used to

distinguish the concrete views of Gedatsu-kai members and the more abstract views of scholars. But there is not, and should not be, an absolute separation between the two. Life histories are clearly "inside" documents because they are the actual testimonies (taiken) of the members, given in the same religious genre as in branch or other Gedatsu-kai meetings. As we comment upon the general features found in the Gedatsu-kai testimonies, comparing and contrasting them with religious experience in other traditions, we enter "outside" territory. In a similar fashion, survey results are "inside" information in the sense that they are the reported perceptions of members. When the survey results are converted to rather objective, statistical tables, and are interpreted in the light of other general knowledge, they enter "outside" territory. Perhaps a better way of distinguishing the life histories and survey results is in terms of intensive and extensive materials: the survey results provide extensive, quantitative information to complement the intensive, dramatic content of life histories. For a standard treatment of the "emic" and "etic" viewpoints, see Pelto and Pelto 1978:54–66. My intention has been to approximate the balance of emic and etic found in Pelto and Pelto's conclusion (p. 66). Geertz (1983:56–57) in his perceptive treatment of the "native's point of view" has discussed the relative merits of various paired terms such as *inside-outside, first person-third person*, and *emic-etic*; he favors following the distinction of psychoanalyst Heinz Kohut between *experience-near* and *experience-distant*, which is similar to my use of *inside* and *outside*.

12. The inability to reduce motive for joining a religious group to a simple response is probably true of many members in various traditions, and would not seem to be a distinctive characteristic of Gedatsu-kai members.

13. Responses for categories in the general areas of Preference and Sickness have been refigured, with the percentage each category represents for each particular area of Preference and Sickness. There were not sufficient responses in categories of other areas for cross-tabulation with other factors; therefore, they are listed here by number of actual responses, and are not refigured as a percentage of their respective general areas.

14. A safe generalization is that female members of Gedatsu-kai are another indication that Japanese women are more "powerful" and influential than popular perception has suspected. The most comprehensive picture of Japanese women in recent times is by Takie Sugiyama Lebra (1984); see also Smith and Wiswell 1982 (especially p. xv), Bernstein 1983, Joyce Lebra 1976, and (for a feminist critique) Sievers 1983. For the life history of a Japanese-American woman, see Kikumura 1981; a dissertation discussing women and religion in Japan is Nefsky 1984.

15. *Michibiku* is the verb, "to recruit"; *michibiki* is the gerund, "recruiting"; and *michibikikata* is the noun, "recruiting person."

16. The controversy over "recruitment" in Japanese new religions is similar to the American debate over "programming" (or "brainwashing") and "deprogramming." See Lifton 1961 for the classic interpretation of Chinese "brainwashing," which he prefers to call *thought control*. Some of the popular notions of brainwashing are presumed in many of the treatments of new religious movements, not only in Japan but in various cultures and many traditions: new religions gain converts by isolating them from their familiar environment (or seeking people away from home and traditional religious association), drastically changing their personal, social, and religious identity by making them part of the new religion, and subjecting them to intense peer pressure to conform to the group's values and practices. In short, the claim is that new religions manipulate or "program" people. The reverse process, when parents or friends attempt to return manipulated or "programmed" people to their "normal" mode of life, is called "deprogramming." In the United States, this has provoked intense controversy, both academic and legal (see Robbins 1981, 1985).

17. The logical impossibility of three females recruited by wife is either coding error or keying error. Table 15 includes the same three females as recruiters of wife.

18. Obviously one of the major factors behind the large percentage of women in Japanese new religions is the *relative* economic freedom Japanese women of recent times are experiencing, as compared with the grueling work days of farm women until the past few decades; the long hours and arduous nature of women's work have been documented by Smith and Wiswell (1982) for the period prior to World War II and by Bernstein (1983) for the 1970s. Most Japanese women today do not work the long, hard hours of their farming forebears, and this does give them relatively more leisure for activities such as involvement

in new religions. For a feminist critique, see Sievers, who has shown that from Meiji times on, the Japanese government openly supported a strong family "nurtured" by the "good wife-wise mother" for the ultimate purpose of building a strong state (1983:22–23).

19. Takie Sugiyama Lebra has pointed out both the androcentrism in Japanese traditional religions and the tendency for women to dominate Japanese new religions (1984:19–20, 257–59).

20. In a study of "the changing social position of women in Japan," results of a 1956 government survey comparing women and men regarding "opinions on the choice of a spouse" showed that women are "more bound by tradition than men" (as indicated by their consistently higher rate of deference to parents' choice over own choice in marriage). See Koyama 1961:43. Within Gedatsu-kai membership, many wives seem to have deferred to the wishes (including religious membership) of husbands at time of marriage; after marriage, many husbands followed wives into Gedatsu-kai.

21. Of the 384 responses indicating more than one recruiting person, the most frequent combination is mother and father; combinations of relative and female family member (mother or sister) are also frequent, as are relative and friend or neighbor; but there are only a few instances of the combination of relative and father.

22. White is of this opinion with Sōka Gakkai members: "The preliminary and as yet empirically deficient assumption I would make from the partial data is that Sōkagakkai believers are born, not made. The Gakkai attracts or at least retains those who are already basically in agreement with Gakkai precepts; it does not successfully resocialize converts into entirely new patterns of thought and action" (1970:254). Of course, this view of "born, not made" depends on what is meant by "entirely new patterns of thought and action," and whether the focus is general cultural values or the concern is individual psychological reorientation. On the broadest level of Japanese culture, we would not expect members of new religions to propose "entirely new patterns of thought and action" in the sense of rejecting filial piety, gratitude to ancestors, veneration of kami, and worship of Buddhas for some "totally new values" or non-Japanese values (such as redemption through Christ or submission to Allah). Gluck has argued effectively that there has been an unwritten "orthodoxy" in the midst of ideological diversity: "the argument here has suggested that orthodoxy—emperor, loyalty, village, family-state—occupied but a portion of the wider ideological landscape as Meiji turned to Taishō. Precisely because its common values were largely unexceptionable and exceedingly general, they coexisted with a diversity of ideological formulations that were often very different from the dominant one" (1985:276). Here, as in all previous discussions of Japanese new religions, some crucial cultural and religious questions are, What is "new" about new religions? How do we distinguish between "old" and "new"? When does the "new" become "old"? From the viewpoint of individual psychological reorientation, the matter of "newness" can be resolved more easily. Members who join new religions, even if they do not assume "entirely new patterns of thought and action" in the sense of new and different for that culture, nevertheless acquire beliefs and values new to each person (or reformulated and reconfigured) and thereby constitute a new orientation, a reorientation. Lebra has demonstrated this effectively for women in Gedatsu-kai in her "Self-reconstruction in Japanese Religious Psychotherapy" (1982).

23. For more detailed charts of the "before-and-after" results of the questionnaire, see Earhart and Miyake 1983:438-45.

24. For works on the imperial institution during and after Tokugawa times, see Earl 1964 Webb 1965, and Hall 1968. It was during the reign of Emperor Meiji (1868–1912) that the emperor first became "popular": "it appears that by the end of the Meiji period virtually all Japanese were conscious of the emperor's existence for the first time in Japanese history" (Gluck 1985:78, 100). Distribution of the emperor's photograph and the Imperial Rescript on Education (1890) was promoted by the Ministry of Education and eagerly accepted by local schools (Gluck 1985:79–80, 89, 92, 100, 106).

25. Dore in his 1951 survey of a Tokyo ward (Shitayama) reports results for attitude toward the emperor that are remarkably similar to our 1979 survey of Gedatsu-kai members, when analyzed by age and historical period (1958:452).

26. It is difficult to make direct comparisons of the Gedatsu-kai percentages of religious practice with the Japanese population as a whole, for such reasons as the different survey instruments and the different means of gathering information. But the general place of

Gedatsu-kai practice within Japanese religious practice can be appreciated by comparison with an NHK (Japan Broadcasting Corporation) survey of the religious attitudes of 2,692 people, conducted in 1981. The survey asked the question, "Do you worship at the kamidana?" and provided answer categories of "worship daily" (16.2%), "worship occasionally" (21.8%), "at some times worship" (14.7%), "do not worship at all" (7.2%), and "have no kamidana" (39.8%). (Those who did not respond or did not understand the question were 0.2%.) For the NHK material, see NHK 1984:6. Ishii (1983c:252) has compared the results of the NHK survey with our Gedatsu-kai survey by grouping all positive responses of worship at kamidana (daily, occasionally, at some times), or 52.7%, and grouping negative responses (no worship at all, no kamidana), or 47.0%. These figures allow the following comparisons:

	NHK	Gedatsu-kai (before joining)	Gedatsu-kai (after joining)
Worship at kamidana	52.7%	55.1%	85.8%
No worship at kamidana	47.0%	26.6%	1.0%
No response	.2%	18.3%	13.1%

Although the results of these two surveys cannot be compared exactly, because of slightly different questions, the general picture is clear: before joining Gedatsu-kai, members worship at kamidana at a rate the same as or a little higher than the population as a whole; after joining, Gedatsu-kai members worship at kamidana at a rate much higher than the population as a whole. Dore reports on kamidana presence and practice in his 1951 survey of a Tokyo ward, with results similar to those of the NHK survey and Gedatsu-kai members before joining. After reporting the mandatory Shinto practices during World War II, he writes, "But today 47% of households in Shitayama-cho have no *kamidana*. (59% of households who have moved into the ward since the end of the war.) And of fifty-five people in a sample of one hundred who said they had *kamidana* in their houses, less than a half said that they bowed to it every day" (1958:306). Robert J. Smith (1974:88) cites percentages of families with kamidana for eight surveys (including Dore's), ranging from a low of 40% for an urban group to a high of 95% for a rural group. Ishii (1983c:253–55) also cross-tabulated worship at kamidana in our Gedatsu-kai survey with age at time of questionnaire, with historical periods by year of entry, and with occupation. For absolute age at time of questionnaire, Ishii compared daily worship at kamidana with "have no kamidana." The highest decade for people without a kamidana is of those in their twenties and thirties, who reach a high of 50% and above, declining to about 20% for age seventy and above. Daily worship at kamidana rises steadily from less than 5% in the first decade of life to about 40% for age seventy and above. For historical period by year of entry, Ishii compared worship at kamidana before and after joining. Worship at kamidana by people entering Gedatsu-kai in the earliest period of Gedatsu-kai, 1929–1937 (prewar), begins at almost 60% worshipping at kamidana and climbs to almost 70% for people entering in the wartime period of 1938–1945, and then declines steadily to less than 50% worshipping at kamidana in the most recent (1974–1980) period. (The peak of highest kamidana practice for people entering during prewar and wartime years corresponds to the peak years for possession of pictures of the imperial household.) Worship at kamidana after entering is consistently high, varying less than ten percentage points in all historical periods, always in the 80% range. When worship at kamidana before and after joining is considered by occupations, farmers-lumbermen-fishermen showed the smallest increase, from 61.4% to 83.5%, while clerical workers showed the greatest increase, from 45.8% to 88.1%.

27. A general picture of Gedatsu-kai members' practice at butsudan in comparison with the Japanese population's practice at butsudan can be drawn from the NHK survey in similar fashion to the comparison of percentages for practice at kamidana. The NHK survey question "Do you worship at the butsudan?" provided answer categories of "worship daily" (27.8%), "worship occasionally" (18.9%), "at some times worship" (10.0%), "do not worship at all" (4.0%), "have no butsudan" (39.2%). (Those who did not respond or did not understand the question were 0.2%.) Ishii (1983c:252) has compared the results of the NHK survey with our Gedatsu-kai survey by grouping all positive responses of worship at butsudan (daily, occasionally, at some times), or 56.7%, and grouping negative responses (no worship at all, no butsudan), or 43.2%. These figures allow the following comparisons:

	NHK	Gedatsu-kai (before joining)	Gedatsu-kai (after joining)
Worship at butsudan	56.7%	66.8%	86.8%
No worship at butsudan	43.2%	16.9%	.9%
No response	.2%	16.3%	12.3%

The same general remarks for the comparison of NHK and Gedatsu-kai surveys of kami-dana hold true for butsudan: although results are not directly comparable, because of slightly different questions, a general picture emerges. Gedatsu-kai members before joining worship at butsudan at a rate significantly higher than the population as a whole; Gedatsu-kai members after joining worship at butsudan at a rate much higher than the population as a whole. (It is worth noting that the most obvious difference in the before-after results of kamidana and butsudan with the NHK results is that Gedatsu-kai members before joining are just slightly above the national figures for worship at kamidana, but more than 10% above the national figures for worship at butsudan.) Dore reports in his 1951 survey of a Tokyo ward that 80% of families established in this ward for more than one generation had a butsudan, while 45% of younger sons had a butsudan (1958:313). Robert J. Smith (1974:88) cites percentages of families with butsudan for eight surveys (including Dore's), ranging from a low of 45% for a Tokyo white-collar group to a high of 92% for a rural group.

Ishii (1983c:253–55) also cross-tabulated worship at butsudan in our Gedatsu-kai survey with age at time of questionnaire, with historical periods by year of entry, and with oc-cupations. For absolute age at time of questionnaire, Ishii compared daily worship at bu-tsudan with "have no butsudan." As with comparable figures for worship at kamidana, the highest decade for people without a butsudan is the thirties, with a high of almost 60%, declining to about 10% for age seventy and above. Daily worship at butsudan rises steadily from about 5% in the first decade of life to age seventy and above, when males are 57% and females are 77%. Worship at butsudan by people entering Gedatsu-kai in the earliest period of Gedatsu-kai, 1929–1937 (prewar), begins at 70% and climbs in the wartime period of 1938–1945 to almost 80%, and then declines steadily to almost 60% in the most recent (1974–1980) period. Worship at butsudan after entering, by historical period, follows a pattern similar to that for worship at kamidana after entering, by historical period: it is consistently high, varying by less than ten percentage points, always in the 80% range. It is not surprising that worship at butsudan, before and after entry, when considered by occupation, reveals the same pattern as the corresponding figures for worship at kamidana: the smallest increase before to after is for farmers-lumbermen-fishermen, from 72.0% to 85.2%; clerical workers showed the greatest increase, from 57.9% to 88.1%. Robert J. Smith's research on ancestor worship reveals information and insights similar to those of our study of Gedatsu-kai, for example, the distinction between the experience of people in prewar and wartime Japan and the experience of people who were born and grew up in postwar Japan (1974:36). For the prewar-postwar conditions and Sōka Gakkai, see White 1970:63. Robert J. Smith's information on the close correlation between daily worship at butsudan and advancing age is similar to that of our survey (see 1974:117).

28. For a brief treatment of sacredness in relation to home and family, and sacred space outside the home, see Earhart 1984:69–100.

29. Dore (1958:300–301) gives a clear picture of the very loose attachment of people in Shitayama-chō (Tokyo) to ujigami in his 1951 study; he reports of one rare individual who regularly visited the local (Soga) ujigami, proving the exception to the rule. This presents a remarkable contrast with the high rate of visits to ujigami by Gedatsu-kai members.

30. For a general treatment of "Family Rites," including treatment of butsudan and the "family temple," see Dore 1958:312–28: He reports that 94% said they had a parish (family) temple; 53% had visited their family temple in the previous year.

31. In Dore's study of a Tokyo ward, "in 1951, half of the kamidana in Shitayama-cho still contained fuda to the Ise shrine" (1958:309).

32. For a critical treatment of this problem, see Murakami 1980:113–14, 158–60, 162–63.

33. This position was advocated by the Gedatsu-kai superintendent (*kyōtō*) in a 1969 speech at the Tokyo Practice Hall, as will be mentioned in chapter 7.

34. Ishii (1983c:262–64) has cross-tabulated visits to Ise and Yasukuni, before and after joining, with other results in the Gedatsu-kai study, as done with other before-and-after categories, revealing similar tendencies.

5. Branch Meetings

1. To preserve anonymity, branch names (which tend to be easily identifiable place names) are abbreviated to a single letter.

2. In Japan, religious membership usually is counted in households, not by individuals.

3. *Dōjō* is a common term for the place of physical or spiritual "exercise." As Davis has pointed out, "Since Japanese religion is more concerned with practice, discipline, and training (*shugyō*) than with theological erudition (*kyō*), one naturally associates dojos with a very 'Japanese' kind of spirituality" (1980:1–2).

4. Striking sparks over an altar is a Shinto form of purification.

5. One of the problems that Gedatsu-kai executives perceive in the present organizational structure is that they cannot provide sufficient guidance to local branches. Ishii concludes from a survey of branch leaders that a headquarters representative provides a guidance talk at a branch once every three months (1983b:88).

6. Hōon Kansha-kai is one of the earliest names of Gedatsu-kai.

7. This brief reference supports the previous interpretation of before-and-after frequencies for ujigami and bodaiji: because the tutelary Shinto shrine (ujigami) is close, it can be visited every day; because the Buddhist parish temple (bodaiji) is distant, it can be visited only when the woman has a day off.

8. As we saw in the responses for recruitment in chapter 4, more wives recruit husbands than husbands recruit wives. It is not surprising that this man appears to have been recruited by his wife. The remarkable point is that he had explored Shinto, Christianity, and Buddhism on his own, but entered Gedatsu-kai following the lead of his wife.

9. Here "faith" as *shinkō* is disparaged in the sense of the founder's critique of automatic, unreflected repetition of ritual simply to ask for personal benefits.

10. *Banbutsu* can mean all of nature, or the entire creation.

11. In his stress of *gaku*, study or scholarship, he was echoing and implicitly criticizing terms in my talk—"It was not a matter of the *study* of religion [*shūkyōGAKU*], it was not *scholarship* [*GAKUmon*]."

12. The higi sanpō, or three mysteries, are the amacha memorial ritual, the purification (kiyome), and the mediation ritual of gohō shugyō. The third of the three mysteries is left out of this young man's account, either inadvertently overlooked by him or not written down in my notes.

13. *Tadashii* means "right," "correct," or "proper"; this Gedatsu-kai member is praising the "right" personal conduct and discipline as conforming to the "right" religion (Gedatsu-kai).

14. For a treatment of the notions of karma and six levels of hell in a literary context, see LaFleur 1983:26–59. LaFleur argues "that Buddhism's cognitive framework . . . functioned quite effectively as what Max Weber called a *theodicy*; that is, it made the world and the vast variety of individual destinies rational and acceptable—something needed perhaps equally by princes and peasants" (p. 27).

15. Batō Kannon is the so-called "horse-headed Kannon." For a treatment of "Hayagrīva: The Mantrayānic Aspect of the Horse-Cult in China and Japan," see Gulik 1935.

16. For Dōsojin, associated with roadside deities, as well as powers of fertility (especially phallic symbols) and Dōsojin couples idealizing conjugal harmony, see Czaja 1974.

17. The only lengthy study in English on hōza (which the author calls "circle of harmony") is Dale 1975. See also the treatment of hōza as "dharma seat" in Hardacre 1987.

18. An incisive treatment of "women and their sexual karma" in the Japanese new religion

Sūkyō Mahikari is provided by Davis 1980:161–200. See also Hardacre 1984:188–223 for the role of women in Reiyū-kai.

19. My notes for this interview give July 14, 1965, as the date in question; either Mr. Yanagida mistakenly said, or I mistakenly heard, *shichigatsu* (July) for *hachigatsu* (August). For dates of the Watts riot and a newspaper description, see Thackrey 1965.

20. A book and article on Gedatsu-kai by Kiyota (1982, 1987) relate Gedatsu-kai to Shingon Mikkyō (esoteric Buddhism) and Shinto-Buddhist syncretism in order to interpret Gedatsu theory and practice in the context of Shingon Mikkyō doctrine (1982:3). Kiyota concludes that "Shingon Mikkyō forms the doctrinal infrastructure of Gedatsu thought" but argues that "the Gedatsu is a lay organization and it addresses itself to people who might not be as concerned with abstract, theoretical issues as with practical issues. Hence it has presented Shingon doctrine in a new way" (ibid., p. 80). As Kiyota has indicated, this abstract version of Gedatsu-kai as an expression of Shingon teaching has not yet reached the members, and it is not yet clear how the beliefs and practices of Gedatsu-kai will be codified and formalized in a more permanent fashion.

6. Branches, Divisions, and Headquarters

1. Gedatsu-kai headquarters is currently preparing a history of the formation of the movement as a companion volume to its life of the founder printed in *Gedatsu Kongō den*.

2. Many aspects of the organization of Gedatsu-kai, naturally, are shared with other Japanese religious and social groups. Rohlen observed the same emphasis on face-to-face work in his anthropological study of a Japanese bank: "This general emphasis on the group context of work . . . arises from something much more elemental—the inclination, found throughout Japanese society, to organize activities into small face-to-face groups, to enjoy this kind of environment, and to work most efficiently in it" (1974:30).

3. This list was taken from a 1979 Gedatsu-kai publication, which was prepared when there were 361 branches; by the time of our research in late 1979, there were 368 branches. When visiting Gedatsu-kai headquarters in the summer of 1987, I was told by an executive that the number of branches had increased to more than 400, even though their policy was not to pursue rapid expansion of the movement.

4. The branch leader in Gedatsu-kai is the crucial or pivotal point in the organization, because the leader is in direct contact with both the face-to-face grassroots group and the central headquarters. The branch leader in Gedatsu-kai is comparable to the "chief" in the Japanese bank studied by Rohlen, because this chief "faces in two directions and has two sets of loyalties" (1974:30).

5. Hardacre (1986:121–24) points out the crucial role of women in leading the religious life of Kurozumi-kyō branches.

6. In his detailed study of Gedatsu-kai's administrative structure, Ishii concludes that the role and responsibility of divisions and division heads are not always clearly specified, but the main consideration is guidance of branches. On the other hand, division heads have the best knowledge of actual conditions within Gedatsu-kai, and for this reason they are regularly gathered at headquarters to discuss actual conditions and to adjust policy in relation to changing conditions (1983b:87).

7. Ishii points out that there are four types of zadankai or discussion groups: independent discussion groups, discussion groups instructed by headquarters, discussion groups instructed by divisions, and discussion groups instructed by branches. The independent discussion groups, which must have thirty families, are for all purposes the same as branches. The other three are less formal gatherings in homes, named by the unit responsible for instructing and guiding them (1983b:85–86).

8. For comparative purposes, see "Structure of the Sōkagakkai in 1951" and "Structure of the Sōkagakkai in January 1970" in White 1970:305–07.

9. Mr. Akiyoshi's shift from participation in the student movement during the 1960s to more conservative behavior as he became older is a trend among Japanese former students noted by many observers. See Krauss 1974:99.

10. Some other members of the publications bureau apparently share his views, because they were upset that we had observed gohō shugyō and might think that this is the distinctive

feature of Gedatsu-kai. Although polite, they firmly insisted that the founder's teaching was his emphasis on ethical values and self-reflection, not such spiritual matters.

11. For the terakoya, or temple schools, see Dore 1965:252–90. For the "content of terakoya education," which is interesting background for values of the founder Okano as well as for Gedatsu-kai generally, see especially pp. 279–84. Dore describes the teaching and morality of the terakoya as Confucianism, "Buddhist-digested Confucianism," and "purely Buddhist" material, all of which encouraged filial piety, warned of the punishment of hell, and advocated honesty and industry while castigating dishonesty and profligacy.

12. After Kishida's death in 1981, the post of kyōtō was abolished, and authority resides jointly in the director general (rijichō) and the newly created post of secretary general of instruction (kyōmu sōchō).

13. In Rohlen's study of the organization and membership of a Japanese bank, there were two factors precluding employees from participating in a political party, a new religion, or any voluntary organization. First, potential employees were screened out of the hiring process if they were active in a political or religious group; second, work at the bank was such a total commitment of time, energy, and loyalty that few employees participated in any voluntary religious organization. The bank actually agreed with the basic values of most new religions, but did not want its employees to divide their loyalties between religion and work. See Rohlen 1974:72.

14. The problems of the organization of Gedatsu-kai and the balance of small face-to-face groups with centralized administration, as well as the advantages/disadvantages of small informal groups versus large formal "churches," are not unique to Gedatsu-kai or Japanese religion. For a recent article in a local American newspaper recommending reorganization of American Christianity along the lines of an "extended family," see McManus 1984. This newspaper article, commenting on George Gallup, Jr.'s, book *Religion in America 1984*, cites the paradox in America of religion growing in importance but morality losing ground. This columnist's recommendation is not more "being saved" and piety, but rather a reorganization of religion as an "extended family."

7. Ritual Life

1. In the Gedatsu-kai publication *English Prayer Book*, an English translation of the *Hannya Shingyō* (or *Prajnaparamitahridaya*) by D. T. Suzuki is given on pages 11–14. For the original publication, including explanatory notes, see Suzuki 1960:26–30. Suzuki mentions that of the three most frequently read sutras in Zen Buddhism, "the *Shingyo* being the shortest is read on almost all occasions" (p. 26). According to Suzuki, the literal meaning of the *Hannya Shingyō* is a reflection or meditation on the "emptiness" of all form (or life), resulting in the perfection of wisdom (*prajnaparamita*) by which all Buddhas "attain to the highest perfect enlightenment" (p. 27). Other translations and modern commentaries on this brief work can be found in Conze 1958:77–107, Conze 1974:140–43, Conze 1968, Hurvitz 1977, and Wayman 1977. As is the case with most Buddhist scriptures in Japan, the *Heart Sutra* is written in Chinese; in Japanese usage this text is chanted phonetically, with the Chinese characters pronounced in a Japanese fashion. Buddhist priests with knowledge of Chinese may understand and appreciate the theoretical and soteriological intent of this Buddhist scripture, but most Japanese laymen have neither the linguistic nor the Buddhological training to appreciate such subtleties; laymen recite the *Shingyō* as an act of piety or repentance. This popular use of the *Hannya Shingyō*, chanting it as a spell, has been compared by Blacker with the chanting of mantras (*shingon*) or *darani* (*dhāranī* in Sanskrit)—the sounds have been preserved, but the meanings have been lost. She gives "the reason for its popularity" in the final phrases of the work: "The Prajnaparamita, it declares, is the great spell, the utmost spell, the unequalled spell which will allay all suffering" (1975:95–96). For similar usage of the *Heart Sutra*, see Hakeda 1972:264–65 and Pye 1977. Gedatsu-kai members utilize the *Hannya Shingyō* in a devotional (rather than strictly ascetic) sense of piety and repentance, both in daily ritual and in special circumstances, as seen in Mr. Abe's life history, when the sutra was chanted as an act of repentance and healing.

2. A mimamori or body protector is a small cloth bag displaying the name of a shrine

or temple, and usually enclosing a paper with writing that indicates the power of that holy place. The purchaser attaches the mimamori to clothing or underwear so that its power can protect the body (or person). Gedatsu-kai's body protector is very similar to those in common Japanese usage; it may differ in the significant aspect that it is not simply the religious token of a local holy site, but is a vehicle of the religious power of Gedatsu-kai as a nationwide voluntary organization.

3. Kawatō 1983a:126–33.

4. I did not visit homes and observe the enshrining of the Gedatsu-kai triad, but when questioning members and branch leaders, I was given the same general answer: the home features a less elaborate altar than those in branch meeting places, but it is the same basic pattern of enshrining the sacred triad. The description of initiation is adapted from Kawatō 1983a:126–36.

5. Gedatsu-kai uses the term *anrei*, literally "quiet spirit" or "to quiet a spirit," for this pacification.

6. This presentation of memorial mass tablets has followed Kawatō 1983a:128–31.

7. On a rectangular piece of plain wood, five Sanskrit words forming a *darani* (*dhāraṇī* in Sanskrit) are written in red; over these are written in black the name of the family and the proper terms and names of spirits. In January 1980 we viewed this work area, which is an inconspicuous part of the headquarters not frequented by ordinary members.

8. Kenkō shidō or health consultation is an interesting aspect of Gedatsu-kai that we did not have sufficient time to explore. Ishii comments that although the formal department for health consultation is rather recent in Gedatsu-kai's institutional history, the rationale of a physical and spiritual harmony that eliminates illness goes back to the founder's teaching. He notes that about a fourth of branches surveyed had monthly meetings for health consultations (1983b:111–14).

9. Another way of interpreting this tension is to distinguish between more "rational," "this-worldly" religion and more "emotional," "other-worldly" religion. The amacha rite and self-reflection (hansei) emphasize analysis and correction of personal defects of the individual, while gohō shugyō focuses on communication with forces outside the realm and power of the individual. This tension seems to be found within most religious traditions, and although one side may be dominant in a particular tradition, each religious group tends to find its form of balance between the two sides.

10. Kawatō sums up the similarities and differences between okiyome and gohō shugyō: they are similar in posture and in placing a booklet between the hands; they are different in that a different booklet is used in each, in okiyome no spirit descends, and okiyome can be performed in a group setting, whereas in gohō shugyō a spirit may descend, and it is performed by an individual. In other words, as Kawatō concludes, okiyome is a kind of meditation or contemplation (1983a:134).

11. Lebra in this and other articles has translated *Gedatsu-kai* as "Salvation Cult." She does not mention the term *gohō shugyō* directly, referring to Gedatsu-kai's "possession ritual," but does deal with okiyome and amacha. Lebra's translation of some terms differs slightly from the English equivalents used herein; some of these are noted in the text.

12. The notion of hansei as reflection or self-criticism is widespread in recent Japanese history, and is not limited to what might be considered conservative or right-wing movements; Lai (1984:20, 26, 28, 31) comments on the use of this notion by Seno'o Girō, "the only leftist prophet of the Lotus Sutra."

13. Hardacre has documented the same pattern of self-accusation in Reiyū-kai. See Hardacre 1984:167–69 and Hardacre 1979.

14. As Kawatō (1983a:136) remarks, the point of division meetings is more mutual friendship among branches than "religion" as such.

15. The same arguments for changing the private legal and financial status of Yasukuni Shrine to state status are still being made by the same conservative groups up to the time of writing. For a critical account of these attempts, see Murakami 1980.

16. The custom of observing an annual calendar of ceremonies is not limited to Japanese religious groups; note the "regularly scheduled ceremonies" of the bank studied by Rohlen, which even include a kind of annual memorial rite for bank "ancestors" (1974:41–42). Even the Grand Festival of Gedatsu-kai has parallels in the larger ceremonies of this bank. In both a new religion and a bank, ritual and organization are clearly interwoven.

17. Another rhythm of spring and fall that probably has influenced the Grand Festivals of Gedatsu-kai is the pattern of spring and fall rites for family dead at equinox, or *higan*, March 23 and September 23. For a general treatment of seasonal festivals in Japan, see Miyake 1972:126–31. The influence of higan on the Grand Festival is probably seen in the performance of the all souls' memorial rite.

18. Pilgrimage is a fascinating subject both in Japanese religion and in comparative perspective. For a discussion of the origins of Japanese pilgrimage dating back to the Heian period, and pilgrimage to sacred mountains, see Earhart 1970b:21–23, 69–71, 108–110; for a recent village "pilgrimage" rite, see Earhart 1968. Every Japanese new religion has its own sacred center(s) and distinctive forms of pilgrimage; for an interesting account of three pilgrimage sites in Reiyū-kai, see Hardacre 1984:69–83. There are some obvious differences between the ancient or traditional Japanese forms of pilgrimage and the pilgrimage practices of new religions such as Gedatsu-kai; there are also some similarities between Gedatsu-kai practices and some pilgrimage practices in earlier Japan and in other traditions. In general, Gedatsu-kai's pilgrimage shares with these other practices retracing the footsteps of the founder (visiting the sites of birth, enlightenment/revelation, death), coming into contact with the power of the place and the person, and thereby being spiritually transformed. For the notion of transformation in the Shikoku pilgrimage of eighty-eight sites sacred to Kōbō Daishi, see Statler 1983:327. Turner and Turner 1978 raise comparative considerations about pilgrimage; following van Gennepp's interpretation of rites of passage, the Turners view pilgrimage as a rite of passage involving transition or potentiality (pp. 2–3). Their general view of pilgrimage as transformation (p.11) is similar to my interpretation of Gedatsu-kai pilgrimage. The Turners' view of pilgrimage and much of their interpretive model describes Gedatsu-kai very well: "the oldest pilgrim centers of the historical religions are generally places mentioned in sacred narratives as connected with the birth, mission and death of the founder and his closest kin and disciples. . . . Believers in the message seek to imitate or to unite with the founder by replicating his actions, either literally or in spirit. Pilgrimage is one way, perhaps the most literal, of imitating the religious founder" (p. 33). For the Ise pilgrimage, see Davis 1983–1984. In general, the Gedatsu-kai practice stands in sharp contrast to the spontaneous and ecstatic practices of pilgrimage to Ise; Gedatsu-kai pilgrimage has much more in common with what Turner and Turner call "modern" examples of pilgrimage (which "are heavily in debt to modern modes of communication and transportation") (p. 18).

19. The close quarters on such pilgrimage buses reveal candid inside views of the dynamics of Japanese religious groups, as Hardacre has documented for Reiyū-kai (1984:70–71). See also Lebra 1984:270–73 for a rare view of how women on an excursion bus relax from the "sexual inhibition and frustration imposed upon their domestic life-style."

20. In a preliminary analysis of 124 branch questionnaires, 54 began with Tenjin Chigi Shrine and concluded with the Sun Monument; a number of other patterns contained so many variations that they are not easily categorized. However, the different orders of pilgrimage do not detract from the character of Goreichi as a "Sacred Land." The rather diffuse character of pilgrimage to this Sacred Land led us to ask question 11 in the survey, "Rank from 1 to 5 in importance the sites you paid homage to in making your individual pilgrimage rounds when you have visited the Sacred Land (Goreichi)." The results are interesting when arranged according to tabulation by rank: first in importance, Tenjin Chigi; second, Gochi Nyorai; third, Gedatsu Kongō; fourth, Yaoyorozu Mitama Matsuri Tō; and fifth, Yaoyorozu Mitama Matsuri Tō. In other words, the Gedatsu-kai triad marks the first three places, and the Yaoyorozu Mitama Matsuri Tō (All Souls' Monument) dominated fourth and fifth place.

Many other interesting observations can be made from the results of this survey. The most conspicuous example is the stupa called Hōkyōin Tō, which ranks no higher than .2% in all five ranks. This is remarkable, because this stupa was a popular pilgrimage site from late Tokugawa times, and may have helped the fledgling Gedatsu-kai attract people to this holy place where the five mystic letters of gohō shugyō were revealed. Fuji Sengen is another interesting negative example, not exceeding .1% in all five ranks. Fuji pilgrimage may have been important to the founder's ancestors, but not so to Gedatsu-kai members. Other negative examples, all of which fall below 1.0% in all five ranks are Renshinkan (Spiritual Training Hall), Kenshū Senta (Study Center), Hōmotsukan (Museum), Okano ke

Notes to Pages 207–233

264 Notes to Pages 207–233

no haka (the Okano family cemetery), and Tamonji. All other sites had significant responses in at least one or more rankings. Taking the number of 100 responses in a single ranking as a measure of significant response (more than 1%), we find the following results. The popularity of the patriotic Taiyō Seishin Hi is demonstrated by the fact that it is the only one of all the sites (including the five most important sites) that has more than 100 responses in all five ranks. Gochi Nyorai, Gedatsu Kongō, and Yaoyorozu Mitama Matsuri Tō share with Goshugo Daijin (protective kami) the distinction of having more than 100 responses in the second through fifth most important ranks. Sites with 100 responses in at least two ranks are Tengoshiki (heavenly kami), Shōtoku Hi, Roku Jizō, Gohonke (the Okana family home), and Tenjin Chigi; the Goreichi Dōjō has more than 100 responses in one rank. It is difficult to lump together the results from these pilgrimage sites, but two general conclusions are obvious: first, some formerly popular pilgrimage sites, such as the Hōkyōin Tō and Fuji Sengen, are no longer observed, and some seemingly important sites such as the Okano family cemetery and the Buddhist temple Tamonji are overlooked; second, patriotic and religious ties are demonstrated in the consistent results for Taiyō Seishin Hi, and typical Japanese diffuse religiosity is illustrated in the general popularity of other protective deities such as Goshugo Daijin and Roku Jizō.

21. The certificate called honshō contains part of a Shingon scripture known as the *Daranikyō* and five characters called *kandakara* (literally "kami treasure").

22. This information is taken from Kawatō 1983a:142, who states that for one ceremony in 1980 the number of certificates was about 150,000 to 200,000.

23. For a treatment of the healing Buddha in the history of Buddhism, see Birnbaum 1979.

24. I did not observe this pilgrimage; the description is taken from the account of Kawatō 1983a:138–39.

25. For a brief account of Kigensetsu and Kenkoku Kinenbi (or Kinen no Hi), see Murakami 1980:132, 158.

26. I did not observe the Sun Monument Spirit Festival. This account is based on the description of Kawatō 1983a:137–38.

27. Gedatsu-kai prefers to be known as *chōshūkyō*, literally "suprareligion," in the sense of not replacing traditional religious practices, but going beyond them.

8. Returning to the Center

1. This section is based in part on a previously published article (Earhart 1980b), modified and reprinted here with permission of The University of Chicago Press.

2. This is not the place to provide complete documentation for the Western interpretation of the origin of new religions; see the second edition of my comprehensive bibliography of Western-language materials on Japanese new religions (Earhart 1983), especially items 1–259, and the items listed under "New Religions, definition of," p. 210 in the Topical Index of this bibliography. Two decades of reading in this literature is my basis for the claim that the "crisis theory" of Japanese new religions has prevailed; except for Rajana earlier and Hardacre more recently, few scholars have dared to criticize this theory.

3. Critiques of the "crisis theory" of the origin of new religions by no means are limited to these three points. Hardacre has raised two other salient critiques. She notes that "the momentary sense of the idea of crisis is strained by the proposition that the crisis has lasted from the mid-eighteenth century to the present" (1984:30). A condition that lasts in a culture for more than 200 years seems to qualify more as an enduring feature than as a turning point. Among other critical arguments Hardacre raises is "the inadequacy of the crisis explanation to account for the origin and persistence of Reiyukai . . . " (1984:33). The same point could be made of the crisis theory's attempt to explain other new religions: even if we accepted the notion that new religions were somehow caused to arise by a crisis condition, this would not be sufficient explanation for their persistence—maintenance and expansion of their membership, facilities, and religious practices.

4. White has addressed this problem in relationship to stress upon working people and their joining Sōka Gakkai or Communism (1970:80).

5. As Fujii Masao (1983:62) has pointed out, belief in the spirits of the dead is strong

in contemporary Japan—about 60% of respondents in a 1981 Asahi Shinbun survey, even though half of this 60% claimed to have no religious affiliation.

6. White has used the combined concepts of "Precipitation and Mobilization" in chapter 3 of his treatment of Sōka Gakkai (1970:39–56); he follows Norman Cohn's concept of precipitation—"For Norman Cohn the key precipitating factor in the production of a new movement is catastrophe," but adds that "Another sort of catalyst is the appearance of a charismatic or otherwise extraordinarily able leader." I have treated the charismatic leader as the personal or innovative factor.

7. My use of this term *the substratum of the new religions* in 1969 was an attempt to refer to the kind of values Gluck has called "orthodoxy." See Gluck 1985:260.

8. For the classic Marxist interpretation, see Lanternari 1963; for my critique see Earhart 1974a:175.

9. The nature of the Japanese village as a social reality and as a conceptual ideal has undergone considerable change during the past few centuries, and has been discussed at some length by Western scholars. This subject falls outside the immediate scope of our study of Gedatsu-kai as a new religion, and cannot be discussed here. See especially the work of Bellah 1957, Thomas C. Smith 1959, Scheiner 1973, Davis 1977, Murakami 1980, and Fujii Masao 1983. The relationship between the actual and ideal village, on the one hand, and Japanese new religions, on the other, is a matter worthy of further study. On the subject of villages, as in other areas, there are three important concerns for the study of all Japanese new religions: first, what is the relationship of prior social and economic conditions to the rise of new religious movements? Second, what is the relationship of new religious movements to subsequent social and economic conditions? And third, how do these events bear upon the continuity and change in (traditional) religious values? Some of these theoretical issues have been discussed in the previous section in this chapter. We cannot hope to resolve all of these issues here; our immediate point is that Gedatsu-kai's perception of their founder's village writ large is its symbolic means of appropriating the past and facing the future. As Tsurumi has pointed out, "On the surface . . . contemporary Japanese society looks like a model mass society. At bottom, however, the primary village community and the fictitious village within the city are still preserved" (1970:211). When we better understand this "fictitious village," we will better be able to interpret the above-mentioned three concerns in the study of Japanese new religions.

10. It is well known that both the state and popular thinkers idealized the family, village, and agrarian values from late Meiji times on, even as radical changes were transforming the family, the former rural dominance over the city, and the prominence of agricultural over industrial occupations. See Gluck 1985:178–87, Dore and Ouchi 1971, Havens 1974:3–14, and for "national villagers," Smethurst 1974:176–78.

As this work goes to press I am gathering materials on the beliefs and practices related to Mount Fuji pilgrimage groups, especially during and after Tokugawa times; the social and religious values associated with Fuji pilgrimages constitute an important example of the "center" to which Gedatsu-kai is returning. Deeper study of the symbolism of Fuji has impressed upon me even more how much continuity there is between Gedatsu-kai and this Tokugawa heritage. My next work will focus on the religious beliefs and practices associated with Mount Fuji.

11. For example, Sievers (1983) has recorded the feminist critique of Japanese "traditional" values. The feminist issue is just one example of the debate over the support of or attack upon traditional values. There is no doubt that the family system and traditional values will change, because societies are constantly changing; and it should be remembered that the "traditional" values and structures such as "family" and "village" are of more recent origin than is idealized in the memory of their supporters. The fundamental question is whether Japanese people wish to gradually modify their present (traditional) values and structures, or whether they wish to quickly and radically overturn them.

12. This book closes with the picture of the microcosm of Gedatsu-kai, but it is at this juncture that a number of debates may begin. To enter these debates would require the writing of a separate work, but the following remarks may serve as a point of departure for those who will take up the issues. Western discussions of Japan have fluctuated sharply from severe criticism to uncritical admiration. Especially in the decades immediately after World War II, the gist of Western discussions was where Japan went wrong in her political

and social policies leading up to and through that war, and how she could learn from her Western counterparts. In the past decade or so there has been a Western rush to praise and emulate Japan's success, not only in industrial and commercial areas but also even in the social realm of school systems. Probably the most famous book of this genre is Vogel's provocatively titled *Japan as Number One: Lessons for America* (1979). Even Vogel has his assessment of "costs and dangers" (pp. 238–52), as do other writers who extol Japanese forms of industry, management, education, and even family life. Japan also has her detractors, not the least of whom are some Japanese themselves—frequently criticizing such features as the aggressive character of the "economic animal," the intense competition in the educational system, and the nervous pace of life generally. Readers who are familiar with the high praise of contemporary Japan but have not heard about problems may wish to see such works as Ben-Dasan 1972, Dore and Ouchi 1971, Frager and Rohlen 1976, Halliday 1975, Hane 1982, Iga 1986, and Smethurst 1974.

The status of Japanese religion in the Western debate is a curious one. Since before World War II, there has been a steady stream of criticism of religious traditions in Japan, especially for their cooperation with and support of nationalism and militarism. Since the war, there has been a curious mixture of Western attitudes toward Japanese religious traditions: on the one hand, there has been a sometimes scholarly, more frequently popular admiration of Japanese religion, notably Zen, as an existential solution for Western people; on the other hand, Western journalists and most scholars have been severely critical of Japanese new religions as exploiting and abusing misguided people. An interesting point to note in this criticism-praise debate is that in recent times those who lionize Japan's success and recommend acceptance of Japanese institutions and techniques have refrained from encouraging adoption of Japanese forms of religion: there is no chapter on religion or spirituality in Vogel's *Japan as Number One*. The enthusiasm for adopting Japanese religious traditions, Zen in particular, has come not from the "establishment" that praises industrial and commercial success, but primarily from the "counter-culture" that advocates withdrawal from economic and technolgical "success" in favor of personal or spiritual fulfillment.

There is a double irony in the vagaries of history: from the time of closer interaction, Japanese (and Asians generally), while conceding Western technological superiority, which they readily adopted, claimed the superiority of "Oriental" or "Eastern" spirituality, which they tried to retain; eventually, at least in appearances, the Japanese were better at receiving and perfecting technology than at retaining (and in persuading others of) a superior spiritual tradition; the West generally (with the exception of counter-culture representatives) has disregarded Japanese spirituality and has focused primarily on the technological and commercial achievements, many of which had their beginnings in the West.

The pioneer work that raised the question of the relationship between religion and "modernization" in Japan is Bellah's *Tokugawa Religion* (1957), which argued for a kind of "Protestant ethic" in Japan. Ooms in his *Tokugawa Ideology* (1985) has carried the argument back into history, claiming that the religious background for the ideology was much more complex (not just Neo-Confucian) and much less a deliberate governmental construct than most scholars have thought. Gluck in her work on Meiji ideology (*Japan's Modern Myths: Ideology in the Late Meiji Period* 1985), in contrast to Ooms's use of ideology as necessarily exploitative, approaches ideology from a more neutral view (as does Geertz 1973), and views the cluster of commonly held beliefs and ideas that formed the "orthodoxy" in the early part of this century—and to a certain extent still do. These three works raise more serious issues and questions about the interrelationship of the religious tradition and the modern Japanese situation.

In assessing Gedatsu-kai and its role in Japanese society, it is easier to discuss previous scholarship such as the debate among Bellah, Ooms, and Gluck; it is more difficult to raise larger cross-cultural or universal issues such as the proper and improper roles of religion in the modern world. However, it is worth noting that Gedatsu-kai concentrates its religious message on guilt and gratitude, the subject of a recent book by Amato (1982). Amato is familiar with Japanese culture and earlier treatments of gratitude in various cultures, although his interest is primarily in the philosophical concepts and their application to American culture. Amato's analysis and interpretation are too complex for brief treatment here, but his distinction between "traditional" guilt and gratitude and "modern" guilt and gratitude is worthy of mention. He writes that "in contrast to traditional society, in which guilt and gratitude mutually fulfilled the conservative function of defending the established order, in modern society guilt and gratitude have become, at least in two of their essential forms, conflicting modalities of human obligation. Gratitude, when serving either private or public purposes, points backward in time toward first gifts. . . . Almost inevitably, gratitude serves the authorities of established tradition. . . . On the other hand, guilt—at least the sort that calls one to serve mankind at large—opens the person to a changing world and the new responsibilities it suggests. The guilt is inseparable from a progressive view of existence that binds all humans in a mutuality of problems and potential" (1982:xviii-xix).

Amato's argument about traditional and modern modes of gratitude and guilt is incisive, and yet there seems to remain an ambiguity in applying the distinction to Gedatsu-kai. On the one hand, Gedatsu-kai seems to possess a "traditional" pattern of gratitude and guilt, since the movement does point "backward toward first gifts" and has tended to serve "the authorities of established tradition." On the other hand, Gedatsu-kai seems to possess some aspects of a "modern" pattern of gratitude and guilt, because the founder established the all souls' memorial rite (manbu kuyō) as a kind of expression of guilt for the spirits of all living creatures. I mention this ambiguity in this all-too-brief application of Amato's distinction to Gedatsu-kai, not to raise issue with his argument but to emphasize that such ambiguity seems to be part and parcel of religious movements and the historical process in general. Even Amato, after his wide-ranging critique, recognizes the necessity for as well as the ambiguity of guilt and gratitude. He says, "We have tried here to understand the guilt and gratitude that war within us, as well as the ambiguities, tensions, and contradictions that have formed around them. . . . Our endeavor has not been to dissolve these ethical sentiments upon which conscience depends, but it has been to restore them to health" (p. 201). As the old tradition becomes the new tradition, as the old religion becomes the new religion, there is always the tension between old and new, between support for status quo and proposal of new ideals and institutions. I hope that this book presents a balanced picture of Gedatsu-kai in its ambiguous position between the old tradition and the new tradition, and thereby throws light on the contemporary Japanese religious scene.

BIBLIOGRAPHY

Many works read over the past two decades have helped frame my thinking about Japanese new religions, but it would be cumbersome to list all of them in the bibliography. Only works cited in the text or directly related to this book are included here. For a comprehensive bibliography of Western-language works on Japanese new religions, see Earhart 1983.

Amato, Joseph Anthony II. 1982. *Guilt and Gratitude: A Study of the Origins of Contemporary Conscience*. Contributions in Philosophy, no. 20. Westport, Conn.: Greenwood.

Anesaki, Masaharu. 1930. *History of Japanese Religion*. London: Kegan Paul, Trench Trubner. Reprint ed. 1963. Rutland, Vt.: Charles E. Tuttle Co.

Anzu, Motohiko, ed. 1968. *Shintō Jiten*. Tokyo: Hori Shoten.

Araki, Michio. 1982. Konkō Daijin and Konkō-kyō: A Case Study of Religious Mediation. Ph.D. dissertation, University of Chicago.

Associated Press. 1984. Advertisement Ends 46 years of Guilt. *Kalamazoo Gazette*, Friday, June 15, 1984.

Beattie, J. H. M. 1959. Understanding and Explanation in Social Anthropology. *British Journal of Sociology* 10(1):45–60.

————. 1964. *Other Cultures: Aims, Methods, and Achievements in Social Anthropology*. New York: Free Press of Glencoe.

Bellah, Robert N. 1957. *Tokugawa Religion: The Values of Pre-industrial Japan*. Glencoe, Ill.: Free Press. Reprint ed. 1970. Boston: Beacon Press.

Ben-Dasan, Isaiah. 1972. *The Japanese and the Jews*. New York and Tokyo: Weatherhill.

Benedict, Ruth. 1946. *The Chrysanthemum and the Sword*. Boston: Houghton Mifflin.

Bernstein, Gail Lee. 1983. *Haruko's World: A Japanese Farm Woman and Her Community*. Stanford, Calif.: Stanford University.

Birnbaum, Raoul. 1979. *The Healing Buddha*. Boulder: Shambhala.

Blacker, Carmen. 1975. *The Catalpa Bow: A Study of Shamanistic Practices in Japan*. London: Allen & Unwin.

Bowen, Roger W. 1980. *Rebellion and Democracy in Meiji Japan: A Study of Commoners in the Popular Rights Movement*. Berkeley: University of California.

Brooks, Anne Page. 1981. Mizuko Kuyō and Japanese Buddhism. *Japanese Journal of Religious Studies* 8(3–4):119–47.

Buchanan, Daniel C. 1935. Inari: Its Origin, Development, and Nature. *Transactions of the Asiatic Society of Japan*, 2d ser. 12:1–191.

Bunkachō. 1980. *Shūkyō Nenkan*. Tokyo: Bunkachō.

Caudill, William. 1976. The Cultural and Interpersonal Context of Everyday Health and Illness in Japan and America. In Charles Leslie, ed., *Asian Medical Systems: A Comparative Study*, pp. 159–77. Berkeley: University of California Press.

Chen, Kenneth. 1968. Filial Piety in Chinese Buddhism. *Harvard Journal of Asiatic Studies* 28:81–97.

Cole, Robert E., and Ken'ichi Tominaga. 1976. Japan's Changing Occupational Structure and Its Significance. In Hugh Patrick, ed., *Japanese Industrialization and Its Social Consequences*, pp. 53–95. Berkeley: University of California.

Coleman, Samuel. 1983. *Family Planning in Japanese Society: Traditional Birth Control in a Modern Urban Culture*. Princeton, N.J.: Princeton University.

Conze, Edward. 1958. *Buddhist Wisdom Books: Containing the Diamond Sutra and the Heart Sutra*. London: George Allen & Unwin.

————. 1968. The Prajñāpāramitā-hṛdaya Sūtra. In Edward Conze, *Thirty Years of Buddhist Studies: Selected Essays*, pp. 148–67. Columbia: University of South Carolina Press.

———. 1974. *The Short Prajñāpāramitā Texts*. London: Luzac.

Czaja, Michael. 1975. *Gods of Myth and Stone: Phallicism in Japanese Folk Religion*. New York: Weatherhill.

Dale, Kenneth J. 1975. *Circle of Harmony: A Case Study in Popular Japanese Buddhism with Implications for Christian Mission*. South Pasadena, Calif.: William Carey Library.

Daniel, E. Valentine. 1983. Conclusion: Karma, the Uses of an Idea. In Charles F. Keyes and E. Valentine Daniel, eds., *Karma: An Anthropological Inquiry*, pp. 287–300. Berkeley: University of California.

Davis, Winston Bradley. 1977. *Toward Modernity: A Developmental Typology of Popular Religious Affiliations in Japan*. Cornell East Asia Papers, no. 12. Ithaca, N.Y.: Cornell China-Japan Program.

———. 1980. *Dojo: Exorcism and Miracles in Modern Japan*. Stanford, Calif.: Stanford University Press.

———. 1983–1984. Pilgrimage and World Renewal: A Study of Religion and Social Values in Tokugawa Japan. Pt. 1, *History of Religions* 23(2):97–116; pt. 2, ibid. 23 (3):197–221.

deBary, Wm. Theodore. 1975. Introduction. In Wm. Theodore deBary, ed., *The Unfolding of Neo-Confucianism*, pp. 1–36. New York: Columbia University Press.

———. 1979. *Principle and Practicality: Essays in Neo-Confucianism and Practical Learning*. New York: Columbia University Press.

———. 1981. *Neo-Confucian Orthodoxy and the Learning of the Mind-and-Heart*. New York: Columbia University Press.

De Vos, George A. (with contributions by Hiroshi Wagatsuma, William Caudill, and Keiichi Mizushima). 1973. *Socialization for Achievement: Essays on the Cultural Psychology of the Japanese*. Berkeley: University of California.

Dollard, John. 1949. *Criteria for Life History: With Analyses of Six Notable Documents*. New York: Peter Smith.

Dore, Ronald P. 1958. *City Life in Japan: A Study of a Tokyo Ward*. Berkeley: University of California.

———. 1965. *Education in Tokugawa Japan*. Berkeley: University of California.

———. 1978. *Shinohata: A Portrait of a Japanese Village*. London: Allen Lane. Reprint ed. 1980. New York: Pantheon Books.

Dore, Ronald P., and Tsutomu Ouchi. 1971. Rural Origins of Japanese Fascism. In James W. Morley, ed., *Dilemmas of Growth in Prewar Japan*, pp. 181–209. Princeton, N.J.: Princeton University.

Dunaway, David K., and Willa K. Baum. 1984. *Oral History: An Interdisciplinary Anthology*. Nashville, Tenn.: American Association for State and Local History in cooperation with the Oral History Association.

Earhart, H. Byron. 1965. Shugendō, the Traditions of En no Gyōja, and Mikkyō Influence. In *Studies of Esoteric Buddhism and Tantrism*, pp. 297–317. Koyasan, Japan: Koyasan University.

———. 1968. The Celebration of Haru-yama (Spring Mountain): An Example of Folk Religious Practices in Contemporary Japan. *Asian Folklore Studies* 27 (1):1–18.

———. 1969. The Interpretation of the "New Religions" of Japan as Historical Phenomena. *Journal of the American Academy of Religion* 37 (3):237–48.

———. 1970a. *The New Religions of Japan: A Bibliography of Western-Language Materials*. Tokyo: Sophia University. Monumenta Nipponica.

———. 1970b. *A Religious Study of the Mount Haguro Sect of Shugendō: An Example of Japanese Mountain Religion*. Tokyo: Sophia University. Monumenta Nipponica.

———. 1970c. The Significance of the "New Religions" for Understanding Japanese Religion. *KBS Bulletin on Japanese Culture* 101:1–9. Reprinted in H. Byron Earhart, *Religion in the Japanese Experience: Sources and Interpretations*. Belmont, Calif.: Wadsworth, 1974

———. 1971. Recent Publications on the Japanese New Religions. *History of Religions* 10 (4):375–85.

———. 1974a. The Interpretation of the "New Religions" of Japan as New Religious Movements. In Robert J. Miller, ed., *Religious Ferment in Asia*, pp. 170–88. Lawrence:

University Press of Kansas.

——. 1974b. The New Religions of Korea: A Preliminary Interpretation. *Transactions of the Korea Branch of the Royal Asiatic Society* 49:7–25.

——. 1974c. *Religion in the Japanese Experience: Sources and Interpretations.* Belmont, Calif.: Wadsworth.

——. 1976. Recent Western Publications on Sōka Gakkai. *History of Religions* 15 (3):264–88.

——. 1980a. Gedatsu-kai: One Life History and Its Significance for Interpreting Japanese New Religions. *Japanese Journal of Religious Studies* 7 (2–3):227–57.

——. 1980b. Toward a Theory of the Formation of the Japanese New Religions: A Case Study of Gedatsu-kai. *History of Religions* 20 (1–2):175–97.

——. 1982. *Japanese Religion: Unity and Diversity.* 3d ed. Belmont, Calif.: Wadsworth.

——. 1983. *The New Religions of Japan: A Bibliography of Western-Language Materials.* 2d ed. Michigan Papers in Japanese Studies, no.9. Ann Arbor: Center for Japanese Studies, University of Michigan.

——. 1984. *Religions of Japan: Many Traditions within One Sacred Way.* San Francisco: Harper & Row.

——. 1987. Japanese Buddhism and the New Religions: Buddhism as Power. In Minoru Kiyota et al., *Japanese Buddhism: Its Tradition, New Religions, and Interaction with Christianity,* pp. 63–70. Tokyo-Los Angeles: Buddhist Books International.

Earhart, H. Byron, and Hitoshi Miyake, eds. 1983. *Dentōteki shūkyō no saisei: Gedatsu-kai no shisō to kōdō.* Tokyo: Meichō.

Earl, David Magarey. 1964. *Emperor and Nation in Japan: Political Thinkers of the Tokugawa Period.* Seattle: University of Washington Press.

Early, Evelyn A. 1982. The Logic of Well Being: Therapeutic Narratives in Cairo, Egypt. *Social Science & Medicine* 16: 1491–1497.

Eliade, Mircea. 1964. *Shamanism: Archaic Techniques of Ecstasy.* Translated by Willard R. Trask. Princeton, N.J.: Princeton University.

——. 1965. Experiences of the Mystic Light. In *The Two and the One,* translated by J. M. Cohen, pp. 19–77. New York: Harper & Row.

Embree, John F. 1939. *Suye Mura.* Chicago: University of Chicago.

Enchi, Fumiko. 1983. *Masks.* Translated by Juliet Winters Carpenter. New York: Knopf.

English Prayer Book. N.D. N.P.: Gedatsu Church of America.

Frager, Robert, and Thomas P. Rohlen. 1976. The Future of a Tradition: Japanese Spirit in the 1980s. In Lewis Austin, ed., *Japan: The Paradox of Progress,* pp. 255–78. New Haven, Conn.: Yale University.

Fujii, Masao. 1983. Maintenance and Change in Japanese Traditional Funerals and Death-Related Behavior. *Japanese Journal of Religious Studies* 10 (1):39–64.

Fujii, Takeshi. 1983. "Kyōso-Okano Seiken no shisō keisei." In H. Byron Earhart and Hitoshi Miyake, eds., *Dentōteki shūkyō no saisei: Gedatsu-kai no shisō to kōdō,* pp. 1–78. Tokyo: Meichō.

Fung, Yu-lan. 1948. *A Short History of Chinese Philosophy.* Edited by Derk Bodde. New York: Macmillan.

Gedatsu-kai. 1976. *Shibuchō-kanji no kokoroe.* Tokyo: Gedatsu-kai.

Gedatsu Shuppanbu. 1979. *Gedatsu Kongō den.* Tokyo: Gedatsu Shuppanbu.

Geertz, Clifford. 1973. Ideology as a Cultural System. In Clifford Geertz, *The Interpretation of Cultures: Selected Essays,* p. 193–233. New York: Basic Books. Reprinted from D. Apter, ed., *Ideology and Discontent,* pp. 47–56. New York: Free Press of Glencoe, 1964.

——. 1983. "From the Native's Point of View": On the Nature of Anthropological Understanding. In Clifford Geertz, *Local Knowledge: Further Essays in Interpretive Anthropology,* pp. 55–70. New York: Basic Books. Reprinted from *Bulletin of the American Academy of Arts and Sciences* 28, no. 1 (1974).

Gluck, Carol. 1985. *Japan's Modern Myths: Ideology in the Late Meiji Period.* Princeton, N.J.: Princeton University.

Gulik, Robert Hans van. 1935. *Hayagrīva: The Mantrayānic Aspect of Horse-Cult in China and Japan.* Leiden: E. J. Brill.

Guthrie, Stewart Elliott. 1976. A Japanese "New Religion": Rissho Kosei Kai in a Japanese

Farming Village. Ph.D. dissertation, Yale University.

———. 1988. *A Japanese "New Religion": Rissho Kosei-kai in a Mountain Hamlet.* Ann Arbor: Center for Japanese Studies, University of Michigan.

Hakeda, Yoshito S. 1972. *Kūkai: Major Works.* New York: Columbia University Press.

Hall, John Whitney. 1968. A Monarch for Modern Japan. In Robert E. Ward, ed., *Political Development in Modern Japan*, pp. 11–64. Princeton, N.J.: Princeton University Press.

Halliday, Jon. 1975. *A Political History of Japanese Capitalism.* New York: Pantheon.

Hane, Mikiso. 1982. *Peasants, Rebels, and Outcastes: The Underside of Modern Japan.* New York: Pantheon Books.

Hardacre, Helen. 1979. Sex Role Norms and Values in Reiyukai. *Japanese Journal of Religious Studies* 6 (3) :445–59.

———. 1982. The Transformation of Healing in the Japanese New Religions. *History of Religions* 20 (3) : 45–60.

———. 1984. *Lay Buddhism in Contemporary Japan: Reiyūkai Kyōdan.* Princeton, N.J.: Princeton University.

———. 1986. *Kurozumikyō and the New Religions of Japan.* Princeton, N.J.: Princeton University.

———. 1987. *Hoza*: The Dharma Seat. In Minoru Kiyota et al., *Japanese Buddhism: Its Tradition, New Religions, and Interaction with Christianity*, pp. 96–105. Tokyo-Los Angeles: Buddhist Books International.

Havens, Thomas R. H. 1974. *Farm and Nation in Modern Japan: Agrarian Nationalism.* Princeton, N.J.: Princeton University.

Hiebert, Paul G. 1983. Karma and Other Explanation Traditions in a South Indian Village. In Charles F. Keyes and E. Valentine Daniel, eds., *Karma: An Anthropological Inquiry*, pp. 119–130. Berkeley: University of California.

Hiemstra, Patty C. 1984. From Horror to Beauty, Couple Claims Miracle. *Kalamazoo Gazette*, Saturday, July 14, 1984.

Hori, Ichirō, et al., eds. 1972. *Japanese Religion.* Tokyo: Kodansha International.

Hurvitz, Leon. 1977. Hsuän-tsang (602–664) and the *Heart Scripture.* In Lewis Lancaster, ed., *Prajñāpāramitā and Related Systems: Studies in Honor of Edward Conze*, pp. 103–121. Berkeley: Berkeley Buddhist Studies Series.

Ichihashi, Nobuhiro. 1986. A Prisoner of Selfishness Set Free. *Dharma World* 13:26–31.

Iga Mamoru 1986. *The Thorn in the Chrysanthemum: Suicide and Economic Success in Modern Japan.* Berkeley: University of California.

Ishii, Kenji. 1983a. Beikoku gedatsu kyōkai—nikkei shinshūkyō no hen'yō. In H. Byron Earhart and Hitoshi Miyake, eds., *Dentōteki shūkyō no saisei: Gedatsukai no shisō to kōdō*, pp. 361–407. Tokyo: Meichō.

———. 1983b. Gedatsukai no keisei to genjō. In H. Byron Earhart and Hitoshi Miyake, eds., *Dentōteki shūkyō no saisei: Gedatsukai no shisō to kōdō*, pp. 79–123. Tokyo: Meichō.

———. 1983c. Kaiin no ishiki to kōdō—shitsumonshi chōsa ni yoru. In H. Byron Earhart and Hitoshi Miyake, eds., *Dentōteki shūkyō no saisei: Gedatsukai no shisō to kōdō*, pp. 227–73. Tokyo: Meichō.

———. 1983d. Transformation of a Japanese New Religion in American Society: A Case Study of Gedatsu Church of America. In Keiichi Yanagawa, ed., *Japanese Religions in California: A Report on Research within and without the Japanese-American Community*, pp. 163–95. Tokyo: Department of Religious Studies, University of Tokyo.

Japanese-English Buddhist Dictionary. 1965. Tokyo: Daitō Shuppansha.

Katō, Genchi. 1917. The Warongo: *Transactions of the Asiatic Society of Japan* 45 (2):1–138.

Kawatō, Hitoshi. 1983a. Gedatsukai no girei. In H. Byron Earhart and Hitoshi Miyake, eds., *Dentōteki shūkyō no saisei: Gedatsukai no shisō to kōdō*, pp. 125–47. Tokyo: Meichō.

———. 1983b. Gedatsukai no shugyō. In H. Byron Earhart and Hitoshi Miyake, eds., *Dentōteki shūkyō no saisei: Gedatsukai no shisō to kōdō*, pp. 187–226. Tokyo: Meichō.

————. 1983c. Gedatsukai no shūkyōteki uchūkan. In H. Byron Earhart and Hitoshi Mi-
    yake, eds., Dentōteki shūkyō no saisei: Gedatsukai no shisō to kōdō, pp. 149–85.
    Tokyo: Meichō.

Keyes, Charles F. 1983a. Introduction: The Study of Popular Ideas of Karma. In Charles
    F. Keyes and E. Valentine Daniel, eds., Karma: An Anthropological Inquiry, pp.
    1–26. Berkeley: University of California.

————. 1983b. Merit-Transference in the Kammic Theory of Popular Theravada Buddhism.
    In Charles F. Keyes and E. Valentine Daniel, eds., Karma: An Anthropological
    Inquiry, pp. 261–86. Berkeley: University of California.

Keyes, Charles F., and E. Valentine Daniel, eds. 1983. Karma: An Anthropological Inquiry.
    Berkeley: University of California.

Kikumura, Akemi. 1981. Through Harsh Winters: The Life of a Japanese Immigrant
    Woman. Novato, Calif.: Chandler & Sharp.

Kishida, Eizan. 1969. The Character and Doctrine of Gedatsu Kongo. Translated by Louis
    K. Ito. N.p.: Gedatsu Church of America.

Kitagawa, Joseph M. 1966. Religion in Japanese History. New York: Columbia University
    Press.

Kiyota, Minoru. 1982. Gedatsukai: Its Theory and Practice (A Study of a Shinto-Buddhist
    Syncretic School in Contemporary Japan). Los Angeles-Tokyo: Buddhist Books In-
    ternational.

————. 1987. Gedatsukai: A Case Study of Shinto-Buddhist Syncretism in Contemporary
    Japan. In Minoru Kiyota et al., Japanese Buddhism: Its Tradition, New Religions,
    and Interaction with Christianity, pp. 83–95. Tokyo-Los Angeles: Buddhist Books
    International.

Kluckhohn, Clyde. 1945. The Personal Document in Anthropological Science. New York:
    Social Science Research Council, Bulletin no. 53.

Koyama, Takashi. 1961. The Changing Social Position of Women in Japan. Paris: Unesco.

Krauss, Ellis S. 1974. Japanese Radicals Revisited: Student Protest in Postwar Japan. Berke-
    ley: University of California.

LaFleur, William R. 1983. The Karma of Words: Buddhism and the Literary Arts in
    Medieval Japan. Berkeley: University of California Press.

Lai, Whalen. 1984. Seno'o Girō and the Dilemma of Modern Buddhism—Leftist Prophet
    of the Lotus Sutra. Japanese Journal of Religious Studies 11(1):7–42.

Lanternari, Vittorio. 1963. The Religions of the Oppressed: A Study of Modern Messianic
    Cults. Translated by Lisa Sergio. New York: Knopf. First published 1960.

Lebra, Joyce, et al. 1976. Women in Changing Japan. Stanford, Calif.: Stanford University
    Press.

Lebra, Takie Sugiyama. 1974. Reciprocity and the Asymmetric Principle: An Analytical
    Reappraisal of the Japanese Concept of On. In Takie Sugiyama Lebra and William
    P. Lebra, eds., Japanese Culture and Behavior: Selected Readings. Honolulu: Uni-
    versity Press of Hawaii. (First published in Psychologia 12(1969) :129–38.)

————. 1976. Japanese Patterns of Behavior. Honolulu: University Press of Hawaii.

————. 1982. Self-reconstruction in Japanese Religious Psychotherapy. In A. J. Marsella
    and G. M. White, eds., Cultural Conceptions of Mental Health and Therapy, pp.
    269–83. The Hague: D. Reidel.

————. 1983. Shame and Guilt: A Psychocultural View of the Japanese Self. Ethos
    11(3):192–209.

————. 1984. Japanese Women: Constraint and Fulfillment. Honolulu: University of Ha-
    waii.

Lebra, Takie Sugiyama, and William P. Lebra, eds. 1974. Japanese Culture and Behavior:
    Selected Readings. Honolulu: University Press of Hawaii.

Lifton, Robert Jay. 1961. Thought Reform and the Psychology of Totalism: A Study of
    "Brainwashing" in China. New York: Norton.

McFarland, H. Neill. 1967. The Rush Hour of the Gods: A Study of the New Religious
    Movements in Japan. New York: Macmillan.

McManus, Michael J. 1984. Gallup Poll on Morals Slide Upholds Small Church Groups.
    Kalamazoo Gazette, Saturday, August 11.

Masuda, Koh. 1974. Kenkyusha's New Japanese-English Dictionary. 4th ed. Tokyo: Kenk-
    yusha.

Matsumoto, Sannosuke. 1978. The Idea of Heaven: A Tokugawa Foundation for Natural Rights Theory. Translated by J. Victor Koschmann. In Tetsuo Najita and Irwin Scheiner, eds., *Japanese Thought in the Tokugawa Period, 1600–1868: Methods and Metaphors*, pp. 181–99. Chicago: University of Chicago.

Matsushita, Konosuke. 1976. *Japan at the Brink*. Translated by Charles S. Terry. Tokyo: Kodansha International.

Mintz, Sidney. 1984. The Anthropological Interview and the Life History. In David K. Dunaway and Willa K. Baum, eds., *Oral History: An Interdisciplinary Anthology*, pp. 306–313. Nashville, Tenn.: American Association for State and Local History in cooperation with the Oral History Association.

Mitchell, Richard H. 1976. *Thought Control in Prewar Japan*. Ithaca, N.Y.: Cornell University.

Miyake, Hitoshi. 1972. Folk Religion. In Ichiro Hori et al., eds., *Japanese Religion*, translated by Yoshiya Abe and David Reid, pp. 121–43. Tokyo: Kodansha International.

———. 1987. The Influence of *Shugendō* on the "New Religions." In Minoru Kiyota et al., *Japanese Buddhism: Its Tradition, New Religions, and Interaction with Christianity*, pp. 71–82. Tokyo-Los Angeles: Buddhist Books International.

Morioka, Kiyomi. 1975. *Religion in Changing Japanese Society*. Tokyo: University of Tokyo.

———. 1977. The Appearance of "Ancestor Religion" in Modern Japan: The Years of Transition from the Meiji to the Taisho Periods. *Japanese Journal of Religious Studies* 4 (2–3): 183–212.

Murakami, Shigeyoshi. 1980. *Japanese Religion in the Modern Century*. Translated by H. Byron Earhart. Tokyo: University of Tokyo.

Murasaki, Shikibu. 1977. *The Tale of Genji*. 2 vols. Translated with an introduction by Edward G. Seidensticker. New York: Alfred A. Knopf.

Murdock, George Peter. 1980. *Theories of Illness: A World Survey*. Pittsburgh: University of Pittsburgh.

Nefsky, Marilyn Felcher. 1984. Women and the Religious Character of Contemporary Japan. Ph.D. dissertation, University of Toronto.

NHK Seron Chōsabu. 1984. *Nihonjin no shūkyō ishiki*. Tokyo: Nihon Hōsō Shuppan Kyōkai.

Niwano, Nikkyo. 1978. *Lifetime Beginner*. Translated by Richard L. Gage. Tokyo: Kosei.

Obeyesekere, Gananath. 1963. The Great Tradition and the Little in the Perspective of Sinhalese Buddhism. *Journal of Asian Studies* 22 (2): 139–53.

———. 1980. The Rebirth Eschatology and Its Transformations: A Contribution to the Sociology of Early Buddhism. In Wendy Doniger O'Flaherty, ed., *Karma and Rebirth in Classical Indian Traditions*, pp. 137–64. Berkeley: University of California.

O'Flaherty, Wendy Doniger, ed. 1980. *Karma and Rebirth in Classical Indian Traditions*. Berkeley: University of California.

Ohnuki-Tierney, Emiko. 1984. *Illness and Culture in Contemporary Japan: An Anthropological View*. Cambridge: Cambridge University.

Onuma, Yūko. 1983. Gedatsukai no kyūsai no ronri. In H. Byron Earhart and Hitoshi Miyake, eds., *Dentōteki shūkyō no saisei: Gedatsukai no shisō to kōdō*, pp. 275–335. Tokyo: Meichō.

Ooms, Herman. 1985. *Tokugawa Ideology: Early Constructs, 1570–1680*. Princeton, N.J.: Princeton University.

Opler, Marvin K. 1950a. Japanese Folk Beliefs and Practices, Tule Lake, California. *Journal of American Folklore* 63:383–97.

———. 1950b. Two Japanese Sects. *Southwestern Journal of Anthropology* 6:60–78.

Otsuka, Yasuo. 1976. Chinese Traditional Medicine in Japan. In Charles Leslie, ed., *Asian Medical Systems: A Comparative Study*, pp. 322–40. Berkeley: University of California.

Patrick, Hugh. 1976. An Introductory Overview. In Hugh Patrick, ed., *Japanese Industrialization and Its Social Consequences*, pp. 1–17. Berkeley: University of California.

Pelto, Pertti J., and Gretel H. Pelto. 1978. *Anthropological Research: The Structure of Inquiry*. 2d ed. Cambridge: Cambridge University.

Pettazzoni, Raffaele. 1931–1932. *La Confession des Péchés*. 2 vols. Translated from the Italian by R. Monnot. Paris: Librairie Ernest Leroux.

Pye, Michael. 1977. The *Heart Sutra* in Japanese Context. In Lewis Lancaster, ed., *Prajñā-*

pāramitā and Related Systems: Studies in Honor of Edward Conze, pp. 123–33. Berkeley: Berkeley Buddhist Studies Series.

Rajana, Eimi Watanabe. 1975. New Religions in Japan: An Appraisal of Two Theories. In W. G. Beasley, ed., *Modern Japan: Aspects of History, Literature, and Society,* pp. 187–97. Berkeley: University of California.

Rehder, Alfred. 1954. *Manual of Cultivated Trees and Shrubs Hardy in North America: Exclusive of the Subtropical and Warmer Temperate Regions.* 2d ed. New York: Macmillan.

Robbins, Thomas. 1981. *Civil Liberties, "Brainwashing," and "Cults": A Select Annotated Bibliography.* Berkeley: Center for the Study of New Religious Movements, Graduate Theological Union.

———. 1985. New Religious Movements, Brainwashing, and Deprogramming—The View from the Law Journals: A Review Essay and Survey. *Religious Studies Review* 11 (4): 361–70.

Robertson, Jennifer. 1979. Rooting the Pine: Shingaku Methods of Organization. *Monumenta Nipponica* 34 (4): 311–32.

Rohlen, Thomas P. 1974. *For Harmony and Strength: Japanese White-Collar Organization in Anthropological Perspective.* Berkeley: University of California.

Scheiner, Irwin. 1973. The Mindful Peasant: Sketches for a Study of Rebellion. *Journal of Asian Studies* 32 (4): 579–92.

Shils, Edward. 1981. *Tradition.* Chicago: University of Chicago.

Shimazono, Susumu. 1979. The Living Kami Idea in the New Religions of Japan. *Japanese Journal of Religious Studies* 6 (3): 389–412.

Shinto Committee for the IXth International Congress for the History of Religions, comp. 1958. *Basic Terms of Shinto.* Tokyo: Jinja Honcho (The Association of Shinto Shrines), Kokugakuin University, Institute for Japanese Culture and Classics.

Sievers, Sharon L. 1983. *Flowers in Salt: The Beginnings of Feminist Consciousness in Modern Japan.* Stanford, Calif.: Stanford University.

Smethurst, Richard J. 1974. *A Social Basis for Prewar Japanese Militarism: The Army and the Rural Community.* Berkeley: University of California.

Smith, Robert J. 1974. *Ancestor Worship in Contemporary Japan.* Stanford, Calif.: Stanford University.

———. 1978. *Kurusu: The Price of Progress in a Japanese Village, 1951–1975.* Stanford, Calif.: Stanford University.

———. 1983. *Japanese Society: Tradition, Self, and the Social Order.* Cambridge: Cambridge University.

Smith, Robert J., and Ella Lury Wiswell. 1982. *The Women of Suye Mura.* Chicago: University of Chicago.

Smith, Thomas C. 1959. *The Agrarian Origins of Modern Japan.* Stanford, Calif.: Stanford University.

Smith, Warren W., Jr. 1959. *Confucianism in Modern Japan: A Study of Conservatism in Japanese Intellectual History.* Tokyo: Hokuseido.

Southwold, Martin. 1983. *Buddhism in Life: The Anthropological Study of Religion and the Sinhalese Practice of Buddhism.* Manchester: Manchester University.

Statistics Bureau, Prime Minister's Office [Japan]. 1981. *Japan Statistical Yearbook* 1981. Tokyo: Japan Statistical Association.

Statler, Oliver. 1983. *Japanese Pilgrimage.* New York: William Morrow.

Steinhoff, Patricia G., and Milton Diamond. 1977. *Abortion Politics: The Hawaii Experience.* Honolulu: University Press of Hawaii.

Stern, William Louis. 1974. Saxifragales. In *Encyclopaedia Britannica,* 15th ed., vol. 16, pp. 290–302. Chicago: Encyclopaedia Britannica.

Stevens, John. 1986. The Loneliness of the Long-Distance Buddha: Japan's Remarkable Running Monks. *East West* 16 (7): 54–58.

Suzuki, Daisetz Teitaro. 1960. *Manual of Zen Buddhism.* New York: Grove Press. Original publication 1935.

Tambiah, S. J. 1968. The Magical Power of Words. *Man: The Journal of the Royal Anthropological Institute,* n.s. 3 (2): 175–208.

Tatz, Mark. 1985. *Buddhism and Healing: Demieville's Article "Byo" from Hobogirin.* Lanham, Md.: University Press of America.

Thackrey, Ted, Jr. 1965. The Los Angeles Riots. In Dan Golenpaul, ed., *Information Please Almanac Atlas and Yearbook* 1966, pp. 51–53. New York: Simon and Schuster.

Tsurumi, Kazuko. 1970. *Social Change and the Individual: Japan before and after Defeat in World War II*. Princeton, N.J.: Princeton University.

Turner, Victor W. 1967. Aspects of Saora Ritual and Shamanism: An Approach to the Data of Ritual. In A. L. Epstein, ed., *The Craft of Social Anthropology*, pp. 181–204. London: Social Science Paperbacks, in association with Tavistock Publications.

Turner, Victor, and Edith Turner. 1978. *Image and Pilgrimage in Christian Culture: Anthropological Perspectives*. New York: Columbia University.

Uetake, Takae. 1986. Serving Others Saved Me from Stress. *Dharma World* 13:32–34.

Umeda, Yoshihiko, ed. 1966. *Shūkyō jiten*. Tokyo: Hori Shoten.

Umehara, Masaki. 1978. Gedatsu-kai—shin, shin rei no jōka to hōon kansha. In Umehara et al., *Shinshūkyō no sekai*, vol. 3, pp. 147–200. Tokyo: Daizō Shuppan.

Unno, Taitetsu. 1985. The Concept of Gratitude in Shin Buddhism. *The Pacific World: Journal of the Institute of Buddhist Studies*, n.s. 1:25–31.

Van Velsen, J. 1967. The Extended-Case Method and Situational Analysis. In A. L. Epstein, ed., *The Craft of Social Anthropology*, pp. 129–49. London: Social Science Paperbacks, in association with Tavistock Publications.

Vogel, Ezra F. 1979. *Japan as Number One: Lessons for America*. Cambridge: Harvard University.

Walters, Barbara. 1985. Hackett Teacher Resigns to Help Families with "Domestic Spirituality." *Kalamazoo Gazette*, Tuesday, August 13, 1985.

Watanabe, Eimi. 1968. Rissho Kosei-kai: A Sociological Observation of Its Members, Their Conversion and Their Activities. *Contemporary Religions in Japan* 9 (1–2): 75–151.

Wayman, Alex. 1977. Secret of the *Heart Sutra*. In Lewis Lancaster, ed., *Prajñāpāramitā and Related Systems: Studies in Honor of Edward Conze*, pp. 135–52. Berkeley: Berkeley Buddhist Studies Series.

Webb, Herschel. 1965. The Development of an Orthodox Attitude toward the Imperial Institution in the Nineteenth Century. In Marius B. Jansen, ed., *Changing Japanese Attitudes toward Modernization*. Princeton, N.J.: Princeton University.

———. 1968. *The Japanese Imperial Institution in the Tokugawa Period*. New York: Columbia University.

White, James W. 1970. *The Sōkagakkai and Mass Society*. Stanford, Calif.: Stanford University.

Woodard, William P. 1972. *The Allied Occupation of Japan, 1945–1952, and Japanese Religions*. Leiden: E. J. Brill.

Yamada, Yutaka. 1984. Purifying the Living and Purifying the Dead: Narratives of the Religious Experience of Japanese-American and Caucasian Members of the Church of World Messianity, Los Angeles, California. Ph.D. dissertation, University of North Carolina at Chapel Hill.

Yasuda, Kenneth. 1957. *The Japanese Haiku: Its Essential Nature, History, and Possibilities in English, with Selected Samples*. Rutland, Vt.: Charles E. Tuttle Co.

Yinger, J. Milton. 1970. *The Scientific Study of Religion*. New York: Macmillan.

Yoshida, Teigo. 1967. Mystical Retribution, Spirit Possession, and Social Structure in a Japanese Village. *Ethnology* 6 (3): 237–62.

INDEX

Many Japanese words, some distinctive to Gedatsu-kai, are used in this book. For ease in identifying and locating these terms, they are listed in the index under the Japanese term, with English translation or equivalent in parentheses. These items are also listed by English term, with cross-reference to the Japanese term. For example, all page references for taiken will be found under "Taiken ('testimonials')"; there is also a cross-reference from the English term [Testimonials. *See* Taiken]. Some terms which are mentioned in the text primarily in English (such as "Human relations") are listed by the English term, with cross-reference from the Japanese term; for example "Ningen kankei. *See* Human relations." Because many terms, such as "ancestors," appear throughout the book, only page numbers for more important treatments are provided.